S0-BII-602

NORTH
CENTRAL
GPS
COMPANION

Iowa
Minnesota
Wisconsin

Copyright © 1998 Wendt Companies, Inc.
Made in U.S.A. All rights reserved.

The GPS Companion is for the hundreds of days when you can't be in the wilderness or on the water.

The Companion makes any portable GPS a useful highway navigation tool. It includes the location of virtually every town in the area, no matter how small, plus landmarks like the Split Rock Light and the Mall of America.

The Companion is compatible with every brand of GPS sold. It also includes handy reference information tailored for the North Central region.

-Lists the coordinates for over 8200 cities and landmarks

-Includes all cities and towns indexed on normal State
 Highway maps plus THOUSANDS more.

-Based on US Government survey data

-Compact size to "go along" in car, boat or backpack

-Useful conversion charts and helpful hints

-After batteries the Companion is the best thing you can buy
 for your GPS.

CONTENTS

DATA FORMAT: DD-MM-SS

DATUM: NAD27

CAUTION: Airport data is not approved for aerial navigation.

NORTH
CENTRAL
GPS
COMPANION

IOWA

Place Name	Latitude	Longitude	Type	Elev

A

Place Name	Latitude	Longitude	Type	Elev
Abbott	42 29 07N	093 03 58W	city/town	
Abbott Crossng-his	42 29 35N	093 04 14W	city/town	
Abingdon	41 04 56N	092 08 20W	city/town	
Ackley	42 33 15N	093 03 11W	city/town	
Ackley Municipal	42 32 45N	093 02 02W	airport	1070
Ackworth	41 22 01N	093 28 21W	city/town	
Adair	41 30 02N	094 38 36W	city/town	
Adaville	42 45 03N	096 24 15W	city/town	
Adaza	42 11 43N	094 29 39W	city/town	
Adel	41 36 52N	094 01 02W	city/town	930
Adelphi	41 32 00N	093 25 34W	city/town	
Afton	41 01 39N	094 11 52W	city/town	
Afton Jct. -hist	41 01 00N	094 07 24W	city/town	
Agency	40 59 42N	092 18 24W	city/town	
Agricola -hist	41 29 57N	092 28 30W	city/town	
Ainsworth	41 17 20N	091 33 08W	city/town	
Akron	42 49 44N	096 33 33W	city/town	
Akron Municipal	42 48 21N	096 33 46W	airport	1143
Albany	42 51 57N	091 45 31W	city/town	
Albaton	42 11 08N	096 17 26W	city/town	

Iowa GPS Companion

Place Name	Latitude	Longitude	Type	Elev
Albert City	42 46 55N	094 56 54W	city/town	
Albia	41 01 36N	092 48 20W	city/town	
Albia Municipal	40 59 40N	092 45 46W	airport	963
Albion	42 06 45N	092 59 18W	city/town	
Alburnett	42 08 54N	091 37 06W	city/town	
Alden	42 31 13N	093 22 33W	city/town	
Alden Station-hist	42 30 15N	093 22 50W	city/town	
Alexander	42 48 21N	093 28 35W	city/town	
Algona	43 04 12N	094 13 58W	city/town	
Algona Municipal	43 04 40N	094 16 18W	airport	1219
Alice	42 11 51N	091 41 44W	city/town	
Allee Exper. Farm	42 36 00N	095 00 44W	locale	
Alleman	41 35 48N	093 36 41W	city/town	
Allen	41 48 18N	095 49 06W	city/town	
Allendorf	43 24 53N	095 38 35W	city/town	
Allerton	40 42 23N	093 21 54W	city/town	
Allison	42 45 10N	092 47 42W	city/town	
Allison Municipal	42 45 50N	092 48 15W	airport	1053
Almont	41 58 31N	090 11 56W	city/town	
Almoral	42 32 08N	091 17 23W	city/town	
Almoral Spring	42 30 59N	091 16 21W	city/town	975
Alpha	42 59 48N	092 02 51W	city/town	

Place Name	Latitude	Longitude	Type	Elev
Alta	42 40 25N	095 17 25W	city/town	
Alta Vista	43 11 55N	092 25 01W	city/town	
Alton	42 59 15N	096 00 37W	city/town	
Altoona	41 38 39N	093 27 52W	city/town	
Alvord	43 20 32N	096 18 03W	city/town	
Amana	41 48 00N	091 52 14W	city/town	
Amana Airport	41 47 45N	091 52 15W	airport	712
Amber	42 07 41N	091 10 48W	city/town	
Ambrose	41 31 53N	092 14 00W	city/town	
Ambrose A Call St.	43 03 10N	094 14 52W	park	
Ames	42 02 05N	093 37 11W	city/town	
Ames Country Club	42 04 26N	093 39 26W	golf	
Ames Municipal	41 59 31N	093 37 17W	airport	955
Amish	41 32 09N	091 47 11W	city/town	
Amund	43 28 24N	093 47 35W	city/town	
Anamosa	42 06 30N	091 17 06W	city/town	
Anderson	40 48 05N	095 36 14W	city/town	
Andover	41 58 45N	090 15 06W	city/town	
Andrew	42 09 13N	090 35 32W	city/town	
Andrews	41 45 12N	093 45 25W	city/town	
Angus	41 53 00N	094 09 26W	city/town	1029
Anita	41 26 43N	094 45 52W	city/town	

Iowa GPS Companion

Place Name	Latitude	Longitude	Type	Elev
Anita Municipal	41 26 25N	094 46 10W	airport	1251
Ankeny	41 43 47N	093 36 20W	city/town	
Ankeny Regional	41 41 32N	093 33 57W	airport	903
Anthon	42 23 18N	095 51 59W	city/town	
Antique Airfield	40 58 40N	092 35 15W	airport	890
Aplington	42 35 03N	092 53 03W	city/town	
Arbor Hill	41 22 00N	094 19 05W	city/town	
Arcadia	42 01 54N	095 02 45W	city/town	
Archer	43 06 55N	095 44 44W	city/town	
Ardon	41 23 42N	091 11 18W	city/town	
Aredale	42 49 59N	093 00 19W	city/town	
Argand	42 16 54N	091 20 43W	city/town	
Argo	41 37 33N	090 25 57W	city/town	
Argyle	40 31 54N	091 33 58W	city/town	
Arion	41 56 57N	095 27 48W	city/town	
Arispe	40 56 58N	094 13 08W	city/town	
Arlington	42 44 57N	091 40 16W	city/town	
Armah	41 31 53N	092 12 33W	city/town	
Armour	42 30 46N	092 15 18W	city/town	
Armstrong	43 23 46N	094 28 41W	city/town	
Arnold	42 48 39N	094 11 54W	city/town	
Arnolds Park	43 22 22N	095 07 25W	city/town	

Iowa GPS Companion

Place Name	Latitude	Longitude	Type	Elev
Artesian	42 43 42N	092 20 13W	city/town	
Arthur	42 20 05N	095 20 50W	city/town	
Asbury	42 30 52N	090 45 05W	city/town	
Ascot	41 24 49N	095 53 53W	city/town	
Ash Grove	40 52 15N	092 33 10W	city/town	
Ashawa	41 34 20N	093 45 22W	city/town	
Ashland	40 57 31N	092 14 11W	city/town	
Ashton	43 18 41N	095 47 27W	city/town	
Aspinwall	41 54 43N	095 08 07W	city/town	1381
Astor	41 52 12N	095 15 59W	city/town	
Atalissa	41 34 16N	091 09 57W	city/town	
Athelstan	40 34 20N	094 32 14W	city/town	
Atkins	41 59 49N	091 51 43W	city/town	
Atlantic	41 24 13N	095 00 49W	city/town	1215
Atlantic C C	41 23 04N	095 00 53W	golf	
Atlantic Municipal	41 24 26N	095 02 47W	airport	1182
Attica	41 13 47N	093 00 57W	city/town	
Atwood	41 19 30N	092 24 21W	city/town	
Auburn	42 15 05N	094 52 39W	city/town	1220
Audubon	41 43 05N	094 55 56W	city/town	1373
Audubon County	41 42 05N	094 55 13W	airport	1287
Augusta	40 45 29N	091 16 32W	city/town	

Iowa GPS Companion

Place Name	Latitude	Longitude	Type	Elev
Aurelia	42 42 46N	095 26 11W	city/town	
Aurelia C C	42 43 02N	095 25 40W	golf	
Aureola	42 58 06N	092 52 40W	city/town	
Aurora (1)	42 37 08N	091 43 42W	city/town	
Aurora (2)	41 29 45N	092 14 22W	city/town	
Austinville	42 35 09N	092 57 25W	city/town	
Avery	41 03 55N	092 42 51W	city/town	
Avoca	41 28 36N	095 20 16W	city/town	
Avon	41 31 43N	093 31 23W	city/town	
Avon Lake	41 31 19N	093 30 03W	city/town	
Ayresville	41 41 05N	091 00 50W	city/town	
Ayrshire	43 02 21N	094 49 57W	city/town	

𝔹

Place Name	Latitude	Longitude	Type	Elev
Backbone State	42 36 58N	091 33 34W	park	
Badger	42 36 52N	094 08 45W	city/town	
Badger Lake	42 09 10N	096 13 58W	lake	1052
Bagley	41 50 46N	094 25 47W	city/town	1106
Bailey	43 27 54N	092 36 28W	city/town	
Baird	41 47 55N	095 39 15W	city/town	
Bald Point	41 59 08N	090 10 12W	cliff	
Baldwin	42 04 27N	090 50 29W	city/town	

Place Name	Latitude	Longitude	Type	Elev
Balfour	41 02 56N	095 40 03W	city/town	
Ballard C C	41 54 46N	093 36 31W	golf	
Balltown	42 38 17N	090 52 07W	city/town	
Balltown Ridge	42 38 15N	090 54 46W	summit	
Ballyclough	42 25 33N	090 43 05W	city/town	
Baltimore -hist	40 51 28N	091 27 35W	city/town	565
Bancroft	43 17 34N	094 13 04W	city/town	
Bangor	42 10 24N	093 05 36W	city/town	
Bankston	42 31 07N	090 57 40W	city/town	
Bard	41 14 25N	091 17 15W	city/town	
Barkley Memorial S	42 08 36N	093 56 18W	park	
Barnes City	41 30 30N	092 28 05W	city/town	
Barney	41 10 00N	094 00 13W	city/town	
Barnum	42 30 31N	094 21 54W	city/town	
Baron Spring	42 43 37N	091 32 54W	spring	
Barrell	40 41 53N	093 52 02W	city/town	
Bartlett	40 53 06N	095 47 41W	city/town	946
Bassett	43 03 47N	092 30 55W	city/town	
Batavia	40 59 39N	092 10 02W	city/town	
Battle Creek	42 18 56N	095 35 54W	city/town	1194
Battle Hill	42 19 43N	095 35 06W	summit	
Bauer	41 12 14N	093 18 25W	city/town	

Place Name	Latitude	Longitude	Type	Elev
Baxter	41 49 34N	093 09 05W	city/town	
Bayard	41 51 07N	094 33 29W	city/town	1135
Beacon	41 16 37N	092 40 46W	city/town	
Beaconsfield	40 48 28N	094 03 01W	city/town	
Beaman	42 13 11N	092 49 24W	city/town	
Bear Hill	42 45 14N	091 42 57W	summit	
Beaver	42 02 18N	094 08 31W	city/town	
Beaver Hill C C	42 34 11N	092 31 10W	golf	
Beaver Island	41 48 45N	090 12 14W	island	
Beaverdale	40 50 48N	091 12 30W	city/town	
Beckwith	41 00 33N	091 51 52W	city/town	
Bedford	40 40 01N	094 43 16W	city/town	
Bedford Municipal	40 38 16N	094 43 45W	airport	1201
Beebeetown	41 31 16N	095 45 19W	city/town	
Beech	41 22 29N	093 21 07W	city/town	
Beeds Lake State	42 46 14N	093 14 41W	park	
Belfast -hist	40 59 23N	091 41 07W	city/town	606
Belinda	41 08 20N	093 11 32W	city/town	
Belknap	40 49 14N	092 25 34W	city/town	
Bell	41 57 26N	095 29 44W	city/town	
Bellair -hist	40 41 30N	092 58 45W	city/town	
Belle Plaine	41 53 49N	092 16 41W	city/town	

10

Place Name	Latitude	Longitude	Type	Elev
Bellefountain	41 16 49N	092 51 41W	city/town	720
Bellevue	42 15 31N	090 25 22W	city/town	
Bellevue State	42 14 50N	090 25 22W	park	
Belmond	42 50 46N	093 36 50W	city/town	
Belmond Municipal	42 51 10N	093 35 40W	airport	1201
Beloit	43 16 53N	096 34 28W	city/town	
Benan -hist.	42 07 23N	094 38 52W	city/town	
Bennett	41 44 25N	090 58 25W	city/town	
Bennettsville	42 21 36N	090 43 41W	city/town	
Benson	42 32 33N	092 32 31W	city/town	
Bentley	41 22 37N	095 37 12W	city/town	
Benton	40 42 12N	094 21 29W	city/town	
Benton City -hist	42 09 30N	091 56 01W	city/town	
Benton Stat. -hist	42 08 43N	092 08 40W	city/town	
Bentonsport	40 43 32N	091 51 13W	city/town	
Berea	41 22 27N	094 40 48W	city/town	
Berkley	41 56 42N	094 06 52W	city/town	973
Berlin	42 25 07N	093 09 37W	city/town	
Bernard	42 18 44N	090 49 54W	city/town	
Berne	42 04 52N	095 39 09W	city/town	
Bernhart	41 00 45N	092 04 04W	city/town	
Bernina	41 24 28N	092 45 57W	city/town	

Place Name	Latitude	Longitude	Type	Elev
Bertram	41 56 59N	091 32 07W	city/town	
Berwick	41 39 54N	093 32 41W	city/town	
Bethany Hall	43 10 38N	092 14 23W	city/town	
Bethel	41 22 23N	091 29 00W	city/town	
Bethelhem	40 50 29N	093 12 43W	city/town	
Bethesda	40 50 35N	095 05 58W	city/town	
Bettendorf	41 31 28N	090 30 56W	city/town	
Bettendorf Museum	41 31 37N	090 30 28W	building	
Beulah	43 01 38N	091 18 29W	city/town	
Bever Zoo	41 59 26N	091 37 27W	locale	
Beverly Depot	41 55 56N	091 43 33W	city/town	
Bevington	41 21 38N	093 47 26W	city/town	
Biddick -hist	41 04 40N	095 04 45W	city/town	
Bidwell	41 01 08N	092 32 18W	city/town	
Big Creek Lake	41 48 44N	093 44 28W	lake	920
Big Creek State	41 48 56N	093 45 31W	park	
Big Rock (1)	42 33 06N	092 17 52W	city/town	
Big Rock (2)	41 46 13N	090 49 34W	city/town	
Big Spring -hist	40 41 00N	093 31 36W	city/town	
Bigelow State Park	42 18 15N	096 19 29W	park	
Bingham	40 44 03N	095 17 19W	city/town	
Birmingham	40 52 44N	091 56 49W	city/town	

Place Name	Latitude	Longitude	Type	Elev
Bixby State Park	42 40 31N	091 23 58W	park	
Black Bridge Sprg	42 39 40N	090 52 55W	spring	
Black Corners	41 41 18N	094 01 23W	city/town	
Black Falls	43 25 04N	092 00 46W	falls	
Black Hawk	41 31 15N	090 38 15W	city/town	
Blackhawk	40 49 46N	092 35 26W	city/town	
Bladensburg	41 02 46N	092 14 13W	city/town	
Blairsburg	42 28 48N	093 38 34W	city/town	
Blairstown	41 54 34N	092 05 03W	city/town	
Blakesburg	40 57 44N	092 38 02W	city/town	
Blanchard	40 34 45N	095 13 17W	city/town	
Blanden	42 34 38N	094 33 40W	city/town	
Blank Ridge	41 56 57N	093 54 11W	ridge	
Blencoe	41 55 49N	096 04 50W	city/town	
Blessing	42 18 42N	092 27 21W	city/town	
Bliedorn	41 54 09N	090 40 41W	city/town	
Blockly	40 39 35N	093 45 17W	city/town	
Blockton	40 36 56N	094 28 37W	city/town	
Bloomfield	40 45 06N	092 24 53W	city/town	
Bloomfield Munic.	40 43 55N	092 25 41W	airport	888
Bloomington	42 03 22N	093 35 14W	city/town	
Blue Grass	41 30 32N	090 45 57W	city/town	

13

Place Name	Latitude	Longitude	Type	Elev
Blue Spring	42 46 58N	091 41 39W	spring	
Bluff Creek	41 08 50N	092 51 00W	city/town	
Bluff Park	40 31 39N	091 24 13W	city/town	
Bluffton	43 24 11N	091 54 42W	city/town	
Bob White State	40 42 37N	093 23 52W	park	
Bode	42 52 06N	094 17 22W	city/town	
Boies	42 36 52N	092 22 37W	city/town	
Bois d'Arc	42 24 56N	092 32 15W	locale	
Bolan	43 22 19N	093 07 09W	city/town	
Bolton	41 15 31N	092 44 09W	city/town	
Bonair	43 25 19N	092 11 33W	city/town	
Bonaparte	40 41 53N	091 48 11W	city/town	
Bondurant	41 42 02N	093 27 43W	city/town	
Boone	42 03 35N	093 52 48W	city/town	
Boone Country Club	42 03 01N	093 52 17W	golf	
Boone Municipal	42 02 58N	093 50 50W	airport	1160
Booneville	41 31 27N	093 53 01W	city/town	
Border Plains	42 23 53N	094 02 52W	city/town	
Botna	41 51 21N	095 07 52W	city/town	1303
Bouton	41 51 05N	094 00 32W	city/town	938
Bowsher	41 38 21N	093 32 30W	city/town	
Boxholm	42 10 33N	094 06 21W	city/town	

Place Name	Latitude	Longitude	Type	Elev
Boyd	43 00 45N	092 15 28W	city/town	
Boyden	43 11 28N	096 00 20W	city/town	
Boyer	42 10 55N	095 14 06W	city/town	
Boyer River	42 11 21N	095 12 16W	city/town	
Braddyville	40 34 44N	095 01 47W	city/town	990
Bradford (1)	42 37 59N	093 14 41W	city/town	
Bradford (2)	42 57 58N	092 30 17W	city/town	
Bradgate	42 48 11N	094 25 04W	city/town	
Brady St. Stadium	41 33 21N	090 33 57W	park	
Brainard	42 55 51N	091 42 18W	city/town	
Brandon	42 18 52N	092 00 07W	city/town	
Brayton	41 32 40N	094 55 26W	city/town	
Brazil	40 45 29N	092 57 15W	city/town	
Breda	42 10 54N	094 58 36W	city/town	
Bremer	42 46 24N	092 23 41W	city/town	
Briar Cliff Coll.	42 31 36N	096 25 33W	univ/coll	
Bricker	40 34 32N	091 27 20W	city/town	
Bridgeport (1)	42 05 22N	090 37 37W	city/town	
Bridgeport (2)	40 45 12N	093 13 53W	city/town	
Bridgeport (3)	41 09 14N	092 39 16W	city/town	
Bridgewater	41 14 42N	094 40 07W	city/town	
Brighton	41 10 29N	091 49 10W	city/town	

Place Name	Latitude	Longitude	Type	Elev
Bristol	43 24 43N	093 28 04W	city/town	1252
Bristow	42 46 26N	092 54 26W	city/town	
Britt	43 05 52N	093 48 06W	city/town	
Broddyville	40 34 42N	095 01 48W	city/town	1103
Brogan -hist	42 12 55N	095 11 30W	city/town	
Bromley	42 07 08N	093 07 46W	city/town	
Brompton	40 55 53N	092 44 04W	city/town	
Bronson	42 24 39N	096 12 49W	city/town	
Brook Mount	42 23 08N	095 15 51W	city/town	
Brookdale	42 34 07N	096 46 55W	city/town	
Brooklyn	41 44 01N	092 26 43W	city/town	
Brooklyn-Victor CC	41 43 12N	092 23 01W	golf	
Brooks	40 57 55N	094 48 17W	city/town	
Brooks C C	43 23 14N	095 07 42W	golf	
Brookville	41 03 20N	092 05 20W	city/town	
Brownells Beach	43 25 34N	095 10 27W	beach	
Browns	42 01 50N	090 29 57W	city/town	
Brownsville	41 30 45N	092 33 22W	city/town	
Brownville	43 20 32N	092 40 33W	city/town	
Brucewell	40 38 45N	093 38 15W	city/town	
Brunsville	42 48 35N	096 16 08W	city/town	
Brush Creek Canyon	42 46 45N	091 41 18W	park	

Iowa GPS Companion

Place Name	Latitude	Longitude	Type	Elev
Brushy	42 25 51N	094 00 36W	city/town	
Brushy Creek State	42 23 30N	093 59 26W	park	
Bryan Hill	40 32 28N	091 37 00W	summit	
Bryant	41 57 48N	090 19 48W	city/town	
Bryantsburg	42 34 29N	091 54 19W	city/town	
Bubona -hist	43 19 38N	094 39 34W	city/town	
Buchanan	41 45 54N	091 14 48W	city/town	
Buck Creek (1)	42 20 14N	091 20 31W	city/town	
Buck Creek (2)	42 45 31N	092 08 26W	city/town	1015
Buck Grove (1)	41 55 05N	095 23 45W	city/town	1302
Buck Grove (2)	42 30 51N	092 50 58W	city/town	
Buckeye	42 25 02N	093 22 29W	city/town	
Buckhorn	42 03 36N	090 45 11W	city/town	
Buckingham	42 15 45N	092 26 51W	city/town	
Buckingham -hist	42 12 38N	092 28 45W	city/town	
Bucknell	41 03 58N	093 02 39W	city/town	
Budd	42 31 59N	090 48 56W	city/town	
Buena Vista	41 44 31N	090 44 25W	city/town	
Buena Vista -hist	40 23 12N	091 26 01W	city/town	
Buena Vista Coll.	42 38 28N	095 12 30W	univ/coll	
Buffalo (1)	41 18 40N	094 00 12W	city/town	
Buffalo (2)	41 27 23N	090 43 24W	city/town	

Place Name	Latitude	Longitude	Type	Elev
Buffalo Bill Home.	41 44 46N	090 26 35W	homestead	600
Buffalo Center	43 23 09N	093 56 47W	city/town	
Buffalo Heights	41 28 21N	090 42 52W	city/town	
Buffalo Ridge	41 56 51N	093 54 08W	ridge	
Bulgers Hollow	41 56 07N	090 11 02W	city/town	
Bullard	40 37 00N	091 24 25W	city/town	
Burchinal	43 03 55N	093 16 41W	city/town	
Burdette	42 34 19N	093 21 36W	city/town	
Burlington	40 48 27N	091 06 46W	city/town	
Burlington Golf	40 50 03N	091 07 17W	golf	
Burlington Munic.	40 46 59N	091 07 31W	airport	698
Burnside	42 20 45N	094 06 24W	city/town	1137
Burr Oak (1)	43 27 32N	091 51 55W	city/town	
Burr Oak (2)	40 56 09N	095 47 15W	city/town	
Burt	43 11 51N	094 13 10W	city/town	
Bushville	40 51 24N	094 44 17W	city/town	
Business Corners	40 51 16N	092 14 37W	city/town	
Bussey	41 12 16N	092 52 57W	city/town	
Butler Center	42 41 51N	092 47 00W	city/town	
Buxton	41 09 30N	092 49 16W	city/town	

Place Name	Latitude	Longitude	Type	Elev
C				
Cairo	41 11 01N	091 19 38W	city/town	
Calamus	41 49 33N	090 45 29W	city/town	
Caldwell Siding	41 27 08N	094 14 13W	city/town	
Calhoun	41 37 54N	095 53 42W	city/town	
California Jct.	41 33 31N	095 59 40W	city/town	1006
Callender	42 21 43N	094 17 44W	city/town	
Calmar	43 11 01N	091 51 50W	city/town	
Caloma	41 16 38N	093 18 33W	city/town	
Calumet	42 56 47N	095 32 59W	city/town	
Camanche	41 47 17N	090 15 22W	city/town	
Cambria	40 50 16N	093 24 08W	city/town	
Cambridge	41 53 54N	093 31 44W	city/town	
Cameron (1)	42 39 58N	090 51 57W	city/town	
Cameron (2)	43 04 58N	093 11 17W	city/town	
Camp Dodge	41 41 59N	093 42 26W	city/town	
Campbell	41 36 38N	093 47 40W	city/town	902
Canby	41 25 02N	094 33 59W	city/town	1440
Canfield	42 30 43N	092 08 28W	city/town	
Canoe	43 21 03N	091 39 14W	city/town	
Canton	42 09 48N	090 53 44W	city/town	

Iowa GPS Companion

Place Name	Latitude	Longitude	Type	Elev
Cantril	40 38 39N	092 04 11W	city/town	
Capitol Heights	41 38 00N	093 31 12W	city/town	
Capoli Mill	43 18 37N	091 14 41W	locale	
Carbon (1)	40 53 47N	092 25 18W	city/town	
Carbon (2)	41 03 00N	094 49 23W	city/town	
Carbondale	41 34 56N	093 30 11W	city/town	
Carl	41 07 12N	094 39 46W	city/town	
Carlisle	41 30 03N	093 29 27W	city/town	
Carmel	43 07 40N	096 14 06W	city/town	
Carnarvon	42 15 13N	095 01 17W	city/town	1260
Carnes	42 55 38N	096 03 24W	city/town	
Carney (1)	41 41 18N	093 36 01W	city/town	
Carney (2)	43 01 45N	092 48 37W	city/town	
Carnforth	41 43 20N	092 20 58W	city/town	
Carpenter	43 24 54N	093 00 53W	city/town	
Carriage Place	41 35 26N	090 25 36W	city/town	721
Carroll	42 03 57N	094 52 00W	city/town	
Carroll -A N Neu	42 02 49N	094 47 23W	airport	1230
Carrollton	41 56 59N	094 44 52W	city/town	1215
Carrville	43 00 32N	092 34 29W	city/town	
Carson	41 14 12N	095 25 04W	city/town	
Carter Lake	41 17 26N	095 55 04W	city/town	

Place Name	Latitude	Longitude	Type	Elev
Cartersville	42 59 40N	093 04 58W	city/town	
Cascade	42 17 55N	091 00 53W	city/town	
Casey	41 30 18N	094 31 09W	city/town	
Casino Beach	42 37 27N	095 13 42W	city/town	
Casino Beach	42 37 34N	095 13 39W	beach	
Cass	42 11 41N	091 20 44W	city/town	
Castalia	43 06 43N	091 40 34W	city/town	
Castana	42 04 28N	095 54 30W	city/town	1166
Castle Grove	42 15 38N	091 19 00W	city/town	
Cathedral Square	42 29 41N	090 40 34W	city/town	850
Cattese	42 27 40N	090 37 52W	city/town	
Cayler Prairie	43 23 47N	095 14 40W	area	
Cedar	41 12 44N	092 31 32W	city/town	
Cedar Bluff	41 47 09N	091 18 29W	city/town	
Cedar City	42 32 26N	092 26 27W	city/town	
Cedar Falls	42 31 40N	092 26 43W	city/town	
Cedar Falls Jct.	42 26 43N	092 25 07W	city/town	
Cedar Hills	41 58 22N	091 44 25W	city/town	
Cedar Lake	41 59 31N	091 40 07W	lake	721
Cedar Lakes	41 43 30N	091 02 51W	lake	775
Cedar Rapids	42 00 30N	091 38 38W	city/town	
Cedar Rapids Mun.	41 53 04N	091 42 38W	airport	864

Iowa GPS Companion

Place Name	Latitude	Longitude	Type	Elev
Cedar Rock State	42 24 22N	091 46 13W	park	
Cedar Valley	41 43 35N	091 14 47W	city/town	
Center Grove	42 29 28N	090 42 55W	city/town	
Center Junction	42 06 58N	091 05 13W	city/town	
Center Lake	43 24 42N	095 08 12W	lake	1416
Center Point	42 11 27N	091 47 06W	city/town	
Centerdale	41 38 31N	091 18 25W	city/town	
Centerville (1)	40 44 03N	092 52 26W	city/town	
Centerville (2)	42 05 34N	093 56 07W	city/town	
Centerville Mun.	40 41 02N	092 54 03W	airport	1028
Central City	42 12 14N	091 31 26W	city/town	
Central Heights	43 08 06N	093 14 30W	city/town	
Central Univ of IA	41 24 04N	092 55 13W	univ/coll	
Centralia	42 28 20N	090 50 10W	city/town	
Ceres	42 49 14N	091 11 10W	city/town	
Chalstroms Beach	43 23 14N	095 06 50W	beach	
Chaney	41 47 41N	090 17 04W	city/town	
Chapel Hill -hist	41 29 32N	090 38 50W	city/town	
Chapin	42 50 01N	093 13 19W	city/town	
Chariton	41 00 50N	093 18 23W	city/town	
Chariton Munic.	41 01 10N	093 21 34W	airport	1050
Charles City	43 03 59N	092 40 20W	city/town	

22

Iowa GPS Companion

Place Name	Latitude	Longitude	Type	Elev
Charles City Mun.	43 04 21N	092 36 38W	airport	1125
Charleston	40 35 27N	091 31 52W	city/town	
Charlotte	41 57 37N	090 27 54W	city/town	
Charter Oak	42 04 06N	095 35 29W	city/town	
Chatsworth	42 54 58N	096 30 58W	city/town	1162
Chautauqua	41 17 27N	095 47 36W	city/town	
Cheever Lake	43 22 22N	094 52 59W	lake	1430
Chelsea	41 55 09N	092 23 40W	city/town	792
Cheney	42 15 15N	091 55 38W	city/town	
Chequest	40 49 42N	092 14 44W	city/town	
Cherokee	42 44 58N	095 33 05W	city/town	
Cherokee Municipal	42 43 51N	095 33 19W	airport	1226
Cherry Lake	41 57 42N	092 35 07W	lake	819
Chester	43 29 28N	092 21 37W	city/town	
Chickasaw	43 02 02N	092 29 42W	city/town	
Chicken Ridge	42 48 48N	091 26 27W	summit	
Chillicothe	41 05 08N	092 31 45W	city/town	
Church	43 21 08N	091 20 20W	city/town	
Churchville	41 23 48N	093 45 03W	city/town	
Churdan	42 09 07N	094 28 27W	city/town	1110
Cincinnati	40 37 51N	092 55 28W	city/town	
Clara	41 21 13N	095 53 48W	city/town	

Iowa GPS Companion

Place Name	Latitude	Longitude	Type	Elev
Clare	42 35 14N	094 20 43W	city/town	
Clarence	41 53 20N	091 03 23W	city/town	
Clarinda	40 44 31N	095 02 17W	city/town	
Clarinda -Schenck	40 43 21N	095 01 32W	airport	994
Clarinda Junction	40 55 56N	095 00 03W	city/town	
Clarion	42 43 54N	093 43 58W	city/town	
Clarion Municipal	42 44 31N	093 45 31W	airport	1162
Clark	40 57 02N	095 32 24W	city/town	
Clark Field House	40 47 58N	091 07 48W	locale	
Clarkdale	40 47 07N	092 54 17W	city/town	
Clarke College	42 30 34N	090 41 26W	univ/coll	
Clarkson -hist	41 20 04N	093 27 08W	city/town	
Clarksville	42 47 05N	092 40 03W	city/town	
Clay County Fairgr	43 09 15N	095 09 10W	fairgrnd	
Clay Mills	42 11 03N	090 56 35W	city/town	
Clayton	42 54 14N	091 08 50W	city/town	
Clayton Center	42 53 00N	091 19 36W	city/town	
Clear Lake	43 07 32N	093 25 28W	lake	1226
Clear Lake	43 08 17N	093 22 45W	city/town	
Clearfield	40 48 03N	094 28 32W	city/town	
Cleghorn	42 48 44N	095 42 45W	city/town	
Clemons	42 06 50N	093 09 21W	city/town	

Place Name	Latitude	Longitude	Type	Elev
Clermont	43 00 13N	091 39 08W	city/town	
Cleves	42 28 22N	093 02 42W	city/town	
Cliffland	40 57 57N	092 19 34W	city/town	
Climax	40 55 50N	095 21 56W	city/town	
Climbing Hill	42 20 30N	096 04 39W	city/town	
Clinton	41 50 40N	090 11 19W	city/town	
Clinton C C	41 49 32N	090 13 33W	golf	
Clinton Center	40 36 33N	093 23 04W	city/town	
Clinton Municipal	41 49 51N	090 19 44W	airport	708
Clinton Stock Yard	41 49 00N	090 13 21W	city/town	
Clio	40 38 06N	093 27 04W	city/town	
Clive	41 36 11N	093 43 26W	city/town	
Cloud	41 10 30N	093 14 06W	city/town	
Cloverdale	43 20 49N	095 41 08W	city/town	
Clucas	41 29 48N	094 03 06W	city/town	
Clutier	42 04 46N	092 24 07W	city/town	
Clyde	41 50 31N	093 15 54W	city/town	
Coal City	40 35 50N	092 43 07W	city/town	
Coal Creek	41 26 16N	092 23 36W	city/town	
Coal Siding -hist	41 40 15N	093 03 21W	city/town	
Coal Valley	42 01 54N	093 57 02W	city/town	
Coalville	42 26 43N	094 07 32W	city/town	

Iowa GPS Companion

Place Name	Latitude	Longitude	Type	Elev
Coburg	40 55 03N	095 15 51W	city/town	1004
Coe College	41 59 11N	091 39 25W	univ/coll	
Coggon	42 16 51N	091 31 49W	city/town	
Coin	40 39 16N	095 13 48W	city/town	
Cold Springs State	41 17 24N	095 05 09W	park	
Colesburg	42 38 22N	091 12 07W	city/town	
Colfax	41 40 40N	093 14 42W	city/town	
College Springs	40 37 09N	095 07 14W	city/town	
Collett	40 54 22N	091 58 39W	city/town	
Collins	41 54 10N	093 18 22W	city/town	
Colo	42 01 04N	093 18 54W	city/town	
Columbia	41 10 31N	093 08 59W	city/town	
Columbus City	41 15 31N	091 22 27W	city/town	
Columbus Junction	41 16 48N	091 21 38W	city/town	
Colwell	43 09 21N	092 35 38W	city/town	
Commerce	41 32 20N	093 45 52W	city/town	
Communia	42 47 24N	091 21 46W	city/town	
Competine	41 07 14N	092 13 38W	city/town	
Conesville	41 22 55N	091 20 59W	city/town	
Confidence	40 51 46N	093 07 31W	city/town	
Conger	41 21 07N	093 45 29W	city/town	
Conover	43 12 59N	091 53 50W	city/town	

Iowa GPS Companion

Place Name	Latitude	Longitude	Type	Elev
Conrad	42 13 29N	092 52 28W	city/town	
Conroy	41 43 45N	091 59 51W	city/town	
Consol	41 04 17N	093 00 06W	city/town	
Conway	40 44 55N	094 37 07W	city/town	
Cool	41 13 24N	093 34 38W	city/town	
Coon Rapids	41 52 15N	094 40 38W	city/town	
Cooper	41 55 13N	094 20 40W	city/town	1079
Coppock	41 09 44N	091 42 40W	city/town	
Coralville	41 40 35N	091 34 49W	city/town	
Cordova	41 25 28N	093 05 45W	city/town	
Corley	41 34 43N	095 19 48W	city/town	
Corn Hill	42 48 22N	091 44 12W	summit	
Cornelia	42 47 24N	093 40 59W	city/town	
Cornelia, Lake	42 47 14N	093 41 21W	lake	1208
Cornell	42 56 40N	095 08 23W	city/town	
Cornell College	41 55 33N	091 25 31W	univ/coll	
Corning	40 59 24N	094 44 26W	city/town	
Corning Municipal	40 59 38N	094 45 17W	airport	1274
Correctionville	42 28 30N	095 47 07W	city/town	
Corwith	42 59 34N	093 57 26W	city/town	
Corydon	40 45 25N	093 19 07W	city/town	
Corydon -hist	41 44 51N	093 41 14W	city/town	

Iowa GPS Companion

Place Name	Latitude	Longitude	Type	Elev
Corydon Bridge-his	41 44 45N	093 42 37W	bridge	
Cosgrove	41 38 34N	091 44 08W	city/town	805
Coster	42 40 18N	092 42 41W	city/town	
Cottage Hill	42 35 07N	090 54 49W	city/town	
Cotter	41 17 31N	091 27 41W	city/town	
Cottonville	42 14 13N	090 36 07W	city/town	
Cou Falls	41 49 02N	091 40 21W	city/town	
Coulter	42 44 14N	093 22 11W	city/town	
Council Bluffs	41 15 43N	095 51 39W	city/town	986
Council Bluffs M.	41 15 31N	095 45 37W	airport	1252
Covington	42 00 26N	091 45 44W	city/town	
Crab Town	42 10 24N	090 48 21W	city/town	
Crab Tree Lake	41 51 58N	093 12 45W	lake	897
Craig	42 53 45N	096 18 34W	city/town	
Crain Creek	42 34 13N	092 15 32W	city/town	
Crandalls Beach	43 29 26N	095 07 29W	beach	
Crandalls Lodge	43 29 50N	095 06 53W	building	
Cranston	41 22 45N	091 15 40W	city/town	
Crathorne	42 48 26N	096 19 52W	city/town	
Crawfordsville	41 14 39N	091 33 43W	city/town	
Creamery	43 13 15N	093 19 45W	city/town	
Credit Island	41 29 36N	090 37 14W	island	550

Place Name	Latitude	Longitude	Type	Elev
Crescent	41 21 54N	095 51 28W	city/town	
Cresco	43 22 53N	092 06 50W	city/town	
Cresco -E Church	43 21 55N	092 07 58W	airport	1279
Creston	41 03 31N	094 21 40W	city/town	
Creston Municipal	41 01 17N	094 21 47W	airport	1294
Crestwood	41 36 22N	093 42 46W	city/town	
Crestwood Golf	41 26 10N	094 46 04W	golf	
Creswell	41 25 15N	092 01 27W	city/town	
Cricket	41 11 02N	092 48 25W	city/town	
Crisp	41 34 42N	095 42 30W	city/town	
Crocker	41 46 29N	093 40 11W	city/town	
Cromwell	41 02 22N	094 27 42W	city/town	
Croton	40 35 25N	091 41 26W	city/town	
Crows Nest Resort	43 22 23N	095 07 24W	city/town	
Crystal Lake	43 13 24N	093 47 32W	city/town	
Cumberland	41 16 27N	094 52 12W	city/town	
Cumming	41 29 00N	093 45 44W	city/town	
Curlew	42 58 44N	094 44 27W	city/town	
Curtis -hist	41 48 15N	091 38 58W	city/town	
Cushing	42 27 53N	095 40 29W	city/town	1327
Cylinder	43 05 20N	094 33 10W	city/town	
Cypsum City -hist	42 28 25N	094 07 40W	city/town	

Place Name	Latitude	Longitude	Type	Elev

D

Place Name	Latitude	Longitude	Type	Elev
Dahlonega	41 03 31N	092 22 11W	city/town	
Dairyville	42 29 05N	092 39 09W	city/town	
Dakota City	42 43 20N	094 11 49W	city/town	
Dalby	43 15 51N	091 16 26W	city/town	
Dale	41 35 45N	094 20 30W	city/town	
Dales Ford	42 12 52N	091 04 00W	city/town	
Dallas Center	41 41 04N	093 57 39W	city/town	1072
Dalton Pond Fishng	42 02 17N	090 22 23W	access	
Dan Green Slough	43 13 18N	095 00 14W	lake	1357
Dana	42 06 27N	094 14 26W	city/town	
Danbury	42 14 03N	095 43 19W	city/town	
Danville	40 51 52N	091 18 52W	city/town	
Danville Center	40 51 25N	091 18 48W	city/town	
Darbyville	40 48 58N	092 52 23W	city/town	
Darling Pool	43 16 13N	094 06 58W	lake	1125
Davenport	41 31 25N	090 34 39W	city/town	
Davenport Art Gal.	41 31 34N	090 36 05W	building	
Davenport C C	41 34 53N	090 24 31W	golf	
Davenport Harbor	41 29 50N	090 37 17W	bay	
Davenport Mun.	41 36 37N	090 35 20W	airport	753

Iowa GPS Companion

Place Name	Latitude	Longitude	Type	Elev
Davis City	40 38 21N	093 48 41W	city/town	
Davis Corners	43 22 15N	092 17 51W	city/town	
Dawson	41 50 34N	094 13 20W	city/town	948
Dayfield	41 27 54N	091 09 04W	city/town	
Dayton (1)	42 15 41N	094 04 06W	city/town	
Dayton (2)	41 51 06N	092 11 09W	city/town	
Dayton -hist	40 43 43N	094 55 32W	city/town	
Daytonville	41 28 34N	091 49 44W	city/town	
De Soto	41 31 54N	094 00 34W	city/town	975
De Witt	41 49 24N	090 32 17W	city/town	
Dean	40 37 39N	092 42 50W	city/town	
Decatur City	40 44 31N	093 50 01W	city/town	
Deception Hol.Fish	42 19 41N	094 01 17W	access	
Decorah	43 18 12N	091 47 08W	city/town	
Decorah Municipal	43 16 31N	091 44 21W	airport	1157
Dedham	41 54 22N	094 49 19W	city/town	
Deep River	41 34 49N	092 22 29W	city/town	
Deer Creek	43 29 58N	093 07 36W	city/town	1206
Deerfield	43 09 49N	092 29 43W	city/town	1145
Defiance	41 49 27N	095 20 33W	city/town	1283
Delaware	42 28 31N	091 20 43W	city/town	
Delhi	42 25 47N	091 19 51W	city/town	

Iowa GPS Companion

Place Name	Latitude	Longitude	Type	Elev
Delmar	42 00 08N	090 36 25W	city/town	
Deloit	42 05 52N	095 19 20W	city/town	1202
Delphos	40 39 49N	094 20 21W	city/town	
Delta	41 19 22N	092 19 48W	city/town	
Denhart	42 57 58N	093 52 19W	city/town	
Denison	42 01 04N	095 21 18W	city/town	
Denison Municipal	41 59 11N	095 22 49W	airport	1273
Denmark	40 44 30N	091 20 14W	city/town	
Denova	40 54 30N	091 38 13W	city/town	
Denver	42 40 17N	092 20 14W	city/town	
Depew	43 11 03N	094 32 32W	city/town	
Derby	40 55 54N	093 27 22W	city/town	
Des Moines	41 36 02N	093 36 32W	city/town	
Des Moines -Morn.	41 39 20N	093 38 38W	airport	805
Des Moines Beach	43 22 37N	095 08 07W	beach	
Des Moines Int'l.	41 32 05N	093 39 37W	airport	957
Devon	43 07 11N	092 21 27W	city/town	
Dewar	42 31 32N	092 13 08W	city/town	
Dewey	41 11 13N	094 45 27W	city/town	
Dexter	41 31 06N	094 13 34W	city/town	1150
Diagonal	40 48 34N	094 20 31W	city/town	
Diamond	40 45 47N	092 57 56W	city/town	

Iowa GPS Companion

Place Name	Latitude	Longitude	Type	Elev
Diamond Lake 1	41 35 15N	092 33 27W	lake	856
Diamond Lake 2	43 28 53N	095 11 28W	lake	1409
Dickens	43 07 53N	095 01 24W	city/town	
Dickierville	41 00 04N	094 53 45W	city/town	
Dike	42 27 51N	092 37 41W	city/town	
Dillon	41 58 37N	092 49 26W	city/town	
Dinsdale	42 15 33N	092 32 41W	city/town	
Dixie	43 16 11N	092 59 40W	city/town	
Dixon	41 44 34N	090 46 56W	city/town	
Dodgeville	40 56 35N	091 10 50W	city/town	
Dolliver	43 27 52N	094 37 30W	city/town	
Dolliver Memorial	42 23 13N	094 05 00W	park	
Donahue	41 41 41N	090 40 31W	city/town	
Donley Station	41 20 03N	093 10 30W	city/town	
Donnan	42 53 46N	091 52 40W	city/town	
Donnelley	41 20 06N	093 10 36W	city/town	767
Donnellson	40 38 34N	091 33 52W	city/town	
Doon	43 16 46N	096 13 57W	city/town	
Dorchester	43 28 11N	091 30 39W	city/town	
Dordt College	43 04 56N	096 10 05W	univ/coll	
Doris	42 28 49N	091 48 51W	city/town	
Doubleday	43 05 11N	092 38 00W	city/town	

Iowa GPS Companion

Place Name	Latitude	Longitude	Type	Elev
Douds	40 50 22N	092 05 11W	city/town	
Dougherty	42 55 20N	093 02 31W	city/town	
Douglass	43 30 00N	091 52 16W	city/town	968
Dover	41 50 53N	092 17 35W	city/town	
Dover Mills	43 01 10N	091 43 45W	city/town	
Dow City	41 55 44N	095 29 37W	city/town	1131
Downers Grove	42 14 42N	091 16 51W	city/town	
Downey	41 36 58N	091 20 54W	city/town	
Dows	42 39 24N	093 30 03W	city/town	
Drake University	41 36 05N	093 39 06W	univ/coll	
Drakesville	40 47 54N	092 28 53W	city/town	
Dresden (1)	42 58 45N	092 19 06W	city/town	
Dresden (2)	41 34 40N	092 21 20W	city/town	
Drew	42 50 50N	093 48 21W	city/town	
Dry Mill Creek	42 50 32N	091 22 23W	stream	
Dubuque Harbor	42 29 42N	090 39 37W	bay	
Dubuque	42 30 02N	090 39 52W	city/town	
Dubuque C C	42 29 05N	090 40 54W	golf	
Dubuque Greyhound	42 31 15N	090 38 40W	park	
Dubuque Regional	42 24 10N	090 42 32W	airport	1076
Dudley	41 05 16N	092 35 30W	city/town	
Dumfries	41 11 13N	095 44 16W	city/town	1254

Iowa GPS Companion

Place Name	Latitude	Longitude	Type	Elev
Dumont	42 45 07N	092 58 31W	city/town	
Dunbar	41 56 27N	092 47 47W	city/town	
Duncan	43 06 17N	093 42 40W	city/town	
Duncombe	42 28 14N	093 59 36W	city/town	
Dundee	42 34 45N	091 32 47W	city/town	998
Dunkerton	42 34 12N	092 09 37W	city/town	
Dunlap	41 51 16N	095 36 01W	city/town	1158
Durango	42 33 37N	090 46 32W	city/town	
Durant	41 35 59N	090 54 38W	city/town	
Durham	41 19 13N	092 57 20W	city/town	
Durr Hill	42 04 28N	095 59 39W	summit	
Dutchtown	42 33 08N	091 24 39W	city/town	
Duttons Cave Campg	42 59 46N	091 46 16W	locale	1190
Dyersville	42 29 04N	091 07 22W	city/town	
Dysart	42 10 18N	092 18 22W	city/town	

E

Eagle Center	42 20 27N	092 21 26W	city/town	
Eagle City	42 28 18N	093 08 42W	city/town	
Eagle Grove	42 39 51N	093 54 15W	city/town	
Eagle Grove C C	42 40 02N	093 56 48W	golf	
Eagle Grove Mun.	42 42 35N	093 54 57W	airport	1133

35

Iowa GPS Companion

Place Name	Latitude	Longitude	Type	Elev
Eagle Lake 1	43 07 44N	093 44 02W	lake	1214
Eagle Lake 2	43 29 17N	094 49 41W	lake	1353
Eagle Lake State	43 07 31N	093 44 29W	park	
Eagle Point	42 32 05N	090 38 40W	city/town	
Eagle Rock	42 10 09N	090 54 56W	pillar	
Eagle Rock	43 05 30N	091 11 10W	cliff	
Earlham	41 29 31N	094 07 26W	city/town	
Earling	41 46 32N	095 25 02W	city/town	1408
Earlville	42 28 54N	091 16 20W	city/town	
Early	42 27 41N	095 09 06W	city/town	
Easley	42 18 40N	094 23 57W	city/town	
East Amana	41 48 33N	091 51 03W	city/town	
East Canton	42 09 50N	090 53 45W	city/town	
East Creston	41 03 30N	094 20 08W	city/town	
East Des Moines	41 34 15N	093 33 08W	city/town	
East Iron Hills	42 08 35N	090 44 15W	city/town	
East Monticello	42 14 56N	091 10 17W	city/town	
East Okoboji Beach	43 24 41N	095 04 26W	beach	
East Okoboji Lake	43 24 17N	095 04 30W	lake	1396
East Ottumwa	41 00 18N	092 22 42W	city/town	
East Peru	41 13 37N	093 55 34W	city/town	
East Pleasant Pln.	41 08 50N	091 51 32W	city/town	

Iowa GPS Companion

Place Name	Latitude	Longitude	Type	Elev
East Port -hist	40 40 44N	095 50 07W	city/town	
East Rapids	41 57 36N	091 38 21W	city/town	
East Rickardsville	42 34 25N	090 51 28W	city/town	
East Twin Lake	42 56 09N	093 42 41W	lake	1188
Eastern Iowa Cent.	41 26 28N	091 01 34W	univ/coll	
Easton Place	41 36 37N	093 33 58W	city/town	
Ebys Mill	42 11 59N	091 03 32W	city/town	
Echo	41 44 31N	095 56 29W	city/town	
Echo Valley State	42 56 40N	091 45 53W	park	
Eckards	42 51 23N	091 06 15W	city/town	
Eddyville	41 09 38N	092 37 52W	city/town	
Eden	42 06 33N	091 58 10W	city/town	
Edenville	41 55 37N	093 11 00W	city/town	1020
Edgewood	42 38 40N	091 24 04W	city/town	
Edinburg	42 08 00N	091 08 02W	city/town	
Edmore	42 33 22N	090 40 43W	city/town	
Edna	43 23 06N	096 05 39W	city/town	
Edwards	42 34 13N	092 15 32W	city/town	
Effigy Mounds Mon.	42 56 26N	091 10 00W	monument	
Egan	43 09 24N	091 17 22W	city/town	
Egralharve	43 24 08N	095 10 22W	city/town	
Ehler	42 18 37N	091 30 45W	city/town	

Iowa GPS Companion

Place Name	Latitude	Longitude	Type	Elev
Eifield -hist	41 24 42N	093 01 57W	city/town	
Elberon	42 00 22N	092 19 00W	city/town	
Eldergrove	43 14 23N	091 13 11W	city/town	
Eldon	40 55 07N	092 13 22W	city/town	
Eldora	42 21 39N	093 05 58W	city/town	1088
Eldora Municipal	42 19 48N	093 06 59W	airport	979
Eldorado	43 03 02N	091 50 07W	city/town	
Eldridge	41 39 29N	090 35 04W	city/town	
Eleanor	42 36 51N	092 50 57W	city/town	
Elgin	42 57 27N	091 37 50W	city/town	
Elk Horn	41 35 30N	095 03 35W	city/town	1363
Elk Lake	43 04 56N	094 55 21W	lake	1393
Elk River Junction	41 58 47N	090 10 26W	city/town	
Elk Run Heights	42 28 01N	092 15 23W	city/town	
Elkader	42 51 14N	091 24 19W	city/town	
Elkhart	41 27 25N	093 31 19W	city/town	
Elkport	42 44 23N	091 16 40W	city/town	
Elkton	42 47 51N	095 22 05W	city/town	
Elliott	41 08 57N	095 09 49W	city/town	1075
Ellmaker	40 58 22N	092 04 57W	city/town	
Ellston	40 50 25N	094 06 30W	city/town	
Ellsworth	42 18 46N	093 34 43W	city/town	

Place Name	Latitude	Longitude	Type	Elev
Elm Lake	42 45 53N	093 40 42W	lake	1204
Elm Spring	43 18 38N	096 29 28W	city/town	
Elma	43 14 48N	092 26 09W	city/town	
Elmcrest C C	42 00 58N	091 38 58W	golf	
Elmira	41 43 22N	091 25 29W	city/town	
Elmwood C C	42 01 30N	092 56 00W	golf	
Elon	43 15 51N	091 19 26W	city/town	
Elrick Junction	41 05 55N	091 07 03W	city/town	
Elvira	41 51 32N	090 21 19W	city/town	
Elwood	41 59 30N	090 44 20W	city/town	
Ely	41 52 25N	091 35 06W	city/town	
Emeline	42 09 19N	090 49 50W	city/town	
Emerson	41 01 02N	095 24 07W	city/town	
Emery	43 08 01N	093 16 48W	city/town	1170
Emmetsburg	43 06 46N	094 40 58W	city/town	
Emmetsburg Mun.	43 06 07N	094 42 15W	airport	1205
Enterprise	41 43 55N	093 31 48W	city/town	1003
Epworth	42 26 42N	090 55 55W	city/town	
Ericson	42 01 43N	093 47 46W	city/town	
Essex	40 50 01N	095 18 29W	city/town	
Estherville	43 24 06N	094 49 57W	city/town	
Estherville Beach	43 25 13N	095 10 39W	beach	

Place Name	Latitude	Longitude	Type	Elev
Estherville Mun.	43 24 26N	094 44 46W	airport	1317
Euclid	41 32 38N	095 51 38W	city/town	
Eureka	40 45 56N	095 50 15W	city/town	
Eureka -hist	41 13 14N	091 42 49W	city/town	
Evander	43 10 43N	095 45 44W	city/town	
Evans	41 18 10N	092 43 37W	city/town	
Evansdale	42 28 09N	092 16 51W	city/town	
Evanston	42 26 03N	094 03 27W	city/town	
Eveland	41 10 11N	092 48 02W	city/town	
Everly	43 09 36N	095 19 38W	city/town	
Ewart	41 38 28N	092 36 37W	city/town	
Exeelsior	41 15 25N	092 30 44W	city/town	
Exira	41 35 27N	094 52 31W	city/town	
Exline	40 38 57N	092 50 25W	city/town	

𝔽

Place Name	Latitude	Longitude	Type	Elev
Faegre Prairie	43 19 35N	091 18 25W	area	
Fairbank	42 38 21N	092 02 49W	city/town	
Fairfax	41 55 10N	091 46 51W	city/town	
Fairfield	41 00 31N	091 57 45W	city/town	778
Fairfield Mun.	41 03 11N	091 58 43W	airport	799
Fairoak Beach	43 24 34N	095 09 38W	beach	

Iowa GPS Companion

Place Name	Latitude	Longitude	Type	Elev
Fairport	41 26 09N	090 54 16W	city/town	
Fairview (1)	42 04 41N	091 19 47W	city/town	
Fairview (2)	42 41 02N	091 12 59W	city/town	
Fairville	43 09 22N	094 27 47W	city/town	
Falling Springs	42 59 45N	091 52 16W	spring	
Fallow	43 11 52N	094 48 07W	city/town	
Fanslers	41 44 58N	094 27 20W	city/town	
Farley	42 26 34N	091 00 22W	city/town	
Farlin	42 04 35N	094 26 54W	city/town	1072
Farmersburg	42 57 40N	091 22 04W	city/town	
Farmington	40 38 25N	091 44 34W	city/town	569
Farnhamville	42 16 34N	094 24 13W	city/town	
Farragut	40 43 19N	095 28 50W	city/town	
Farrar	41 48 21N	093 22 11W	city/town	
Farson	41 07 20N	092 15 18W	city/town	
Faulkner	42 36 55N	093 05 09W	city/town	
Fayette	42 50 31N	091 48 07W	city/town	
Fejervary Home	41 32 49N	090 33 12W	locale	
Fenton	43 13 11N	094 25 49W	city/town	
Ferguson	41 56 13N	092 51 56W	city/town	
Fern	42 29 05N	092 46 13W	city/town	1060
Fernald	42 04 15N	093 23 41W	city/town	

Place Name	Latitude	Longitude	Type	Elev
Fertile	43 15 52N	093 25 05W	city/town	
Festina	43 07 10N	091 52 01W	city/town	
Fielding	42 39 47N	095 48 00W	city/town	
Fillmore	42 19 09N	090 55 00W	city/town	
Finchford	42 37 38N	092 32 37W	city/town	
Findley	41 31 43N	095 52 44W	city/town	
Fire Point	43 05 40N	091 10 50W	cliff	
Fiscus	41 44 20N	095 05 34W	city/town	
Fisher Lake	42 32 08N	092 24 45W	lake	844
Fisk	41 12 04N	094 31 40W	city/town	
Five Flags Theater	42 45 52N	090 39 57W	building	
Five Points	42 33 05N	090 51 30W	city/town	
Flagler	41 19 29N	093 01 18W	city/town	
Florence	42 42 09N	093 49 06W	city/town	
Florenceville	43 29 57N	092 07 57W	city/town	
Floris	40 51 54N	092 19 58W	city/town	
Floyd	43 07 40N	092 44 10W	city/town	
Floyd Crossing	43 05 28N	092 44 31W	city/town	
Floyds Bluff	42 27 46N	096 22 39W	cliff	
Flugstad	42 26 55N	093 55 54W	city/town	
Flugstad -hist	42 28 18N	093 56 13W	city/town	
Folletts	41 44 55N	090 21 17W	city/town	

Place Name	Latitude	Longitude	Type	Elev
Folsom	41 05 24N	095 49 02W	city/town	
Fonda	42 34 53N	094 50 45W	city/town	
Fontanelle	41 17 23N	094 33 41W	city/town	
Forbush	40 46 08N	092 52 37W	city/town	
Ford	41 29 06N	093 23 18W	city/town	
Forest City	43 15 45N	093 38 13W	city/town	
Forest City Munic.	43 14 05N	093 37 26W	airport	1230
Forest Park Mobile	43 16 24N	093 38 08W	city/town	
Forestville	42 35 48N	091 31 42W	city/town	
Forneys Lake	41 51 15N	095 46 49W	lake	934
Forsyth	43 15 20N	094 28 22W	city/town	
Fort Atkinson	43 08 36N	091 55 57W	city/town	
Fort Defiance -his	43 24 04N	094 50 12W	military	
Fort Defiance St.	43 23 31N	094 51 56W	park	
Fort Des Moines	41 31 13N	093 36 56W	city/town	
Fort Dodge	42 29 51N	094 10 04W	city/town	
Fort Dodge Point	43 22 33N	095 08 26W	cape	
Fort Dodge Reg.	42 33 05N	094 11 32W	airport	1157
Fort Madison	40 37 47N	091 18 54W	city/town	
Fort Madison Mun.	40 39 33N	091 19 36W	airport	724
Fort Sumter Rock	42 43 22N	092 53 18W	summit	
Foster	40 55 58N	092 45 26W	city/town	

Iowa GPS Companion

Place Name	Latitude	Longitude	Type	Elev
Fostoria	43 14 32N	095 09 19W	city/town	
Fountain Mill Spng	42 36 13N	091 18 56W	spring	
Foursome C C	42 39 11N	091 55 19W	golf	
Frank Gotch State	42 40 37N	094 12 07W	park	
Frankel Ridge	41 57 10N	093 54 20W	ridge	
Frankfort -hist	41 01 58N	095 08 02W	city/town	
Franklin	40 40 05N	091 30 40W	city/town	
Frankville	43 11 21N	091 37 02W	city/town	
Fraser	42 07 38N	093 57 53W	city/town	
Frederic	41 05 27N	092 40 41W	city/town	
Fredericksburg	42 57 55N	092 11 58W	city/town	
Frederika	42 52 54N	092 18 29W	city/town	
Fredonia	41 17 05N	091 20 19W	city/town	
Fredsville	42 29 03N	092 34 26W	city/town	
Freeman	43 12 47N	093 11 59W	city/town	1151
Freeport	43 18 08N	091 44 36W	city/town	
Fremont	41 12 45N	092 26 07W	city/town	
Fremont County	40 43 03N	095 38 42W	golf	
Frith Spur	42 32 59N	090 42 06W	city/town	
Froelich	43 00 24N	091 19 18W	city/town	
Fruitland	41 21 22N	091 07 45W	city/town	
Fullers Mill -hist	42 11 14N	091 01 43W	locale	

Place Name	Latitude	Longitude	Type	Elev
Fulton	42 09 13N	090 40 41W	city/town	

G

Place Name	Latitude	Longitude	Type	Elev
Gait	42 41 37N	093 36 07W	city/town	1212
Galbraith	42 58 50N	094 09 32W	city/town	
Galesburg	41 33 32N	092 56 46W	city/town	
Galland	40 30 02N	091 22 28W	city/town	
Galt	42 41 37N	093 36 19W	city/town	
Galva	42 30 25N	095 25 01W	city/town	
Gambrill -hist	41 45 07N	090 32 08W	city/town	
Garber	42 44 31N	091 15 43W	city/town	
Garden City	42 14 44N	093 23 43W	city/town	
Garden Grove	40 49 38N	093 36 25W	city/town	1110
Gardiner	41 49 28N	094 01 40W	city/town	
Gardner	41 40 28N	094 45 49W	city/town	
Garfield	40 46 07N	093 00 06W	city/town	
Garland	41 03 33N	091 13 03W	city/town	
Garnavillo	42 52 07N	091 14 09W	city/town	
Garner	43 06 09N	093 36 06W	city/town	
Garretville	41 31 03N	094 04 47W	city/town	
Garrison	42 08 39N	092 08 37W	city/town	
Garry Owen	42 17 00N	090 49 54W	city/town	

Iowa GPS Companion

Place Name	Latitude	Longitude	Type	Elev
Garwin	42 05 37N	092 40 32W	city/town	
Gates College	42 29 43N	092 20 28W	univ/coll	
Gatesville	42 26 30N	091 49 56W	city/town	
Gaza	43 01 13N	095 34 47W	city/town	
Geneva (1)	42 40 32N	093 07 45W	city/town	
Geneva (2)	42 07 01N	092 07 27W	city/town	
Geneva C C	41 26 58N	091 03 22W	golf	
Genoa	40 36 15N	093 06 50W	city/town	
Genoa Bluff	41 41 43N	092 09 12W	locale	
Geode State Park	40 49 57N	091 23 06W	park	
George	43 20 38N	096 00 07W	city/town	
George, Lake	43 13 07N	093 52 31W	lake	1248
Georgetown	41 00 46N	092 57 18W	city/town	
Gerled	43 23 00N	094 11 15W	city/town	
German Valley	43 16 12N	094 01 45W	city/town	
Germantown	42 57 12N	095 46 50W	city/town	
Germanville	41 06 15N	091 46 09W	city/town	
Giard	43 00 20N	091 17 21W	city/town	
Giard Station -his	43 02 05N	091 16 04W	city/town	
Gibbsville	41 48 03N	093 49 25W	city/town	
Gibson	41 28 52N	092 23 36W	city/town	
Gifford	42 17 18N	093 05 25W	city/town	

Place Name	Latitude	Longitude	Type	Elev
Gilbert	42 06 25N	093 38 58W	city/town	
Gilbertville	42 24 58N	092 12 53W	city/town	
Gilead	41 10 21N	094 35 08W	city/town	
Gillett Grove	43 00 57N	095 02 14W	city/town	
Gilliatt	41 17 28N	095 45 30W	city/town	
Gilman	41 52 44N	092 47 21W	city/town	
Gilmore City	42 43 46N	094 26 51W	city/town	
Gilt Edge	42 26 27N	091 12 17W	city/town	
Givin	41 13 30N	092 39 45W	city/town	
Gladbrook	42 11 16N	092 42 54W	city/town	
Glade	43 20 34N	093 09 39W	city/town	
Gladstone	41 57 50N	092 29 50W	city/town	
Gladwin	41 21 35N	091 27 03W	city/town	
Glasgow	40 56 27N	091 46 49W	city/town	
Glasgow -hist	42 36 18N	092 20 53W	city/town	
Glen Ellen	42 25 07N	096 19 12W	city/town	
Glendon	41 35 40N	094 24 07W	city/town	
Glenwood	41 02 49N	095 44 32W	city/town	
Glidden	42 03 25N	094 43 43W	city/town	
Goddard	41 43 03N	093 11 34W	city/town	
Godfield	42 44 14N	093 55 12W	city/town	
Golden	42 23 26N	091 28 13W	city/town	

Place Name	Latitude	Longitude	Type	Elev
Goldfield	42 44 09N	093 55 14W	city/town	1130
Gonoa Bluff	41 41 36N	092 09 09W	city/town	
Goodell	42 55 23N	093 36 58W	city/town	
Goose Lake	41 58 03N	090 22 58W	city/town	
Goose Lake	42 06 45N	094 24 10W	lake	1081
Goose Lake Quarry	41 58 34N	090 22 19W	locale	
Goose Rock	42 09 02N	090 52 38W	summit	
Gosport	41 12 17N	093 09 02W	city/town	
Gowrie	42 16 50N	094 17 26W	city/town	1137
Grable	41 28 15N	095 53 58W	city/town	
Grace Hill	41 15 49N	091 49 47W	city/town	
Graettinger	43 14 16N	094 45 04W	city/town	
Graf	42 29 35N	090 52 16W	city/town	
Grafton	43 19 48N	093 04 09W	city/town	
Graham -hist	41 40 31N	091 27 21W	city/town	
Grand Junction	42 01 54N	094 14 26W	city/town	
Grand Mound	41 49 27N	090 38 52W	city/town	
Grand River	40 49 10N	093 57 44W	city/town	
Grandview	41 16 33N	091 11 18W	city/town	
Grandview College	41 37 15N	093 36 16W	univ/coll	
Granger	41 45 40N	093 49 27W	city/town	
Granger Hill	42 02 35N	095 52 43W	summit	

Place Name	Latitude	Longitude	Type	Elev
Granger Homesteads	41 45 52N	093 50 20W	city/town	
Granite	43 28 08N	096 33 22W	city/town	
Grant	41 08 34N	094 59 04W	city/town	
Grant City	42 16 03N	094 53 15W	city/town	
Granville	42 59 08N	095 52 24W	city/town	
Granville -hist	41 29 46N	092 46 27W	city/town	
Gravel Pit	42 04 13N	094 17 28W	city/town	
Gravity	40 45 38N	094 44 36W	city/town	
Gray	41 50 22N	094 58 58W	city/town	1374
Great Oaks	41 35 39N	090 25 17W	city/town	650
Greeley	42 35 09N	091 20 29W	city/town	
Green Acres	41 34 12N	090 36 36W	city/town	
Green Bay -hist	40 54 55N	093 46 27W	city/town	
Green Brier	41 55 19N	094 25 06W	city/town	
Green Castle	41 44 46N	093 15 41W	city/town	
Green Castle -hist	41 46 28N	091 39 58W	city/town	
Green Center	41 32 25N	091 53 11W	city/town	
Green Island	42 09 13N	090 19 19W	city/town	
Green Mountain	42 06 06N	092 49 13W	city/town	
Green Valley State	41 06 52N	094 22 58W	park	
Greenbush (1)	41 25 28N	093 39 23W	city/town	
Greenbush (2)	41 25 30N	093 27 05W	city/town	

Iowa GPS Companion

Place Name	Latitude	Longitude	Type	Elev
Greene	42 53 45N	092 48 08W	city/town	
Greenfield	41 18 19N	094 27 40W	city/town	
Greenfield Mun.	41 19 37N	094 26 51W	airport	1361
Greenville	43 01 00N	095 08 45W	city/town	
Gridley	43 23 58N	094 34 23W	city/town	
Griffen	42 11 16N	093 47 41W	city/town	
Grimes	41 41 18N	093 47 27W	city/town	
Grinnell	41 44 35N	092 43 20W	city/town	
Grinnell College	41 44 55N	092 43 12W	univ/coll	
Grinnell Regional	41 42 33N	092 44 05W	airport	1008
Griswold	41 14 06N	095 08 14W	city/town	
Grove City -hist	41 23 14N	094 57 43W	city/town	
Groveland -hist	40 59 04N	093 47 53W	city/town	
Grovers Lake	43 29 54N	095 09 27W	lake	1414
Grundy Center	42 21 42N	092 46 06W	city/town	1026
Grundy Center Mun.	42 21 03N	092 50 36W	airport	1075
Gruver	43 23 36N	094 42 18W	city/town	
Guard Lake	41 59 19N	096 06 17W	lake	1033
Guernsey	41 38 55N	092 20 33W	city/town	
Gull Point	43 22 15N	095 09 31W	cape	
Gull Point State	43 22 16N	095 09 53W	park	
Gunder	42 58 18N	091 30 47W	city/town	

Iowa GPS Companion

Place Name	Latitude	Longitude	Type	Elev
Gunwald	41 05 16N	093 15 16W	city/town	
Guss	40 50 31N	094 51 28W	city/town	
Guthrie Center	41 40 38N	094 30 11W	city/town	1150
Guthrie County	41 41 16N	094 26 06W	airport	1230
Guttenberg	42 47 09N	091 05 58W	city/town	625

Ⓗ

Place Name	Latitude	Longitude	Type	Elev
Hagerty (1)	43 18 47N	095 19 44W	city/town	
Hagerty (2)	41 04 37N	092 51 36W	city/town	
Halbur	42 00 25N	094 58 11W	city/town	
Hale	42 00 45N	091 03 33W	city/town	
Haley	41 54 22N	095 33 22W	city/town	
Halfa	43 21 07N	094 32 30W	city/town	
Halls Lake	41 06 40N	091 04 56W	lake	539
Ham House Museum	42 44 27N	090 39 00W	locale	740
Hamburg	40 36 16N	095 39 27W	city/town	914
Hamerville	42 18 45N	091 53 22W	city/town	
Hamilton	41 10 09N	092 54 11W	city/town	
Hamilton Technical	41 34 50N	090 34 02W	univ/coll	
Hamlin	41 40 01N	094 54 20W	city/town	1266
Hammondsburgh -his	41 18 25N	093 28 22W	city/town	
Hampton	42 44 31N	093 12 08W	city/town	

Iowa GPS Companion

Place Name	Latitude	Longitude	Type	Elev
Hampton Municipal	42 43 25N	093 13 34W	airport	1176
Hancock	41 23 24N	095 21 44W	city/town	
Hanford	43 04 27N	093 08 29W	city/town	
Hanging Rock	43 06 30N	091 10 50W	pillar	
Hanley	41 17 17N	093 50 02W	city/town	
Hanlontown	43 16 49N	093 22 43W	city/town	
Hanna	42 56 57N	094 01 14W	city/town	
Hanover	43 21 39N	091 31 14W	city/town	
Hansell	42 45 28N	093 06 14W	city/town	
Harcourt	42 15 46N	094 10 32W	city/town	
Hard Scratch	41 36 48N	095 42 50W	city/town	1220
Hardin	43 04 49N	091 29 03W	city/town	1039
Hardy	42 48 38N	094 03 04W	city/town	
Harlan	41 39 11N	095 19 31W	city/town	1250
Harlan Junction	41 29 53N	095 21 48W	city/town	
Harlan Municipal	41 35 01N	095 20 20W	airport	1218
Harmon Tunnel	41 17 46N	094 04 27W	other	
Harper	41 21 45N	092 03 03W	city/town	
Harpers Ferry	43 12 02N	091 09 11W	city/town	
Harris	43 26 43N	095 26 02W	city/town	
Harrisburg	40 46 14N	091 46 37W	city/town	
Harrison	41 17 14N	094 11 06W	city/town	

Iowa GPS Companion

Place Name	Latitude	Longitude	Type	Elev
Hart	42 15 50N	094 59 39W	city/town	
Hartford	41 27 34N	093 24 17W	city/town	
Hartley	43 10 48N	095 28 36W	city/town	
Hartley -Lamb. F.	43 09 45N	095 28 00W	airport	1452
Hartwick	41 47 05N	092 20 36W	city/town	
Harvard	40 41 24N	093 16 09W	city/town	
Harvey	41 18 57N	092 55 26W	city/town	
Haskins	41 19 41N	091 32 12W	city/town	
Hastie	41 33 46N	093 29 22W	city/town	
Hastings	41 01 22N	095 29 56W	city/town	
Hauntown	42 00 03N	090 11 56W	city/town	
Havelock	42 50 10N	094 42 01W	city/town	
Haven	41 53 30N	092 28 44W	city/town	
Haverhill	41 56 42N	092 57 38W	city/town	
Havre	41 15 13N	091 36 36W	city/town	
Hawarden	42 59 45N	096 29 06W	city/town	
Hawarden Municipal	43 02 13N	096 29 34W	airport	1174
Hawkeye	42 56 19N	091 57 00W	city/town	
Hawkeye Downs	41 56 03N	091 40 51W	locale	
Hawley	43 12 46N	093 40 46W	city/town	
Hawleyville	40 46 36N	094 56 10W	city/town	
Hawthorne	41 00 06N	095 20 12W	city/town	

Place Name	Latitude	Longitude	Type	Elev
Hayesville	41 15 52N	092 14 56W	city/town	
Hayfield	43 10 36N	093 41 42W	city/town	
Hayfield Junction	43 08 02N	093 35 57W	city/town	
Hazleton	42 37 15N	091 54 00W	city/town	
Hebron	41 15 17N	094 17 06W	city/town	
Hedrick	41 10 21N	092 18 31W	city/town	
Heery Woods State	42 46 30N	092 40 32W	park	
Hefel Ridge	42 40 40N	090 58 52W	summit	
Heinz Field	41 26 24N	091 01 42W	locale	
Helena	41 55 15N	092 28 27W	city/town	
Henderson	41 08 26N	095 25 51W	city/town	
Henshaw	40 50 33N	094 53 42W	city/town	
Hentons -hist	41 05 33N	095 49 58W	city/town	
Hepburn	40 50 57N	095 01 01W	city/town	
Herndon	41 50 44N	094 20 57W	city/town	1058
Hesper	43 29 11N	091 46 06W	city/town	
Hiattsville	40 49 38N	092 48 37W	city/town	
Hiawatha	42 02 09N	091 40 55W	city/town	
Hickory Grove	41 39 17N	090 44 58W	city/town	690
Hickory Grove C C	42 38 58N	091 54 05W	golf	
Hickory Grove Lake	41 59 09N	093 21 12W	lake	970
Hicks	42 21 58N	092 32 02W	city/town	

Place Name	Latitude	Longitude	Type	Elev
High Amana	41 48 12N	091 56 17W	city/town	
High Creek	40 35 15N	095 27 01W	city/town	
High Point	40 45 40N	093 35 39W	city/town	
Highland	42 53 38N	091 35 49W	city/town	
Highland Center	41 07 35N	092 21 11W	city/town	
Highland Park	43 03 17N	096 20 35W	city/town	
Highlandville	43 26 32N	091 40 06W	city/town	
Highview	42 28 19N	093 54 14W	city/town	1128
Hillcrest C C 1	41 37 54N	093 59 06W	golf	
Hillcrest C C 2	41 54 52N	091 24 32W	golf	
Hills	41 33 15N	091 32 05W	city/town	
Hillsboro (1)	40 50 12N	091 42 56W	city/town	
Hillsboro (2)	41 17 15N	091 21 45W	city/town	
Hillsdale	41 00 27N	095 40 14W	city/town	
Hilltop	42 28 34N	092 16 13W	city/town	
Hinton	42 37 40N	096 17 29W	city/town	
Hiteman	41 03 32N	092 53 31W	city/town	
Hobarton	43 04 14N	094 16 55W	city/town	
Hocking	40 59 27N	092 49 13W	city/town	
Hodge	40 40 52N	093 24 13W	city/town	
Hogback, The	42 05 33N	091 48 40W	summit	
Holbrook	41 35 27N	091 54 46W	city/town	

Place Name	Latitude	Longitude	Type	Elev
Holiday Lake	41 49 09N	092 26 53W	lake	867
Holland	42 23 56N	092 48 01W	city/town	
Holly Springs	42 16 14N	096 04 39W	city/town	1078
Holmes	42 44 21N	093 50 01W	city/town	
Holstein	42 29 21N	095 32 41W	city/town	1437
Holt	40 53 40N	094 44 17W	city/town	
Holy Cross (1)	42 35 43N	091 13 24W	city/town	
Holy Cross (2)	42 36 02N	090 59 44W	city/town	
Homer	42 22 26N	093 55 24W	city/town	
Homestead	41 45 34N	091 52 01W	city/town	
Homewood Golf	42 02 36N	093 36 24W	golf	
Honey Creek	41 25 50N	095 51 58W	city/town	
Hoover Birthplace	41 40 09N	091 20 51W	park	
Hopeville	40 56 34N	093 59 47W	city/town	
Hopkinton	42 20 38N	091 14 54W	city/town	
Hoprig	43 16 12N	094 37 09W	city/town	
Hornick	42 13 50N	096 05 50W	city/town	1067
Horseshoe Bluff	42 27 46N	090 38 06W	cliff	
Horton	42 50 51N	092 28 31W	city/town	
Hospers	43 04 19N	095 54 15W	city/town	
Hottes Lake	43 28 45N	095 08 25W	lake	1402
Houghton	40 47 01N	091 36 10W	city/town	

Place Name	Latitude	Longitude	Type	Elev
Howard County Mus.	43 22 37N	092 07 16W	museum	
Howardville	43 11 27N	092 42 44W	city/town	
Howe	41 24 11N	094 22 33W	city/town	
Howell -hist	41 22 45N	092 58 05W	city/town	
Hubbard	42 18 20N	093 18 00W	city/town	
Hudson	42 24 24N	092 27 19W	city/town	
Hughs	42 23 51N	093 09 27W	city/town	
Hull	43 11 19N	096 08 00W	city/town	
Humboldt	42 43 15N	094 12 54W	city/town	
Humboldt Municipal	42 44 10N	094 14 42W	airport	1110
Humeston	40 51 32N	093 29 50W	city/town	
Huntington	43 29 30N	094 47 30W	city/town	
Hurley	43 00 33N	093 13 52W	city/town	
Huron	41 02 12N	091 02 02W	city/town	
Hurstville	42 05 51N	090 40 59W	city/town	
Hutchins	43 05 30N	093 52 51W	city/town	1200
Huxley	41 53 43N	093 36 02W	city/town	
Hyperion C C	41 41 41N	093 42 23W	golf	
Icarid -hist	40 59 43N	094 41 14W	city/town	
Ice Harbor Empor.	42 29 43N	090 45 51W	locale	730

Place Name	Latitude	Longitude	Type	Elev
Iconium	40 53 29N	092 57 18W	city/town	993
Ida Grove	42 20 42N	095 28 17W	city/town	1236
Ida Grove Munic.	42 19 57N	095 26 40W	airport	1245
Idlewild State	43 09 59N	092 45 26W	park	
Illinois Grove	42 11 27N	093 13 24W	city/town	
Illyria	42 53 55N	091 38 06W	city/town	
Imogene	40 52 46N	095 25 36W	city/town	
Independence	42 28 07N	091 53 21W	city/town	
Independence Mun.	42 27 13N	091 56 50W	airport	978
Indian Creek C C 1	41 58 33N	093 26 43W	golf	
Indian Creek C C 2	42 02 48N	091 35 35W	golf	
Indian Spring -his	42 40 57N	094 16 45W	spring	
Indian Village St.	42 58 44N	095 25 36W	park	
Indiana	41 12 16N	093 01 30W	city/town	
Indianapolis	41 23 49N	092 26 00W	city/town	
Indianola	41 21 29N	093 33 26W	city/town	
Indianola Junction	41 02 25N	093 21 23W	city/town	
Indiantown -hist	41 18 45N	095 06 28W	city/town	
Ingersoll -hist	41 43 55N	093 49 15W	city/town	
Inwood	43 18 26N	096 25 54W	city/town	
Ioka -historic	41 10 57N	092 07 44W	city/town	
Iola -historic	41 19 58N	095 22 47W	city/town	

Place Name	Latitude	Longitude	Type	Elev
Ion	43 06 46N	091 15 43W	city/town	
Ionia	43 02 04N	092 27 20W	city/town	
Iowa Center	41 55 43N	093 24 18W	city/town	
Iowa City	41 39 40N	091 31 48W	city/town	
Iowa City Munic.	41 38 21N	091 32 46W	airport	668
Iowa Falls	42 31 24N	093 15 04W	city/town	
Iowa Falls Jct.	42 30 55N	093 15 48W	city/town	
Iowa Falls Munic.	42 28 14N	093 16 11W	airport	1137
Iowa Junction -his	41 29 33N	091 32 06W	city/town	
Iowa St Exper Farm	41 54 34N	093 48 13W	locale	
Iowa St Fair Campg	41 35 41N	093 32 29W	locale	
Iowa St U Agronomy	42 01 16N	093 46 23W	farm	
Iowa St U Experim.	41 42 41N	093 37 58W	farm	
Iowa St U Experim.	42 03 28N	093 40 55W	farm	
Iowa St U Experim.	42 03 47N	095 50 09W	station	
Iowa St U Experim.	42 06 31N	093 35 17W	farm	
Iowa St University	42 01 34N	093 38 54W	univ/coll	960
Iowa State Capitol	41 35 28N	093 36 13W	building	
Ira	41 46 40N	093 12 20W	city/town	
Ireton	42 58 29N	096 19 05W	city/town	
Ironhills	42 08 30N	090 46 11W	city/town	
Irving	41 56 54N	092 17 42W	city/town	

Place Name	Latitude	Longitude	Type	Elev
Irvington	43 00 27N	094 11 43W	city/town	
Irwin	41 47 30N	095 12 20W	city/town	1264
ISU Arboretum	42 01 08N	093 39 19W	locale	
Ivester	42 20 23N	092 56 38W	city/town	1120
Iveyville	40 54 03N	094 47 44W	city/town	
Ivy	41 36 02N	093 25 01W	city/town	

J

Place Name	Latitude	Longitude	Type	Elev
J Dubuque Monument	42 26 36N	090 29 23W	park	
Jackson	42 09 15N	091 21 09W	city/town	
Jackson Junction	43 06 54N	092 01 56W	city/town	
Jacksonville (1)	41 38 43N	095 08 59W	city/town	1274
Jacksonville (2)	43 07 10N	092 12 32W	city/town	
Jacksonville -hist	41 06 20N	093 33 30W	city/town	
Jacobs	41 39 54N	092 40 07W	city/town	
Jamaica	41 50 46N	094 18 34W	city/town	1048
James	42 34 37N	096 19 02W	city/town	
Jamestown (1)	41 25 45N	092 21 17W	city/town	
Jamestown (2)	41 29 40N	090 42 29W	city/town	
Jamison	41 07 18N	093 43 29W	city/town	
Janesville	42 38 46N	092 27 46W	city/town	
Jay	41 06 24N	093 35 11W	city/town	

Place Name	Latitude	Longitude	Type	Elev
Jefferson	42 00 55N	094 22 38W	city/town	1078
Jefferson Munic.	42 00 37N	094 20 31W	airport	1048
Jeffersonville	40 36 35N	091 26 45W	city/town	
Jerico	43 11 03N	092 33 19W	city/town	
Jerome	40 43 08N	093 01 41W	city/town	
Jesup	42 28 32N	092 03 49W	city/town	
Jewell	42 18 25N	093 38 24W	city/town	
John Vardy House	41 58 28N	091 39 45W	building	
Johnson -hist	42 08 57N	091 01 58W	city/town	
Johnston	41 40 23N	093 41 51W	city/town	
Joice	43 21 46N	093 27 13W	city/town	
Jolley	42 28 44N	094 43 07W	city/town	
Jollyville Hill	40 41 11N	091 14 09W	summit	
Jones Siding	42 40 48N	094 12 28W	city/town	
Jordan	42 02 57N	093 47 02W	city/town	
Jordans Grove	42 09 21N	091 29 54W	city/town	
Jubilee	42 23 03N	092 06 13W	city/town	
Judd	42 28 20N	094 02 58W	city/town	
Julien	42 28 52N	090 46 46W	city/town	
Julien Dubuque Mon	42 28 07N	090 38 45W	monument	
Junction -hist	43 05 07N	091 37 45W	city/town	
Junction Switch	42 16 36N	091 12 10W	city/town	

Place Name	Latitude	Longitude	Type	Elev
Juniata	42 34 49N	095 08 52W	city/town	

𝕂

Place Name	Latitude	Longitude	Type	Elev
Kalo	42 25 52N	094 07 54W	city/town	
Kalona	41 28 59N	091 42 21W	city/town	
Kalsow St Prairie	42 34 07N	094 33 55W	park	
Kamrar	42 23 32N	093 43 45W	city/town	
Kanawha	42 56 16N	093 47 35W	city/town	
Keb -historic	41 05 00N	092 27 30W	city/town	
Kellerton	40 42 39N	094 02 59W	city/town	
Kelley	41 57 02N	093 39 54W	city/town	
Kellogg	41 43 05N	092 54 26W	city/town	
Kellys Beach	43 22 54N	095 06 13W	beach	
Kellys Bluff	42 29 45N	090 40 07W	cliff	750
Kemling -hist	41 10 00N	095 16 42W	city/town	
Kemper	40 44 38N	091 07 24W	city/town	
Kendallville	43 26 22N	092 02 10W	city/town	
Kenfield	41 34 35N	094 43 10W	city/town	
Kennebec	42 05 51N	096 00 45W	city/town	
Kennedy	41 36 24N	094 07 29W	city/town	
Kensett	43 21 13N	093 12 37W	city/town	1225
Kent	40 57 09N	094 27 15W	city/town	

Iowa GPS Companion

Place Name	Latitude	Longitude	Type	Elev
Kentner	42 10 00N	094 49 22W	city/town	
Kenwood	42 00 31N	095 30 35W	city/town	
Keokuk	40 23 50N	091 23 05W	city/town	
Keokuk Municipal	40 27 35N	091 25 42W	airport	671
Keomah Village	41 17 18N	092 32 11W	city/town	
Keosauqua	40 43 49N	091 57 44W	city/town	
Keosauqua Munic.	40 44 05N	091 56 55W	airport	580
Keota	41 21 50N	091 57 13W	city/town	
Kesley	42 39 45N	092 54 36W	city/town	
Keswick	41 27 09N	092 14 21W	city/town	
Keteban Switch	40 38 47N	091 41 56W	city/town	
Key West	42 26 56N	090 41 02W	city/town	
Keystone	41 59 54N	092 11 50W	city/town	
Kidder	42 27 51N	090 55 40W	city/town	
Kilbourn	40 48 22N	091 58 11W	city/town	
Killduff	41 36 29N	092 54 16W	city/town	
Kimballton	41 37 43N	095 04 22W	city/town	1290
Kimze	41 59 39N	095 23 22W	city/town	
King	42 24 19N	090 35 30W	city/town	
Kingsley	42 35 18N	095 58 02W	city/town	
Kingston (1)	40 48 51N	093 50 06W	city/town	
Kingston (2)	40 58 39N	091 02 25W	city/town	

Iowa GPS Companion

Place Name	Latitude	Longitude	Type	Elev
Kinross	41 27 39N	091 59 12W	city/town	
Kirkman	41 43 43N	095 15 54W	city/town	
Kirkville	41 08 44N	092 30 14W	city/town	
Kiron	42 11 44N	095 19 39W	city/town	1341
Klacks Island Park	42 50 35N	091 49 00W	park	
Klemme	43 00 25N	093 36 10W	city/town	
Kline	40 55 20N	091 12 32W	city/town	
Klinger	42 39 24N	092 13 09W	city/town	
Klondike	43 23 16N	096 31 14W	city/town	
Knierim	42 27 20N	094 27 24W	city/town	1175
Knittel	42 42 55N	092 15 30W	city/town	
Knoke	42 31 01N	094 45 46W	city/town	
Knowlton	40 49 35N	094 19 55W	city/town	
Knoxville	41 19 15N	093 06 33W	city/town	
Knoxville Munic.	41 17 56N	093 06 49W	airport	928
Koch Lake	41 42 30N	091 05 55W	lake	755
Konigsmark	41 53 24N	091 41 32W	city/town	
Kossuth	41 00 38N	091 08 04W	city/town	
Koszta	41 49 38N	092 12 19W	city/town	

𝕃

La Crew	40 44 00N	091 35 01W	city/town	

64

Iowa GPS Companion

Place Name	Latitude	Longitude	Type	Elev
La Motte	42 17 45N	090 37 15W	city/town	915
La Porte City	42 18 54N	092 11 31W	city/town	
Lacey	41 24 03N	092 38 24W	city/town	
Lacey-Keosauqua St	40 42 37N	091 58 53W	park	
Lacona	41 11 23N	093 22 58W	city/town	
Ladoga	40 44 30N	094 47 42W	city/town	
Ladora	41 45 17N	092 11 00W	city/town	
Lafayette (1)	42 08 49N	091 40 48W	city/town	
Lafayette (2)	41 17 15N	091 21 45W	city/town	
Lainsville	42 07 47N	090 12 16W	city/town	
Lake Ahquabi State	41 17 15N	093 35 33W	park	
Lake Anita State	41 25 27N	094 46 21W	park	
Lake City	42 16 03N	094 44 01W	city/town	
Lake Darling State	41 11 30N	091 53 44W	park	
Lake Keomah State	41 17 24N	092 32 26W	park	
Lake Macbride St	41 47 38N	091 33 57W	park	
Lake Manawa State	41 12 28N	095 51 25W	park	
Lake Mills	43 25 10N	093 31 59W	city/town	
Lake of Three Fire	40 43 00N	094 41 30W	park	
Lake Park	43 27 20N	095 19 14W	city/town	
Lake View	42 18 42N	095 03 11W	city/town	1270
Lake Wapello State	40 48 57N	092 35 18W	park	

Place Name	Latitude	Longitude	Type	Elev
Lakeside	42 37 17N	095 10 23W	city/town	
Lakeside Beach	42 36 55N	095 10 46W	beach	
Lakeview	42 18 25N	095 03 05W	city/town	1245
Lakewood	41 30 06N	093 40 26W	city/town	
Lakewood Corner	43 20 46N	096 10 33W	city/town	
Lakonta	41 11 36N	092 43 49W	city/town	
Lakota	43 22 38N	094 05 37W	city/town	
Lambs Grove	41 42 11N	093 04 45W	city/town	
LaMoille	42 01 50N	093 02 18W	city/town	
Lamoni	40 37 22N	093 56 02W	city/town	
Lamoni Municipal	40 38 00N	093 54 07W	airport	1131
Lamont	42 35 55N	091 38 31W	city/town	
Lanesboro	42 11 04N	094 41 28W	city/town	1149
Langdon	43 12 57N	095 05 16W	city/town	
Langworthy	42 11 28N	091 13 26W	city/town	
Lanscaster	41 16 32N	092 09 53W	city/town	
Lansing	43 21 44N	091 12 59W	city/town	
Lansing Ridge	43 20 32N	091 22 01W	ridge	
Lansrud	43 27 07N	093 28 07W	city/town	
Lanyon	42 13 21N	094 11 42W	city/town	
LaPorte City -Nich	42 19 00N	092 17 00W	airport	950
Larchwood	43 27 13N	096 26 02W	city/town	

Place Name	Latitude	Longitude	Type	Elev
Larland	41 43 54N	094 45 46W	city/town	
Larrabee	42 51 39N	095 32 42W	city/town	
Last Chance	40 57 23N	093 33 12W	city/town	
Latimer	42 45 48N	093 22 05W	city/town	
Lattnerville	42 29 08N	090 52 58W	city/town	
Latty	40 54 12N	091 07 18W	city/town	
Laurel	41 53 03N	092 55 19W	city/town	
Laurens	42 50 48N	094 51 06W	city/town	
Lavinia	42 24 28N	094 44 47W	city/town	
Lawler	43 04 14N	092 09 00W	city/town	
Lawn Hill	42 17 52N	093 10 18W	city/town	
Lawrenceburg	41 13 38N	093 32 54W	city/town	
Lawton	42 28 43N	096 11 01W	city/town	1179
Lazy Brook C C	41 40 43N	091 21 58W	golf	
Le Claire	41 35 55N	090 20 36W	city/town	
Le Grand	42 00 25N	092 46 31W	city/town	
Le Mars	42 47 39N	096 09 55W	city/town	1231
Le Mars Municipal	42 46 40N	096 11 36W	airport	1196
Le Roy	40 52 40N	093 35 33W	city/town	
Leando	40 50 01N	092 05 19W	city/town	
Lear	42 31 39N	092 44 19W	city/town	
Lebanon (1)	40 43 33N	092 04 56W	city/town	

Place Name	Latitude	Longitude	Type	Elev
Lebanon (2)	43 05 55N	096 21 23W	city/town	
Ledges State Park	41 59 00N	093 53 12W	park	
Ledyard	43 25 18N	094 09 43W	city/town	
Lee -histor.	40 35 16N	094 06 38W	city/town	
Leeds	42 32 28N	096 21 35W	city/town	
Lehigh	42 21 36N	094 03 07W	city/town	
Leighton	41 20 14N	092 47 13W	city/town	
Leland	43 20 14N	093 38 06W	city/town	
Lemont -hist	41 19 58N	094 28 10W	city/town	
Lena	42 13 14N	094 17 15W	city/town	
Lenox	40 52 54N	094 33 42W	city/town	
Leon	40 44 23N	093 44 51W	city/town	
Leslie	40 56 34N	093 47 52W	city/town	
Lester	43 26 41N	096 19 58W	city/town	
Letts	41 19 42N	091 14 13W	city/town	
Leverett	42 54 24N	094 58 24W	city/town	
Levey	41 32 47N	093 31 18W	city/town	
Lewis	41 18 21N	095 04 59W	city/town	
Lewis &Clark -1804	41 37 15N	096 06 48W	campsite	1010
Lewis And Clark St	42 02 32N	096 10 03W	park	
Lexington (1)	40 41 57N	091 48 52W	city/town	560
Lexington (2)	41 23 52N	091 48 25W	city/town	

Place Name	Latitude	Longitude	Type	Elev
Liberty	41 08 43N	093 39 14W	city/town	
Liberty Center	41 12 17N	093 29 55W	city/town	
Libertyville	40 57 27N	092 03 04W	city/town	
Lidderdale	42 07 28N	094 46 58W	city/town	
Lidtke Mill	43 27 52N	092 16 41W	city/town	
Lighthouse Marina	42 06 45N	096 16 00W	locale	
Lily Lake	43 23 44N	095 01 20W	lake	1520
Lily Pond	41 47 55N	091 53 09W	lake	718
Lima	42 52 06N	091 44 34W	city/town	928
Lime City	41 38 52N	091 04 38W	city/town	
Lime Springs	43 25 48N	092 18 00W	city/town	1250
Linby	41 09 02N	092 08 28W	city/town	
Lincoln (1)	42 15 46N	092 41 30W	city/town	
Lincoln (2)	42 25 40N	092 39 41W	city/town	
Lincoln Center	41 06 57N	094 52 19W	city/town	
Lincolnway Village	41 55 17N	091 39 55W	city/town	
Linden	41 38 40N	094 16 08W	city/town	1120
Lindle Lake	41 30 01N	091 08 54W	lake	615
Lineville	40 34 53N	093 31 25W	city/town	
Linn Grove	42 53 30N	095 14 47W	city/town	
Linn Junction	42 01 08N	091 43 14W	city/town	
Linwood (1)	41 25 30N	094 37 26W	city/town	

Iowa GPS Companion

Place Name	Latitude	Longitude	Type	Elev
Linwood (2)	41 27 56N	090 40 44W	city/town	
Lisbon	41 55 16N	091 23 07W	city/town	
Liscomb	42 11 24N	093 00 13W	city/town	
Little Cedar	43 22 49N	092 43 32W	city/town	
Little Groves	41 32 15N	090 41 19W	city/town	759
Little Rock	43 26 39N	095 52 59W	city/town	
Little Sioux	41 48 34N	096 01 15W	city/town	1033
Little Sioux C C	42 54 16N	095 09 42W	golf	
Little Turkey	43 07 47N	092 06 03W	city/town	
Littleport	42 45 17N	091 22 09W	city/town	708
Littleton	42 32 00N	092 01 24W	city/town	
Livermore	42 52 07N	094 11 06W	city/town	
Lizard -hist	42 38 05N	094 30 39W	city/town	
Lizard Lake Access	42 40 17N	094 29 58W	park	1190
Loch Burns	41 01 32N	092 21 00W	city/town	
Lock and Dam #10	42 47 06N	091 05 42W	dam	
Lock and Dam #11	42 32 25N	090 38 39W	dam	
Lock and Dam #13	41 53 54N	090 09 24W	dam	
Lock and Dam #14	41 34 24N	090 23 56W	dam	
Lock and Dam #15	41 31 07N	090 34 08W	dam	
Lock and Dam #16	41 25 32N	091 00 34W	dam	
Lock and Dam #17	41 11 30N	091 03 30W	dam	

Place Name	Latitude	Longitude	Type	Elev
Lock and Dam #18	40 52 58N	091 01 26W	dam	
Lock and Dam #19	40 23 42N	091 22 25W	dam	
Lockman	41 05 00N	092 44 21W	city/town	
Lockridge	40 59 41N	091 44 53W	city/town	
Locust	43 25 18N	091 43 20W	city/town	
Logan	41 38 35N	095 47 19W	city/town	1104
Logan-Missouri V.	41 35 52N	095 50 00W	golf	
Logansport	42 04 03N	093 56 48W	city/town	
Lohrville	42 16 13N	094 32 54W	city/town	
Lone Rock	43 13 07N	094 19 36W	city/town	
Lone Tree	41 29 17N	091 25 33W	city/town	
Long Grove	41 41 51N	090 34 57W	city/town	
Long Point	41 56 43N	092 29 01W	city/town	
Lonia	43 02 03N	092 27 21W	city/town	
Lorah	41 28 13N	094 57 18W	city/town	1222
Loras College	42 30 15N	090 40 53W	univ/coll	
Lore	42 31 05N	090 47 59W	city/town	
Lorimor	41 07 42N	094 03 11W	city/town	
Loring	41 50 05N	093 26 06W	city/town	
Lost Island Lake	43 10 20N	094 54 18W	lake	1347
Lost Island Lake	43 10 24N	094 53 31W	park	
Lost Nation	41 57 50N	090 49 03W	city/town	

71

Iowa GPS Companion

Place Name	Latitude	Longitude	Type	Elev
Lotts Creek	43 09 24N	094 21 58W	city/town	
Louisa	42 01 53N	091 40 02W	city/town	
Louise	42 21 36N	092 17 55W	city/town	
Lourdes	43 15 44N	092 17 55W	city/town	
Loveland	41 29 50N	095 53 23W	city/town	
Lovilia	41 08 09N	092 54 14W	city/town	
Lovington	41 38 45N	093 41 11W	city/town	
Low Moor	41 48 06N	090 21 17W	city/town	
Lowden	41 51 27N	090 55 41W	city/town	
Lowe Pool	43 14 17N	094 09 30W	lake	1125
Lowell	40 50 00N	091 26 11W	city/town	
Lowther Station	43 19 08N	092 30 21W	city/town	
Lu Verne	42 54 30N	094 04 25W	city/town	
Luana	43 03 37N	091 27 14W	city/town	
Lucas	41 01 42N	093 27 35W	city/town	
Lucas County Mus.	41 00 56N	093 19 10W	building	
Ludlow	43 13 35N	091 34 00W	city/town	1217
Lundgren	42 22 07N	094 10 28W	city/town	
Lunsford	40 36 10N	092 26 07W	city/town	
Luray	41 59 26N	092 59 59W	city/town	
Luther	41 58 04N	093 49 07W	city/town	
Luther College	43 18 45N	091 48 17W	univ/coll	

Place Name	Latitude	Longitude	Type	Elev
Lutherische Kirche	41 09 20N	095 45 46W	locale	
Luton	42 20 23N	096 13 34W	city/town	1081
Luxemburg	42 36 10N	091 04 26W	city/town	1180
Luzerne	41 53 53N	092 10 47W	city/town	
Lycurgus	43 19 52N	091 25 26W	city/town	
Lyman	41 13 52N	094 59 03W	city/town	
Lyndale	43 17 56N	091 17 00W	city/town	
Lynnville	41 34 39N	092 47 00W	city/town	
Lyons	41 52 02N	090 11 10W	city/town	
Lytton	42 25 23N	094 51 34W	city/town	

M

M and M Country C	41 54 16N	095 10 48W	golf	
Macedonia	41 11 34N	095 25 31W	city/town	
Macey	42 32 22N	093 08 52W	city/town	
Mackey	42 09 59N	093 45 24W	city/town	
Macksburg	41 12 53N	094 11 06W	city/town	
Maclay -hist	42 58 09N	095 04 22W	city/town	
Madrid	41 52 36N	093 49 23W	city/town	
Magill	41 31 08N	095 30 19W	city/town	
Magnolia	41 41 45N	095 52 35W	city/town	
Maine	40 51 22N	092 51 41W	city/town	

Iowa GPS Companion

Place Name	Latitude	Longitude	Type	Elev
Malcom	41 42 30N	092 33 32W	city/town	
Mallard	42 56 11N	094 40 55W	city/town	
Maloy	40 40 28N	094 24 43W	city/town	
Malta	41 58 15N	093 06 45W	city/town	
Malvern	41 00 10N	095 35 06W	city/town	
Mammen	42 51 05N	096 17 31W	city/town	
Manatheka -hist	42 13 40N	091 52 13W	city/town	
Manchester	42 29 03N	091 27 19W	city/town	
Manchester Munic.	42 29 36N	091 29 54W	airport	987
Manilla	41 53 23N	095 13 55W	city/town	1317
Manly	43 17 14N	093 12 07W	city/town	1198
Manning	41 54 33N	095 03 53W	city/town	1355
Manson	42 31 45N	094 32 02W	city/town	1221
Manteno	41 49 57N	095 32 13W	city/town	
Maple Hill	43 23 32N	094 37 30W	city/town	
Maple Leaf	43 19 15N	092 22 44W	city/town	
Maple Lndg -hist	42 05 32N	096 12 48W	city/town	
Maple River	42 05 53N	094 56 06W	city/town	
Mapleside	43 00 09N	095 37 25W	city/town	
Mapleton	42 09 57N	095 47 34W	city/town	1157
Mapleton Municipal	42 10 41N	095 47 36W	airport	1116
Maquoketa	42 04 08N	090 39 56W	city/town	

Iowa GPS Companion

Place Name	Latitude	Longitude	Type	Elev
Maquoketa Caves Br	42 07 02N	090 46 51W	arch	
Maquoketa Caves St	42 07 03N	090 46 50W	park	
Maquoketa Munic.	42 03 00N	090 44 19W	airport	769
Marathon	42 51 42N	094 58 56W	city/town	
Marble Beach	43 28 12N	095 07 26W	beach	
Marble Lake	43 28 27N	095 08 05W	lake	1402
Marble Rock	42 57 55N	092 52 06W	city/town	
Marcus	42 49 33N	095 48 26W	city/town	
Marcus Community	42 48 42N	095 48 15W	golf	
Marengo	41 47 53N	092 04 14W	city/town	
Margo Frankel Wood	41 40 22N	093 36 59W	park	
Marietta	42 04 59N	093 00 01W	city/town	
Marion	42 02 03N	091 35 51W	city/town	
Marion Airport	42 01 52N	091 31 45W	airport	862
Mark	40 39 37N	092 30 41W	city/town	
Mark Twain Overlk	41 25 37N	091 02 01W	locale	
Marne	41 27 05N	095 06 40W	city/town	
Marquette	43 02 40N	091 10 41W	city/town	
Marquisville	41 39 24N	093 36 02W	city/town	
Marsh	41 06 06N	091 21 08W	city/town	
Marshall -hist	40 43 30N	094 19 40W	city/town	
Marshalltown	42 02 58N	092 54 28W	city/town	

Place Name	Latitude	Longitude	Type	Elev
Marshalltown Mun.	42 06 45N	092 55 03W	airport	974
Martelle	42 01 18N	091 21 35W	city/town	
Martensdale	41 22 23N	093 44 08W	city/town	
Martinsburg	41 10 44N	092 15 06W	city/town	
Martinstown⁄	40 41 14N	092 57 32W	city/town	1026
Mary Hill	42 44 08N	095 41 18W	city/town	
Marycrest College	41 31 50N	090 35 54W	univ/coll	
Marysville	41 10 50N	092 56 56W	city/town	
Marysville -hist	41 17 17N	092 13 43W	city/town	
Maryville	42 41 16N	091 38 43W	city/town	
Mason City	43 09 13N	093 12 03W	city/town	
Mason City Jct	43 07 07N	093 11 20W	city/town	
Mason City Munic.	43 09 28N	093 19 51W	airport	1213
Masonville	42 28 46N	091 35 28W	city/town	
Massena	41 15 15N	094 46 05W	city/town	
Massey	42 25 49N	090 35 06W	city/town	
Massillon	41 54 53N	090 55 21W	city/town	
Matlock	43 14 38N	095 56 06W	city/town	
Maud	43 13 35N	091 22 13W	city/town	
Maulsby	42 08 41N	092 55 23W	city/town	
Maurice	42 57 59N	096 10 49W	city/town	
Max	43 11 10N	095 35 42W	city/town	

Place Name	Latitude	Longitude	Type	Elev
Maxon	41 02 27N	092 46 33W	city/town	
Maxwell	41 53 31N	093 23 58W	city/town	
May City	43 19 15N	095 28 27W	city/town	
Maynard	42 46 26N	091 52 56W	city/town	
Maysville	41 38 55N	090 43 00W	city/town	
McBride	41 25 55N	093 56 08W	city/town	
McCallsburg	42 09 59N	093 23 08W	city/town	
McCausland	41 44 46N	090 26 35W	city/town	
McClelland	41 19 46N	095 41 01W	city/town	
McClelland Beach	43 29 49N	095 05 32W	beach	
McCloy -hist	42 13 54N	095 09 47W	city/town	
McFarlane State	42 19 11N	092 08 20W	park	
McGargels Ford	42 13 59N	090 55 16W	city/town	
McGregor	43 01 06N	091 10 57W	city/town	
McGregor Heights	43 02 02N	091 10 38W	city/town	
McIntire	43 26 09N	092 35 37W	city/town	
McIntosh Woods St	43 07 39N	093 27 07W	park	
McNally	42 56 26N	096 23 26W	city/town	
McPaul	40 49 19N	095 48 09W	city/town	941
McPherson (1)	41 00 41N	095 20 11W	city/town	
McPherson (2)	41 14 25N	094 07 06W	city/town	
Meadowview C C	42 12 18N	091 30 40W	golf	

Iowa GPS Companion

Place Name	Latitude	Longitude	Type	Elev
Mechanicsville	41 54 16N	091 15 16W	city/town	
Mederville	42 45 47N	091 25 22W	city/town	
Mediapolis	41 00 29N	091 09 50W	city/town	
Medora	41 11 13N	093 36 09W	city/town	
Mekee	42 29 33N	091 02 44W	city/town	1062
Melbourne	41 56 29N	093 06 11W	city/town	
Melcher-Dallas	41 13 30N	093 14 28W	city/town	
Melrose	40 58 34N	093 03 01W	city/town	
Meltonville	43 26 50N	093 01 34W	city/town	
Melvin	43 17 15N	095 36 32W	city/town	
Memorial Field	42 30 26N	096 24 54W	locale	
Mendota -hist	40 35 43N	092 55 28W	city/town	
Menlo	41 31 09N	094 24 15W	city/town	1265
Mercer	40 56 36N	094 38 56W	city/town	
Meriden	42 47 41N	095 38 03W	city/town	
Merle Junction	40 46 54N	094 35 33W	city/town	
Merrill	42 43 11N	096 14 54W	city/town	
Merrimac	41 05 14N	091 43 07W	city/town	
Meservey	42 54 46N	093 28 41W	city/town	1246
Mesquakie Indian S	41 58 56N	092 38 33W	city/town	
Mestad Spring	43 26 47N	091 41 24W	spring	
Metz	41 39 59N	093 08 08W	city/town	

Iowa GPS Companion

Place Name	Latitude	Longitude	Type	Elev
Meyer	43 27 28N	092 41 33W	city/town	
Miami	41 08 50N	092 50 23W	city/town	
Middle Amana	41 47 44N	091 53 58W	city/town	
Middle Pond	41 48 30N	091 54 25W	lake	765
Middleburg	43 06 49N	096 04 07W	city/town	
Middletown	40 49 42N	091 15 32W	city/town	
Midland	43 28 35N	096 06 00W	city/town	
Midvale	41 55 46N	093 36 36W	city/town	
Midway (1)	42 06 22N	091 41 48W	city/town	
Midway (2)	43 00 19N	092 36 19W	city/town	
Midway (3)	42 22 15N	095 43 43W	city/town	
Midway -hist	41 37 08N	091 26 20W	city/town	
Midway Beach	41 27 33N	090 49 42W	city/town	
Miles	42 02 54N	090 18 56W	city/town	
Milford	43 19 29N	095 08 59W	city/town	
Milford -Fuller	43 19 59N	095 09 31W	airport	1439
Mill Creek State	42 59 04N	095 40 06W	park	
Miller	43 11 03N	093 36 00W	city/town	
Millersburg	41 34 24N	092 09 35W	city/town	
Millerton	40 50 58N	093 18 19W	city/town	
Millman	41 32 28N	093 40 38W	city/town	
Millnerville	42 41 55N	096 29 17W	city/town	

Iowa GPS Companion

Place Name	Latitude	Longitude	Type	Elev
Millrock	42 03 18N	090 50 21W	city/town	
Mills	41 01 07N	095 45 56W	city/town	
Millville	42 42 00N	091 04 27W	city/town	
Millville Siding	42 30 22N	091 04 22W	city/town	
Milo	41 17 30N	093 26 32W	city/town	
Milton	40 40 24N	092 09 43W	city/town	
Minburn	41 45 23N	094 01 38W	city/town	1042
Minden	41 28 01N	095 32 33W	city/town	
Mineola	41 08 35N	095 41 43W	city/town	
Miner	42 42 53N	092 06 04W	city/town	
Minerva	42 06 59N	093 05 16W	city/town	
Mines of Spain St	42 27 45N	090 39 45W	park	
Mingo	41 46 03N	093 17 00W	city/town	
Mini Wakan State P	43 29 51N	095 06 11W	park	
Missouri Valley	41 33 23N	095 53 15W	city/town	1019
Mitchell	43 19 19N	092 52 03W	city/town	
Mitchellville	41 40 07N	093 21 27W	city/town	
Modale	41 37 11N	096 00 42W	city/town	1013
Mohrs Lake	41 57 38N	092 54 19W	lake	945
Moingona	42 01 01N	093 55 56W	city/town	
Mona	43 29 14N	092 56 28W	city/town	
Mondamin	41 42 38N	096 01 17W	city/town	

Iowa GPS Companion

Place Name	Latitude	Longitude	Type	Elev
Moneek	43 09 37N	091 37 27W	city/town	
Moneta	43 07 45N	095 23 25W	city/town	
Monette	41 05 05N	094 04 19W	city/town	
Moningers	42 06 33N	093 02 03W	city/town	
Monmouth	42 04 37N	090 52 47W	city/town	
Monona	43 03 06N	091 23 21W	city/town	
Monona Municipal	43 01 50N	091 20 45W	airport	1147
Monroe	41 31 20N	093 06 06W	city/town	
Montauk Historical	43 00 32N	091 38 53W	site	
Monteith	41 37 53N	094 25 42W	city/town	1037
Monterey	40 39 08N	092 35 16W	city/town	953
Montezuma	41 35 09N	092 31 38W	city/town	
Montezuma -Sig Fld	41 32 45N	092 32 00W	airport	929
Montgomery	43 26 27N	095 12 09W	city/town	
Monti	42 22 37N	091 38 14W	city/town	
Monticello	42 14 18N	091 11 13W	city/town	
Monticello Munic.	42 13 33N	091 10 01W	airport	846
Montour	41 58 53N	092 42 53W	city/town	
Montpelier	41 27 33N	090 48 25W	city/town	
Montrose	40 31 56N	091 24 53W	city/town	530
Mooar	40 26 37N	091 27 08W	city/town	
Mooney Ridge	43 15 43N	091 09 27W	ridge	

Iowa GPS Companion

Place Name	Latitude	Longitude	Type	Elev
Moores Beach	43 23 19N	095 05 16W	beach	
Moores Siding-hist	43 27 33N	094 07 40W	city/town	
Mooreville -hist	42 14 44N	092 18 01W	city/town	
Moorhead	41 55 21N	095 51 04W	city/town	1200
Moorland	42 26 30N	094 17 41W	city/town	
Moran	41 48 39N	093 54 27W	city/town	
Moravia	40 53 27N	092 48 54W	city/town	
Morgan	40 36 34N	093 37 18W	city/town	
Morgin Vly -hist	41 29 24N	093 17 30W	city/town	
Morhain	42 38 39N	093 40 34W	city/town	
Morley	42 00 22N	091 14 46W	city/town	
Mormon Ridge	42 07 45N	093 03 40W	ridge	
Morning Sun	41 05 46N	091 15 27W	city/town	
Morningside	42 28 08N	096 21 32W	city/town	
Morningside Coll.	42 28 29N	096 21 33W	univ/coll	
Morrisburgh -hist	41 36 00N	094 19 04W	city/town	
Morrison	42 20 39N	092 40 25W	city/town	
Morse	41 44 58N	091 26 04W	city/town	
Morse Lake	42 50 21N	093 41 35W	lake	1229
Mortimer -hist	40 53 04N	094 19 10W	city/town	
Morton Mills	41 04 47N	094 59 04W	city/town	
Moscow	41 34 30N	091 04 57W	city/town	

Iowa GPS Companion

Place Name	Latitude	Longitude	Type	Elev
Motor	42 48 25N	091 21 04W	city/town	
Moulton	40 41 09N	092 40 38W	city/town	
Mount Auburn	42 15 18N	092 05 33W	city/town	
Mount Ayr	40 42 53N	094 14 06W	city/town	
Mount Carmel	42 09 09N	094 54 30W	city/town	
Mount Clare	40 31 23N	091 27 07W	city/town	
Mount Etna	41 07 14N	094 44 06W	city/town	
Mount Hamill	40 45 02N	091 36 47W	city/town	
Mount Joy	41 36 54N	090 33 56W	city/town	
Mount Lucia	42 32 26N	096 27 52W	city/town	1391
Mount Mercy Col.	42 00 07N	091 39 00W	univ/coll	
Mount Pleasant	40 57 49N	091 33 28W	city/town	
Mount Pleasant Mun	40 56 47N	091 30 39W	airport	734
Mount Saint Clare	41 51 04N	090 11 53W	univ/coll	
Mount Sterling	40 37 04N	091 55 55W	city/town	
Mount Union	41 03 28N	091 23 25W	city/town	
Mount Vernon	41 55 19N	091 25 00W	city/town	
Mount Zion	40 47 19N	091 56 01W	city/town	
Moville	42 29 20N	096 04 20W	city/town	
Mt Ayr -Jdge Lewis	40 42 20N	094 13 25W	airport	1265
Munterville	41 02 08N	092 37 12W	city/town	
Murphy	41 39 30N	092 58 25W	city/town	

Place Name	Latitude	Longitude	Type	Elev
Murray	41 02 30N	093 56 57W	city/town	
Muscatine	41 25 28N	091 02 35W	city/town	585
Muscatine Commun.	41 26 27N	091 01 32W	univ/coll	
Muscatine Munic.	41 22 00N	091 08 43W	airport	547
Muskrat Lake	41 12 26N	091 12 08W	lake	557
Mystic	40 46 39N	092 56 37W	city/town	

N

Place Name	Latitude	Longitude	Type	Elev
Nahant	41 29 15N	090 38 16W	city/town	
Nanito	41 18 56N	094 17 22W	city/town	
Nansen	43 06 43N	092 14 15W	city/town	
Napier	41 58 47N	093 43 04W	city/town	
Narrows Point, The	43 24 41N	095 04 46W	cape	
Nashua	42 57 10N	092 32 10W	city/town	
Nashville	42 03 45N	090 47 01W	city/town	
Nasset	43 17 04N	091 40 00W	city/town	
Navan	43 05 52N	092 03 45W	city/town	
Nemaha	42 30 57N	095 05 17W	city/town	
Neola	41 26 56N	095 36 55W	city/town	
Neptune	42 39 49N	096 09 21W	city/town	
Neska	41 24 30N	092 30 48W	city/town	
Nevada	42 01 22N	093 27 08W	city/town	1003

Iowa GPS Companion

Place Name	Latitude	Longitude	Type	Elev
Nevinville	41 08 50N	094 30 02W	city/town	
New Albin	43 29 48N	091 17 22W	city/town	
New Albion	42 38 34N	092 43 53W	city/town	
New Boston	40 33 38N	091 30 19W	city/town	
New Dixon	41 44 05N	090 46 16W	city/town	
New Era	41 27 58N	090 53 31W	city/town	
New Hampton	43 03 33N	092 19 03W	city/town	
New Hampton Munic.	43 05 14N	092 20 35W	airport	1173
New Hartford	42 34 01N	092 37 19W	city/town	
New Haven	43 17 04N	092 38 31W	city/town	
New Liberty	41 43 04N	090 52 44W	city/town	
New London	40 55 37N	091 23 58W	city/town	
New Market	40 43 52N	094 53 58W	city/town	
New Providence	42 16 52N	093 10 17W	city/town	1130
New Sharon	41 28 12N	092 39 04W	city/town	
New Vienna	42 32 53N	091 06 51W	city/town	
New Virginia	41 10 56N	093 43 43W	city/town	
New York	40 51 06N	093 15 35W	city/town	1657
Newbern	41 09 39N	093 18 30W	city/town	
Newburg	41 49 07N	092 46 27W	city/town	
Newell	42 36 20N	095 00 09W	city/town	
Newhall	41 59 44N	091 58 03W	city/town	899

Iowa GPS Companion

Place Name	Latitude	Longitude	Type	Elev
Newkirk	43 04 12N	095 58 40W	city/town	
Newport (1)	41 05 20N	091 10 58W	city/town	
Newport (2)	42 02 43N	091 12 02W	city/town	
Newport (3)	41 44 19N	091 28 26W	city/town	
Newton	41 41 59N	093 02 52W	city/town	
Newton Speedway	41 43 07N	093 02 50W	locale	
Newtown -hist	41 27 13N	095 20 10W	city/town	
Nezekaw Point	43 05 00N	091 10 55W	cliff	
Nichols	41 28 52N	091 18 27W	city/town	
Nilesville	43 08 26N	092 36 48W	city/town	
Nine Eagles State	40 35 50N	093 45 08W	park	
Nira	41 27 15N	091 55 56W	city/town	
Nishna	41 41 45N	094 55 07W	city/town	1284
Nishna Hills Golf	41 23 50N	094 59 30W	golf	
Noble	41 09 59N	091 37 10W	city/town	
Nodaway	40 56 14N	094 53 41W	city/town	
Noel -historic	41 45 02N	090 35 31W	city/town	
Nora Junction	43 08 24N	093 00 58W	city/town	
Nora Springs	43 08 34N	093 00 15W	city/town	
Nordness	43 14 04N	091 46 18W	city/town	
Norris Siding	42 33 56N	092 38 06W	city/town	
North Bellevue	42 16 42N	090 26 04W	city/town	

Place Name	Latitude	Longitude	Type	Elev
North Branch	41 38 45N	094 42 54W	city/town	
North Buena Vista	42 40 47N	090 57 23W	city/town	
North Cedar	42 33 17N	092 27 20W	city/town	
North English	41 30 50N	092 04 34W	city/town	815
North Liberty	41 44 57N	091 35 52W	city/town	
North Overlook C.	41 22 49N	092 58 11W	campgrnd	800
North Washington	43 07 05N	092 25 00W	city/town	
North Welton	41 54 49N	090 36 16W	city/town	
Northboro	40 36 28N	095 17 29W	city/town	
Northfield	41 03 32N	091 07 18W	city/town	
Northwood	43 26 39N	093 13 15W	city/town	
Norwalk	41 28 32N	093 40 43W	city/town	
Norway	41 54 10N	091 55 17W	city/town	796
Norway Center	41 20 45N	094 52 20W	city/town	
Norwich	40 44 33N	095 15 23W	city/town	
Norwood	41 07 00N	093 28 43W	city/town	
Norwoodville	41 38 38N	093 33 39W	city/town	
Nuel	42 37 34N	093 57 52W	city/town	
Nugent	41 12 22N	092 11 23W	city/town	
Numa	40 41 17N	092 58 40W	city/town	
Nyman	40 52 51N	095 12 13W	city/town	

Place Name	Latitude	Longitude	Type	Elev
O				
Oak Grove State	43 03 38N	096 28 06W	park	
Oak Lake	43 07 29N	094 10 16W	lake	1151
Oakdale	41 42 23N	091 36 10W	city/town	
Oakfield	41 32 00N	094 54 27W	city/town	
Oakland (1)	41 18 33N	095 23 47W	city/town	1103
Oakland (2)	42 34 52N	093 26 35W	city/town	
Oakland Acres	41 43 02N	092 49 13W	city/town	
Oakland Mills	40 56 10N	091 36 59W	city/town	
Oakland Mills St.	40 55 50N	091 37 00W	park	
Oakley	41 06 04N	093 21 54W	city/town	
Oaks Golf Course	42 04 32N	093 37 23W	golf	
Oakville	41 05 59N	091 02 40W	city/town	
Oakwood	43 00 33N	092 46 37W	city/town	
Oakwood Station	41 56 14N	093 30 58W	city/town	
Oasis	41 42 22N	091 23 07W	city/town	804
Ocheyedan	43 24 58N	095 32 04W	city/town	
Ocheyedan Mound	43 24 10N	095 31 15W	summit	
Odebolt	42 18 44N	095 15 01W	city/town	1377
Oelwein	42 40 24N	091 54 48W	city/town	
Oelwein Municipal	42 40 51N	091 58 27W	airport	1076

Place Name	Latitude	Longitude	Type	Elev
Ogden	42 02 21N	094 01 39W	city/town	1092
Okamanpeedam State	43 29 23N	094 37 30W	park	
Okoboji	43 23 11N	095 08 53W	city/town	
Okoboji Golf	43 24 44N	095 11 06W	golf	
Olaf	42 53 12N	093 43 28W	city/town	
Old Balltown	42 37 54N	090 51 30W	city/town	
Old Peru	41 14 09N	093 56 42W	city/town	
Old Pine Crk Mill	41 28 03N	090 52 03W	locale	
Old Shot Tower	42 29 45N	090 39 28W	building	
Old Town	43 18 49N	095 08 38W	city/town	
Old Tripoli	42 49 34N	092 15 55W	city/town	
Olds	41 08 03N	091 32 41W	city/town	
OLeary	42 42 24N	096 03 30W	city/town	
Olin	41 59 53N	091 08 29W	city/town	
Olivet	41 18 49N	092 49 48W	city/town	
Ollie	41 11 53N	092 05 32W	city/town	
Olmitz	41 04 54N	093 10 09W	city/town	
Omaha Beach	43 23 55N	095 09 11W	beach	
Onawa	42 01 36N	096 05 49W	city/town	1052
Onawa Junction	42 43 30N	095 33 27W	city/town	
Onawa Municipal	42 00 35N	096 06 30W	airport	1046
Oneida	42 32 34N	091 21 12W	city/town	

Iowa GPS Companion

Place Name	Latitude	Longitude	Type	Elev
O'Neill	42 36 32N	090 53 12W	city/town	
Onslow	42 06 25N	091 00 54W	city/town	
Ontario	42 02 09N	093 40 53W	city/town	
Open Bible College	41 33 43N	093 38 43W	univ/coll	
Oralabor	41 42 00N	093 35 16W	city/town	
Oran	42 42 05N	092 04 28W	city/town	
Orange	42 25 33N	092 21 23W	city/town	
Orange City	43 00 26N	096 03 29W	city/town	
Orange City Mun.	42 59 25N	096 03 45W	airport	1414
Orchard	43 13 39N	092 46 19W	city/town	
Ord	41 15 04N	094 04 15W	city/town	
Orient	41 12 11N	094 24 52W	city/town	
Orillia	41 30 35N	093 43 43W	city/town	
Orleans (1)	43 26 50N	095 05 32W	city/town	
Orleans (2)	40 43 32N	092 39 26W	city/town	
Orleans Beach	43 26 55N	095 05 31W	beach	
Orleans Cheese Fac	43 22 50N	091 59 15W	factory	
Orleans State Park	43 26 35N	095 06 14W	park	
Ormanville	40 54 31N	092 28 59W	city/town	
Orson	41 46 46N	095 58 59W	city/town	
Orton	41 35 19N	095 48 36W	city/town	
Ortonville	41 36 54N	093 57 34W	city/town	

Iowa GPS Companion

Place Name	Latitude	Longitude	Type	Elev
Osage	43 17 03N	092 48 39W	city/town	
Osage Municipal	43 17 33N	092 47 45W	airport	1168
Osborne	42 47 31N	091 26 43W	city/town	
Osceola	41 02 02N	093 45 55W	city/town	
Osceola Munic.	41 03 08N	093 41 22W	airport	1110
Osgood	43 11 36N	094 42 04W	city/town	
Oskaloosa	41 17 47N	092 38 39W	city/town	
Oskaloosa Col -his	41 17 35N	092 39 56W	locale	
Oskaloosa Munic.	41 13 34N	092 29 37W	airport	840
Ossian	43 08 47N	091 45 52W	city/town	
Osterdock	42 44 01N	091 09 28W	city/town	
Oswalt	41 41 45N	093 17 51W	city/town	
Otho	42 25 29N	094 09 00W	city/town	
Otis	41 57 05N	091 37 23W	city/town	
Otley	41 27 32N	093 02 08W	city/town	875
Oto	42 17 02N	095 53 34W	city/town	
Otranto	43 27 30N	092 59 08W	city/town	
Ottawa (1)	41 18 43N	093 30 07W	city/town	
Ottawa (2)	41 01 48N	093 35 27W	city/town	
Otter Creek	42 14 26N	090 40 57W	city/town	
Otterville	42 30 31N	091 56 47W	city/town	
Ottosen	42 53 42N	094 22 47W	city/town	

Place Name	Latitude	Longitude	Type	Elev
Ottumwa	41 00 15N	092 22 25W	city/town	
Ottumwa Heights C.	41 02 41N	092 23 40W	univ/coll	
Ottumwa Indus.	41 06 24N	092 26 53W	airport	845
Ottumwa Junction	41 02 54N	092 26 22W	city/town	
Ovia	40 51 18N	093 19 03W	city/town	
Owasa	42 26 01N	093 12 25W	city/town	1085
Owego	42 16 46N	096 09 15W	city/town	
Owen	43 02 15N	093 04 55W	city/town	
Oxford	41 43 24N	091 47 25W	city/town	
Oxford Junction	41 59 01N	090 57 22W	city/town	
Oxford Mills	41 58 13N	090 57 35W	city/town	
Oyens	42 49 13N	096 03 27W	city/town	
Ozark	42 11 43N	090 52 31W	city/town	
Ozark -historic	42 09 27N	090 52 27W	city/town	
Ozark Springs	42 12 54N	090 52 08W	spring	

ℙ

Place Name	Latitude	Longitude	Type	Elev
Pacific City	41 02 52N	095 48 00W	city/town	
Pacific Junction	41 01 07N	095 47 56W	city/town	
Packard	42 51 03N	092 43 55W	city/town	953
Packwood	41 07 58N	092 04 57W	city/town	
Page Center	40 42 44N	095 07 46W	city/town	

Iowa GPS Companion

Place Name	Latitude	Longitude	Type	Elev
Palestine -hist	40 41 40N	091 47 38W	city/town	620
Palisades-Kepler	41 54 27N	091 30 22W	park	
Palm Grove	42 19 34N	094 10 26W	city/town	1165
Palmer	42 37 50N	094 36 01W	city/town	
Palmyra	41 26 10N	093 26 17W	city/town	
Palo	42 03 58N	091 47 43W	city/town	
Palsville	42 52 45N	093 32 23W	city/town	
Pammel State Park	41 17 30N	094 04 32W	park	
Panama	41 43 35N	095 28 19W	city/town	1325
Panora	41 41 30N	094 21 46W	city/town	1071
Panorama Park	41 33 20N	090 27 11W	city/town	
Panther	41 41 18N	094 06 22W	city/town	
Paralta	42 01 53N	091 26 33W	city/town	
Paris (1)	40 47 19N	092 35 32W	city/town	
Paris (2)	42 14 19N	091 34 44W	city/town	
Paris -historic	42 14 06N	091 27 29W	city/town	
Park View	41 41 39N	090 32 44W	city/town	
Parkersburg	42 34 39N	092 47 12W	city/town	
Parkhurst -hist	41 36 22N	091 24 00W	city/town	750
Parksville -hist	40 52 08N	091 55 37W	city/town	745
Parnell	41 34 59N	092 00 14W	city/town	
Parsons College	41 01 00N	091 58 00W	univ/coll	

Place Name	Latitude	Longitude	Type	Elev
Paton	42 09 52N	094 15 18W	city/town	
Patterson (1)	40 44 23N	091 08 23W	city/town	
Patterson (2)	41 20 54N	093 52 49W	city/town	
Patterson Lake	40 43 56N	091 08 19W	lake	520
Paullina	42 58 45N	095 41 16W	city/town	
Paullina Munic.	42 59 18N	095 39 51W	airport	1385
Payne	40 40 11N	095 45 36W	city/town	921
Pekin	41 09 46N	092 09 34W	city/town	
Pella	41 24 29N	092 54 58W	city/town	
Pella Municipal	41 24 01N	092 56 43W	airport	880
Peoria (1)	41 27 43N	092 48 04W	city/town	
Peoria (2)	40 46 59N	093 22 29W	city/town	
Peosta	42 27 02N	090 51 01W	city/town	
Percival	40 44 56N	095 48 48W	city/town	
Percy -historic	41 28 54N	093 15 01W	city/town	
Perkins	43 11 17N	096 11 07W	city/town	
Perlee	41 05 02N	091 54 12W	city/town	
Perry	41 50 19N	094 06 25W	city/town	998
Perry Municipal	41 49 40N	094 09 34W	airport	1014
Perry Yard	41 50 40N	094 05 14W	city/town	
Pershing	41 15 47N	093 00 22W	city/town	
Persia	41 34 48N	095 34 04W	city/town	1273

Iowa GPS Companion

Place Name	Latitude	Longitude	Type	Elev
Peter	41 21 17N	095 39 14W	city/town	
Petersburg (1)	42 33 18N	091 12 47W	city/town	
Petersburg (2)	41 33 36N	090 47 38W	city/town	
Peterson	42 55 05N	095 20 37W	city/town	
Petersville	41 58 03N	090 32 01W	city/town	
Pettis	42 22 07N	094 56 08W	city/town	
Philby	43 04 11N	095 48 05W	city/town	
Phillips	41 03 14N	092 25 36W	city/town	
Pickerel Lake	42 54 24N	094 55 17W	lake	1347
Pickering	41 56 27N	092 48 59W	city/town	
Pickwick	41 00 30N	092 25 06W	city/town	
Pictured Rocks St.	42 13 10N	091 06 20W	park	
Pierson	42 32 39N	095 52 02W	city/town	
Pigeon	41 37 46N	095 45 54W	city/town	
Pikes Peak State	42 59 52N	091 09 48W	park	
Pikes Point	43 24 56N	095 09 08W	cape	
Pikes Point State	43 24 56N	095 09 41W	park	
Pillsbury Point	43 22 01N	095 08 27W	cape	
Pillsbury Point St	43 22 01N	095 08 27W	park	
Pilot Grove	40 45 46N	091 32 12W	city/town	
Pilot Knob Lake	43 15 04N	093 33 39W	lake	1309
Pilot Knob State	43 14 57N	093 33 26W	park	

Iowa GPS Companion

Place Name	Latitude	Longitude	Type	Elev
Pilot Mound	42 09 52N	094 00 59W	city/town	
Pilot Rock	42 46 26N	092 50 58W	city/town	
Pine Lake State	42 22 15N	093 04 41W	park	
Pine Mills -hist	41 28 10N	090 52 15W	city/town	
Pioneer	42 39 14N	094 23 32W	city/town	
Pioneer State Park	43 20 28N	092 40 46W	park	
Piper	42 21 54N	094 33 12W	city/town	
Pisgah	41 49 53N	095 55 31W	city/town	1060
Pittsburg	40 44 47N	091 59 30W	city/town	
Pitzer	41 22 26N	094 11 08W	city/town	
Plainfield	42 50 51N	092 32 13W	city/town	
Plainview	41 40 06N	090 46 57W	city/town	
Plano	40 45 20N	093 02 47W	city/town	
Plato	41 44 17N	091 18 30W	city/town	
Platteville	40 38 24N	094 33 23W	city/town	
Pleasant Corner	41 06 15N	092 40 40W	city/town	
Pleasant Creek	42 11 58N	090 22 57W	city/town	
Pleasant Grove (1)	40 58 03N	091 17 16W	city/town	
Pleasant Grove (2)	42 23 23N	090 55 34W	city/town	
Pleasant Hill	41 35 02N	093 31 11W	city/town	
Pleasant Hill -his	40 43 37N	091 57 28W	city/town	
Pleasant Lake	43 24 16N	095 01 36W	lake	1520

Iowa GPS Companion

Place Name	Latitude	Longitude	Type	Elev
Pleasant Plain	41 08 50N	091 51 32W	city/town	
Pleasant Prairie	41 31 28N	090 52 19W	city/town	
Pleasant Valley	41 34 11N	090 25 23W	city/town	
Pleasant View -his	40 49 31N	092 22 45W	city/town	
Pleasanton	40 34 50N	093 44 37W	city/town	
Pleasantville	41 23 09N	093 16 09W	city/town	
Plessis	43 14 01N	095 32 52W	city/town	
Plover	42 52 42N	094 37 13W	city/town	
Plum Creek C C	42 58 00N	092 12 47W	golf	
Plymouth (1)	43 14 45N	093 07 22W	city/town	1128
Plymouth (2)	40 39 12N	091 44 42W	city/town	
Plymouth Junction	43 13 39N	093 07 50W	city/town	
Pocahontas	42 44 08N	094 40 08W	city/town	
Pocahontas Mun.	42 44 34N	094 38 48W	airport	1224
Poker Rock	42 09 36N	090 54 00W	pillar	
Polen	40 53 06N	094 23 45W	city/town	
Polk City	41 46 17N	093 42 46W	city/town	889
Polk City Junction	41 48 09N	093 41 52W	city/town	
Pomeroy	42 33 04N	094 41 01W	city/town	
Popejoy	42 35 38N	093 25 33W	city/town	
Poplar	41 41 18N	095 05 36W	city/town	
Port Allen -hist	41 20 16N	091 21 11W	city/town	

Iowa GPS Companion

Place Name	Latitude	Longitude	Type	Elev
Port Louisa	41 14 21N	091 07 52W	city/town	
Portland	43 07 43N	093 07 24W	city/town	
Portsmouth	41 39 01N	095 31 06W	city/town	1237
Postville	43 05 05N	091 34 05W	city/town	
Postville -Delight	43 04 44N	091 36 54W	airport	1200
Potosia	42 39 49N	096 22 18W	city/town	
Potter	41 57 36N	092 40 30W	city/town	
Powersville	42 56 11N	092 41 13W	city/town	
Prairie City	41 35 58N	093 14 06W	city/town	
Prairie Grove	40 52 45N	091 15 08W	city/town	
Prairie Lake	43 22 49N	095 03 48W	lake	1486
Prairie Rose Lake	41 36 14N	095 13 04W	lake	1225
Prairie Rose State	41 36 19N	095 12 57W	park	
Prairiebell	41 36 52N	093 18 35W	city/town	
Prairieburg	42 14 18N	091 25 20W	city/town	
Predonia -hist	42 03 18N	092 48 15W	city/town	
Preparation Canyon	41 53 34N	095 54 19W	park	
Prescott	41 01 23N	094 36 48W	city/town	
Preston	42 03 01N	090 24 50W	city/town	
Primghar	43 05 13N	095 37 37W	city/town	
Primghar Airport	43 05 00N	095 36 45W	airport	1481
Primrose	40 40 32N	091 38 17W	city/town	

Iowa GPS Companion

Place Name	Latitude	Longitude	Type	Elev
Princeton	41 40 29N	090 20 25W	city/town	
Probstei	41 34 53N	090 39 45W	city/town	
Prole	41 24 33N	093 43 37W	city/town	
Promise City	40 44 51N	093 08 49W	city/town	
Protivin	43 12 58N	092 05 27W	city/town	
Prussia	41 22 26N	094 30 22W	city/town	
Pulaski	40 41 49N	092 16 23W	city/town	
Purdy	41 09 38N	093 13 59W	city/town	
Putnam Museum	41 31 34N	090 36 05W	building	

Q

Place Name	Latitude	Longitude	Type	Elev
Quandahl	43 27 00N	091 36 23W	city/town	
Quarry (1)	42 01 02N	092 48 18W	city/town	
Quarry (2)	41 31 41N	094 04 48W	city/town	
Quasqueton	42 23 40N	091 45 39W	city/town	
Queen City -hist	41 00 19N	094 42 35W	city/town	
Quick	41 17 24N	095 40 12W	city/town	
Quilhart -hist	41 43 07N	093 31 57W	city/town	
Quimby	42 37 49N	095 38 30W	city/town	
Quincy	41 02 25N	094 47 24W	city/town	

Place Name	Latitude	Longitude	Type	Elev
R				
Racine	42 28 13N	093 19 45W	city/town	
Radcliffe	42 18 55N	093 26 03W	city/town	
Radcliffe -Drake	42 19 00N	093 25 00W	airport	1179
Rafferty Field	42 29 18N	090 39 50W	park	
Railroad Lake	42 34 50N	092 30 08W	lake	859
Rake	43 29 02N	093 55 07W	city/town	
Raleigh	43 20 22N	094 52 07W	city/town	
Ralston	42 02 30N	094 37 58W	city/town	
Randalia	42 51 47N	091 53 08W	city/town	
Randall	42 14 18N	093 36 02W	city/town	
Randolph	40 52 23N	095 33 58W	city/town	977
Rands	42 19 30N	094 34 43W	city/town	
Rathbun	40 48 04N	092 53 19W	city/town	
Raymar	42 27 19N	092 14 24W	city/town	
Raymond	42 28 08N	092 13 10W	city/town	
Readers Mills -his	41 36 15N	095 43 37W	locale	
Readlyn	42 42 08N	092 13 31W	city/town	
Reasnor	41 34 42N	093 01 23W	city/town	
Red Haw Lake State	40 59 45N	093 16 45W	park	
Red Line	41 43 02N	095 09 03W	city/town	

Place Name	Latitude	Longitude	Type	Elev
Red Oak	41 00 35N	095 13 31W	city/town	
Red Oak C C	41 00 51N	095 11 08W	golf	
Red Oak Municipal	41 00 37N	095 15 35W	airport	1044
Redding	40 36 17N	094 23 15W	city/town	
Redfield	41 35 22N	094 11 45W	city/town	
Redman -hist	41 58 09N	092 17 57W	city/town	
Reeceville	42 07 36N	090 17 54W	city/town	
Reeve	42 40 20N	093 15 37W	city/town	
Reilly Settlement	43 09 20N	092 10 50W	city/town	
Reinbeck	42 19 25N	092 35 57W	city/town	
Rembrandt	42 49 32N	095 09 58W	city/town	
Remicker -hist	42 28 38N	093 42 05W	city/town	
Remsen	42 48 53N	095 58 23W	city/town	
Renwick	42 49 41N	093 58 51W	city/town	
Republic	42 57 04N	092 23 50W	city/town	
Rex 4 Mine	41 06 44N	092 53 26W	mine	
Rexfield	41 04 54N	092 57 08W	city/town	
Rhodes	41 55 32N	093 11 10W	city/town	
Rice Lake State	43 23 00N	093 30 07W	park	
Riceville	43 21 50N	092 33 14W	city/town	
Riceville -hist	43 23 06N	092 33 47W	city/town	
Richard	42 25 40N	094 31 46W	city/town	

Place Name	Latitude	Longitude	Type	Elev
Richfield	42 57 01N	092 03 45W	city/town	
Richland	41 11 08N	091 59 34W	city/town	
Richmond	41 26 59N	091 41 50W	city/town	
Richmond Spring	42 38 18N	091 33 27W	spring	
Rickardsville	42 35 00N	090 53 02W	city/town	
Ricketts	42 07 37N	095 34 29W	city/town	1366
Rider	41 38 39N	093 46 10W	city/town	
Ridgeport	42 10 37N	093 55 02W	city/town	
Ridgeview Park	41 35 33N	090 36 21W	city/town	
Ridgeway	43 17 52N	091 59 15W	city/town	
Ridley	43 03 53N	091 30 30W	city/town	
Ridotto	42 49 46N	094 40 36W	city/town	
Riggs	42 00 18N	090 31 48W	city/town	
Rinard	42 20 23N	094 29 18W	city/town	
Ringgold -hist	40 35 02N	094 11 30W	city/town	
Ringsted	43 17 41N	094 30 41W	city/town	
Rippey	41 56 02N	094 12 04W	city/town	1077
Rising Sun	41 35 36N	093 28 53W	city/town	
Ritter	43 14 39N	095 49 21W	city/town	
River Junction	41 29 26N	091 29 48W	city/town	
River Sioux	41 48 21N	096 02 46W	city/town	
River View Stadium	41 50 54N	090 11 06W	park	

Iowa GPS Companion

Place Name	Latitude	Longitude	Type	Elev
Riverboat Museum	42 45 55N	090 39 42W	building	
Riverdale	41 32 40N	090 27 29W	city/town	
Riverside (1)	42 31 08N	096 28 55W	city/town	
Riverside (2)	41 28 47N	091 34 52W	city/town	
Riverton	40 41 13N	095 34 06W	city/town	
Roberts	42 25 37N	094 10 27W	city/town	1129
Robertson	42 30 23N	093 07 38W	city/town	
Robins	42 04 16N	091 40 00W	city/town	
Robinson	42 20 31N	091 34 43W	city/town	
Robison-Whitaker A	41 55 33N	093 26 06W	city/town	
Rochester	41 40 26N	091 09 30W	city/town	
Rock Creek	43 14 06N	092 55 07W	city/town	
Rock Creek State	41 45 12N	092 50 13W	park	
Rock Falls	43 12 27N	093 05 04W	city/town	
Rock Rapids	43 25 38N	096 10 32W	city/town	
Rock Rapids Mun.	43 27 08N	096 10 46W	airport	1363
Rock Valley	43 12 19N	096 17 41W	city/town	
Rockaway -hist	42 06 11N	090 24 44W	city/town	
Rockdale	42 27 51N	090 40 42W	city/town	
Rockford	43 03 08N	092 56 54W	city/town	
Rockingham -hist	41 28 57N	090 38 00W	city/town	550
Rockton	42 03 11N	092 50 13W	city/town	

Place Name	Latitude	Longitude	Type	Elev
Rockville	42 25 07N	091 08 31W	city/town	
Rockwell	42 59 07N	093 11 30W	city/town	
Rockwell City	42 23 43N	094 38 01W	city/town	
Rockwell City Mun.	42 23 32N	094 37 15W	airport	1217
Rodman	43 01 43N	094 31 51W	city/town	
Rodney	42 12 20N	095 57 08W	city/town	1122
Roelyn	42 24 49N	094 21 26W	city/town	1160
Rogers	42 11 48N	091 34 43W	city/town	
Rogersville	42 06 31N	092 13 53W	city/town	
Roland	42 09 59N	093 30 06W	city/town	
Rolfe	42 48 46N	094 31 36W	city/town	
Rolfe -historic	42 50 15N	094 28 37W	city/town	
Rome	40 58 53N	091 40 56W	city/town	
Rorbeck	41 32 53N	095 08 00W	city/town	
Roscoe	41 01 25N	091 15 35W	city/town	
Rose	42 34 55N	090 41 57W	city/town	
Rose Hill	41 19 19N	092 27 43W	city/town	
Roselle	42 00 01N	094 54 55W	city/town	
Rosendale	42 12 48N	093 43 05W	city/town	
Rosetta -hist	41 24 35N	092 21 47W	city/town	
Roseville	43 00 33N	092 48 35W	city/town	1029
Ross	41 46 27N	094 55 07W	city/town	

Iowa GPS Companion

Place Name	Latitude	Longitude	Type	Elev
Rosserdale	41 24 10N	094 24 51W	city/town	
Rossie	43 00 48N	095 11 18W	city/town	
Rossville	43 11 22N	091 22 32W	city/town	
Rough Woods Hill	42 21 39N	093 12 31W	city/town	
Round Lake	40 43 30N	091 08 00W	lake	518
Rowan	42 44 27N	093 33 09W	city/town	
Rowley	42 22 12N	091 50 38W	city/town	
Roxie	42 50 53N	092 25 03W	city/town	
Royal	43 03 56N	095 17 01W	city/town	
Rubens Siding	42 49 15N	094 34 47W	city/town	
Rubio	41 13 16N	091 56 15W	city/town	
Ruble	42 48 29N	096 24 34W	city/town	
Rudd	43 07 34N	092 54 20W	city/town	
Ruddy Pool	43 18 11N	094 07 01W	lake	1124
Runnells	41 30 40N	093 21 26W	city/town	
Rush Lake	42 56 47N	094 52 21W	lake	1312
Rushville	41 45 37N	092 56 44W	city/town	
Rusk	42 40 00N	094 44 11W	city/town	
Russell	40 58 55N	093 11 54W	city/town	
Russellville (1)	40 46 58N	091 38 43W	city/town	
Russellville (2)	40 40 30N	092 33 13W	city/town	
Ruthven	43 07 45N	094 53 56W	city/town	

Iowa GPS Companion

Place Name	Latitude	Longitude	Type	Elev
Rutland	42 45 33N	094 17 51W	city/town	
Rutledge	41 03 40N	092 25 16W	city/town	
Ryan	42 21 05N	091 28 53W	city/town	
Ryan House	42 30 03N	090 39 58W	building	

S

Place Name	Latitude	Longitude	Type	Elev
Sabula	42 04 16N	090 10 26W	city/town	
Sac City	42 25 20N	094 59 22W	city/town	
Sac City Jct -hist	42 16 05N	095 04 22W	city/town	
Sac City Municipal	42 22 46N	094 58 45W	airport	1250
Sageville	42 33 10N	090 42 32W	city/town	
Saint Ambrose Coll	41 32 21N	090 34 51W	univ/coll	
Saint Ansgar	43 22 42N	092 55 07W	city/town	1171
Saint Anthony	42 07 20N	093 11 41W	city/town	
Saint Benedict	43 02 17N	094 03 51W	city/town	
Saint Charles	41 17 18N	093 48 33W	city/town	
Saint Donatus	42 21 39N	090 32 21W	city/town	
Saint Joseph	42 54 48N	094 13 37W	city/town	
Saint Josephs Ch.	42 06 51N	091 21 17W	church	
Saint Lucas	43 03 59N	091 56 00W	city/town	
Saint Marys	41 18 29N	093 43 46W	city/town	1033
Saint Olaf	42 55 43N	091 23 10W	city/town	

Iowa GPS Companion

Place Name	Latitude	Longitude	Type	Elev
Saint Paul	40 46 10N	091 31 01W	city/town	
Saint Sebald	42 44 18N	091 32 45W	city/town	
Salem	40 51 10N	091 37 12W	city/town	
Salina	41 02 45N	091 49 59W	city/town	
Salix	42 18 30N	096 17 15W	city/town	1083
Samoa	42 04 40N	090 11 48W	city/town	
Sanborn	43 10 54N	095 39 19W	city/town	
Sand Hill	41 41 19N	091 42 04W	summit	
Sand Springs	42 19 03N	091 11 21W	city/town	
Sandusky	40 27 52N	091 23 14W	city/town	
Sandyville	41 22 15N	093 23 10W	city/town	
Santiago	41 42 36N	093 22 29W	city/town	
Saratoga	43 22 17N	092 24 21W	city/town	
Sargents Spur	40 59 14N	095 47 59W	ridge	955
Sattre	43 23 32N	091 38 22W	city/town	
Saude	43 11 53N	092 09 40W	city/town	1147
Savannah	40 37 27N	092 27 15W	city/town	
Sawyer	40 41 47N	091 21 18W	city/town	
Sawyers Rock	42 13 20N	090 54 20W	pillar	
Saxon	40 45 11N	093 27 25W	city/town	
Saylor	41 39 58N	093 35 47W	city/town	
Saylor Station	41 40 50N	093 35 44W	city/town	

Iowa GPS Companion

Place Name	Latitude	Longitude	Type	Elev
Saylorville	41 40 43N	093 37 46W	city/town	
Scandia Br. -hist	41 50 56N	093 50 29W	bridge	
Scarville	43 28 14N	093 37 03W	city/town	
Schaefer Field	41 00 59N	092 23 50W	park	
Schaller	42 29 59N	095 17 34W	city/town	1439
Schleswig	42 09 55N	095 26 12W	city/town	1497
Schley	43 18 12N	092 13 08W	city/town	
Sciola	41 02 02N	094 59 07W	city/town	
Scotch Grove	42 10 22N	091 06 27W	city/town	
Scotch Ridge	41 28 21N	093 33 30W	city/town	
Scott	42 42 07N	091 45 55W	city/town	
Scranton	42 01 21N	094 32 42W	city/town	1185
Searsboro	41 34 50N	092 42 12W	city/town	
Secor -historic	42 18 40N	093 04 18W	city/town	
Sedan	40 39 25N	092 50 00W	city/town	
Seigel	42 50 24N	092 21 21W	city/town	
Selection	40 57 50N	092 46 59W	city/town	
Selma	40 52 13N	092 09 11W	city/town	
Seneca	43 17 57N	094 23 02W	city/town	
Seney	42 51 10N	096 07 50W	city/town	
Sergeant Bluff	42 24 00N	096 21 00W	cliff	
Sergeant Bluff	42 24 14N	096 21 30W	city/town	1092

Iowa GPS Companion

Place Name	Latitude	Longitude	Type	Elev
Seven Bridges C.	42 39 33N	092 09 32W	park	
Severs	41 39 06N	093 12 47W	city/town	
Sewal	40 38 39N	093 15 31W	city/town	
Sexton	43 04 58N	094 05 20W	city/town	
Seymour	40 40 57N	093 07 15W	city/town	
Shady Grove	42 22 50N	092 03 17W	city/town	
Shady Oak	42 27 42N	094 09 24W	city/town	
Shaffton	41 45 22N	090 19 55W	city/town	
Shambaugh	40 39 32N	095 01 54W	city/town	
Shannon City	40 54 06N	094 15 47W	city/town	
Sharon (1)	41 40 27N	094 59 43W	city/town	1318
Sharon (2)	40 43 35N	091 39 37W	city/town	
Sharon Bluffs St.	40 43 14N	092 48 00W	park	
Sharon Center	41 34 09N	091 39 40W	city/town	
Sharpsburg	40 48 09N	094 38 32W	city/town	
Shawondasse	42 26 22N	090 35 29W	city/town	
Sheffield	42 53 36N	093 12 54W	city/town	
Shelby	41 30 58N	095 27 00W	city/town	1338
Sheldahl	41 51 52N	093 41 49W	city/town	
Sheldon	43 10 52N	095 51 21W	city/town	
Sheldon C C	43 12 34N	095 49 19W	golf	
Sheldon Municipal	43 12 30N	095 49 59W	airport	1419

Iowa GPS Companion

Place Name	Latitude	Longitude	Type	Elev
Shell Rock	42 42 37N	092 34 58W	city/town	
Shellsburg	42 05 40N	091 52 09W	city/town	
Shenandoah	40 45 56N	095 22 19W	city/town	
Shenandoah Munic.	40 45 07N	095 24 45W	airport	970
Shepard -hist	40 59 25N	094 09 14W	city/town	
Sheridan	41 50 02N	092 35 28W	city/town	
Sherman	42 21 14N	093 22 25W	city/town	
Sherrill	42 36 14N	090 47 04W	city/town	
Sherrill Mound	42 36 19N	090 47 55W	summit	
Sherton Heights	41 35 33N	090 25 35W	city/town	645
Sherwood	42 21 33N	094 43 36W	city/town	
Shipley	41 58 48N	093 30 41W	city/town	
Shueyville	41 51 02N	091 38 47W	city/town	
Shunem	40 46 36N	092 17 50W	city/town	
Siam	40 37 40N	094 53 07W	city/town	
Sibley	43 23 57N	095 45 06W	city/town	
Sibley Municipal	43 22 10N	095 45 22W	airport	1537
Sibyl -historic	41 56 57N	090 11 07W	city/town	
Sidney	40 44 54N	095 38 50W	city/town	
Siewers Spring	43 16 22N	091 46 42W	park	
Sigourney	41 20 00N	092 12 16W	city/town	
Silver City	41 06 48N	095 38 13W	city/town	

Place Name	Latitude	Longitude	Type	Elev
Silver Lake	43 01 55N	094 53 12W	lake	1322
Silver Lake	43 28 51N	093 21 59W	city/town	
Simpson College	41 21 54N	093 33 48W	univ/coll	
Sinclair	42 30 00N	092 43 54W	city/town	
Sioux Center	43 04 47N	096 10 31W	city/town	
Sioux Center Mun.	43 08 00N	096 11 13W	airport	1448
Sioux City	42 30 00N	096 24 00W	city/town	1117
Sioux City -Gatewy	42 24 13N	096 23 00W	airport	1098
Sioux Empire Col.	43 00 42N	096 28 37W	univ/coll	
Sioux Rapids	42 53 36N	095 09 03W	city/town	
Sixmile	41 54 35N	090 17 43W	city/town	
Sixteen	43 07 36N	091 18 57W	city/town	
Skunk River	40 43 36N	091 12 02W	city/town	
Slater	41 52 40N	093 40 42W	city/town	
Slifer	42 20 29N	094 22 42W	city/town	1139
Sloan	42 13 58N	096 13 40W	city/town	
Smith Pool	43 14 56N	094 08 47W	lake	1125
Smithland	42 13 45N	095 55 50W	city/town	1090
Smiths	42 19 21N	090 25 51W	city/town	
Smoky Hollow Mine	41 02 36N	092 53 58W	mine	
Smyrna	40 56 32N	093 36 34W	city/town	
Snefs	42 44 27N	091 08 27W	city/town	

Iowa GPS Companion

Place Name	Latitude	Longitude	Type	Elev
Soldier	41 59 07N	095 46 45W	city/town	
Sollberg	42 44 20N	093 38 12W	city/town	
Solomon	40 54 19N	095 26 30W	city/town	
Solon	41 48 26N	091 29 38W	city/town	
Somber	43 25 21N	093 23 56W	city/town	
Somers	42 22 42N	094 25 47W	city/town	
South Amana	41 46 34N	091 58 02W	city/town	
South Amana Pond	41 46 14N	091 58 55W	lake	808
South Augusta	40 45 08N	091 16 38W	city/town	
South English	41 27 08N	092 05 25W	city/town	
South Garry Owen	42 13 50N	090 48 25W	city/town	
South River Cross.	41 13 04N	093 44 45W	city/town	
South Spring	42 42 29N	091 32 15W	spring	
South Switch Jct.	42 28 17N	090 39 00W	city/town	
Spaulding	41 09 45N	094 22 12W	city/town	
Spencer	43 08 29N	095 08 39W	city/town	1321
Spencer C C	43 09 18N	095 10 30W	golf	
Spencer Municipal	43 09 52N	095 12 06W	airport	1338
Spencers Grove	42 17 04N	091 52 08W	city/town	
Sperry	40 57 25N	091 09 23W	city/town	
Spillville	43 12 18N	091 57 03W	city/town	
Spirit Lake	43 25 20N	095 06 07W	city/town	

Iowa GPS Companion

Place Name	Latitude	Longitude	Type	Elev
Spirit Lake	43 28 38N	095 05 52W	lake	1402
Spirit Lake Munic.	43 23 15N	095 08 20W	airport	1434
Sportsman Park Rac	40 24 33N	091 26 00W	track	
Spragueville	42 04 21N	090 26 06W	city/town	
Spring Fountain	42 49 58N	092 10 49W	city/town	
Spring Grove	40 44 23N	091 09 29W	city/town	
Spring Hill	41 24 41N	093 38 41W	city/town	
Spring Lake	42 03 45N	094 17 20W	lake	1014
Spring Lake State	42 03 52N	094 17 19W	park	1014
Spring Valley	41 24 54N	092 29 01W	city/town	
Springbrook	42 09 51N	090 28 35W	city/town	
Springbrook State	41 46 36N	094 27 34W	park	
Springdale (1)	41 40 14N	091 15 32W	city/town	
Springdale (2)	42 31 24N	096 22 11W	city/town	
Springhole	42 13 06N	091 05 51W	city/town	
Springville	42 03 34N	091 26 33W	city/town	
Springwater	43 22 47N	091 44 34W	city/town	
Squaw Creek Munic.	42 00 38N	091 33 17W	golf	
Stacyville	43 26 10N	092 46 56W	city/town	
Stacyville Jct	43 26 45N	092 55 57W	city/town	
Stanhope	42 17 20N	093 47 45W	city/town	
Stanley	42 38 34N	091 48 45W	city/town	

Iowa GPS Companion

Place Name	Latitude	Longitude	Type	Elev
Stanton (1)	40 58 54N	095 06 14W	city/town	
Stanton (2)	41 04 23N	095 05 43W	city/town	
Stanwood	41 53 35N	091 09 02W	city/town	
Stanzel	41 18 57N	094 15 39W	city/town	
State Center	42 01 00N	093 09 48W	city/town	
State Center Jct	41 56 32N	093 02 49W	city/town	
Steamboat Rock	42 24 01N	093 04 32W	cliff	
Steamboat Rock	42 24 34N	093 03 56W	city/town	
Steamboat Rock	43 20 28N	092 06 31W	summit	
Steamboat Rock Way	42 24 29N	093 04 22W	park	
Stennett	41 05 23N	095 11 39W	city/town	
Sterling	42 04 36N	090 15 10W	city/town	
Steuben	40 43 25N	092 23 18W	city/town	
Stevens	43 25 54N	094 00 14W	city/town	
Stiles	40 38 06N	092 21 04W	city/town	
Stillwell	41 31 26N	092 40 06W	city/town	
Stilson	43 02 18N	093 53 06W	city/town	
Stimsons -hist	42 21 15N	094 36 00W	city/town	
Stockport	40 51 27N	091 50 06W	city/town	
Stockton	41 35 29N	090 51 31W	city/town	
Stone Beach Gardnr	43 21 48N	095 08 10W	cabin	
Stone City	42 06 50N	091 20 57W	city/town	

Iowa GPS Companion

Place Name	Latitude	Longitude	Type	Elev
Stone State Park	42 32 56N	096 27 59W	park	
Stonega	42 28 36N	093 42 52W	city/town	
Storm Lake	42 38 28N	095 12 34W	city/town	
Storm Lake Munic.	42 35 52N	095 14 25W	airport	1488
Story City	42 11 14N	093 35 44W	city/town	
Stout	42 31 35N	092 42 42W	city/town	1020
Strahan	40 56 59N	095 29 56W	city/town	
Strand	41 04 20N	094 54 06W	city/town	
Stratford	42 16 17N	093 55 37W	city/town	
Strawberry Point	42 41 01N	091 32 02W	city/town	
Streepyville	40 41 46N	092 54 57W	city/town	1016
String Prairie	40 34 29N	091 36 13W	area	
Stringtown	40 58 44N	094 33 27W	city/town	
Struble	42 53 43N	096 11 42W	city/town	
Stuart	41 30 12N	094 19 06W	city/town	1210
Sugar Creek -hist	40 24 28N	091 30 18W	city/town	
Sugar Creek Mills	41 36 45N	091 04 13W	locale	
Sugar Loaf	42 38 36N	090 57 36W	summit	1065
Sully	41 34 42N	092 50 41W	city/town	
Sully Municipal	41 34 20N	092 50 50W	airport	922
Sulphur Springs	42 37 19N	095 05 49W	city/town	
Summerset	41 25 53N	093 32 41W	city/town	

Place Name	Latitude	Longitude	Type	Elev
Summerset Jct -his	41 26 40N	093 32 39W	city/town	
Summit (1)	41 30 31N	091 01 20W	city/town	
Summit (2)	41 55 15N	091 37 52W	city/town	
Summit (3)	40 49 45N	095 25 04W	city/town	
Summit -hist	40 39 55N	091 20 06W	city/town	
Summitville	40 28 22N	091 26 55W	city/town	
Sumner	42 50 51N	092 05 29W	city/town	
Sunbury	41 40 12N	090 55 51W	city/town	
Sunny Brae Golf	43 15 23N	092 49 20W	golf	
Sunnyside C C	42 30 54N	092 18 53W	golf	
Sunshine	40 44 23N	092 55 30W	city/town	
Superior	43 25 49N	094 56 46W	city/town	
Sutherland	42 58 27N	095 29 50W	city/town	
Sutliff	41 50 21N	091 23 29W	city/town	
Swaledale	42 58 43N	093 26 17W	city/town	1150
Swan	41 27 55N	093 18 40W	city/town	
Swan Lake 1	41 46 27N	091 40 35W	lake	714
Swan Lake 2	43 27 33N	094 57 04W	lake	1374
Swan Lake State	42 02 26N	094 50 36W	park	
Swanton	42 30 00N	092 41 32W	city/town	
Swanwood	41 39 05N	093 35 25W	city/town	
Swea -historic	43 24 53N	094 23 00W	city/town	

Place Name	Latitude	Longitude	Type	Elev
Swea City	43 23 04N	094 18 53W	city/town	1181
Swedesburg	41 06 19N	091 32 49W	city/town	
Sweetland Center	41 29 36N	090 58 10W	city/town	
Swisher	41 50 44N	091 41 34W	city/town	
T				
T F Clark State	42 13 35N	092 25 14W	park	
Tabor	40 53 54N	095 40 16W	city/town	
Taintor	41 30 04N	092 44 18W	city/town	
Talleyrand	41 17 42N	091 57 54W	city/town	
Talmage	41 01 37N	094 06 42W	city/town	
Tama	41 58 00N	092 34 36W	city/town	
Tara	42 30 01N	094 17 44W	city/town	
Tarkio City -hist	40 43 57N	095 11 43W	city/town	
Taylor	41 16 17N	095 31 11W	city/town	
Taylorsville	42 46 02N	091 38 48W	city/town	
Teeds Grove	42 00 42N	090 14 51W	city/town	
Temple Hill	42 13 33N	090 58 34W	city/town	
Templeton	41 55 06N	094 56 33W	city/town	
Tenmile	41 56 44N	090 20 02W	city/town	
Tennant	41 35 37N	095 26 27W	city/town	1382
Tenville	41 00 31N	094 59 31W	city/town	

Iowa GPS Companion

Place Name	Latitude	Longitude	Type	Elev
Terre Haute	40 41 00N	093 51 59W	city/town	
Terril	43 18 21N	094 58 17W	city/town	
Thayer	41 01 41N	094 03 02W	city/town	1107
Thirty	40 41 46N	092 52 03W	city/town	1022
Thomasville	42 45 14N	091 34 51W	city/town	
Thompson	43 22 17N	093 46 24W	city/town	
Thompson Corner	43 15 59N	091 13 50W	city/town	
Thor	42 41 17N	094 02 57W	city/town	
Thornburg	41 27 17N	092 20 08W	city/town	
Thornton	42 56 41N	093 23 04W	city/town	
Thorpe	42 33 58N	091 26 57W	city/town	
Thoten	43 18 35N	091 38 23W	city/town	
Thurman	40 49 12N	095 44 51W	city/town	
Ticonic	42 09 58N	095 57 08W	city/town	1086
Tiffin	41 42 21N	091 39 46W	city/town	
Tileville	41 20 53N	093 56 09W	city/town	
Tilton	41 30 35N	092 21 08W	city/town	
Tingley	40 51 10N	094 11 42W	city/town	
Tioga	41 17 49N	092 25 20W	city/town	
Tipperary	41 06 49N	093 09 15W	city/town	
Tipton	41 46 11N	091 07 40W	city/town	
Tipton -Mathews	41 45 48N	091 09 10W	airport	840

118

Place Name	Latitude	Longitude	Type	Elev
Titonka	43 14 13N	094 02 28W	city/town	
Titu	41 16 30N	091 47 30W	city/town	
Toddville	42 05 57N	091 43 00W	city/town	
Toeterville	43 26 32N	092 53 25W	city/town	
Togo (historical)	40 37 14N	093 53 07W	city/town	
Toledo	41 59 44N	092 34 36W	city/town	
Toledo Municipal	41 59 30N	092 33 42W	airport	960
Tom Bruner Field	41 24 41N	091 04 07W	locale	
Toolesboro	41 08 31N	091 03 43W	city/town	
Toronto	41 54 18N	090 51 50W	city/town	
Tower Rock	42 24 11N	092 55 27W	cliff	
Tower Stat. -hist	41 01 37N	092 52 22W	city/town	
Tracy	41 16 35N	092 52 31W	city/town	775
Traer	42 11 37N	092 27 55W	city/town	
Traer Municipal	42 11 57N	092 27 28W	airport	892
Trappers Bay	43 27 16N	095 19 53W	bay	
Trappers Bay State	43 27 13N	095 20 04W	park	
Trenton	41 03 42N	091 38 14W	city/town	
Treynor	41 13 57N	095 36 46W	city/town	
Tri-State Fairgr.	40 48 57N	091 07 55W	fairgrnd	
Triboji Beach	43 25 37N	095 10 28W	city/town	
Trinity College	42 31 39N	096 22 37W	univ/coll	

Iowa GPS Companion

Place Name	Latitude	Longitude	Type	Elev
Tripoli	42 48 29N	092 15 29W	city/town	
Troy	40 44 55N	092 12 09W	city/town	
Troy -historic	41 02 12N	093 25 32W	city/town	
Troy Mills	42 17 24N	091 40 56W	city/town	
Truesdale	42 43 45N	095 10 57W	city/town	
Trumbull Lake	43 11 31N	094 56 55W	lake	1341
Truro	41 12 35N	093 50 47W	city/town	1082
Turin	42 01 10N	095 57 58W	city/town	
Turkey River	42 42 22N	091 01 33W	city/town	
Turner -hist	41 42 08N	092 49 04W	city/town	
Twelvemile Lake	43 17 22N	094 52 33W	lake	1453
Twin Lakes State	42 29 34N	094 37 06W	park	
Twin Pines Golf	42 01 20N	091 41 42W	golf	
Twin Springs (1)	43 07 31N	091 51 30W	city/town	
Twin Springs (2)	42 07 55N	090 17 01W	city/town	
Twin Springs (3)	42 30 55N	090 50 25W	city/town	
Twin View Heights	41 48 38N	091 34 23W	city/town	
Tyrone	40 58 40N	092 56 47W	city/town	

U

Udell	40 46 51N	092 44 31W	city/town	
Ulmer	42 16 04N	094 56 59W	city/town	1272

Iowa GPS Companion

Place Name	Latitude	Longitude	Type	Elev
Underwood	41 23 13N	095 40 35W	city/town	
Union	42 14 44N	093 03 52W	city/town	
Union Burg -hist	41 32 21N	095 38 29W	city/town	
Union Center	42 41 33N	096 03 29W	city/town	
Union Grove State	42 08 09N	092 43 26W	park	
Union Mills	41 27 09N	092 34 14W	city/town	
Unionville	40 49 06N	092 41 43W	city/town	
Unique	42 43 02N	094 20 42W	city/town	
Univ. of Dubuque	42 29 53N	090 41 35W	univ/coll	
Univ. of Iowa Med.	41 39 45N	091 32 46W	univ/coll	
Univ. of N. Iowa	42 30 57N	092 27 26W	univ/coll	
University Heights	41 39 18N	091 33 24W	city/town	785
University Of Iowa	41 39 42N	091 32 10W	univ/coll	698
University Park	41 17 13N	092 37 06W	city/town	
Updegraff	42 41 02N	091 14 13W	city/town	
Upper Iowa Univ.	42 50 26N	091 47 58W	univ/coll	
Upper South Amana	41 45 57N	091 58 04W	city/town	
Urbana	42 13 27N	091 52 27W	city/town	
Urbandale	41 37 36N	093 42 43W	city/town	
Urbandale C C	41 37 59N	093 44 21W	golf	
Ute	42 03 01N	095 42 22W	city/town	
Utica	40 48 53N	091 50 05W	city/town	

Place Name	Latitude	Longitude	Type	Elev
V				
Vail	42 03 43N	095 11 59W	city/town	
Valdora -hist	43 01 27N	091 20 42W	city/town	
Valeria	41 43 48N	093 19 30W	city/town	
Valley Junction	41 34 09N	093 42 34W	city/town	
Van	41 56 23N	093 01 07W	city/town	1039
Van Buren	42 05 04N	090 21 53W	city/town	
Van Cleve	41 55 53N	093 01 08W	city/town	
Van Horne	42 00 31N	092 05 27W	city/town	
Van Meter	41 31 55N	093 57 14W	city/town	
Van Wert	40 52 11N	093 47 34W	city/town	
Vandalia	41 32 22N	093 18 21W	city/town	
Varina	42 39 29N	094 53 51W	city/town	
Veenker Memorial	42 02 23N	093 39 08W	golf	
Vennard College	41 17 22N	092 37 07W	univ/coll	
Ventura	43 07 35N	093 28 39W	city/town	
Ventura Heights	43 07 04N	093 28 26W	city/town	
Veo	41 09 15N	091 54 28W	city/town	
Vernon (1)	40 43 21N	091 51 18W	city/town	
Vernon (2)	41 41 07N	091 36 06W	city/town	
Vernon Springs	43 21 00N	092 08 17W	city/town	

Iowa GPS Companion

Place Name	Latitude	Longitude	Type	Elev
Vernon View	41 58 32N	091 34 22W	city/town	
Victor	41 43 54N	092 17 52W	city/town	
Viele	40 36 47N	091 26 01W	city/town	
Viking Lake State	40 58 21N	095 02 14W	park	
Village Creek	43 18 33N	091 14 06W	city/town	
Villisca	40 55 47N	094 58 33W	city/town	
Vincennes	40 29 47N	091 34 11W	city/town	
Vincent	42 35 31N	094 01 12W	city/town	
Vining	41 59 24N	092 22 47W	city/town	
Vinje	43 28 24N	093 40 36W	city/town	
Vinton	42 10 07N	092 01 24W	city/town	
Vinton C C	42 10 22N	092 00 33W	golf	
Vinton Veterans M.	42 13 03N	092 01 43W	airport	845
Viola	42 05 27N	091 26 15W	city/town	
Viola Center	41 48 21N	094 48 07W	city/town	1446
Virgin Lake	43 06 11N	094 53 40W	lake	1395
Vista	42 24 48N	091 59 13W	city/town	
Volga	42 48 17N	091 32 27W	city/town	
Volney	43 07 50N	091 22 25W	city/town	
Voorhies	42 20 09N	092 28 57W	city/town	
Vulcan -hist	41 25 13N	092 22 11W	city/town	

Place Name	Latitude	Longitude	Type	Elev
W				
Wacky Waters Park	41 31 07N	090 38 00W	park	
Wadena	42 50 34N	091 39 24W	city/town	
Wadleigh	42 28 25N	094 24 11W	city/town	
Wahpeton	43 21 58N	095 10 18W	city/town	
Wakonda C C	41 33 02N	093 38 29W	golf	
Walcott	41 35 05N	090 46 19W	city/town	
Wald	41 50 16N	091 07 56W	city/town	
Wales	41 07 01N	095 19 37W	city/town	1204
Walford	41 52 42N	091 50 04W	city/town	
Walker	42 17 12N	091 46 50W	city/town	
Wall Lake	42 16 16N	095 05 34W	city/town	
Wall Lake Munic.	42 15 00N	095 06 00W	airport	1224
Wall Lake Station	42 15 23N	095 15 25W	city/town	
Wallace	43 16 12N	095 19 44W	city/town	
Wallin	41 03 36N	095 03 21W	city/town	
Wallingford	43 19 11N	094 47 33W	city/town	
Walnut	41 28 39N	095 13 18W	city/town	
Walnut City	40 48 44N	092 56 41W	city/town	
Walnut Grove	41 28 13N	090 39 40W	city/town	
Walnut Woods St.	41 32 33N	093 44 28W	park	

Place Name	Latitude	Longitude	Type	Elev
Wanamaker	40 38 45N	094 06 34W	city/town	
Wanata State Park	42 54 44N	095 20 26W	park	
Waneta	40 37 48N	092 16 10W	city/town	
Wanetta Corner	40 37 28N	092 16 09W	city/town	
Wantea Point	42 01 42N	090 09 51W	cliff	
Wapello	41 10 53N	091 11 07W	city/town	
Wapsie	42 42 54N	092 11 57W	city/town	
Wapsipinicon C C	42 28 59N	091 55 53W	golf	
Wapsipinicon State	42 05 43N	091 16 59W	park	
Ward	41 01 46N	092 53 11W	city/town	
Ware	42 47 25N	094 45 32W	city/town	
Wartburg Col. -hist	41 50 06N	090 13 51W	univ/coll	
Wartburg College	42 43 40N	092 28 52W	univ/coll	
Washburn	42 24 42N	092 16 02W	city/town	
Washington (1)	41 17 57N	091 41 34W	city/town	
Washington (2)	42 44 52N	093 16 16W	city/town	
Washington Mills	42 18 02N	090 46 56W	city/town	
Washington Munic.	41 16 33N	091 40 23W	airport	754
Washington Prairie	43 16 13N	091 36 49W	city/town	
Washta	42 34 32N	095 43 02W	city/town	
Wassonville -hist	41 29 30N	091 52 45W	city/town	
Waterloo	42 29 34N	092 20 34W	city/town	

Iowa GPS Companion

Place Name	Latitude	Longitude	Type	Elev
Waterloo Municipal	42 33 24N	092 24 00W	airport	866
Waterman	42 57 21N	095 26 40W	city/town	
Waterville	43 12 28N	091 17 51W	city/town	
Watkins	41 53 28N	091 59 10W	city/town	
Watson	43 04 31N	091 19 48W	city/town	1179
Watterson	40 36 07N	094 14 00W	city/town	
Waubeek	42 09 57N	091 27 54W	city/town	
Waubonsie State	40 40 39N	095 41 30W	park	
Waucoma	43 03 22N	092 01 59W	city/town	
Waukee	41 36 42N	093 53 06W	city/town	
Waukon	43 16 10N	091 28 32W	city/town	
Waukon Junction	43 09 12N	091 11 17W	city/town	
Waukon Municipal	43 16 49N	091 28 09W	airport	1281
Waupeton	42 40 04N	090 52 56W	city/town	613
Waverly	42 43 33N	092 28 31W	city/town	
Waverly Junction	42 40 04N	092 31 41W	city/town	
Waverly Municipal	42 44 31N	092 30 27W	airport	992
Wayland	41 08 50N	091 39 38W	city/town	
Webb	42 56 55N	095 00 42W	city/town	
Webster (1)	41 19 45N	094 13 52W	city/town	
Webster (2)	41 26 18N	092 10 08W	city/town	
Webster City	42 28 10N	093 48 57W	city/town	

Place Name	Latitude	Longitude	Type	Elev
Webster City Mun.	42 26 09N	093 52 07W	airport	1121
Weldon	40 53 51N	093 44 05W	city/town	
Weller	41 06 26N	093 02 57W	city/town	
Wellman	41 27 51N	091 50 17W	city/town	
Wellsburg	42 27 33N	092 56 18W	city/town	
Welsh Lake	43 27 38N	095 10 20W	lake	1434
Welton	41 54 29N	090 35 43W	city/town	
Wesley	43 05 18N	093 59 24W	city/town	
Wesleyan College	40 58 21N	091 33 08W	univ/coll	
West Amana	41 48 29N	091 57 49W	city/town	
West Bend	42 57 25N	094 26 27W	city/town	
West Branch	41 40 17N	091 20 47W	city/town	
West Burlington	40 49 30N	091 09 23W	city/town	
West Cedar Rapids	41 57 30N	091 40 07W	city/town	
West Chester	41 20 20N	091 49 03W	city/town	
West Des Moines	41 34 38N	093 42 40W	city/town	
West Ft Dodge -his	42 28 52N	094 12 40W	city/town	
West Grove	40 43 29N	092 33 36W	city/town	
West Iron Hills	42 08 32N	090 47 30W	city/town	
West Le Mars	42 47 35N	096 13 33W	city/town	
West Liberty	41 34 12N	091 15 49W	city/town	
West Liberty C C	41 33 41N	091 16 32W	golf	

Iowa GPS Companion

Place Name	Latitude	Longitude	Type	Elev
West Okoboji	43 21 12N	095 09 44W	city/town	
West Okoboji Lake	43 23 04N	095 09 33W	lake	1396
West Point	40 43 00N	091 27 00W	city/town	
West Saint Marys	41 18 29N	093 44 22W	city/town	
West Twin Lake	42 56 18N	093 43 51W	lake	1218
West Union	42 57 46N	091 48 29W	city/town	
West Union -hist	42 11 26N	092 26 47W	city/town	
West Union -Scott	42 59 06N	091 47 25W	airport	1232
West Yards	43 02 33N	091 12 02W	city/town	
Western	41 51 55N	091 38 35W	city/town	
Westfield (1)	42 45 20N	096 36 20W	city/town	
Westfield (2)	41 42 15N	092 45 38W	city/town	
Westgate	42 46 12N	091 59 46W	city/town	
Westmar College	42 46 50N	096 09 44W	univ/coll	
Weston	41 20 27N	095 44 27W	city/town	
Westphalia	41 43 11N	095 23 40W	city/town	1402
Westside	42 03 33N	095 05 52W	city/town	
Westwood	40 57 56N	091 37 25W	city/town	700
Wever	40 42 38N	091 13 51W	city/town	
What Cheer	41 24 05N	092 21 16W	city/town	
Wheatland	41 49 54N	090 50 17W	city/town	
Wheelerwood	43 14 30N	093 03 50W	city/town	

Iowa GPS Companion

Place Name	Latitude	Longitude	Type	Elev
White Cloud	40 59 03N	095 31 22W	city/town	
White Elm	40 51 05N	092 12 23W	city/town	
White Oak	41 40 30N	093 32 03W	city/town	
White Pine Hollow	42 37 47N	091 06 43W	park	
Whitebreast	41 02 22N	093 21 45W	city/town	
Whitefield -hist	40 59 42N	092 02 37W	city/town	
Whiting	42 07 39N	096 08 57W	city/town	
Whittemore	43 03 43N	094 25 36W	city/town	
Whittemore Golf	43 04 34N	094 23 09W	golf	
Whitten	42 15 39N	093 00 19W	city/town	
Whittier	42 05 41N	091 27 45W	city/town	
Wichita	41 44 00N	094 36 14W	city/town	
Wick	41 20 41N	093 44 19W	city/town	
Wightman	42 13 57N	094 36 34W	city/town	
Wildcat Bluff	42 11 31N	091 53 11W	cliff	
Wildcat Cave Acc.	42 23 03N	093 05 27W	access	
Wildcat Den State	41 28 04N	090 52 52W	park	
Wilke	42 29 48N	093 28 09W	city/town	
Wilkins	42 24 34N	090 32 28W	city/town	
Willard	41 00 22N	092 35 22W	city/town	
Willett	41 41 50N	095 44 42W	city/town	
Willey	41 58 45N	094 49 19W	city/town	

Iowa GPS Companion

Place Name	Latitude	Longitude	Type	Elev
William M. Black M.	42 29 40N	090 39 30W	museum	
William Penn Col.	41 18 33N	092 38 48W	univ/coll	
Williams	42 29 18N	093 32 41W	city/town	
Williamsburg	41 39 40N	092 00 32W	city/town	
Williamson (1)	41 08 37N	094 33 57W	city/town	
Williamson (2)	41 05 16N	093 15 17W	city/town	
Williamstown (1)	42 57 55N	092 19 04W	city/town	
Williamstown (2)	41 34 12N	091 43 56W	city/town	
Willow Creek Golf	41 31 29N	093 42 13W	golf	
Willsburg -hist	40 35 57N	095 15 15W	city/town	
Wilmar	42 49 06N	092 49 47W	city/town	
Wilson -hist	41 38 04N	093 04 08W	city/town	
Wilson Island St.	41 28 58N	096 00 17W	park	
Wilton	41 35 20N	091 01 00W	city/town	
Winchester	40 51 01N	091 53 59W	city/town	
Windham	41 36 32N	091 45 43W	city/town	
Windsor Heights	41 35 52N	093 42 29W	city/town	
Winfield	41 07 23N	091 26 28W	city/town	
Winkelmans	41 58 16N	094 20 18W	city/town	
Winterset	41 19 51N	094 00 49W	city/town	
Winterset -Madison	41 21 46N	094 01 15W	airport	1110
Winthrop	42 28 24N	091 44 03W	city/town	

Place Name	Latitude	Longitude	Type	Elev
Wiota	41 24 01N	094 53 12W	city/town	
Wiscotta	41 34 49N	094 11 24W	city/town	
Wise	42 28 57N	092 01 22W	city/town	
Woden	43 13 59N	093 54 32W	city/town	
Wolf	42 08 08N	094 01 38W	city/town	
Wolf Hill	42 35 15N	091 32 10W	summit	
Wolf Lake Addition	41 59 43N	092 53 08W	city/town	
Wood	42 39 27N	091 19 57W	city/town	
Woodbine	41 44 18N	095 42 09W	city/town	1078
Woodbine Municipal	41 44 10N	095 41 00W	airport	1068
Woodburn	41 00 43N	093 35 56W	city/town	
Woodland	40 41 46N	093 35 52W	city/town	
Woodland Hills	41 33 12N	093 27 43W	city/town	
Woodmans Hollow St	42 25 16N	094 06 06W	park	
Woodthrush State	40 58 54N	091 48 27W	park	
Woodward	41 51 25N	093 55 18W	city/town	
Woolstock	42 34 00N	093 50 37W	city/town	
Worthington	42 23 47N	091 07 11W	city/town	
Worthington Acres	41 55 46N	091 37 41W	city/town	
Wren	42 38 44N	096 17 10W	city/town	
Wright	41 14 57N	092 31 33W	city/town	
Wyman	41 11 32N	091 28 26W	city/town	

Place Name	Latitude	Longitude	Type	Elev
Wyoming	42 03 33N	091 00 26W	city/town	
X				
Xenia (1)	42 18 40N	093 04 50W	city/town	
Xenia (2)	41 51 25N	093 53 35W	city/town	
Y				
Yale	41 46 36N	094 21 28W	city/town	
Yampa	41 00 36N	092 13 25W	city/town	
Yarmouth	41 01 35N	091 19 24W	city/town	
Yatton -hist	41 27 49N	091 35 01W	city/town	
Yellow River	43 05 16N	091 11 16W	city/town	
Yeomans	42 35 05N	096 24 53W	city/town	
Yetter	42 18 58N	094 50 45W	city/town	1216
York	42 38 04N	091 26 35W	city/town	
York Center	41 22 34N	095 33 20W	city/town	1322
Yorkshire	41 31 14N	095 34 47W	city/town	
Yorktown	40 44 00N	095 09 24W	city/town	
Z				
Zaneta	42 23 37N	092 33 07W	city/town	
Zearing	42 09 40N	093 17 49W	city/town	

Iowa GPS Companion

Place Name	Latitude	Longitude	Type	Elev
Zenorsville	42 06 26N	093 43 04W	city/town	
Zero	40 59 00N	093 07 37W	city/town	
Zion	41 12 02N	094 17 55W	city/town	
Zwingle	42 17 52N	090 41 15W	city/town	

Add your own coordinates here

133

Place Name	Latitude	Longitude	Type	Elev

Add your own coordinates here

NORTH
CENTRAL
GPS
COMPANION

MINNESOTA

DATA FORMAT: DD-MM-SS

DATUM: NAD27

CAUTION: Airport data is not approved for aerial navigation.

Place Name	Latitude	Longitude	Type	Elev

A

Place Name	Latitude	Longitude	Type	Elev
Acton	45 05 03N	094 39 38W	city/town	
Ada	47 17 59N	096 30 54W	city/town	907
Ada -Norman Co.	47 15 37N	096 24 01W	airport	954
Adams	43 33 55N	092 43 09W	city/town	
Adolph	46 46 43N	092 16 48W	city/town	1277
Adrian	43 38 06N	095 55 57W	city/town	1541
Afton	44 54 10N	092 47 00W	city/town	
Afton State Park	44 51 45N	092 47 00W	park	
Ah-gwah-ching	47 04 19N	094 34 05W	city/town	1342
Airlie	44 01 12N	096 26 16W	city/town	1660
Aitkin	46 31 59N	093 42 36W	city/town	1217
Aitkin Municipal	46 32 51N	093 40 36W	airport	1205
Akeley	47 00 15N	094 43 36W	city/town	
Albany	45 37 48N	094 34 11W	city/town	
Albert Lea	43 38 53N	093 22 05W	city/town	
Albert Lea Municip	43 40 53N	093 22 02W	airport	1259
Alberta	45 34 24N	096 02 50W	city/town	
Albertville	45 14 16N	093 39 15W	city/town	
Albion Center	45 10 37N	094 04 24W	city/town	
Alborn	46 58 23N	092 34 33W	city/town	1304

Minnesota GPS Companion

Place Name	Latitude	Longitude	Type	Elev
Albright	45 07 46N	094 06 51W	city/town	
Alden	43 40 13N	093 34 33W	city/town	
Alder	47 33 42N	093 42 13W	city/town	
Aldrich	46 22 35N	094 56 11W	city/town	
Aldrich Arena	44 59 50N	093 01 22W	building	
Alexander Ramsey S	44 33 05N	095 07 46W	park	
Alexandria	45 53 07N	095 22 38W	city/town	
Alexandria Mun.	45 52 00N	095 23 42W	airport	1425
Alford	46 37 55N	092 23 00W	city/town	
Alger	47 08 50N	091 41 33W	city/town	
Alida	47 23 01N	095 14 04W	city/town	1522
Allen	47 30 59N	092 05 55W	city/town	1510
Alma City	44 01 21N	093 43 40W	city/town	
Almelund	45 29 29N	092 47 07W	city/town	
Almora	46 14 47N	095 21 55W	city/town	
Alpha	43 38 20N	094 52 14W	city/town	1387
Alton Heights Lkt.	47 11 09N	095 11 17W	tower	
Altura	44 04 18N	091 56 22W	city/town	
Alvarado	48 11 39N	096 59 45W	city/town	812
Alvwood	47 43 50N	094 16 04W	city/town	1380
Amboy	43 53 17N	094 09 23W	city/town	1044
Amherst	43 36 31N	091 53 41W	city/town	1049

Minnesota GPS Companion

Place Name	Latitude	Longitude	Type	Elev
Amiret	44 19 00N	095 41 48W	city/town	
Amor	46 24 45N	095 44 42W	city/town	
Anchor Hill	47 11 55N	095 19 07W	summit	1895
Andersons Crossing	46 41 57N	094 52 55W	city/town	
Andover	45 14 00N	093 17 28W	city/town	891
Andree	45 43 42N	093 13 25W	city/town	959
Andrusia	47 29 10N	094 39 49W	city/town	
Andyville	43 43 26N	092 59 22W	city/town	
Angle Inlet	49 20 43N	095 03 45W	city/town	
Angleworm Lookout	48 05 08N	091 53 33W	tower	1570
Anglim	47 47 42N	096 35 51W	city/town	
Angora	47 46 30N	092 38 02W	city/town	1349
Angus	48 04 52N	096 42 10W	city/town	
Annandale	45 15 46N	094 07 27W	city/town	
Anoka	45 11 52N	093 23 13W	city/town	
Anthony	47 20 46N	096 39 57W	city/town	
Antlers Park	44 39 47N	093 15 55W	city/town	
Apple Valley	44 43 55N	093 13 03W	city/town	955
Appleton	45 11 49N	096 01 10W	city/town	
Appleton Municipal	45 13 40N	096 00 19W	airport	1021
Arago	47 03 04N	095 09 41W	city/town	1501
Arbutus	48 18 25N	093 02 51W	city/town	1286

Minnesota GPS Companion

Place Name	Latitude	Longitude	Type	Elev
Arco	44 23 01N	096 11 00W	city/town	
Arcola	45 07 24N	092 45 59W	city/town	865
Arden Hills	45 03 01N	093 09 23W	city/town	
Arendahl	43 49 31N	091 54 34W	city/town	1190
Argonne	44 41 45N	093 17 08W	city/town	
Argyle	48 19 58N	096 49 14W	city/town	847
Arlberg	46 55 24N	092 36 50W	city/town	
Arlington	44 36 30N	094 04 49W	city/town	
Armour No. 2 Mine	46 29 06N	093 58 06W	city/town	
Armstrong (1)	43 39 53N	093 28 04W	city/town	
Armstrong (2)	45 00 41N	093 41 12W	city/town	
Arnessen	48 57 27N	095 04 02W	city/town	
Arnold	46 52 49N	092 05 25W	city/town	1438
Arrow Lookout	47 50 57N	091 18 36W	tower	1678
Arrowhead Lookout	46 50 03N	092 42 53W	tower	1610
Arthyde	46 21 22N	093 05 21W	city/town	1285
Artichoke	45 23 57N	096 09 26W	city/town	1096
Asbury	44 52 44N	095 32 01W	city/town	1043
Ash Creek	43 32 18N	096 11 38W	city/town	
Ash Lake	48 13 08N	092 54 57W	city/town	
Ash River Falls	48 22 38N	092 49 09W	falls	
Ash River Lookout	48 24 24N	092 47 13W	tower	1372

Minnesota GPS Companion

Place Name	Latitude	Longitude	Type	Elev
Ashby	46 05 35N	095 49 02W	city/town	1298
Askov	46 11 12N	092 46 56W	city/town	
Askov Lookout	46 14 27N	092 43 14W	tower	1271
Assumption	44 41 17N	093 53 19W	city/town	1009
Atkinson	46 36 44N	092 33 55W	city/town	1147
Atwater	45 08 20N	094 46 40W	city/town	1215
Atwood	44 51 47N	093 21 49W	city/town	
Audubon	46 51 48N	095 58 53W	city/town	
Augsburg College	44 57 58N	093 14 30W	univ/coll	
Augusta	44 48 18N	093 41 16W	city/town	982
Aure	47 40 24N	095 07 13W	city/town	
Aurora	47 31 48N	092 14 13W	city/town	1480
Austin	43 40 00N	092 58 28W	city/town	
Austin Acres	43 39 08N	093 00 04W	city/town	
Austin C C	43 40 38N	092 55 32W	golf	
Austin Municipal	43 39 53N	092 56 00W	airport	1233
Automba	46 31 15N	093 01 06W	city/town	1284
Averill	46 58 15N	096 32 49W	city/town	916
Avoca	43 56 55N	095 38 43W	city/town	
Avon	45 36 33N	094 27 05W	city/town	1129

Place Name	Latitude	Longitude	Type	Elev
𝔹				
B I R Airport	46 25 10N	094 16 30W	airport	1210
Babbitt	47 42 31N	091 56 40W	city/town	
Backus	46 49 13N	094 30 58W	city/town	
Backus Municipal	46 49 36N	094 30 25W	airport	1355
Baden (1)	47 00 37N	092 35 18W	city/town	
Baden (2)	44 42 51N	093 35 17W	city/town	
Badger	48 46 57N	096 00 51W	city/town	1082
Badoura	46 51 44N	094 45 57W	city/town	
Badoura Lookout	46 51 41N	094 43 24W	tower	1423
Bagley	47 31 18N	095 23 53W	city/town	1441
Bagley C C	47 31 47N	095 23 17W	golf	
Bagley Municipal	47 31 29N	095 21 39W	airport	1500
Bailey	45 19 01N	093 39 54W	city/town	927
Bain	46 47 27N	093 35 22W	city/town	1264
Baker (1)	47 07 18N	094 31 08W	city/town	1298
Baker (2)	46 42 47N	096 33 06W	city/town	936
Balaton	44 14 00N	095 52 19W	city/town	1523
Bald Eagle	45 06 07N	093 00 49W	city/town	
Bald Eagle Center	47 24 04N	094 25 07W	city/town	
Bald Rock Light	48 37 26N	093 10 56W	locale	1115

Minnesota GPS Companion

Place Name	Latitude	Longitude	Type	Elev
Ball Bluff	46 57 17N	093 16 23W	city/town	1247
Ball Bluff Lookout	46 56 21N	093 14 38W	tower	
Ball Club	47 19 33N	093 56 09W	city/town	
Balsam	46 46 52N	093 09 21W	city/town	1238
Bancroft	43 42 06N	093 21 18W	city/town	1236
Banning	46 09 38N	092 51 06W	city/town	
Baptism Crossing	47 31 47N	091 20 28W	city/town	1912
Baptism River St.	47 20 25N	091 12 13W	park	
Bar-L Ranch C C	45 30 23N	093 16 16W	golf	
Barden	44 47 26N	093 24 37W	city/town	
Barnesville	46 39 08N	096 25 10W	city/town	
Barnesville Munic	46 39 54N	096 26 28W	airport	980
Barnum	46 30 11N	092 41 18W	city/town	1103
Baroda	43 43 15N	093 40 29W	city/town	
Barrett	45 54 38N	095 53 24W	city/town	1166
Barrows	46 18 04N	094 15 13W	city/town	1206
Barry	45 33 29N	096 33 32W	city/town	
Bartlett	46 54 45N	092 20 28W	city/town	1365
Bass Brook -subd.	47 14 18N	093 38 47W	city/town	1280
Bass Lake Lookout	47 42 52N	093 55 04W	tower	
Basswood	46 27 20N	095 41 35W	city/town	
Basswood Falls	48 06 21N	091 38 54W	falls	1308

143

Place Name	Latitude	Longitude	Type	Elev
Basswood Grove	44 49 38N	092 47 57W	city/town	
Bath	43 49 32N	093 23 23W	city/town	1262
Battle Lake	46 16 50N	095 42 48W	city/town	1372
Baudette	48 42 45N	094 35 59W	city/town	
Baudette Intern.	48 43 42N	094 36 43W	airport	1084
Baxter	46 20 36N	094 17 11W	city/town	1208
Bay Lake	46 24 34N	093 52 25W	city/town	1288
Bayport	45 01 17N	092 46 51W	city/town	
Bayview (1)	46 07 08N	093 36 11W	city/town	
Bayview (2)	46 44 50N	092 11 43W	city/town	1196
Bear Head Lake St.	47 47 47N	092 04 36W	park	
Bear River	47 46 40N	093 04 58W	city/town	1288
Bear Valley	44 18 12N	092 28 38W	city/town	
Beardsley	45 33 30N	096 42 43W	city/town	1098
Bearskin Lookout	48 03 41N	090 23 39W	tower	
Beatty Portage	48 16 39N	092 17 39W	portage	
Beauford	44 00 27N	093 57 30W	city/town	1011
Beaulieu	47 20 08N	095 48 15W	city/town	
Beaver	44 09 12N	092 00 44W	city/town	
Beaver Bay	47 15 28N	091 18 01W	city/town	
Beaver Creek	43 36 51N	096 21 51W	city/town	
Beaver Creek Vly	43 38 34N	091 34 54W	park	

Minnesota GPS Companion

Place Name	Latitude	Longitude	Type	Elev
Beaver Crossing	47 14 32N	091 31 29W	city/town	1329
Beaver Falls	44 34 59N	095 02 49W	city/town	
Beaver River Falls	47 15 55N	091 17 51W	falls	801
Bechyn	44 39 02N	095 04 33W	city/town	
Becida	47 21 15N	095 04 51W	city/town	1425
Becker	45 23 36N	093 52 36W	city/town	
Beckville	45 02 40N	094 33 49W	city/town	1194
Bee	43 30 04N	091 34 14W	city/town	
Bejou	47 26 29N	095 58 33W	city/town	1222
Belden	46 19 20N	092 18 47W	city/town	1266
Belgrade (1)	45 27 11N	095 00 15W	city/town	1266
Belgrade (2)	47 31 52N	092 22 26W	city/town	
Bell Harbor	47 23 21N	091 08 19W	city/town	608
Bellaire	45 04 11N	092 59 40W	city/town	
Belle Creek	44 26 18N	092 46 14W	city/town	
Belle Plaine	44 37 22N	093 46 06W	city/town	
Belle Plaine ARS	44 40 00N	093 47 00W	airport	955
Belle Prairie	46 02 02N	094 20 14W	city/town	
Belle River	45 59 28N	095 13 43W	city/town	1362
Bellechester	44 22 06N	092 30 40W	city/town	
Bellingham	45 08 10N	096 17 14W	city/town	
Bellwood Oaks Golf	44 38 54N	092 50 21W	golf	

Minnesota GPS Companion

Place Name	Latitude	Longitude	Type	Elev
Beltrami	47 32 33N	096 31 48W	city/town	903
Belvidere Mills	44 27 09N	092 30 33W	city/town	
Belview	44 36 19N	095 19 45W	city/town	
Bemidji	47 28 25N	094 52 48W	city/town	
Bemidji State Col.	47 28 54N	094 52 27W	univ/coll	
Bemidji-Beltrami	47 30 33N	094 56 01W	airport	1390
Ben Linn Landing	48 15 02N	093 53 07W	city/town	
Bena	47 20 27N	094 12 25W	city/town	
Benedict	47 09 29N	094 41 25W	city/town	1316
Bengal	47 16 06N	093 03 57W	city/town	
Bennett	47 24 58N	093 05 05W	city/town	
Bennettville	46 24 07N	093 44 55W	city/town	1266
Benning	44 12 12N	093 59 41W	city/town	
Benoit	47 42 06N	096 23 40W	city/town	1022
Benson	45 18 54N	095 35 59W	city/town	
Benson Municipal	45 19 54N	095 39 02W	airport	1039
Benton	44 46 34N	093 46 51W	city/town	
Bergen	43 47 24N	094 59 40W	city/town	
Bergville	47 47 15N	094 15 51W	city/town	
Bernadotte	44 27 19N	094 18 03W	city/town	
Berne	44 09 49N	092 46 45W	city/town	
Berner	47 48 16N	095 28 22W	city/town	

Minnesota GPS Companion

Place Name	Latitude	Longitude	Type	Elev
Berning Mill	45 12 25N	093 37 27W	city/town	
Beroun	45 54 37N	092 57 18W	city/town	
Bertha	46 16 00N	095 03 45W	city/town	
Bethany	44 01 27N	091 54 41W	city/town	
Bethany College	44 10 00N	093 59 26W	univ/coll	
Bethel	45 24 14N	093 16 03W	city/town	
Bethel College	44 59 06N	093 09 57W	univ/coll	
Big Bear Landing	47 20 12N	095 28 36W	city/town	
Big Bend City	45 08 35N	095 46 18W	city/town	
Big Falls	48 11 28N	093 48 23W	city/town	
Big Falls Municip	48 11 44N	093 46 00W	airport	1232
Big Lake	45 19 57N	093 44 45W	city/town	942
Big Lake Chapel	46 43 18N	092 35 48W	city/town	1311
Big Meadows Look.	47 48 32N	095 11 24W	tower	
Big Spring	43 34 00N	092 03 08W	city/town	
Big Stone Colony	45 31 45N	096 28 26W	city/town	
Big Stone Lake St.	45 22 57N	096 30 46W	park	
Big Thunder Peak	47 07 21N	093 40 37W	summit	1752
Big Woods	48 18 41N	097 06 28W	city/town	801
Bigelow	43 30 19N	095 41 23W	city/town	
Bigfork	47 44 40N	093 39 14W	city/town	1318
Bigfork Municipal	47 46 44N	093 39 00W	airport	1343

Minnesota GPS Companion

Place Name	Latitude	Longitude	Type	Elev
Bingham Lake	43 54 24N	095 02 46W	city/town	
BIR Speedway	46 25 00N	094 16 28W	locale	
Birch	47 02 03N	092 35 31W	city/town	1323
Birch Beach	48 57 09N	094 55 54W	city/town	1066
Birch Coulee State	44 34 33N	094 58 29W	park	1027
Birch Hill Lookout	47 27 23N	094 21 50W	tower	1352
Birch Knob Lookout	47 40 47N	092 39 26W	tower	
Birch Lake Lookout	46 58 10N	094 31 03W	tower	1552
Birch Lake State F	45 45 56N	094 46 11W	park	
Birchdale	48 37 37N	094 06 06W	city/town	
Birchdale Lookout	48 37 37N	094 04 50W	tower	
Birchmont	47 32 47N	094 51 37W	city/town	
Birchwood	45 03 40N	092 58 33W	city/town	
Bird Island	44 46 03N	094 53 43W	city/town	
Biscay	44 49 39N	094 16 29W	city/town	
Biwabik	47 31 59N	092 20 24W	city/town	1448
Bixby	43 56 40N	093 05 49W	city/town	
Black Bay Lookout	48 35 58N	093 10 26W	tower	1179
Black Hammer	43 36 59N	091 39 39W	city/town	1179
Blackberry	47 10 51N	093 23 25W	city/town	
Blackduck	47 43 59N	094 32 54W	city/town	1383
Blackduck Lookout	47 41 12N	094 33 13W	tower	1448

Minnesota GPS Companion

Place Name	Latitude	Longitude	Type	Elev
Blackhoof	46 31 58N	092 27 43W	city/town	968
Blaine	45 09 39N	093 14 05W	city/town	
Blakeley	44 36 39N	093 51 11W	city/town	
Blomford	45 30 01N	093 08 32W	city/town	946
Blomkest	44 56 34N	095 01 23W	city/town	
Blooming Prairie	43 52 00N	093 03 03W	city/town	
Bloomington	44 50 27N	093 17 53W	city/town	
Bloomington Ferry	44 47 59N	093 23 03W	city/town	
Blue Earth	43 38 15N	094 06 07W	city/town	
Blue Earth Municip	43 35 43N	094 05 34W	airport	1107
Blue Fin Bay	48 27 48N	092 56 14W	bay	
Blue Grass	46 32 34N	095 00 35W	city/town	
Blue Hill	45 29 55N	093 42 47W	summit	1090
Blue Mounds State	43 42 25N	096 11 12W	park	
Blueberry Hill	47 21 40N	093 06 34W	summit	1495
Blueberry Hill Lkt	47 21 28N	093 45 13W	tower	1476
Blufton	46 28 09N	095 13 58W	city/town	
Bock	45 47 06N	093 33 24W	city/town	1105
Bodum	45 31 18N	093 12 15W	city/town	982
Boisberg	45 55 13N	096 33 40W	city/town	
Bombay	44 17 01N	092 53 29W	city/town	1178
Bonanza Grove	45 26 44N	096 42 33W	city/town	

Place Name	Latitude	Longitude	Type	Elev
Bonga Landing	47 22 26N	095 29 03W	city/town	
Bongards	44 45 45N	093 50 54W	city/town	984
Bonnie Glen	45 21 32N	092 54 13W	city/town	
Borden Lake Lkt.	46 16 43N	093 51 26W	tower	
Border	48 41 48N	094 16 41W	city/town	1097
Borup	47 10 49N	096 30 21W	city/town	912
Boulder Hill Lkt.	47 20 26N	094 14 40W	tower	1348
Bovey	47 17 44N	093 25 07W	city/town	
Bowlus	45 49 10N	094 24 33W	city/town	1108
Bowstring	47 32 35N	093 47 47W	city/town	1314
Bowstring Municip	47 33 30N	093 52 08W	airport	1372
Boy River	47 10 05N	094 07 19W	city/town	1329
Boy River Lookout	47 09 33N	094 05 43W	tower	
Boyd	44 50 55N	095 54 10W	city/town	
Bradford	45 31 21N	093 22 07W	city/town	
Braham	45 43 22N	093 10 14W	city/town	
Brainerd	46 21 29N	094 12 02W	city/town	
Brainerd-Crow Wing	46 23 52N	094 08 13W	airport	1226
Branch -subd.	45 29 07N	092 57 42W	city/town	
Brandon	45 57 55N	095 35 54W	city/town	
Bratsberg	43 44 06N	091 46 13W	city/town	
Breckenridge	46 15 49N	096 35 16W	city/town	

Minnesota GPS Companion

Place Name	Latitude	Longitude	Type	Elev
Breda	47 18 43N	091 53 08W	city/town	
Breezy Point	46 37 00N	094 13 00W	city/town	
Breezy Point Arprt	46 35 59N	094 13 00W	airport	1250
Bremen	44 12 31N	092 18 38W	city/town	1108
Brennyville	45 48 31N	093 54 20W	city/town	1234
Brevik	47 04 59N	094 17 18W	city/town	
Brewster	43 41 55N	095 28 06W	city/town	
Bricelyn	43 33 44N	093 48 42W	city/town	
Brickton	45 36 26N	093 36 21W	city/town	
Bridgeman	46 23 02N	094 34 49W	city/town	1303
Briggs Lake	45 30 31N	093 56 09W	city/town	993
Brimson	47 16 36N	091 52 01W	city/town	1516
Bristol	43 32 40N	092 10 09W	city/town	1334
Britt	47 38 25N	092 31 31W	city/town	1477
Brittmount	47 35 48N	092 34 55W	city/town	1495
Brook Park	45 56 58N	093 04 31W	city/town	
Brooklyn	47 26 23N	092 55 15W	city/town	
Brooklyn Center	45 04 34N	093 19 57W	city/town	
Brooklyn Park	45 05 39N	093 21 22W	city/town	
Brooks	47 48 52N	096 00 07W	city/town	
Brookston	46 52 04N	092 36 13W	city/town	1228
Brookview C C	44 58 36N	093 23 07W	golf	

Minnesota GPS Companion

Place Name	Latitude	Longitude	Type	Elev
Brooten	45 30 04N	095 07 27W	city/town	
Brooten Municipal	45 29 59N	095 06 46W	airport	1305
Browerville	46 05 09N	094 51 56W	city/town	1283
Brownell	46 40 38N	092 20 17W	city/town	1113
Browns Valley	45 35 43N	096 49 59W	city/town	
Brownsdale	43 44 25N	092 52 09W	city/town	
Brownsville	43 41 39N	091 16 47W	city/town	
Brownton	44 43 55N	094 21 00W	city/town	1021
Bruce	43 31 20N	096 23 53W	city/town	
Brule Lake Lookout	47 55 04N	090 38 24W	tower	2120
Brule Mountain	47 55 50N	090 26 48W	summit	2226
Bruno	46 16 45N	092 39 51W	city/town	1151
Brunswick	45 47 20N	093 16 32W	city/town	962
Brush Creek	43 38 41N	093 50 53W	city/town	1134
Brush Hill	46 29 53N	094 31 04W	summit	1499
Brushvale	46 22 10N	096 38 35W	city/town	957
Buck Hill	44 43 23N	093 17 13W	summit	1195
Buckman	45 53 51N	094 05 36W	city/town	
Bucks Mill	46 43 23N	095 54 53W	city/town	1331
Bucksnort	43 49 04N	092 03 03W	city/town	
Bud Hill Lookout	47 14 29N	091 30 40W	tower	1389
Buena Vista Ski	47 39 30N	094 52 40W	ski area	

Minnesota GPS Companion

Place Name	Latitude	Longitude	Type	Elev
Buffalo	45 10 19N	093 52 28W	city/town	967
Buffalo Lake	44 44 14N	094 37 00W	city/town	1074
Buffalo Municipal	45 09 32N	093 50 35W	airport	967
Buffalo Ridge	43 58 49N	096 00 37W	ridge	
Buffalo River St.	46 51 56N	096 28 03W	park	
Buhl	47 29 37N	092 46 40W	city/town	1533
Buhl Lookout	47 32 14N	092 45 18W	tower	
Bunde	44 56 05N	095 18 36W	city/town	1079
Bunker Prairie Lkt	45 12 48N	093 17 46W	tower	
Burchard	44 15 22N	095 59 24W	city/town	1665
Burnett	46 54 03N	092 31 27W	city/town	1306
Burnsville	44 46 04N	093 16 39W	city/town	975
Burntside	47 53 40N	091 55 43W	city/town	
Burntside Lake	47 53 34N	092 02 04W	city/town	1408
Burr	44 44 54N	096 21 32W	city/town	1326
Burschville	45 07 30N	093 38 10W	city/town	
Burtrum	45 52 03N	094 41 05W	city/town	1285
Burwell	47 44 43N	096 30 10W	city/town	
Bush Landing	47 19 54N	095 28 23W	city/town	
Butler	46 41 17N	095 21 10W	city/town	1462
Butterfield	43 57 30N	094 47 40W	city/town	
Butterfly Lake	47 45 30N	091 28 45W	city/town	

Place Name	Latitude	Longitude	Type	Elev
Butternut	44 08 16N	094 19 44W	city/town	988
Buyck	48 07 19N	092 31 24W	city/town	1235
Bygland	47 48 42N	096 55 55W	city/town	
Byron	44 01 58N	092 38 43W	city/town	1262

ℂ

Place Name	Latitude	Longitude	Type	Elev
Cable	45 30 42N	094 04 26W	city/town	
Caledonia	43 38 05N	091 29 48W	city/town	1174
Caledonia -Houston	43 35 46N	091 30 14W	airport	1179
Calhoun Beach	44 56 59N	093 18 55W	city/town	
Callaway	46 58 57N	095 54 34W	city/town	1370
Calumet	47 19 19N	093 16 36W	city/town	1392
Cambria	44 14 19N	094 18 51W	city/town	
Cambridge	45 34 22N	093 13 27W	city/town	962
Cambridge Municip	45 33 30N	093 15 52W	airport	945
Camden State Park	44 21 45N	095 55 29W	park	
Camp Ripley Jct.	46 04 13N	094 19 41W	city/town	1139
Campbell	46 05 52N	096 24 16W	city/town	
Canby	44 42 32N	096 16 34W	city/town	
Canby Municipal	44 43 40N	096 15 47W	airport	1190
Canfield Portage	47 53 10N	092 17 34W	portage	
Canisteo	47 17 16N	093 27 14W	city/town	

Minnesota GPS Companion

Place Name	Latitude	Longitude	Type	Elev
Cannon C C	44 31 15N	092 55 52W	golf	
Cannon City	44 19 45N	093 12 40W	city/town	
Cannon Falls	44 30 25N	092 54 19W	city/town	838
Canton	43 31 47N	091 55 47W	city/town	1345
Canyon	47 02 24N	092 28 14W	city/town	1355
Cardigan Junction	45 03 10N	093 06 33W	city/town	
Caribou	48 58 57N	096 26 57W	city/town	
Caribou Falls	47 28 08N	091 01 55W	falls	
Carimona	43 39 37N	092 09 27W	city/town	
Carleton College	44 27 43N	093 09 18W	univ/coll	
Carley State Park	44 07 00N	092 10 33W	park	
Carlisle	46 22 06N	096 11 22W	city/town	
Carlos	45 58 21N	095 17 31W	city/town	
Carlton	46 39 50N	092 25 29W	city/town	1091
Carlton Peak	47 35 00N	090 51 36W	summit	1526
Carmel	48 16 54N	095 26 39W	city/town	1212
Carmody	45 39 06N	093 28 16W	city/town	
Carnelian Junction	45 07 29N	092 49 48W	city/town	
Carp	48 30 19N	094 38 49W	city/town	
Carpenters Corner	48 09 29N	096 26 14W	city/town	1032
Carriage Hills C C	44 49 35N	093 08 25W	golf	
Carver	44 45 49N	093 37 32W	city/town	

Minnesota GPS Companion

Place Name	Latitude	Longitude	Type	Elev
Carver Beach	44 52 41N	093 32 15W	city/town	
Cascade Falls	47 42 31N	090 31 26W	falls	
Cascade Lookout	47 43 56N	090 35 13W	tower	1881
Cascade River St.	47 42 03N	090 31 10W	park	695
Casco	47 15 29N	092 42 06W	city/town	
Casey	45 03 58N	094 26 28W	city/town	1087
Cashtown	45 17 55N	096 26 20W	city/town	
Casino	46 25 37N	094 32 24W	city/town	1365
Casperson	48 34 34N	095 41 13W	city/town	
Cass Lake	47 22 46N	094 36 14W	city/town	
Castle Danger	47 07 15N	091 30 11W	city/town	634
Castle Rock	44 32 38N	093 09 08W	city/town	
Castlewood C C	45 15 58N	092 57 30W	golf	
Cazenovia	44 04 01N	096 22 03W	city/town	674
Cedar	45 19 11N	093 17 09W	city/town	
Cedar Beach	44 09 42N	092 27 53W	city/town	
Cedar Grove	44 48 17N	093 12 36W	city/town	
Cedar Lake	44 35 14N	093 26 24W	city/town	947
Cedar Mills	44 56 35N	094 31 20W	city/town	1091
Cee Jefferson	43 30 51N	091 16 49W	city/town	662
Celina	47 51 57N	093 03 42W	city/town	1315
Center City	45 23 38N	092 48 59W	city/town	

Minnesota GPS Companion

Place Name	Latitude	Longitude	Type	Elev
Centerville (1)	43 56 35N	091 38 08W	city/town	
Centerville (2)	45 09 47N	093 03 20W	city/town	
Central	48 41 58N	094 20 34W	city/town	
Cerro Gordo	45 03 09N	096 01 54W	city/town	1040
Ceylon	43 32 01N	094 37 53W	city/town	
Chamberlain	46 54 19N	094 43 17W	city/town	1475
Champlin	45 11 20N	093 23 50W	city/town	
Chandler	43 55 45N	095 56 49W	city/town	1651
Chanhassen	44 51 44N	093 31 50W	city/town	976
Charles Lindbergh	45 57 32N	094 23 42W	park	
Charlesville	45 56 57N	096 16 06W	city/town	1011
Chaska	44 47 22N	093 36 07W	city/town	728
Chatfield	43 50 44N	092 11 20W	city/town	
Chatfield Flying A	43 49 10N	092 20 00W	airport	1300
Cherry	47 24 03N	092 42 25W	city/town	1353
Cherry Grove	43 35 15N	092 17 19W	city/town	1327
Chester	44 00 25N	092 20 42W	city/town	
Chickamaw Beach	46 44 37N	094 23 06W	city/town	
Childs	46 03 56N	096 32 03W	city/town	977
Chipmunk Falls	48 10 45N	092 35 51W	falls	
Chippewa City	47 45 35N	090 18 07W	city/town	667
Chisago City	45 22 25N	092 53 23W	city/town	

157

Minnesota GPS Companion

Place Name	Latitude	Longitude	Type	Elev
Chisago Lakes Golf	45 22 16N	092 50 37W	golf	
Chisholm	47 29 21N	092 53 01W	city/town	1578
Choice	43 39 35N	091 47 26W	city/town	818
Chokio	45 34 18N	096 10 23W	city/town	
Chosen Valley Golf	43 50 02N	092 10 04W	golf	
Churchill (1)	45 01 19N	095 52 00W	city/town	
Churchill (2)	44 49 06N	094 40 14W	city/town	1091
Circle Pines	45 08 55N	093 09 05W	city/town	
Clappers	47 26 08N	091 57 53W	city/town	
Clara City	44 57 18N	095 21 58W	city/town	1062
Claremont	44 02 40N	092 59 51W	city/town	
Clarissa	46 07 49N	094 56 54W	city/town	
Clarissa Municipal	46 06 46N	094 54 24W	airport	1308
Clarkfield	44 47 26N	095 48 30W	city/town	
Clarks Grove	43 45 50N	093 19 44W	city/town	
Claybank	44 26 30N	092 37 54W	city/town	
Clear Lake	47 38 24N	091 07 10W	city/town	
Clear Lake -Leader	45 26 39N	093 58 15W	airport	990
Clearbrook	47 41 31N	095 25 51W	city/town	
Clearwater	45 25 10N	094 02 55W	city/town	
Clements	44 22 54N	095 03 08W	city/town	
Clementson	48 41 27N	094 26 10W	city/town	1086

Minnesota GPS Companion

Place Name	Latitude	Longitude	Type	Elev
Cleveland	44 19 32N	093 50 15W	city/town	1051
Clifton	46 52 53N	091 55 13W	city/town	
Climax	47 36 28N	096 49 00W	city/town	865
Clinton	45 27 37N	096 26 00W	city/town	
Clinton Falls	44 08 20N	093 14 48W	city/town	1133
Clitherall	46 16 30N	095 37 51W	city/town	1348
Clontarf	45 22 35N	095 40 42W	city/town	1050
Cloquet	46 43 18N	092 27 33W	city/town	1204
Cloquet Carlton Co	46 42 00N	092 30 19W	airport	1279
Cloquet Golf Club	46 43 15N	092 28 32W	golf	
Cloquet Lookout	47 25 48N	091 28 15W	tower	2067
Cloquet Valley Lkt	47 15 16N	092 07 49W	tower	1603
Clotho	46 01 11N	095 02 33W	city/town	
Cloverdale	46 00 44N	092 44 23W	city/town	972
Cloverton	46 10 05N	092 19 10W	city/town	1099
Clyde	43 53 41N	091 58 45W	city/town	
Coates	44 43 02N	093 02 04W	city/town	
Cobden	44 17 11N	094 50 55W	city/town	
Coffee Mill C C	44 21 17N	092 02 05W	golf	
Coffee Pot Landing	47 20 58N	095 10 58W	city/town	
Cohasset	47 15 49N	093 37 12W	city/town	
Coin	45 44 06N	093 18 23W	city/town	

Minnesota GPS Companion

Place Name	Latitude	Longitude	Type	Elev
Cokato	45 04 33N	094 11 23W	city/town	1052
Colby	47 32 31N	092 10 11W	city/town	
Cold Spring	45 27 21N	094 25 43W	city/town	1091
Coleraine	47 17 20N	093 25 39W	city/town	
Coleraine Junction	46 58 02N	092 34 20W	city/town	
Coll. of St Cath.	44 55 32N	093 11 01W	univ/coll	
Coll. of St Teresa	44 03 04N	091 40 10W	univ/coll	
Collegeville	45 35 40N	094 21 46W	city/town	1094
Collis	45 38 48N	096 25 31W	city/town	
Cologne	44 46 18N	093 46 52W	city/town	948
Columbia Heights	45 02 27N	093 15 46W	city/town	
Comfrey	44 06 37N	094 54 16W	city/town	1301
Comstock	46 39 34N	096 44 53W	city/town	
Comus	44 23 06N	093 15 26W	city/town	
Conception	44 15 56N	092 06 35W	city/town	1170
Concord	44 08 51N	092 50 10W	city/town	
Concordia College	46 51 56N	096 46 06W	univ/coll	
Conger	43 36 54N	093 31 41W	city/town	1289
Constance	45 15 19N	093 17 07W	city/town	902
Cook	47 51 09N	092 41 22W	city/town	1306
Cook Airport	47 49 23N	092 41 29W	airport	1332
Cooley	47 21 30N	093 11 31W	city/town	1444

Minnesota GPS Companion

Place Name	Latitude	Longitude	Type	Elev
Coon Creek	45 09 06N	093 18 03W	city/town	
Coon Lake Beach	45 18 29N	093 09 21W	city/town	
Coon Rapids	45 07 12N	093 17 15W	city/town	
Coon Rapids Dam	45 08 40N	093 18 38W	dam	
Coopers Corner	45 23 57N	093 14 04W	city/town	931
Copas	45 14 05N	092 45 52W	city/town	
Corcoran	45 05 43N	093 32 50W	city/town	
Cordova	44 20 11N	093 40 17W	city/town	
Cormorant	46 43 50N	096 03 55W	city/town	
Corning	43 45 40N	093 02 57W	city/town	1280
Corona	46 40 14N	092 45 58W	city/town	1298
Correll	45 13 51N	096 09 33W	city/town	
Cort	47 19 58N	093 14 49W	city/town	
Corvuso	44 56 10N	094 36 16W	city/town	
Cosmos	44 56 10N	094 41 47W	city/town	
Cottage Grove	44 49 40N	092 56 37W	city/town	
Cotton	47 10 10N	092 28 34W	city/town	1329
Cotton Lookout	47 10 03N	092 30 15W	tower	
Cottonwood	44 36 32N	095 40 26W	city/town	
Courtland	44 16 06N	094 20 24W	city/town	
Cove	46 06 31N	093 37 06W	city/town	
Covill	47 47 43N	090 09 38W	city/town	622

Minnesota GPS Companion

Place Name	Latitude	Longitude	Type	Elev
Craigville	47 54 11N	093 36 46W	city/town	
Cramer	47 31 38N	091 05 24W	city/town	
Crane Lake	48 16 00N	092 29 18W	city/town	
Crane Lake Lookout	48 14 59N	092 32 08W	tower	
Credit River	44 40 28N	093 22 44W	city/town	990
Crescent Beach	44 54 52N	093 35 54W	city/town	
Cresson	44 06 40N	096 26 06W	city/town	1688
Croftville	47 45 54N	090 16 32W	city/town	
Cromwell	46 40 51N	092 53 02W	city/town	1311
Crookston	47 46 27N	096 36 28W	city/town	
Crookston Junction	47 45 23N	096 37 19W	city/town	
Crookston Municip	47 50 30N	096 37 17W	airport	899
Crosby	46 28 56N	093 57 27W	city/town	1261
Crosby Beach	46 28 18N	093 56 58W	city/town	1266
Cross Lake	46 39 34N	094 06 49W	city/town	
Crow River	45 14 38N	094 43 27W	city/town	1156
Crow Wing	46 16 48N	094 17 32W	city/town	1194
Crown	45 26 41N	093 27 36W	city/town	953
Crystal	45 01 58N	093 21 36W	city/town	
Crystal Bay	44 57 11N	093 34 34W	city/town	
Crystal Spring	44 04 29N	091 59 10W	city/town	759
Cuba Hill Lookout	47 20 33N	094 29 20W	tower	1430

Place Name	Latitude	Longitude	Type	Elev
Culver	46 55 33N	092 33 30W	city/town	1289
Cummingsville	43 52 29N	092 15 36W	city/town	
Current Lake	44 08 19N	095 56 35W	city/town	1665
Currie	44 04 17N	095 39 58W	city/town	
Curtain Falls	48 14 12N	091 54 22W	falls	
Cushing	46 08 23N	094 34 36W	city/town	
Cusson	48 06 07N	092 50 34W	city/town	1333
Cutfoot Sioux Info	47 31 12N	094 02 30W	center	1330
Cuyuna	46 31 01N	093 55 22W	city/town	
Cuyuna Lookout	46 30 32N	093 56 15W	tower	
Cuyuna Range	46 22 00N	094 10 00W	range	
Cyrus	45 36 53N	095 44 16W	city/town	1138

D

Place Name	Latitude	Longitude	Type	Elev
Dads Corner	46 19 58N	093 15 32W	city/town	1265
Dahlgren	44 46 36N	093 41 00W	city/town	979
Dakomin	45 43 30N	096 40 18W	city/town	
Dakota	43 54 49N	091 21 35W	city/town	691
Dakota Junction	48 09 32N	096 11 39W	city/town	
Dalbo	45 39 32N	093 23 55W	city/town	
Dale	46 54 19N	096 13 10W	city/town	
Dalton	46 10 26N	095 54 55W	city/town	

Minnesota GPS Companion

Place Name	Latitude	Longitude	Type	Elev
Danesville	44 05 38N	092 40 43W	city/town	1228
Danube	44 47 31N	095 05 49W	city/town	
Danvers	45 16 55N	095 45 06W	city/town	1027
Darby Junction	47 21 34N	091 37 55W	city/town	1708
Darfur	44 03 05N	094 50 16W	city/town	1148
Darling Observtry	46 46 48N	092 06 44W	building	
Darwin	45 05 47N	094 24 38W	city/town	1132
Dassel	45 04 54N	094 18 24W	city/town	1091
Davidson	47 52 36N	096 50 49W	city/town	
Davies	46 36 02N	095 18 39W	city/town	1444
Dawson	44 55 58N	096 03 15W	city/town	1058
Day	45 42 33N	093 22 45W	city/town	
Day Lake Lookout	47 29 56N	093 38 53W	tower	
Days High Landing	47 15 08N	093 48 20W	city/town	1287
Dayton	45 14 38N	093 30 53W	city/town	
Dayton Hollow Dam	46 13 52N	096 07 01W	dam	
De Forest	47 27 36N	092 34 45W	city/town	1418
De Graff	45 15 48N	095 28 03W	city/town	
Deadmans Rapids	48 08 32N	093 29 16W	falls	
Debs	47 43 53N	095 07 40W	city/town	1343
Deephaven	44 55 47N	093 31 20W	city/town	
Deer Creek	46 23 28N	095 19 16W	city/town	1393

Place Name	Latitude	Longitude	Type	Elev
Deer Lane	47 02 24N	094 58 40W	city/town	
Deer Park	44 42 07N	093 19 03W	city/town	
Deer River	47 19 59N	093 47 33W	city/town	1291
Deer River Municip	47 21 08N	093 48 00W	airport	1311
Deerfield	44 10 03N	093 21 34W	city/town	
Deerwood (1)	48 33 30N	096 35 30W	city/town	998
Deerwood (2)	46 28 25N	093 53 55W	city/town	1277
Delano	45 02 31N	093 47 20W	city/town	944
Delavan	43 46 04N	094 01 10W	city/town	1063
Delft	43 59 11N	095 05 19W	city/town	
Delhi	44 35 57N	095 12 39W	city/town	1030
Dell	43 37 27N	093 54 53W	city/town	
Dellwood	45 05 24N	092 58 20W	city/town	
Delorme	47 45 53N	096 17 20W	city/town	
Denham	46 21 50N	092 56 34W	city/town	1203
Dennison	44 24 25N	093 02 21W	city/town	
Dent	46 33 13N	095 42 58W	city/town	
Dentaybow Lookout	48 12 52N	093 30 02W	tower	
Detroit Lakes	46 49 02N	095 50 42W	city/town	
Detroit Lakes Aprt	46 49 30N	095 53 08W	airport	1396
Detroit Mountain	46 48 59N	095 46 59W	summit	1624
Devilfish Lookout	47 58 48N	090 06 15W	tower	

Minnesota GPS Companion

Place Name	Latitude	Longitude	Type	Elev
Devils Cascade	48 12 18N	092 15 02W	falls	
Dexter	43 43 08N	092 42 16W	city/town	
Diamond Corner	43 59 38N	096 06 13W	city/town	1791
Dilworth	46 52 36N	096 42 11W	city/town	
Ditter	45 00 50N	093 31 20W	city/town	
Dixon Lake Lookout	47 37 41N	094 17 28W	tower	1356
Dodge Center	44 01 41N	092 51 16W	city/town	1293
Dodge Center Aprt	44 01 05N	092 50 03W	airport	1298
Domaas	48 06 56N	094 33 00W	city/town	
Donaldson	48 34 20N	096 53 46W	city/town	
Donehower	43 57 40N	091 24 23W	city/town	
Donnelly	45 41 26N	096 00 44W	city/town	1133
Dora Lake	47 44 19N	094 02 24W	city/town	1324
Doran	46 11 03N	096 28 56W	city/town	975
Dorothy	47 55 40N	096 26 47W	city/town	
Dorset	46 57 23N	094 57 08W	city/town	1476
Dorset Lookout	46 57 19N	094 58 33W	tower	
Dotson	44 10 19N	094 59 40W	city/town	
Douglas	44 06 29N	092 34 25W	city/town	1032
Dover	43 58 25N	092 08 20W	city/town	
Dovray	44 03 10N	095 32 59W	city/town	
Downer	46 45 15N	096 29 12W	city/town	

Minnesota GPS Companion

Place Name	Latitude	Longitude	Type	Elev
Doyle	44 22 13N	093 34 29W	city/town	
Draper Lookout	46 55 33N	093 55 29W	tower	1548
Dresbach	43 53 44N	091 20 35W	city/town	
Dudley	44 25 30N	095 41 28W	city/town	
Duelm	45 34 20N	093 56 03W	city/town	
Duesler	46 30 43N	092 30 30W	city/town	1015
Dugdale	47 42 06N	096 15 58W	city/town	
Duluth	46 47 00N	092 06 23W	city/town	
Duluth -Sky Harbor	46 43 18N	092 02 36W	airport	610
Duluth Harbor Mar.	46 46 22N	092 05 25W	marina	605
Duluth Heights	46 48 03N	092 07 54W	city/town	
Duluth Internat'l	46 50 27N	092 11 00W	airport	1428
Duluth Junction	45 04 36N	092 53 59W	city/town	980
Dumblane	47 08 49N	092 36 53W	city/town	
Dumfries	44 20 42N	092 07 12W	city/town	
Dumont	45 42 57N	096 25 32W	city/town	
Dunbar	47 39 30N	094 13 28W	city/town	1351
Dundas	44 25 46N	093 12 06W	city/town	958
Dundee	43 50 49N	095 28 00W	city/town	
Dunnell	43 33 34N	094 46 27W	city/town	
Dunvilla	46 39 47N	096 00 57W	city/town	
Dunwoody Junction	47 27 07N	092 52 02W	city/town	

Place Name	Latitude	Longitude	Type	Elev
Dupont	45 05 45N	093 35 55W	city/town	
Duquette	46 22 11N	092 33 11W	city/town	1147
Duxbury	46 07 40N	092 30 31W	city/town	

E

Place Name	Latitude	Longitude	Type	Elev
Eagan	44 48 15N	093 10 00W	city/town	955
Eagle Bend	46 09 54N	095 02 20W	city/town	1369
Eagle Lake	44 09 54N	093 52 52W	city/town	1014
Eagle Mountain	47 53 51N	090 33 36W	highest	2301
Eaglehead Lookout	46 07 44N	092 36 17W	tower	1130
Eagles Nest	47 50 24N	092 05 47W	city/town	1491
East Beaver Bay	47 16 04N	091 16 58W	city/town	
East Bethel	45 19 10N	093 12 08W	city/town	
East Chain	43 33 32N	094 21 54W	city/town	
East Cottage Grove	44 50 30N	092 52 53W	city/town	
East Grand Forks	47 55 48N	097 01 27W	city/town	
East Gull Lake	46 24 29N	094 21 20W	city/town	1252
East Gull Lake Air	46 22 59N	094 21 43W	airport	1236
East Lake	46 32 18N	093 17 00W	city/town	
East Lake Francis	45 30 14N	093 19 25W	city/town	
East Union	44 43 05N	093 40 53W	city/town	
Easton	43 45 57N	093 54 03W	city/town	

Minnesota GPS Companion

Place Name	Latitude	Longitude	Type	Elev
Eastwood Golf	44 00 29N	092 24 33W	golf	
Ebro	47 29 44N	095 31 45W	city/town	
Echo	44 37 01N	095 25 02W	city/town	
Echols	43 55 26N	094 40 29W	city/town	
Eden	44 05 17N	092 53 05W	city/town	
Eden Prairie	44 51 17N	093 28 14W	city/town	
Eden Valley	45 19 34N	094 32 45W	city/town	
Edgerton	43 52 21N	096 07 42W	city/town	1573
Edgewater Golf	47 35 29N	095 47 10W	golf	
Edgewood	45 32 11N	093 13 50W	city/town	959
Edina	44 53 23N	093 20 59W	city/town	
Edina Country Club	44 54 38N	093 20 25W	golf	
Edwards	46 26 56N	095 59 19W	city/town	1395
Effie	47 50 25N	093 38 34W	city/town	1381
Egg Lake Lookout	47 01 27N	095 37 51W	tower	1645
Eggleston	44 37 12N	092 40 19W	city/town	
Eidswold	44 33 43N	093 17 01W	city/town	
Eitzen	43 30 29N	091 27 41W	city/town	
Elba	44 05 19N	092 01 07W	city/town	
Elbow Lake	45 59 39N	095 58 35W	city/town	1222
Elbow Lake Municip	45 59 09N	095 59 31W	airport	1205
Elbow Lake Village	47 08 48N	095 33 06W	city/town	

Minnesota GPS Companion

Place Name	Latitude	Longitude	Type	Elev
Elcor	47 30 19N	092 26 27W	city/town	1573
Eldes Corner	46 42 36N	092 16 47W	city/town	
Eldred	47 40 58N	096 46 48W	city/town	
Elephant Lake Lkt.	48 10 03N	092 45 01W	tower	1495
Elevenmile Corner	47 11 45N	093 57 22W	city/town	1304
Elgin	44 07 49N	092 15 05W	city/town	
Elizabeth	46 22 47N	096 07 44W	city/town	
Elk River	45 18 14N	093 34 01W	city/town	900
Elk River C C	45 20 03N	093 36 06W	golf	
Elko	44 33 53N	093 19 36W	city/town	
Elkton	43 39 46N	092 42 30W	city/town	
Ellendale	43 52 22N	093 18 04W	city/town	
Ellerth	48 21 18N	096 28 38W	city/town	1057
Ellis	46 30 51N	094 41 48W	city/town	1330
Ellson	46 19 03N	093 00 40W	city/town	1251
Ellsworth	43 31 05N	096 01 05W	city/town	
Elm Park	45 40 23N	093 16 33W	city/town	
Elmdale	45 50 00N	094 29 32W	city/town	1169
Elmer	47 06 13N	092 46 37W	city/town	
Elmore	43 30 18N	094 05 16W	city/town	
Elrosa	45 33 46N	094 56 49W	city/town	
Ely	47 54 12N	091 52 01W	city/town	

Minnesota GPS Companion

Place Name	Latitude	Longitude	Type	Elev
Ely Municipal Aprt	47 49 30N	091 50 00W	airport	1450
Elysian	44 11 55N	093 40 25W	city/town	
Embarrass	47 39 33N	092 11 52W	city/town	1421
Emily	46 43 52N	093 57 28W	city/town	
Emily Lookout	46 40 50N	093 55 57W	tower	
Emmaville	47 03 56N	094 58 49W	city/town	1556
Emmons	43 30 07N	093 29 17W	city/town	
Empire	44 39 33N	093 00 52W	city/town	
Enfield	45 21 27N	093 55 52W	city/town	
Englund	48 29 09N	096 37 40W	city/town	965
Enok	48 39 14N	096 45 29W	city/town	
Epsom	44 15 44N	093 03 21W	city/town	
Erdahl	45 59 31N	095 49 03W	city/town	1265
Erhard	46 29 08N	096 05 54W	city/town	
Ericsburg	48 29 16N	093 19 52W	city/town	
Erskine	47 40 03N	096 00 35W	city/town	
Esko	46 42 21N	092 21 47W	city/town	1170
Espelie	48 13 25N	095 40 48W	city/town	1177
Essig	44 19 27N	094 36 15W	city/town	
Esterdy	46 28 36N	094 43 56W	city/town	
Estes Brook	45 38 56N	093 44 13W	city/town	1053
Etna	43 36 08N	092 20 48W	city/town	

Minnesota GPS Companion

Place Name	Latitude	Longitude	Type	Elev
Etter	44 39 42N	092 44 37W	city/town	
Euclid	47 58 19N	096 38 19W	city/town	
Eureka -subd.	44 54 04N	093 36 15W	city/town	
Eureka Center	44 35 14N	093 13 04W	city/town	
Evan	44 21 15N	094 50 28W	city/town	
Evansville	46 00 15N	095 40 57W	city/town	1359
Eveleth	47 27 45N	092 32 23W	city/town	
Eveleth Golf	47 25 28N	092 31 11W	golf	
Eveleth-Virginia	47 25 27N	092 29 51W	airport	1378
Everdell	46 16 03N	096 24 28W	city/town	991
Evergreen	46 45 36N	095 27 02W	city/town	1548
Excelsior	44 54 12N	093 33 58W	city/town	
Eyota	43 59 18N	092 13 42W	city/town	1241

F

Fairbanks	47 22 14N	091 55 35W	city/town	1653
Fairfax	44 31 45N	094 43 14W	city/town	
Fairfield	45 23 02N	095 58 24W	city/town	
Fairhaven	45 19 18N	094 12 40W	city/town	
Fairland	48 28 03N	094 09 16W	city/town	1140
Fairmont	43 39 08N	094 27 39W	city/town	
Fairmont Municipal	43 38 38N	094 24 56W	airport	1162

Minnesota GPS Companion

Place Name	Latitude	Longitude	Type	Elev
Faith	47 17 13N	096 05 55W	city/town	
Falcon Heights	44 59 30N	093 09 58W	city/town	
Falls Junction	48 36 10N	093 20 34W	city/town	
Faribault	44 17 42N	093 16 07W	city/town	
Faribault Municip	44 19 28N	093 18 38W	airport	1060
Farley Hill Lkt.	47 34 23N	094 07 52W	tower	
Farley Hill Look.	47 34 38N	094 05 59W	locale	1982
Farming	45 30 55N	094 35 52W	city/town	
Farmington	44 38 25N	093 08 36W	city/town	904
Farquhar Knob	47 52 46N	090 00 27W	summit	1771
Farquhar Peak	47 52 39N	089 55 15W	summit	1254
Farris	47 22 36N	094 42 09W	city/town	
Farwell	45 45 08N	095 37 01W	city/town	
Father Hennepin St	46 08 41N	093 29 16W	park	
Faunce	48 35 35N	094 57 08W	city/town	1288
Federal Dam	47 14 43N	094 12 39W	city/town	
Felton	47 04 43N	096 30 22W	city/town	910
Fergus Falls	46 16 59N	096 04 38W	city/town	
Fergus Falls Munic	46 17 03N	096 09 24W	airport	1182
Fernando	44 39 06N	094 27 27W	city/town	1057
Fernberg Lookout	47 56 41N	091 29 46W	tower	1718
Ferndale C C	43 47 16N	091 43 27W	golf	

173

Minnesota GPS Companion

Place Name	Latitude	Longitude	Type	Elev
Fertile	47 32 10N	096 16 48W	city/town	
Fertile Municipal	47 32 50N	096 17 15W	airport	1136
Fifty Lakes	46 44 21N	094 05 34W	city/town	
Fiftysix Rapids	48 14 06N	092 20 19W	falls	
Fillmore	43 44 55N	092 16 05W	city/town	
Finkle	46 48 50N	096 44 49W	city/town	
Finland	47 24 53N	091 14 56W	city/town	1330
Finland Lookout	47 27 23N	091 13 55W	tower	1883
Finlayson	46 12 06N	092 54 57W	city/town	
Fire Tower Hill	46 26 45N	093 40 29W	summit	1403
Fish Lake Dam	46 57 24N	092 16 42W	dam	
Fisher	47 48 01N	096 48 04W	city/town	
Five Corners	46 48 28N	092 16 47W	city/town	1388
Five Points	45 36 28N	094 15 39W	city/town	
Flag Island	49 19 29N	094 53 06W	island	
Flaming	47 27 24N	096 16 13W	city/town	
Flandrau State	44 17 18N	094 28 24W	park	
Flat Lake Lookout	46 57 33N	095 38 53W	tower	1498
Flensburg	45 57 19N	094 32 05W	city/town	
Fletcher	45 10 21N	093 32 28W	city/town	
Flom	47 09 58N	096 07 50W	city/town	
Floodwood	46 55 45N	092 55 10W	city/town	1253

Place Name	Latitude	Longitude	Type	Elev
Florence	44 14 14N	096 03 06W	city/town	
Florian	48 26 32N	096 37 40W	city/town	957
Foldahl	48 20 00N	096 33 00W	city/town	986
Foley	45 39 53N	093 54 34W	city/town	
Fond du Lac	46 39 35N	092 16 23W	city/town	607
Forada	45 47 32N	095 21 19W	city/town	1414
Forbes	47 22 18N	092 36 14W	city/town	1347
Forest Center	47 47 42N	091 18 27W	city/town	
Forest City	45 12 23N	094 27 58W	city/town	
Forest Grove	47 58 36N	094 13 52W	city/town	1365
Forest Lake	45 16 44N	092 59 06W	city/town	909
Forest Lake Arpt	45 14 51N	092 59 39W	airport	925
Forest Mills	44 17 52N	092 38 26W	city/town	
Foreston	45 44 04N	093 42 37W	city/town	
Forestville	43 38 34N	092 12 53W	city/town	
Forsman	47 42 29N	092 34 43W	city/town	
Fort Charlotte	48 00 17N	089 49 35W	site	
Fort Lookout	48 07 38N	093 18 10W	tower	1322
Fort Ridgely State	44 27 09N	094 43 50W	park	
Fort Ripley	46 09 58N	094 21 36W	city/town	
Fort Saint Charles	49 21 43N	094 58 50W	city/town	
Fort Snelling Natl	44 52 20N	093 13 08W	cemetery	

Minnesota GPS Companion

Place Name	Latitude	Longitude	Type	Elev
Fort Snelling St.	44 53 09N	093 10 40W	park	
Fosston	47 34 35N	095 45 04W	city/town	1298
Fosston Municipal	47 35 34N	095 46 24W	airport	1277
Fossum	47 14 19N	096 10 33W	city/town	
Foster	45 24 59N	096 40 32W	city/town	
Fountain	43 44 24N	092 08 10W	city/town	1305
Four Corners	46 51 12N	092 16 48W	city/town	
Four Town	48 16 52N	095 20 07W	city/town	1225
Fox	48 50 20N	095 53 55W	city/town	
Fox Lake	43 40 36N	094 39 31W	city/town	
Foxhome	46 16 38N	096 18 35W	city/town	1029
Frames Landing C.	46 37 47N	094 52 08W	city/town	
Franconia	45 22 13N	092 41 29W	city/town	
Franklin	44 31 42N	094 52 49W	city/town	
Franklin -subd.	47 32 16N	092 31 08W	city/town	
Frazee	46 43 41N	095 42 02W	city/town	
Fredenberg	46 58 26N	092 13 01W	city/town	1393
Freeborn	43 45 57N	093 33 50W	city/town	
Freeburg	43 36 40N	091 21 51W	city/town	
Freedhem	46 03 23N	094 12 30W	city/town	
Freeman	47 49 10N	096 45 38W	city/town	
Freeport	45 39 46N	094 41 23W	city/town	

Place Name	Latitude	Longitude	Type	Elev
Freiheit Spring	43 42 21N	092 19 02W	city/town	
Fremont	43 54 50N	091 53 56W	city/town	
French	46 17 17N	096 12 05W	city/town	
French Lake	45 12 00N	094 11 07W	city/town	1061
French River	46 53 53N	091 53 49W	city/town	
Frenchmans Bluff	47 11 57N	096 10 56W	summit	1354
Fridley	45 05 10N	093 15 47W	city/town	
Friesland	46 05 08N	092 55 46W	city/town	1141
Frogner	46 33 15N	092 18 23W	city/town	
Frontenac	44 30 40N	092 21 23W	city/town	717
Frontenac `State	44 30 27N	092 19 34W	park	
Frontier	48 39 23N	094 15 23W	city/town	
Frost	43 35 11N	093 55 35W	city/town	
Fruitville	45 42 47N	094 04 45W	city/town	1140
Fugles Mill Hist.	43 53 20N	092 24 30W	locale	
Fulda	43 52 14N	095 36 00W	city/town	1532
Funkley	47 47 01N	094 25 52W	city/town	

G

Galls Golf Club	45 02 18N	093 00 03W	golf	
Gappas Landing C.	48 26 22N	093 01 21W	city/town	
Garden City	44 02 50N	094 09 53W	city/town	

Place Name	Latitude	Longitude	Type	Elev
Garfield	45 56 27N	095 29 30W	city/town	
Garnes	47 54 23N	095 52 50W	city/town	1156
Garrison	46 17 40N	093 49 36W	city/town	
Garvin	44 12 52N	095 45 20W	city/town	
Gary (1)	47 22 17N	096 16 02W	city/town	
Gary (2)	46 40 13N	092 13 32W	city/town	
Gates Corner (1)	48 13 09N	094 06 09W	city/town	1191
Gates Corner (2)	48 27 10N	095 19 08W	city/town	1248
Gatzke	48 25 28N	095 47 02W	city/town	
Gaylord	44 33 11N	094 13 13W	city/town	
Gem Lake	45 03 27N	093 01 56W	city/town	954
Gem Lake Golf	45 03 48N	093 02 03W	golf	
Gemmell	47 58 24N	094 07 25W	city/town	
Geneva	43 49 24N	093 16 03W	city/town	
Genoa (1)	44 06 36N	092 36 26W	city/town	
Genoa (2)	47 27 52N	092 30 31W	city/town	
Genola	45 57 37N	094 06 58W	city/town	1161
Gentilly	47 47 21N	096 26 56W	city/town	
Georgetown	47 04 48N	096 47 38W	city/town	
Georgeville	45 25 43N	094 55 37W	city/town	1247
Gheen	47 58 05N	092 48 29W	city/town	1360
Gheen Corner	47 57 51N	092 49 44W	city/town	1339

Place Name	Latitude	Longitude	Type	Elev
Ghent	44 30 46N	095 53 27W	city/town	1164
Giants Ridge Ski	47 34 32N	092 18 02W	ski area	1830
Gibbon	44 32 02N	094 31 34W	city/town	
Giese	46 12 58N	093 06 59W	city/town	1275
Gilbert	47 29 20N	092 27 53W	city/town	
Gilfillan	44 27 33N	094 59 39W	city/town	
Gilman	45 44 07N	093 56 56W	city/town	
Girard	47 43 43N	096 40 26W	city/town	
Glacial Lakes St.	45 32 15N	095 31 18W	park	
Gladstone	45 00 06N	093 01 49W	city/town	
Glen	46 25 07N	093 30 54W	city/town	1302
Glen Lake	44 54 12N	093 28 02W	city/town	
Glen Lookout	46 27 48N	093 30 44W	tower	1384
Glencoe	44 46 09N	094 09 05W	city/town	
Glencoe Municipal	44 45 23N	094 04 56W	airport	992
Glendale (1)	44 45 40N	093 23 20W	city/town	989
Glendale (2)	48 01 57N	092 49 51W	city/town	
Glendorado	45 34 41N	093 46 10W	city/town	
Glenn Avon Falls	47 15 56N	091 20 35W	falls	941
Glenville	43 34 21N	093 16 52W	city/town	
Glenwood	45 39 01N	095 23 22W	city/town	
Glenwood Junction	44 59 14N	093 19 57W	city/town	

Minnesota GPS Companion

Place Name	Latitude	Longitude	Type	Elev
Glenwood Municipal	45 38 41N	095 19 14W	airport	1393
Glory	46 25 03N	093 36 01W	city/town	1266
Gloster	45 00 05N	093 02 39W	city/town	
Gluek	44 59 07N	095 28 23W	city/town	
Glyndon	46 52 31N	096 34 43W	city/town	922
Gneiss Lake Port.	48 10 13N	090 48 10W	portage	
Godahl	44 06 32N	094 38 23W	city/town	
Golden Hill	43 59 18N	092 28 05W	city/town	
Golden Tee C C	45 13 20N	093 15 07W	golf	
Golden Valley	45 00 35N	093 20 56W	city/town	
Golden Valley C C	44 59 16N	093 22 03W	golf	
Goldenrod	47 05 40N	095 14 02W	city/town	1568
Gonvick	47 44 15N	095 30 48W	city/town	
Good Thunder	44 00 17N	094 03 56W	city/town	
Goodhue	44 24 02N	092 37 25W	city/town	
Goodland	47 09 43N	093 08 08W	city/town	1416
Goodrich Golf	44 59 54N	093 01 08W	golf	
Goodridge	48 08 36N	095 48 33W	city/town	1170
Goodview	44 03 45N	091 41 44W	city/town	
Gooseberry Falls	47 08 35N	091 28 03W	falls	
Gooseberry Falls S	47 08 49N	091 27 47W	park	
Gordonsville	43 30 46N	093 15 12W	city/town	

Place Name	Latitude	Longitude	Type	Elev
Gotha	44 43 02N	093 47 18W	city/town	969
Gowan	46 51 51N	092 50 49W	city/town	1260
Gracelock	45 03 02N	095 34 49W	city/town	
Graceton	48 44 28N	094 50 10W	city/town	1136
Graceville	45 34 09N	096 26 03W	city/town	1116
Graceville -Kapaun	45 33 00N	096 27 06W	airport	1122
Graff	46 34 21N	094 32 48W	city/town	
Grainwood	44 43 20N	093 26 21W	city/town	
Granada	43 41 44N	094 20 51W	city/town	
Grand Falls	48 11 55N	093 47 33W	city/town	
Grand Lake	46 52 00N	092 28 04W	city/town	1337
Grand Marais	47 45 02N	090 20 03W	city/town	688
Grand Marais Mar.	47 44 55N	090 20 24W	marina	605
Grand Marais-Cook	47 50 17N	090 22 59W	airport	1798
Grand Meadow	43 42 21N	092 34 19W	city/town	1341
Grand Mound St.	48 30 56N	093 42 34W	park	
Grand Portage	47 57 45N	089 41 00W	locale	
Grand Portage	47 57 50N	089 41 05W	city/town	
Grand Portage Mar.	47 57 23N	089 41 22W	marina	603
Grand Portage Natl	47 59 47N	089 44 03W	park	
Grand Rapids Air.	47 12 39N	093 30 35W	airport	1355
Grand Rapids	47 14 14N	093 31 48W	city/town	1290

Minnesota GPS Companion

Place Name	Latitude	Longitude	Type	Elev
Grand View Heights	46 36 48N	095 31 22W	city/town	
Grandy	45 38 07N	093 11 42W	city/town	
Granger	43 30 08N	092 08 19W	city/town	
Granite Falls	44 48 36N	095 32 43W	city/town	920
Granite Falls Muni	44 48 33N	095 30 18W	airport	1053
Granite Riv. Port.	48 09 35N	090 47 36W	portage	
Grant	47 29 36N	092 47 50W	city/town	
Grass Lake	45 46 41N	093 10 03W	city/town	
Grasston	45 47 41N	093 08 56W	city/town	
Grayling	46 37 45N	093 12 38W	city/town	
Greaney	47 58 02N	093 01 15W	city/town	1306
Great Cherry Port.	48 06 29N	090 07 39W	portage	
Greely	45 44 41N	093 04 05W	city/town	
Green Isle	44 40 45N	094 00 29W	city/town	1000
Green Valley	44 31 37N	095 45 25W	city/town	
Greenbush	48 42 02N	096 10 53W	city/town	
Greenfield	45 06 12N	093 41 28W	city/town	1052
Greenhaven C C	45 12 33N	093 23 55W	golf	
Greenland	44 12 24N	093 43 38W	city/town	
Greenleaf	44 59 47N	094 29 57W	city/town	
Greenleafton	43 34 49N	092 12 33W	city/town	1357
Greenview	47 37 33N	096 33 37W	city/town	

Minnesota GPS Companion

Place Name	Latitude	Longitude	Type	Elev
Greenwald	45 36 06N	094 51 35W	city/town	1263
Greenwood	44 54 54N	093 33 11W	city/town	
Greenwood Junction	47 26 27N	091 34 47W	city/town	
Gregory	45 56 22N	094 21 22W	city/town	
Grey Eagle	45 49 31N	094 44 47W	city/town	1222
Grogan	44 00 59N	094 32 11W	city/town	1043
Groningen	46 09 03N	092 55 26W	city/town	
Gross Golf Course	45 00 38N	093 12 37W	golf	
Grove City	45 09 02N	094 40 58W	city/town	
Grove Lake	45 36 51N	095 09 26W	city/town	1353
Groveland	44 56 30N	093 29 09W	city/town	
Grygla	48 18 03N	095 37 05W	city/town	
Guckeen	43 39 05N	094 13 29W	city/town	
Gull Lake Lookout	46 26 35N	094 22 37W	tower	
Gully	47 46 07N	095 37 21W	city/town	
Gunflint Camp	47 59 14N	090 20 47W	locale	
Gunflint Lookout	48 05 28N	090 50 43W	tower	2064
Gunflint Ranger St	47 44 58N	090 20 28W	station	635
Gunflint Trail	48 03 22N	090 31 27W	portage	
Gunn	47 12 58N	093 28 30W	city/town	
Gustafson Hill	47 11 28N	091 33 12W	summit	1339
Gustavus Adolphus	44 19 24N	093 58 13W	univ/coll	

Minnesota GPS Companion

Place Name	Latitude	Longitude	Type	Elev
Gutches Grove	45 56 39N	094 57 33W	city/town	
Guthrie	47 18 01N	094 47 27W	city/town	

H

Place Name	Latitude	Longitude	Type	Elev
Hackensack	46 55 51N	094 31 13W	city/town	
Hackett	48 48 57N	094 43 06W	city/town	1073
Hader	44 21 56N	092 48 03W	city/town	
Hadler	47 22 07N	096 32 06W	city/town	
Hadley	44 00 04N	095 51 13W	city/town	
Hagan	45 08 55N	095 46 33W	city/town	
Haley	47 55 16N	092 43 57W	city/town	1338
Hallock	48 46 28N	096 56 46W	city/town	817
Hallock Municipal	48 45 09N	096 56 34W	airport	819
Halma	48 39 40N	096 36 00W	city/town	1001
Halstad	47 21 06N	096 49 42W	city/town	872
Ham Lake	45 15 01N	093 14 59W	city/town	911
Hamburg	44 44 00N	093 58 01W	city/town	
Hamel	45 02 28N	093 31 31W	city/town	
Hamilton	43 45 42N	092 26 54W	city/town	1252
Hamline University	44 57 53N	093 09 49W	univ/coll	
Hammond	44 13 20N	092 22 24W	city/town	
Hampton	44 36 37N	093 00 07W	city/town	980

Minnesota GPS Companion

Place Name	Latitude	Longitude	Type	Elev
Hancock	45 29 51N	095 47 47W	city/town	1151
Hanley Falls	44 41 34N	095 37 18W	city/town	1046
Hannine Falls	47 52 05N	092 54 27W	falls	
Hanover	45 09 21N	093 39 58W	city/town	
Hanska	44 08 56N	094 29 38W	city/town	
Happy Land Lookout	48 21 40N	093 37 01W	tower	
Happy Wanderer	47 41 32N	091 41 32W	city/town	1662
Harding	46 06 58N	094 02 26W	city/town	
Hardwick	43 46 30N	096 11 57W	city/town	607
Harlis	46 24 44N	092 18 45W	city/town	1303
Harliss	44 34 57N	092 39 19W	city/town	
Harmony	43 33 19N	092 00 36W	city/town	
Harnell Park	46 53 15N	092 23 46W	city/town	
Harney	46 43 18N	092 20 00W	city/town	1201
Harold	47 42 08N	096 29 50W	city/town	
Harris	45 35 11N	092 58 28W	city/town	902
Hartland	43 48 14N	093 29 12W	city/town	1252
Hartley Spur	46 59 49N	093 01 30W	city/town	
Hassman	46 36 07N	093 36 46W	city/town	1206
Hastings	44 44 36N	092 51 08W	city/town	730
Hasty	45 22 16N	093 58 22W	city/town	
Hatfield	43 57 27N	096 11 42W	city/town	

Minnesota GPS Companion

Place Name	Latitude	Longitude	Type	Elev
Haug	48 49 11N	096 11 03W	city/town	
Havana	44 03 59N	093 08 46W	city/town	1223
Hawick	45 20 52N	094 49 37W	city/town	
Hawley	46 52 51N	096 18 59W	city/town	
Hawley Municipal	46 53 01N	096 21 03W	airport	1208
Hay Creek	44 29 31N	092 32 37W	city/town	832
Haydenville	45 00 34N	096 18 34W	city/town	
Hayes Lake State	48 37 24N	095 30 27W	park	
Hayfield	43 53 26N	092 50 51W	city/town	
Haypoint	46 53 59N	093 36 49W	city/town	1275
Hayward	43 39 02N	093 14 38W	city/town	
Hazel	48 01 12N	096 06 54W	city/town	1113
Hazel Park	44 59 15N	092 59 04W	city/town	
Hazel Run	44 45 07N	095 42 53W	city/town	1062
Hazeltine	44 50 13N	093 36 04W	city/town	
Hazelton	44 57 24N	093 57 05W	city/town	
Hazelwood	44 31 21N	093 17 09W	city/town	
Headwaters C C	46 57 08N	095 02 40W	golf	
Heatwole	44 50 03N	094 23 58W	city/town	1068
Hector	44 44 38N	094 42 55W	city/town	1078
Hector Municipal	44 43 51N	094 42 52W	airport	1077
Heiberg	47 16 59N	096 16 32W	city/town	

186

Minnesota GPS Companion

Place Name	Latitude	Longitude	Type	Elev
Heidelberg	44 29 29N	093 37 34W	city/town	
Height of Land	48 05 59N	090 33 56W	portage	
Height of Land Lkt	47 13 54N	095 30 11W	tower	2005
Heinola	46 27 22N	095 24 25W	city/town	1415
Henderson	44 31 42N	093 54 27W	city/town	
Hendricks	44 30 26N	096 25 26W	city/town	
Hendrickson Lndg.	48 18 00N	093 49 12W	city/town	
Hendrum	47 15 52N	096 48 40W	city/town	
Henning	46 19 18N	095 26 42W	city/town	
Henning Municipal	46 18 13N	095 26 22W	airport	1455
Henriette	45 52 18N	093 07 02W	city/town	996
Henrytown	43 35 40N	091 55 45W	city/town	1108
Heritage Lookout	48 03 47N	093 06 34W	tower	
Herman	45 48 31N	096 08 35W	city/town	1073
Herman Municipal	45 49 47N	096 09 38W	airport	1068
Hermann Monument	44 18 26N	094 28 21W	locale	
Hermantown	46 48 25N	092 14 17W	city/town	1365
Heron Lake	43 47 42N	095 19 12W	city/town	
Hewitt	46 19 32N	095 05 11W	city/town	
Hiawatha Municipal	44 55 13N	093 14 41W	golf	
Hibbing	47 25 38N	092 56 15W	city/town	1489
Hibbing -Chisholm	47 23 11N	092 50 20W	airport	1353

Minnesota GPS Companion

Place Name	Latitude	Longitude	Type	Elev
Hickory Hill	46 25 57N	093 43 35W	summit	1311
Hidden Falls	47 33 24N	090 52 27W	falls	
High Forest	43 50 42N	092 32 59W	city/town	
High Landing	48 02 58N	095 48 30W	city/town	1159
Highland (1)	45 07 23N	094 01 57W	city/town	1003
Highland (2)	47 12 18N	091 43 09W	city/town	1634
Highland (3)	43 40 51N	091 52 12W	city/town	
Highwood	44 54 53N	093 00 51W	city/town	
Hill -Annex Mine	47 20 04N	093 16 20W	mine	
Hill City	46 59 36N	093 35 54W	city/town	1357
Hill City-Quadna	46 57 19N	093 35 48W	airport	1289
Hillcrest Golf	44 59 27N	093 00 30W	golf	
Hillman	46 00 15N	093 53 37W	city/town	1315
Hills	43 31 41N	096 21 30W	city/town	
Hilltop	45 03 12N	093 14 50W	city/town	
Hillview	46 40 49N	095 15 27W	city/town	
Hinckley	46 00 41N	092 56 39W	city/town	1031
Hines	47 41 10N	094 37 57W	city/town	1404
Hinsdale	47 36 04N	092 08 52W	city/town	
Hitterdal	46 58 39N	096 15 32W	city/town	
Hixon	47 49 03N	096 40 31W	city/town	
Hoffman	45 49 46N	095 47 30W	city/town	1254

Place Name	Latitude	Longitude	Type	Elev
Hoffmans Corner	45 03 01N	093 01 54W	city/town	
Hokah	43 45 34N	091 20 47W	city/town	
Holdingford	45 43 52N	094 28 11W	city/town	
Holland	44 05 30N	096 11 18W	city/town	
Hollandale	43 45 39N	093 12 14W	city/town	
Hollandale Jct.	43 39 49N	093 11 21W	city/town	
Hollow Rock	47 55 02N	089 44 50W	arch	
Holloway	45 14 55N	095 54 28W	city/town	
Hollydale Golf	45 02 20N	093 29 43W	golf	
Hollywood	44 54 21N	093 58 16W	city/town	976
Holman	47 18 36N	093 22 17W	city/town	1373
Holmes City	45 50 01N	095 32 27W	city/town	
Holt	48 17 31N	096 11 32W	city/town	1155
Holyoke	46 28 03N	092 23 18W	city/town	1037
Homer	44 01 17N	091 33 23W	city/town	
Honeymoon Bluff	48 03 23N	090 24 50W	overlook	1842
Honeymoon Lookout	47 43 27N	090 49 47W	tower	1896
Honeymoon Mountain	47 43 27N	090 49 47W	summit	1896
Honeywell C C	44 41 25N	093 18 57W	golf	
Hope	43 57 43N	093 16 33W	city/town	
Hopkins	44 55 30N	093 27 45W	city/town	
Hopper	47 30 36N	092 34 51W	city/town	

Minnesota GPS Companion

Place Name	Latitude	Longitude	Type	Elev
Hornby	47 20 36N	091 54 07W	city/town	1619
Horrigan Hill	44 26 01N	092 18 38W	summit	1154
Horton	46 48 40N	095 05 49W	city/town	
Houpt	47 48 02N	094 23 28W	city/town	
Houston	43 45 48N	091 34 06W	city/town	684
Hovland	47 50 20N	089 58 19W	city/town	
Hovland Lookout	47 52 46N	089 59 58W	tower	1777
Howard Lake	45 03 39N	094 04 23W	city/town	1018
Hoyt Lakes	47 31 11N	092 08 18W	city/town	1469
Hubbard	46 50 12N	095 00 36W	city/town	
Hugo	45 09 36N	092 59 35W	city/town	935
Hull	47 11 51N	092 55 23W	city/town	
Humboldt	48 55 16N	097 05 35W	city/town	
Humphrey Metrodome	44 58 26N	093 15 17W	building	
Hunters Park	46 49 45N	092 04 23W	city/town	
Huntersville	46 46 33N	094 53 33W	city/town	
Huntley	43 43 54N	094 14 14W	city/town	1091
Huot	47 51 55N	096 25 23W	city/town	
Hutchinson	44 53 16N	094 22 10W	city/town	1056
Hutchinson Municip	44 51 32N	094 22 54W	airport	1060
Hutton	43 36 58N	092 02 41W	city/town	1064
Hydes Lake	44 49 08N	093 50 57W	city/town	993

Place Name	Latitude	Longitude	Type	Elev
I				
Iberia	44 14 21N	094 41 42W	city/town	1010
Idington	47 44 00N	092 39 06W	city/town	
Ihlen	43 54 26N	096 22 01W	city/town	
Illgen City	47 20 49N	091 11 22W	city/town	
Illgen Falls	47 21 30N	091 12 50W	falls	
Imogene	43 39 37N	094 20 43W	city/town	
Independence (1)	45 01 31N	093 42 26W	city/town	
Independence (2)	46 57 30N	092 27 37W	city/town	1308
Indian Pines Lkt.	48 29 31N	094 11 07W	tower	1170
Indus	48 37 31N	093 50 15W	city/town	
Inez	47 51 37N	094 34 48W	city/town	1294
Inger	47 33 15N	093 59 06W	city/town	1328
Inguadona	46 59 00N	094 07 48W	city/town	1310
Inspiration Peak S	46 08 12N	095 34 39W	park	
Inspiration Point	47 26 34N	094 07 27W	cape	
Interlachen C C	44 54 54N	093 22 46W	golf	
International Fls.	48 35 43N	093 25 54W	airport	1110
International Fls.	48 36 04N	093 24 39W	city/town	1128
Interstate State	45 23 42N	092 40 10W	park	
Inver Grove Hts.	44 50 53N	093 02 33W	city/town	

Minnesota GPS Companion

Place Name	Latitude	Longitude	Type	Elev
Iona	43 54 56N	095 47 02W	city/town	
Iron Junction	47 25 08N	092 36 12W	city/town	
Ironton	46 28 39N	093 58 39W	city/town	
Isabella	47 37 02N	091 21 17W	city/town	1927
Isanti	45 29 25N	093 14 51W	city/town	
Isinours	43 42 37N	092 03 20W	city/town	
Island	46 59 10N	093 00 48W	city/town	1269
Island Lake	47 47 20N	095 01 04W	city/town	1342
Island Park	44 55 29N	093 38 17W	city/town	
Island View	48 35 43N	093 10 00W	city/town	
Island View Lodge	48 35 55N	093 10 06W	locale	1115
Isle	46 08 17N	093 28 14W	city/town	
Isle Airport	46 09 34N	093 27 40W	airport	1271
Isle Harbor Lkt.	46 05 50N	093 29 25W	tower	1259
Itasca State Park	47 11 51N	095 12 06W	park	
Ivanhoe	44 27 48N	096 14 49W	city/town	
Iverson	46 39 59N	092 31 45W	city/town	1230

J

Jack Pine	47 23 00N	095 31 13W	city/town	1479
Jack Pine Hill	47 15 23N	095 30 10W	summit	1951
Jack Pine Mountain	47 43 51N	091 33 18W	summit	1817

Minnesota GPS Companion

Place Name	Latitude			Longitude			Type	Elev
Jackson	43	37	15N	094	59	18W	city/town	
Jackson C C	43	37	59N	094	59	44W	golf	
Jackson Municipal	43	39	00N	094	59	11W	airport	1446
Jacobs Prairie	45	29	13N	094	23	34W	city/town	1151
Jacobson	47	00	03N	093	16	02W	city/town	
Jakeville	45	45	01N	093	59	11W	city/town	1202
Jameson	48	36	14N	093	21	57W	city/town	
Janesville	44	06	58N	093	42	28W	city/town	1069
Jarrett	44	14	10N	092	20	20W	city/town	792
Jasper	43	51	00N	096	23	54W	city/town	
Jasper Peak	47	48	50N	092	12	55W	summit	1706
Jay Cooke State	46	38	59N	092	19	50W	park	
Jay See Landing	47	32	45N	091	28	40W	city/town	
Jeffers	44	03	21N	095	11	47W	city/town	
Jelle	48	14	17N	095	24	00W	city/town	1216
Jenkins	46	38	46N	094	20	04W	city/town	
Jennie	45	00	28N	094	20	52W	city/town	1109
Jessenland	44	34	19N	093	55	23W	city/town	
Jessie Lake	47	36	04N	093	49	01W	city/town	1377
Jessie Lake Lkt.	47	35	03N	093	50	58W	tower	1421
Jessie Lake Pit	47	34	45N	093	50	55W	tower	1375
John Latsch State	44	09	43N	091	49	19W	park	

Minnesota GPS Companion

Place Name	Latitude	Longitude	Type	Elev
Johnsburg	43 30 20N	092 46 08W	city/town	
Johnsdale	46 01 58N	093 47 18W	city/town	1315
Johnson	45 34 22N	096 17 42W	city/town	
Johnson Falls	48 03 41N	090 15 47W	falls	
Johnsville	45 11 50N	093 14 03W	city/town	902
Jordan (1)	44 40 01N	093 37 36W	city/town	
Jordan (2)	47 22 35N	091 37 48W	city/town	1741
Josephine, Mount	47 59 00N	089 39 33W	summit	1348
Judge	43 53 57N	092 28 33W	city/town	
Judge C R Magney S	47 51 05N	090 03 30W	park	1740
Judson	44 11 47N	094 11 42W	city/town	803
Jurgenson	47 19 56N	093 13 46W	city/town	

K

Place Name	Latitude	Longitude	Type	Elev
Kabekona Corner	47 14 05N	094 52 35W	city/town	
Kabekona Lookout	47 13 00N	094 52 38W	tower	1654
Kabetogama	48 26 16N	093 01 38W	city/town	
Kabetogama Lkt.	48 21 18N	093 00 26W	tower	
Kadunce River St.	47 47 38N	090 09 15W	park	
Kanaranzi	43 34 33N	096 05 39W	city/town	
Kandiyohi	45 07 56N	094 55 51W	city/town	1223
Kaplan Woods State	44 03 43N	093 14 07W	park	

Minnesota GPS Companion

Place Name	Latitude	Longitude	Type	Elev
Karlstad	48 34 39N	096 31 13W	city/town	1048
Karlstad Municipal	48 34 44N	096 32 31W	airport	1025
Kasota	44 17 33N	093 57 53W	city/town	
Kasson	44 01 48N	092 45 02W	city/town	1242
Keenan	47 23 00N	092 36 15W	city/town	1352
Keewatin	47 23 59N	093 04 20W	city/town	1469
Kekekabic Lookout	48 03 57N	091 08 41W	tower	1919
Keller Golf Course	45 00 13N	093 03 13W	golf	
Kelliher	47 56 30N	094 26 53W	city/town	1361
Kellogg	44 18 31N	091 59 44W	city/town	
Kelly Lake	47 25 03N	093 00 23W	city/town	1509
Kelly Landing	47 40 36N	091 20 09W	city/town	1778
Kelsey	47 09 14N	092 35 57W	city/town	
Kelso Mountain	47 55 09N	090 55 52W	summit	2100
Kennedy	48 38 31N	096 54 31W	city/town	
Kennedy Landing	47 22 46N	091 09 02W	city/town	
Kenneth	43 45 13N	096 04 20W	city/town	
Kensington	45 46 41N	095 41 45W	city/town	
Kent	46 26 11N	096 41 04W	city/town	
Kenyon	44 16 20N	092 59 07W	city/town	
Kerkhoven	45 11 35N	095 19 13W	city/town	1109
Kerns	44 12 40N	094 06 35W	city/town	994

Minnesota GPS Companion

Place Name	Latitude	Longitude	Type	Elev
Kerr	47 25 25N	092 58 47W	city/town	
Kerrick	46 20 20N	092 35 08W	city/town	
Kettle Falls	48 29 58N	092 38 20W	falls	
Kettle Falls	48 30 10N	092 38 22W	city/town	
Kettle Falls Dam	48 29 59N	092 38 19W	dam	
Kettle River	46 29 30N	092 52 40W	city/town	1182
Kevin	47 20 55N	093 11 37W	city/town	1423
Key West	47 56 05N	096 46 59W	city/town	
Kiester	43 32 11N	093 42 43W	city/town	
Kilkenny	44 18 48N	093 34 26W	city/town	
Killen Woods State	43 43 36N	095 03 46W	park	
Kimball	45 18 45N	094 18 00W	city/town	
Kimberly	46 33 39N	093 27 58W	city/town	
Kinbrae	43 49 33N	095 29 13W	city/town	1464
Kingsdale	46 14 18N	092 18 41W	city/town	
Kingsley Corner	44 04 42N	092 06 51W	city/town	
Kingston	45 11 49N	094 18 47W	city/town	1027
Kinney	47 30 51N	092 43 50W	city/town	
Kirk	47 24 55N	092 39 45W	city/town	
Kitzville	47 27 08N	092 53 51W	city/town	
Klondyke	46 26 30N	093 57 57W	city/town	
Klossner	44 21 57N	094 25 32W	city/town	

Place Name	Latitude	Longitude	Type	Elev
Knapp	45 09 08N	094 13 34W	city/town	1032
Knife River	46 56 58N	091 46 44W	city/town	
Knutson Dam	47 27 07N	094 28 59W	dam	
Komensky	44 54 26N	094 16 36W	city/town	1063
Koochiching Falls	48 36 30N	093 24 10W	falls	
Koronis Hills Golf	45 21 56N	094 43 51W	golf	
Kost	45 29 31N	092 52 04W	city/town	876
Kragnes	46 59 18N	096 45 05W	city/town	890
Kroschel	46 04 18N	093 04 33W	city/town	1110

L

Place Name	Latitude	Longitude	Type	Elev
La Crescent	43 49 41N	091 18 14W	city/town	
La Prairie	47 13 42N	093 29 20W	city/town	
La Salle	44 04 15N	094 34 10W	city/town	
LaBelle	46 52 58N	096 03 44W	city/town	
Lac qui Parle	45 00 02N	095 54 21W	city/town	
Lac qui Parle Dam	45 01 19N	095 52 07W	dam	
Lafayette	44 26 48N	094 23 42W	city/town	1014
Lafayette Country	44 56 37N	093 35 35W	golf	
Lagoona Beach	45 21 59N	096 29 07W	city/town	
Lake Bemidji State	47 32 11N	094 49 21W	park	
Lake Benton	44 15 40N	096 17 14W	city/town	

Minnesota GPS Companion

Place Name	Latitude	Longitude	Type	Elev
Lake Bronson	48 44 08N	096 39 45W	city/town	
Lake Bronson State	48 43 29N	096 36 11W	park	
Lake Carlos State	45 59 51N	095 20 10W	park	
Lake City	44 26 58N	092 16 00W	city/town	701
Lake City C C	44 27 53N	092 17 48W	golf	
Lake Crystal	44 06 21N	094 13 07W	city/town	1000
Lake Elmo	44 59 45N	092 52 45W	city/town	
Lake Elysian	44 08 55N	093 42 48W	city/town	1017
Lake Eunice	46 44 46N	095 58 08W	city/town	
Lake Fremont	45 26 36N	093 35 23W	city/town	992
Lake George	47 12 02N	094 59 36W	city/town	1429
Lake Henry	45 27 38N	094 47 46W	city/town	
Lake Hubert	46 30 08N	094 15 26W	city/town	1204
Lake Itasca	47 15 14N	095 12 44W	city/town	1515
Lake Lillian	44 56 37N	094 52 47W	city/town	
Lake Netta	45 16 48N	093 11 30W	city/town	
Lake Park	46 53 11N	096 05 39W	city/town	
Lake Saint Croix B	44 55 15N	092 46 00W	city/town	1000
Lake Sarah	45 04 19N	093 41 24W	city/town	996
Lake Shetek State	44 06 08N	095 41 23W	park	
Lake Shore	46 29 08N	094 21 37W	city/town	1242
Lake Shore Park	45 04 18N	093 00 40W	city/town	

Place Name	Latitude	Longitude	Type	Elev
Lake Wilson	43 59 48N	095 57 09W	city/town	
Lakefield	43 40 39N	095 10 17W	city/town	1476
Lakeland	44 57 23N	092 45 56W	city/town	
Lakeland Shores	44 56 53N	092 45 50W	city/town	
Lakeside	44 50 03N	094 33 32W	city/town	1070
Lakeside C C 1	44 05 44N	093 29 26W	golf	
Lakeside C C 2	46 37 01N	095 34 13W	golf	
Lakeville	44 38 59N	093 14 33W	city/town	974
Lakewood	46 51 50N	091 57 45W	city/town	662
Lamberton	44 13 52N	095 15 50W	city/town	1151
Lamoille	44 00 08N	091 28 20W	city/town	
Lamon Lookout	48 30 47N	093 46 46W	tower	1093
Lamson	44 59 25N	094 16 28W	city/town	
Lancaster	48 51 30N	096 48 14W	city/town	
Landfall	44 57 03N	092 58 35W	city/town	
Lanesboro	43 43 15N	091 58 36W	city/town	846
Langdon	44 48 36N	092 55 43W	city/town	
Langor	47 46 51N	094 35 29W	city/town	1326
Lansing	43 44 43N	092 58 12W	city/town	
Laporte	47 12 50N	094 45 14W	city/town	
Largo	47 28 49N	092 34 13W	city/town	
Larsmont	46 58 45N	091 44 44W	city/town	668

Minnesota GPS Companion

Place Name	Latitude	Longitude	Type	Elev
LaSalle Lookout	47 18 57N	095 11 18W	tower	
Last Falls	48 06 52N	091 42 36W	falls	1248
Lastrup	46 02 22N	094 03 47W	city/town	
Lauderdale	44 59 55N	093 12 20W	city/town	
Laurel	48 30 54N	093 40 28W	city/town	
Lauren	47 11 05N	091 41 51W	city/town	1548
Lavinia (1)	47 28 21N	092 56 46W	city/town	
Lavinia (2)	47 30 54N	094 48 41W	city/town	
Lawler	46 32 10N	093 10 13W	city/town	1312
Lawler Lookout	46 32 02N	093 07 52W	tower	
Lawndale	46 33 25N	096 21 36W	city/town	
Lawrence	44 39 29N	093 41 04W	city/town	1760
Lax Lake	47 20 39N	091 18 31W	city/town	
Le Center	44 23 22N	093 43 48W	city/town	1052
Le Roy	43 30 35N	092 30 13W	city/town	
Le Sueur	44 27 41N	093 54 54W	city/town	
Le Sueur C C	44 25 37N	093 53 08W	golf	
Le Sueur Municipal	44 26 14N	093 54 45W	airport	868
Leader	46 31 43N	094 39 17W	city/town	1366
Leaf River	46 29 19N	095 04 53W	city/town	1323
Leaf Valley	46 02 58N	095 27 28W	city/town	
Leander	47 48 11N	092 39 01W	city/town	1319

Minnesota GPS Companion

Place Name	Latitude	Longitude	Type	Elev
Leavenworth	44 13 21N	094 48 06W	city/town	
Leetonia	47 25 45N	092 59 06W	city/town	
Legionville	46 26 50N	094 11 57W	city/town	
LeHillier	44 09 07N	094 02 06W	city/town	
Leighton	45 03 55N	093 37 12W	city/town	1051
Lemond	43 58 57N	093 22 48W	city/town	
Lengby	47 30 57N	095 38 08W	city/town	
Lennox	46 14 37N	094 20 34W	city/town	
Lenora	43 34 21N	091 52 56W	city/town	1104
Leo	48 45 39N	096 15 01W	city/town	1030
Leonard	47 39 07N	095 16 19W	city/town	
Leonidas	47 27 42N	092 34 18W	city/town	
Leota	43 50 02N	096 00 48W	city/town	
Lerdal	43 43 26N	093 16 08W	city/town	1269
Lesser Cherry Port	48 06 42N	090 08 41W	portage	
Lester Park	46 50 15N	092 01 10W	city/town	
Lester Prairie	44 53 02N	094 02 29W	city/town	1004
Leveaux Mountain	47 36 56N	090 47 51W	summit	1550
Lewis Lake	45 46 00N	093 22 07W	city/town	1010
Lewiston	43 59 04N	091 52 09W	city/town	
Lewisville	43 55 24N	094 26 14W	city/town	
Lexington (1)	45 08 33N	093 09 47W	city/town	

Minnesota GPS Companion

Place Name	Latitude	Longitude	Type	Elev
Lexington (2)	44 26 33N	093 42 08W	city/town	
Libby	46 47 03N	093 19 30W	city/town	1229
Lilydale	44 54 58N	093 07 33W	city/town	
Lima Mountain	47 59 13N	090 24 13W	summit	2238
Lime Creek	43 53 23N	095 33 42W	city/town	
Lincoln	46 12 37N	094 38 26W	city/town	
Linden	44 10 53N	094 24 33W	city/town	995
Linden Grove	47 51 47N	092 52 13W	city/town	1307
Linder Lookout	48 19 54N	095 16 40W	tower	
Lindford	48 24 39N	093 46 54W	city/town	
Lindstrom	45 23 22N	092 50 52W	city/town	
Link Lake Lookout	47 39 18N	093 24 45W	tower	1467
Lino Lakes	45 09 37N	093 05 19W	city/town	
Linwood	45 21 25N	093 06 41W	city/town	
Lismore	43 44 52N	095 56 49W	city/town	
Litchfield	45 07 38N	094 31 40W	city/town	
Litchfield Municip	45 05 49N	094 30 26W	airport	1140
Litomysl	43 56 50N	093 11 09W	city/town	
Little American F.	47 55 14N	093 37 17W	falls	
Little Canada	45 01 37N	093 05 15W	city/town	
Little Chicago	44 28 45N	093 19 19W	city/town	1080
Little Elbow Lake	47 10 33N	095 36 15W	park	

Minnesota GPS Companion

Place Name	Latitude	Longitude	Type	Elev
Little Falls	45 56 57N	094 20 49W	airport	1122
Little Falls	45 58 35N	094 21 44W	city/town	
Little Flat Lake L	46 59 52N	095 39 52W	tower	1486
Little Knife Port.	48 09 00N	091 08 00W	locale	
Little Mantrap Lkt	47 09 06N	095 08 22W	tower	
Little Marais	47 24 39N	091 06 36W	city/town	641
Little Pine	46 44 44N	093 51 40W	city/town	1276
Little Rock	45 49 57N	094 05 33W	city/town	1202
Little Rock Falls	48 07 08N	090 46 26W	falls	
Little Sauk	45 51 50N	094 55 05W	city/town	1260
Little Swan	47 17 50N	092 49 51W	city/town	1291
Littlefork	48 23 56N	093 33 20W	city/town	
Littlefork Municip	48 24 59N	093 35 10W	airport	1145
Lockhart	47 26 24N	096 33 03W	city/town	
Loerch	46 24 12N	094 04 20W	city/town	
Loman	48 30 46N	093 48 10W	city/town	
London (1)	43 31 34N	093 03 45W	city/town	
London (2)	47 12 10N	091 34 10W	city/town	1291
Long Beach	45 39 17N	095 25 02W	city/town	
Long Lake	44 59 12N	093 34 17W	city/town	981
Long Point	48 58 38N	094 57 35W	city/town	
Long Portage	48 05 46N	090 23 10W	portage	

Place Name	Latitude	Longitude	Type	Elev
Long Prairie A.	45 53 54N	094 52 24W	airport	1333
Long Prairie	45 58 29N	094 51 55W	city/town	
Longville	46 59 11N	094 12 40W	city/town	
Longville Lookout	46 58 24N	094 12 22W	tower	
Longville Municip	46 59 22N	094 12 15W	airport	1335
Longworth	48 58 57N	095 21 53W	city/town	
Lonsdale	44 28 49N	093 25 42W	city/town	
Lookout Mountain	47 34 24N	092 32 08W	summit	1851
Loon Falls	48 14 13N	092 19 33W	falls	
Loretto	45 03 17N	093 38 07W	city/town	
Lorne	44 44 46N	095 34 27W	city/town	
Lost Spur C C	44 51 31N	093 10 27W	golf	
Louisburg	45 09 58N	096 10 15W	city/town	
Louriston	45 05 40N	095 27 06W	city/town	1050
Lower Basswood Fls	48 06 49N	091 42 41W	falls	1252
Lowry	45 42 18N	095 31 04W	city/town	
Lowville	44 04 00N	095 52 00W	city/town	1650
Lucan	44 24 35N	095 24 37W	city/town	
Luce	46 39 28N	095 39 09W	city/town	
Lucknow	47 30 04N	092 44 10W	city/town	
Ludlow Lookout	48 17 16N	094 33 14W	tower	
Luna	48 15 13N	096 47 36W	city/town	

Place Name	Latitude	Longitude	Type	Elev
Lutsen	47 38 50N	090 40 29W	city/town	671
Lutsen Ski Area	47 39 51N	090 42 44W	ski area	1651
Luverne	43 39 15N	096 12 45W	city/town	
Luverne Municipal	43 37 14N	096 13 07W	airport	1431
Luxemburg	45 27 10N	094 14 46W	city/town	1106
Lydia	44 39 10N	093 30 03W	city/town	950
Lyle	43 30 19N	092 56 38W	city/town	
Lyman	46 20 24N	095 14 54W	city/town	
Lynd	44 23 10N	095 53 24W	city/town	1320
Lyndale	44 58 57N	093 43 54W	city/town	

M

Place Name	Latitude	Longitude	Type	Elev
Mabel	43 31 14N	091 46 10W	city/town	1134
Macalester College	44 56 19N	093 10 05W	univ/coll	
Madelia	44 03 03N	094 25 05W	city/town	1029
Madison	45 00 35N	096 11 44W	city/town	
Madison Lake	44 12 16N	093 48 55W	city/town	
Madison-Lac Qui Pa	44 59 10N	096 10 39W	airport	1082
Mae	46 49 56N	093 51 55W	city/town	1303
Magnolia	43 38 43N	096 04 44W	city/town	
Mahkonce	47 19 28N	095 36 55W	city/town	
Mahnomen	47 18 55N	095 58 06W	city/town	

Minnesota GPS Companion

Place Name	Latitude	Longitude	Type	Elev
Mahnomen County	47 15 35N	095 55 41W	airport	1244
Mahnomen County CC	47 18 56N	095 56 31W	golf	
Mahoning	47 26 57N	092 58 19W	city/town	
Mahtomedi	45 04 11N	092 57 05W	city/town	
Mahtowa	46 34 26N	092 37 54W	city/town	1152
Maine	46 24 44N	095 49 01W	city/town	
Makinen	47 21 26N	092 22 03W	city/town	1405
Malcolm	48 19 28N	095 20 07W	city/town	1229
Mall of America	44 51 16N	093 14 36W	locale	820
Mallard	47 18 40N	095 16 00W	city/town	1500
Mallory	47 52 36N	096 54 41W	city/town	
Malmo	46 20 02N	093 31 09W	city/town	
Malung	48 46 21N	095 43 26W	city/town	
Manannah	45 15 13N	094 37 02W	city/town	1151
Manchester	43 43 32N	093 27 06W	city/town	1283
Maney	46 59 25N	092 36 28W	city/town	
Manganese	46 31 39N	094 00 34W	city/town	
Manhattan Beach	46 43 42N	094 08 04W	city/town	
Manitoba Junction	46 54 24N	096 14 50W	city/town	
Manitou	48 37 42N	093 59 34W	city/town	1120
Manitou Junction	47 34 07N	091 15 30W	city/town	
Mankato	44 09 49N	093 59 57W	city/town	

Minnesota GPS Companion

Place Name	Latitude	Longitude	Type	Elev
Mankato Golf Club	44 11 32N	093 58 40W	golf	
Mankato Municipal	44 13 17N	093 55 07W	airport	1020
Mankato State Coll	44 08 50N	093 59 49W	univ/coll	
Manley	43 35 25N	096 25 51W	city/town	
Mansfield	43 34 21N	093 36 31W	city/town	1247
Mantorville	44 04 09N	092 45 20W	city/town	
Maple (1)	44 52 54N	093 48 56W	city/town	
Maple (2)	47 27 29N	091 09 06W	city/town	1357
Maple Bay	47 38 09N	096 13 29W	city/town	
Maple Grove	45 04 21N	093 27 20W	city/town	
Maple Hill	47 48 28N	090 18 17W	city/town	
Maple Island (1)	45 10 27N	092 51 18W	city/town	954
Maple Island (2)	43 45 42N	093 09 49W	city/town	
Maple Lake	45 13 45N	094 00 06W	city/town	
Maple Lake Municip	45 14 09N	093 59 08W	airport	1028
Maple Plain	45 00 26N	093 39 20W	city/town	
Maple Springs	44 24 35N	092 09 42W	city/town	
Maple Valley C C	43 53 49N	092 22 42W	golf	
Mapleton	43 55 44N	093 57 21W	city/town	
Mapleview	43 41 20N	092 58 45W	city/town	
Maplewood	44 57 11N	092 59 42W	city/town	
Maplewood State	46 32 01N	095 56 56W	park	

Minnesota GPS Companion

Place Name	Latitude	Longitude	Type	Elev
Maraboeuf Lake Por	48 11 06N	090 49 39W	portage	
Marble	47 19 14N	093 17 54W	city/town	
Marble Lookout	47 17 22N	091 37 42W	tower	1765
Marcell	47 35 35N	093 41 26W	city/town	1386
March	48 11 42N	096 53 49W	city/town	
Marcoux Corners	47 45 35N	096 15 58W	locale	1095
Margie	48 05 43N	093 56 23W	city/town	
Marietta	45 00 30N	096 25 02W	city/town	
Marine on St Croix	45 12 00N	092 46 15W	city/town	
Mariner Mountain	47 17 18N	091 17 59W	summit	1212
Marion	43 56 37N	092 20 53W	city/town	
Markham	47 17 57N	092 13 06W	city/town	1465
Markville	46 05 31N	092 19 50W	city/town	1005
Marna	43 36 21N	094 00 27W	city/town	
Marsh Lake Dam	45 10 21N	096 05 29W	dam	
Marshall	44 26 49N	095 47 17W	city/town	
Marshall Municipal	44 27 00N	095 49 20W	airport	1180
Martin Lake	45 22 52N	093 05 41W	city/town	
Martin Landing	47 44 42N	091 18 13W	city/town	
Martin Luther Coll	44 18 21N	094 28 15W	univ/coll	
Marty	45 23 59N	094 19 57W	city/town	1138
Marysburg	44 14 25N	093 49 00W	city/town	

Minnesota GPS Companion

Place Name	Latitude	Longitude	Type	Elev
Marystown	44 43 15N	093 32 28W	city/town	
Matawan	43 51 29N	093 38 09W	city/town	
Mattson	48 41 22N	097 04 24W	city/town	794
Maud, Mount	47 58 31N	089 45 31W	summit	1754
Mavie	48 08 41N	095 56 19W	city/town	1162
Max	47 36 53N	094 04 04W	city/town	1373
Mayer	44 53 06N	093 53 15W	city/town	979
Mayhew	45 42 48N	094 06 38W	city/town	
Maynard	44 54 25N	095 28 07W	city/town	1029
Mayo Clinic	44 01 20N	092 27 56W	hospital	
Mayville	43 45 50N	092 54 33W	city/town	
Mazeppa	44 16 23N	092 32 41W	city/town	931
McCarthy Beach St.	47 40 22N	093 01 48W	park	
McCauleyville	46 26 30N	096 42 27W	city/town	
McComber	47 50 56N	092 03 55W	city/town	1472
McGrath	46 14 24N	093 16 20W	city/town	
McGregor	46 36 24N	093 18 49W	city/town	1233
McIntosh	47 38 13N	095 53 10W	city/town	1223
McKinley	47 30 46N	092 24 39W	city/town	1438
McNair	47 19 12N	091 40 21W	city/town	
Meadow Brook	47 51 46N	092 57 16W	city/town	1285
Meadowbrook Golf	44 55 22N	093 22 02W	golf	

Minnesota GPS Companion

Place Name	Latitude	Longitude	Type	Elev
Meadowlands	47 04 19N	092 43 56W	city/town	
Medford	44 10 27N	093 14 46W	city/town	
Medicine Lake	44 59 43N	093 24 55W	city/town	
Medina	45 02 07N	093 34 56W	city/town	
Meire Grove	45 37 47N	094 52 08W	city/town	
Melby	46 03 50N	095 44 08W	city/town	
Melrose	45 40 29N	094 48 26W	city/town	1213
Melrude	47 14 44N	092 25 01W	city/town	
Melvin	47 37 15N	096 23 20W	city/town	
Menahga	46 45 14N	095 05 52W	city/town	
Mendota	44 53 14N	093 09 51W	city/town	
Mendota C C	44 52 53N	093 07 39W	golf	
Mendota Heights	44 53 01N	093 08 17W	city/town	
Mentor	47 41 54N	096 08 27W	city/town	
Meriden	44 04 27N	093 23 12W	city/town	1140
Merriam	44 44 16N	093 35 39W	city/town	756
Merrifield	46 27 54N	094 10 21W	city/town	1219
Merton	44 08 46N	093 08 47W	city/town	1260
Mesaba	47 34 08N	092 07 54W	city/town	1519
Mesaba C C	47 22 48N	092 56 03W	golf	
Mesabi Range	47 28 00N	092 45 01W	range	
Mesabi Regional	47 24 35N	092 55 43W	airport	1359

Minnesota GPS Companion

Place Name	Latitude	Longitude	Type	Elev
Middle Falls	48 00 46N	089 36 57W	falls	
Middle River	48 26 03N	096 09 50W	city/town	
Midland Hills C C	45 00 05N	093 11 48W	golf	
Midland Junction	44 19 16N	092 00 05W	city/town	
Midvale	44 58 18N	092 59 41W	city/town	
Midway (1)	46 46 55N	095 15 36W	city/town	1522
Midway (2)	47 29 28N	092 31 32W	city/town	
Midway Stadium	44 58 20N	093 09 47W	locale	
Miesville	44 36 02N	092 48 46W	city/town	
Milaca	45 45 21N	093 39 15W	city/town	1079
Milaca Municipal	45 46 20N	093 37 55W	airport	1100
Milan	45 06 31N	095 54 47W	city/town	1005
Mildred	46 45 18N	094 27 52W	city/town	
Milford Monument	44 21 24N	094 35 36W	locale	
Mille Lacs Kathio	46 07 44N	093 44 25W	park	
Mille Lacs Lookout	45 58 06N	093 37 11W	tower	
Millersburg	44 25 40N	093 19 54W	city/town	
Millerville	46 04 03N	095 33 44W	city/town	1392
Millstone Landing	43 32 21N	091 16 32W	access	
Millville	44 14 41N	092 17 44W	city/town	
Miloma	43 45 46N	095 22 05W	city/town	
Milroy	44 25 04N	095 33 11W	city/town	

211

Minnesota GPS Companion

Place Name	Latitude	Longitude	Type	Elev
Miltona	46 02 39N	095 17 28W	city/town	
Minakwa C C	47 47 13N	096 37 01W	golf	
Minerva	47 22 09N	095 22 55W	city/town	1515
Minikahda Golf	44 56 19N	093 19 31W	golf	
Minneapolis	44 58 48N	093 15 49W	city/town	
Minneapolis C C	44 57 51N	093 23 42W	golf	
Mpls. -Airlake	44 37 40N	093 13 41W	airport	960
Mpls. -Anoka Co	45 08 41N	093 12 40W	airport	912
Mpls. -Crystal	45 03 43N	093 21 14W	airport	869
Mpls. -Flying Cld	44 49 37N	093 27 14W	airport	906
Mpls. -Internatnl.	44 53 01N	093 13 17W	airport	828
Minnehaha Falls	44 54 53N	093 12 35W	falls	
Minneiska	44 11 42N	091 52 18W	city/town	
Minnemishinona F.	44 10 12N	094 05 05W	falls	
Minneopa State	44 09 44N	094 06 07W	park	
Minneota	44 33 32N	095 59 07W	city/town	1168
Minnesota Boys T.	45 33 24N	093 10 35W	city/town	
Minnesota City	44 05 38N	091 44 58W	city/town	
Minnesota Falls	44 47 29N	095 30 00W	falls	
Minnesota Lake	43 50 31N	093 49 54W	city/town	
Minnesota Nat'l Sp	44 34 10N	093 19 52W	track	
Minnesota Vly C C	44 47 33N	093 21 46W	golf	

Minnesota GPS Companion

Place Name	Latitude	Longitude	Type	Elev
Minnetonka	44 54 48N	093 30 11W	city/town	
Minnetonka Beach	44 56 23N	093 34 35W	city/town	
Minnetonka C C	44 53 54N	093 35 27W	golf	
Minnetonka Mills	44 56 28N	093 26 30W	city/town	
Minnetrista	44 56 18N	093 43 03W	city/town	1012
Minnewankon Falls	44 11 00N	094 06 10W	falls	
Minnewaska Golf	45 39 40N	095 24 58W	golf	
Minnewawa	46 41 55N	093 16 29W	city/town	
Mirror Lake Lkt.	46 58 30N	092 10 33W	tower	1523
Missabe Junction	46 45 34N	092 07 42W	city/town	
Mission	46 35 17N	094 03 03W	city/town	
Mission Creek	45 58 13N	092 56 59W	city/town	
Mission Farms	45 01 06N	093 25 26W	city/town	
Mississippi Headw.	47 26 16N	095 03 29W	forest	1358
Mississippi River	29 09 00N	089 15 00W	stream	
Mitchell	47 26 44N	092 53 42W	city/town	
Mizpah	47 55 27N	094 12 13W	city/town	1385
Moland	44 11 48N	093 03 41W	city/town	
Molde Lookout	47 01 10N	091 50 00W	tower	1387
Money Creek	43 49 17N	091 36 48W	city/town	
Monson Lake Memor.	45 19 14N	095 16 29W	park	
Montevideo	44 56 33N	095 43 24W	city/town	

Minnesota GPS Companion

Place Name	Latitude	Longitude	Type	Elev
Montevideo Air.	44 58 08N	095 42 37W	airport	1034
Montgomery	44 26 20N	093 34 52W	city/town	1065
Monticello	45 18 20N	093 47 38W	city/town	
Monticello Air.	45 19 05N	093 46 38W	airport	943
Montrose	45 03 54N	093 54 39W	city/town	
Moorhead	46 52 26N	096 46 02W	city/town	
Moorhead Mun.	46 50 24N	096 39 48W	airport	917
Moose Lake	46 27 15N	092 45 42W	city/town	1062
Moose Lake Carlton	46 25 07N	092 48 16W	airport	1076
Moose Lake Lookout	46 26 52N	092 48 35W	tower	1234
Moose Mountain 1	46 51 55N	091 59 17W	summit	1148
Moose Mountain 2	47 39 05N	090 44 05W	summit	1688
Moose Mountain 3	48 06 24N	090 08 44W	summit	2012
Moose River Port.	48 07 12N	092 05 57W	locale	1342
Mora	45 52 37N	093 17 37W	city/town	1010
Mora Municipal Air	45 53 09N	093 16 18W	airport	1012
Morgan	44 25 01N	094 55 31W	city/town	
Morgan Park	46 41 18N	092 12 36W	city/town	
Morrill	45 50 20N	093 58 10W	city/town	
Morris	45 35 10N	095 54 49W	city/town	1133
Morris Municipal	45 33 59N	095 58 03W	airport	1130
Morristown	44 13 38N	093 26 40W	city/town	996

Minnesota GPS Companion

Place Name	Latitude	Longitude	Type	Elev
Mort	45 21 38N	093 11 07W	city/town	
Morton	44 33 05N	094 59 03W	city/town	
Moscow	43 42 26N	093 05 53W	city/town	
Motley	46 20 12N	094 38 45W	city/town	1229
Motley -Moreys	46 19 24N	094 38 18W	airport	1225
Motley Lookout	46 21 57N	094 36 00W	tower	
Mound	44 56 12N	093 39 57W	city/town	942
Mounds View	45 06 18N	093 12 30W	city/town	
Mountain Iron	47 31 57N	092 37 24W	city/town	1474
Mountain Lake	43 56 20N	094 55 46W	city/town	1305
Muckland	43 44 41N	093 11 20W	city/town	
Mud River Lookout	47 48 12N	094 53 12W	tower	
Mudbaden	44 41 30N	093 37 03W	city/town	
Munger	46 48 03N	092 20 37W	city/town	1367
Murdock	45 13 26N	095 23 35W	city/town	1090
Murdock Municipal	45 13 19N	095 24 04W	airport	1082
Murphy City	47 30 35N	091 19 28W	city/town	
Murray	47 48 58N	092 10 49W	city/town	1442
Murtaugh	43 36 00N	093 19 41W	city/town	
Muskoda	46 51 42N	096 24 23W	city/town	
Mustinka Dam	45 52 20N	096 07 10W	dam	
Myre State Park	43 37 26N	093 17 20W	park	

Place Name	Latitude	Longitude	Type	Elev
Myrtle	43 33 52N	093 09 48W	city/town	
N				
Nakoda	48 30 54N	093 27 29W	city/town	1145
Nansen	44 21 01N	092 55 54W	city/town	
Nary	47 22 01N	094 49 23W	city/town	1426
Nary National	47 22 33N	094 47 52W	airport	1389
Nashua	46 02 15N	096 18 28W	city/town	
Nashville Center	43 50 03N	094 18 27W	city/town	
Nashwauk	47 22 49N	093 10 05W	city/town	
Nassau	45 03 59N	096 26 22W	city/town	
Naytahwaush	47 15 46N	095 37 33W	city/town	
Nebish	47 46 17N	094 50 50W	city/town	
Nebo, Mount	46 21 22N	095 06 25W	summit	1511
Nelson	45 53 22N	095 15 50W	city/town	
Nemadji	46 28 46N	092 35 40W	city/town	
Nerstrand	44 20 31N	093 04 04W	city/town	
Nerstrand Woods St	44 20 43N	093 06 26W	park	
Nett Lake	48 06 40N	093 05 38W	city/town	1326
Nett Lake Ranger	48 03 29N	093 06 18W	station	
Nevers Dam	45 32 13N	092 43 32W	dam	
Nevis	46 57 55N	094 50 21W	city/town	1470

Minnesota GPS Companion

Place Name	Latitude	Longitude	Type	Elev
New Auburn	44 40 25N	094 13 46W	city/town	1002
New Brighton	45 03 56N	093 12 06W	city/town	
New Duluth	46 39 36N	092 13 34W	city/town	
New Germany	44 53 03N	093 58 13W	city/town	
New Hartford	43 52 43N	091 28 32W	city/town	
New Hope	45 02 17N	093 23 11W	city/town	
New London	45 18 04N	094 56 38W	city/town	
New Market	44 34 23N	093 21 12W	city/town	
New Munich	45 37 49N	094 45 12W	city/town	
New Prague	44 32 36N	093 34 33W	city/town	
New Richland	43 53 38N	093 29 37W	city/town	1184
New Rome	44 32 36N	094 05 32W	city/town	1000
New Sweden	44 24 27N	094 11 23W	city/town	
New Trier	44 36 05N	092 56 02W	city/town	980
New Ulm	44 18 45N	094 27 37W	city/town	
New Ulm C C	44 17 12N	094 27 27W	golf	
New Ulm Municipal	44 19 10N	094 30 08W	airport	1011
New York Mills	46 31 05N	095 22 33W	city/town	
New York Mills Mun	46 30 07N	095 20 15W	airport	1401
Newburg	43 34 02N	091 48 52W	city/town	
Newfolden	48 21 20N	096 19 47W	city/town	
Newhouse	43 31 30N	091 42 00W	city/town	

Minnesota GPS Companion

Place Name	Latitude	Longitude	Type	Elev
Newport	44 51 59N	093 00 01W	city/town	743
Newton Falls	47 58 10N	091 43 22W	falls	
Nichols	46 19 37N	093 47 05W	city/town	1260
Nickerson	46 24 39N	092 29 57W	city/town	1156
Nickerson Lookout	46 23 43N	092 31 14W	tower	
Nicollet	44 16 34N	094 11 14W	city/town	
Nicollet Landing	44 16 58N	094 12 58W	city/town	
Nicols	44 49 20N	093 13 13W	city/town	
Nicolville	43 40 29N	092 52 41W	city/town	
Nielsville	47 31 39N	096 48 53W	city/town	
Nimrod	46 38 20N	094 52 50W	city/town	
Nininger	44 46 09N	092 54 07W	city/town	
Nisswa	46 31 14N	094 17 18W	city/town	1231
Nodine	43 54 18N	091 26 10W	city/town	
Norcross	45 52 09N	096 11 50W	city/town	
Normania	44 38 48N	095 48 30W	city/town	
Norris Hill	47 16 13N	095 32 43W	summit	1926
Norris Lookout	48 37 17N	095 08 56W	tower	1279
Norseland	44 24 46N	094 06 59W	city/town	
Norshor Junction	47 22 00N	091 37 32W	city/town	
North Benton	45 46 46N	093 56 45W	city/town	1236
North Branch	45 30 41N	092 58 48W	city/town	896

Minnesota GPS Companion

Place Name	Latitude	Longitude	Type	Elev
North Hennepin St.	45 07 13N	093 24 25W	univ/coll	
North Mankato	44 10 24N	094 02 01W	city/town	
North Oaks	45 06 10N	093 04 44W	city/town	
North Oaks Golf	45 05 05N	093 05 52W	golf	
North Prairie	45 48 03N	094 20 57W	city/town	
North Redwood	44 33 48N	095 05 39W	city/town	847
North Saint Paul	45 00 45N	092 59 30W	city/town	
North Shore	45 48 10N	094 44 16W	city/town	1217
North Star	44 17 26N	094 04 45W	city/town	
Northcote	48 50 43N	097 00 03W	city/town	802
Northdale	45 10 43N	093 16 48W	city/town	
Northfield	44 27 30N	093 09 41W	city/town	
Northland C C	46 49 32N	092 02 52W	golf	
Northome	47 52 21N	094 16 49W	city/town	1429
Northome Lookout	47 51 57N	094 18 50W	tower	1492
Northome Municipal	47 53 29N	094 15 00W	airport	1427
Northrop	43 44 11N	094 26 10W	city/town	
Northrop College	44 58 11N	093 17 35W	univ/coll	
Norway Lake	45 17 01N	095 08 05W	city/town	
Norway Lookout	48 02 37N	092 16 18W	tower	1545
Norwegian Grove	46 36 33N	096 13 13W	city/town	1347
Norwood	44 46 05N	093 55 38W	city/town	

Place Name	Latitude	Longitude	Type	Elev
Nowthen	45 19 41N	093 28 12W	city/town	941
Noyes	48 59 51N	097 12 15W	city/town	
Noyes Junction	47 47 41N	096 36 19W	city/town	884
Nushka Lookout	47 21 43N	094 06 48W	tower	1353

◎

O L Kipp State	43 56 47N	091 23 57W	park	
Oak Center	44 21 14N	092 24 01W	city/town	1154
Oak Grove	45 20 27N	093 19 36W	city/town	915
Oak Knoll	44 58 17N	093 25 40W	city/town	
Oak Park (1)	45 10 05N	093 15 56W	city/town	914
Oak Park (2)	45 41 52N	093 49 04W	city/town	
Oak Park Heights	45 01 53N	092 47 34W	city/town	
Oak Ridge C C	44 56 09N	093 24 23W	golf	
Oak Terrace	44 53 46N	093 28 13W	city/town	
Oakbury	44 56 56N	092 56 01W	city/town	
Oakdale	44 57 47N	092 57 53W	city/town	1074
Oakland	43 40 26N	093 05 19W	city/town	1264
Oakridge	44 07 15N	091 55 11W	city/town	1226
Oaks Corner	48 25 28N	094 56 59W	city/town	1197
Oberg Mountain	47 37 45N	090 46 32W	summit	1555
O'Brien Lookout	47 45 33N	094 41 55W	tower	1357

Place Name	Latitude	Longitude	Type	Elev
Odessa	45 15 35N	096 19 43W	city/town	
Odin	43 51 59N	094 44 33W	city/town	
Ogema	47 06 10N	095 55 29W	city/town	
Ogilvie	45 49 56N	093 25 34W	city/town	1047
Okabena	43 44 22N	095 18 56W	city/town	1424
Oklee	47 50 21N	095 51 15W	city/town	
Oklee Racetrack	47 50 50N	095 52 59W	locale	
Old Frontenac	44 31 34N	092 19 55W	city/town	
Old Mesaba	47 34 56N	092 07 56W	city/town	
Old Mill State	48 21 41N	096 34 12W	park	
Olga	47 41 14N	095 39 48W	city/town	
Olivia	44 46 35N	094 59 22W	city/town	
Olivia Regional	44 46 42N	095 01 58W	airport	1076
Onamia	46 04 14N	093 40 03W	city/town	
Onega	47 19 07N	092 49 38W	city/town	
Oneota	46 44 47N	092 09 57W	city/town	
Onigum	47 06 34N	094 32 40W	city/town	
Opole	45 44 48N	094 22 07W	city/town	
Opstead	46 14 02N	093 28 19W	city/town	1312
Orchard Garden	44 43 32N	093 17 45W	city/town	
Oreland	46 27 03N	093 55 07W	city/town	
Org	43 34 53N	095 39 05W	city/town	

Place Name	Latitude	Longitude	Type	Elev
Orleans	48 55 34N	096 56 11W	city/town	
Ormsby	43 50 54N	094 41 51W	city/town	
Orono	44 58 17N	093 36 15W	city/town	
Orono Country Club	44 58 28N	093 33 30W	golf	
Oronoco	44 09 58N	092 32 05W	city/town	
Oronoco State Park	44 10 04N	092 32 24W	park	
Orr	48 03 13N	092 49 51W	city/town	1304
Orr Regional Arpt	48 00 57N	092 51 21W	airport	1311
Orrock	45 26 38N	093 44 10W	city/town	987
Orth	47 50 21N	094 18 54W	city/town	
Ortonville	45 18 17N	096 26 40W	city/town	
Ortonville Municip	45 18 20N	096 25 27W	airport	1100
Orwell Dam	46 12 58N	096 10 43W	dam	
Osage	46 55 13N	095 15 24W	city/town	
Osakis	45 52 01N	095 09 07W	city/town	
Oshawa (1)	46 48 14N	094 38 19W	city/town	1480
Oshawa (2)	44 18 01N	094 06 18W	city/town	
Oslo (1)	48 11 43N	097 07 54W	city/town	
Oslo (2)	43 53 32N	092 44 18W	city/town	1295
Oslund	47 39 20N	094 01 59W	city/town	
Osseo	45 07 10N	093 24 08W	city/town	
Oster	44 58 48N	093 58 55W	city/town	998

222

Place Name	Latitude	Longitude	Type	Elev
Ostrander	43 36 49N	092 25 40W	city/town	
Otisco	43 58 43N	093 30 07W	city/town	1149
Otisville	45 14 49N	092 45 53W	city/town	791
Otsego	45 16 27N	093 35 28W	city/town	889
Ottawa	44 22 56N	093 56 44W	city/town	
Otter Creek	46 37 31N	092 32 19W	city/town	1150
Ottertail	46 25 32N	095 33 25W	city/town	
Otto	48 05 17N	094 36 26W	city/town	1179
Outing	46 49 14N	093 56 52W	city/town	
Owanka	44 07 34N	095 40 32W	city/town	
Owatonna	44 05 02N	093 13 33W	city/town	
Owatonna Municipal	44 07 15N	093 15 20W	airport	1148
Oxboro	44 49 35N	093 17 30W	city/town	
Oxlip	45 30 01N	093 23 19W	city/town	956
Oylen	46 34 29N	094 47 54W	city/town	

ℙ

Place Name	Latitude	Longitude	Type	Elev
Padua	45 36 51N	095 03 24W	city/town	1349
Page	45 53 15N	093 39 48W	city/town	1211
Palisade	46 42 48N	093 29 18W	city/town	
Palmdale	45 27 20N	092 44 00W	city/town	
Palmer	44 09 11N	093 32 30W	city/town	

Minnesota GPS Companion

Place Name	Latitude	Longitude	Type	Elev
Palmers	46 55 29N	091 51 02W	city/town	684
Palo	47 24 55N	092 15 34W	city/town	1401
Pancake Falls	47 21 07N	091 21 58W	falls	
Parent	45 37 57N	093 59 10W	city/town	1121
Park Rapids	46 55 20N	095 03 30W	city/town	
Park Rapids Muni	46 54 02N	095 04 23W	airport	1443
Parkdale	46 14 00N	096 00 45W	city/town	
Parkers Prairie	46 09 11N	095 19 43W	city/town	1464
Parkville	47 31 52N	092 34 44W	city/town	
Partridge Falls	47 59 38N	089 50 43W	falls	
Paupores	46 52 21N	092 45 51W	city/town	1240
Payne	47 05 46N	092 35 57W	city/town	1315
Paynesville	45 22 50N	094 42 42W	city/town	
Peabody Hill	47 28 14N	091 36 30W	summit	2015
Peary	47 22 19N	092 33 22W	city/town	1336
Pease	45 41 53N	093 38 52W	city/town	
Pelan	48 38 37N	096 23 35W	city/town	
Pelican Rapids	46 34 15N	096 04 58W	city/town	
Pelican Rapids Mun	46 38 29N	096 06 16W	airport	1389
Pelland	48 31 22N	093 34 30W	city/town	1111
Pemberton	44 00 31N	093 46 59W	city/town	
Penasse	49 22 04N	094 57 31W	city/town	

Place Name	Latitude	Longitude	Type	Elev
Pencer	48 41 57N	095 38 15W	city/town	1096
Pengilly	47 19 58N	093 11 49W	city/town	
Pennington	47 29 01N	094 28 47W	city/town	
Pennock	45 08 56N	095 10 34W	city/town	1131
Pequaywan Lookout	47 11 27N	091 52 22W	tower	
Pequot Lakes	46 36 11N	094 18 33W	city/town	1280
Pequot Lookout	46 36 14N	094 17 47W	tower	
Perault	47 48 45N	096 17 23W	city/town	
Perham	46 35 40N	095 34 20W	city/town	
Perham Municipal	46 36 14N	095 36 16W	airport	1371
Perkins	43 46 59N	091 38 39W	city/town	
Perley	47 10 40N	096 48 18W	city/town	
Perth	44 04 47N	094 21 31W	city/town	
Petersburg	43 31 49N	094 55 07W	city/town	
Peterson	43 47 11N	091 50 05W	city/town	
Petran	43 39 24N	093 12 32W	city/town	
Peyla	47 47 07N	092 21 47W	city/town	1468
Pezhekee Golf	45 36 43N	095 24 43W	golf	
Pfingsten	43 48 20N	095 40 24W	city/town	1600
Phelps	46 22 49N	095 49 13W	city/town	
Philbin	47 09 36N	093 20 28W	city/town	1293
Philbrook	46 17 00N	094 43 00W	city/town	

Minnesota GPS Companion

Place Name	Latitude	Longitude	Type	Elev
Pickwick	43 58 54N	091 29 40W	city/town	
Pictured Rocks	48 03 14N	091 54 14W	other	
Pierz	45 58 54N	094 06 16W	city/town	
Pigeon Falls	48 00 17N	089 35 52W	falls	
Pike River Falls	47 47 28N	092 22 06W	falls	1350
Pillager	46 19 48N	094 28 26W	city/town	1209
Pillager Dam	46 18 56N	094 29 03W	dam	1199
Pillsbury	45 56 00N	094 41 00W	city/town	1183
Pillsbury College	44 04 58N	093 13 12W	univ/coll	
Pilot Grove	43 31 45N	094 13 39W	city/town	1128
Pine Bend (1)	47 25 35N	095 35 27W	city/town	1464
Pine Bend (2)	44 46 45N	093 02 05W	city/town	
Pine Brook	45 35 13N	093 23 18W	city/town	969
Pine Center	46 12 52N	093 54 51W	city/town	
Pine City	45 49 34N	092 58 06W	city/town	950
Pine City Municip	45 50 45N	092 57 29W	airport	971
Pine Creek	43 50 43N	091 24 12W	city/town	
Pine Island	44 12 05N	092 38 46W	city/town	
Pine Island Lkt.	48 18 39N	094 09 20W	tower	1230
Pine Knoll	46 34 38N	093 45 27W	city/town	1206
Pine Mountain	47 53 42N	090 19 35W	summit	2190
Pine Mountain Lkt.	46 49 27N	094 36 11W	tower	1606

Minnesota GPS Companion

Place Name	Latitude	Longitude	Type	Elev
Pine Point	46 58 40N	095 23 00W	city/town	1538
Pine Portage	48 07 56N	090 47 38W	portage	
Pine River	46 43 05N	094 24 14W	city/town	
Pine River Region	46 43 29N	094 23 00W	airport	1295
Pine Springs	45 02 09N	092 57 15W	city/town	
Pine Tree State	47 43 54N	094 35 07W	park	
Pinecreek	48 58 42N	095 56 33W	city/town	1047
Pinetop	47 54 21N	094 06 06W	city/town	1344
Pineville	47 32 10N	092 17 38W	city/town	1380
Pinewood	47 35 50N	095 07 39W	city/town	
Piney Pinecreek	48 59 44N	095 58 45W	airport	1071
Pipestone	44 00 02N	096 19 02W	city/town	1738
Pipestone C C	43 59 36N	096 18 22W	golf	
Pipestone Falls	48 00 07N	091 43 53W	falls	
Pipestone Municip	43 58 59N	096 18 01W	airport	1736
Pipestone Nat'l	44 00 48N	096 19 30W	monument	
Pisgah Dam	46 16 47N	096 06 11W	dam	
Pitt	48 43 03N	094 44 09W	city/town	1112
Plainview	44 09 54N	092 10 17W	city/town	1155
Plato	44 46 28N	094 02 23W	city/town	
Platte	46 06 20N	094 04 55W	city/town	
Pleasant Beach	45 46 41N	094 44 06W	city/town	1245

Minnesota GPS Companion

Place Name	Latitude	Longitude	Type	Elev
Pleasant Grove	43 52 09N	092 23 08W	city/town	
Pleasant Lake	45 29 52N	094 17 11W	city/town	
Pleasant Valley	46 32 18N	092 23 05W	city/town	922
Plum Creek Lookout	47 52 33N	093 49 52W	tower	1325
Plummer	47 54 41N	096 02 29W	city/town	
Plymouth	45 00 38N	093 27 19W	city/town	
Point Douglas	44 45 04N	092 49 04W	city/town	
Pomme de Terre C C	45 32 50N	095 52 05W	golf	
Pomroy	47 49 03N	093 59 34W	city/town	1372
Ponemah	48 01 14N	094 54 49W	city/town	1192
Ponemah Lookout	48 02 11N	094 55 15W	tower	
Ponsford	46 58 12N	095 23 01W	city/town	
Ponsford Landing	47 19 53N	095 27 17W	city/town	
Pontoria	46 51 48N	094 20 11W	city/town	
Poor Farm Landing	44 19 44N	094 14 27W	city/town	
Poplar	46 35 12N	094 41 47W	city/town	1359
Popple Creek	45 39 43N	094 01 27W	city/town	
Pork City Hill	47 00 45N	091 41 14W	summit	848
Port Cargill	44 47 18N	093 19 51W	city/town	
Portage Falls	47 59 59N	090 02 07W	falls	
Porter	44 38 11N	096 09 55W	city/town	
Post Town	44 05 26N	092 38 19W	city/town	

Place Name	Latitude	Longitude	Type	Elev
Potsdam	44 09 56N	092 20 20W	city/town	1139
Prairie Portage	48 03 03N	091 26 19W	city/town	1341
Prairieville	44 17 02N	093 11 31W	city/town	
Pratt	44 01 21N	093 09 33W	city/town	
Predmore	43 56 17N	092 19 43W	city/town	
Preston	43 40 13N	092 04 59W	city/town	
Preston -Fillmore	43 40 35N	092 10 46W	airport	1276
Priam	45 04 06N	095 08 26W	city/town	1110
Princeton	45 34 12N	093 34 53W	city/town	983
Princeton Municip	45 33 35N	093 36 29W	airport	985
Prinsburg	44 56 02N	095 11 14W	city/town	1104
Prior Lake	44 42 48N	093 25 21W	city/town	
Proctor	46 44 50N	092 13 31W	city/town	1248
Prosit	46 59 53N	092 37 03W	city/town	
Prosper	43 30 28N	091 52 10W	city/town	1357
Prosper Lookout	48 55 37N	094 57 30W	tower	1146
Providence	44 50 04N	096 06 46W	city/town	1081
Puposky	47 40 40N	094 54 25W	city/town	
Purvis Ober State	47 49 12N	092 00 14W	park	1520

Q

Quadna Mountain	46 57 47N	093 35 12W	summit	1589

Place Name	Latitude	Longitude	Type	Elev
Quamba	45 54 56N	093 10 23W	city/town	
Queens Bluff	43 57 26N	091 24 02W	cliff	
Quest End Golf	44 48 08N	093 19 22W	golf	
Quiring	47 52 57N	094 41 58W	city/town	1206
ℝ				
Racine	43 46 34N	092 28 58W	city/town	
Radium	48 13 46N	096 36 48W	city/town	
Rainy Junction	47 29 55N	092 32 42W	city/town	
Ramey	45 50 07N	093 56 15W	city/town	1288
Ramsey (1)	43 42 35N	092 58 10W	city/town	
Ramsey (2)	45 14 46N	093 27 07W	city/town	870
Ramshaw	47 25 39N	092 34 52W	city/town	1410
Randall	46 05 28N	094 30 12W	city/town	
Randolph	44 31 34N	093 01 11W	city/town	
Ranier	48 36 47N	093 20 55W	city/town	
Ransom	43 32 38N	095 47 38W	city/town	1624
Ranum	47 27 20N	096 07 53W	city/town	1204
Rapidan	44 05 40N	094 04 06W	city/town	986
Rassat	45 09 08N	093 59 30W	city/town	975
Rattlesnake Hill	44 24 12N	092 09 15W	summit	1166
Rauch	47 57 32N	093 08 44W	city/town	

Place Name	Latitude	Longitude	Type	Elev
Ray	48 24 39N	093 12 37W	city/town	
Raymond	45 00 57N	095 14 18W	city/town	
Reading	43 42 13N	095 42 46W	city/town	
Reads Landing	44 24 08N	092 04 44W	city/town	
Red Lake	47 52 35N	095 01 00W	city/town	1216
Red Lake Falls	47 52 56N	096 16 26W	city/town	1037
Red Lake Falls Mun	47 49 29N	096 15 28W	airport	1061
Red Rock	47 55 15N	089 44 18W	city/town	
Red Wing	44 33 45N	092 32 01W	city/town	750
Red Wing C C	44 33 26N	092 32 50W	golf	
Red Wing Mun.	44 35 24N	092 29 12W	airport	785
Redby	47 52 43N	094 54 46W	city/town	
Redore	47 26 37N	092 53 56W	city/town	
Redtop	46 10 34N	093 23 50W	city/town	1283
Redwood Falls	44 32 22N	095 07 00W	city/town	1044
Redwood Falls Muni	44 32 49N	095 04 56W	airport	1023
Regal	45 24 26N	094 50 43W	city/town	
Remer	47 03 22N	093 54 57W	city/town	1340
Remer Lookout	47 01 48N	094 02 01W	tower	
Remer Municipal	47 04 04N	093 54 50W	airport	1350
Reno (1)	47 25 05N	091 57 01W	city/town	1692
Reno (2)	43 36 04N	091 16 30W	city/town	

Minnesota GPS Companion

Place Name	Latitude	Longitude	Type	Elev
Renova	43 44 19N	092 45 56W	city/town	
Renville	44 47 21N	095 12 41W	city/town	1069
Revere	44 13 26N	095 21 51W	city/town	1151
Rice	45 45 07N	094 13 12W	city/town	
Rice Lake (1)	44 06 38N	093 02 45W	city/town	
Rice Lake (2)	45 00 51N	094 08 39W	city/town	1025
Riceford	43 34 34N	091 43 36W	city/town	1019
Rich Valley	44 44 46N	093 02 37W	city/town	859
Richards	46 50 10N	095 54 43W	city/town	
Richdale	46 33 17N	095 28 29W	city/town	
Richfield	44 53 00N	093 16 58W	city/town	842
Richmond	45 27 15N	094 31 05W	city/town	1119
Richville	46 30 24N	095 37 31W	city/town	
Richwood	46 58 29N	095 49 21W	city/town	1476
Ridge	47 37 21N	092 02 09W	city/town	1632
Ridge Lookout	48 03 35N	095 15 22W	tower	
Ridgeview C C	46 50 55N	092 06 05W	golf	
Ridgeway	43 54 43N	091 33 36W	city/town	
Riley	47 21 47N	092 55 47W	city/town	1395
Rindal	47 29 58N	096 07 52W	city/town	1158
Ringe	44 06 29N	092 23 57W	city/town	1209
River Junction	43 50 46N	091 17 50W	city/town	

Minnesota GPS Companion

Place Name	Latitude	Longitude	Type	Elev
River Point	43 56 21N	093 14 42W	city/town	
River Valley	48 01 13N	095 46 55W	city/town	
Riverside	46 42 36N	092 12 14W	city/town	
Riverside C C	43 42 36N	094 08 28W	golf	
Riverside Dam	47 56 28N	097 02 39W	dam	
Riverside Heights	43 39 53N	094 06 37W	city/town	
Riverton	46 27 36N	094 03 06W	city/town	1228
Roan	48 09 00N	096 44 35W	city/town	
Robbin	48 34 22N	097 08 32W	city/town	
Robbinsdale	45 01 56N	093 20 18W	city/town	
Robinson	47 51 34N	092 02 30W	city/town	1480
Rochert	46 51 36N	095 41 15W	city/town	
Rochester	44 01 18N	092 28 11W	city/town	
Rochester C C	44 01 03N	092 30 40W	golf	
Rochester Municip	43 54 37N	092 29 48W	airport	1291
Rock Creek	45 45 27N	092 57 44W	city/town	938
Rock Cut Lookout	48 00 12N	093 35 33W	tower	1305
Rock Dell	43 55 15N	092 38 18W	city/town	
Rockford	45 05 18N	093 44 03W	city/town	916
Rockville	45 28 19N	094 20 26W	city/town	1084
Rogers (1)	45 11 20N	093 33 10W	city/town	
Rogers (2)	44 15 38N	093 34 42W	city/town	

Minnesota GPS Companion

Place Name	Latitude	Longitude	Type	Elev
Roland	47 56 39N	095 46 43W	city/town	
Rollag	46 44 24N	096 14 16W	city/town	1366
Rolling Green C C	45 02 59N	093 32 05W	golf	
Rollingstone	44 05 52N	091 49 00W	city/town	759
Rollins	47 15 24N	091 50 42W	city/town	1504
Ronald	46 26 50N	093 03 18W	city/town	1305
Ronneby	45 40 53N	093 51 52W	city/town	
Roosevelt	48 48 13N	095 05 48W	city/town	1163
Root River C C	43 37 19N	092 23 26W	golf	
Rosby	47 24 36N	094 48 23W	city/town	1348
Roscoe (1)	45 26 02N	094 38 22W	city/town	
Roscoe (2)	44 13 31N	092 46 17W	city/town	
Roscoe Center	44 15 40N	092 43 37W	city/town	
Rose City	46 04 39N	095 09 59W	city/town	1431
Rose Creek	43 36 13N	092 49 54W	city/town	
Roseau	48 50 46N	095 45 45W	city/town	1048
Roseau Municipal	48 51 21N	095 41 49W	airport	1059
Roseland	44 56 33N	095 06 19W	city/town	
Rosemount	44 44 22N	093 07 32W	city/town	970
Rosen	45 09 13N	096 24 04W	city/town	
Rosendale	45 02 26N	094 42 23W	city/town	1178
Roseport	44 46 33N	093 02 58W	city/town	

Place Name	Latitude	Longitude	Type	Elev
Roseville	45 00 22N	093 09 23W	city/town	950
Rosewood	48 11 22N	096 17 24W	city/town	
Ross (1)	48 54 22N	095 55 12W	city/town	1035
Ross (2)	47 47 51N	096 44 22W	city/town	
Rossburg	46 32 07N	093 34 47W	city/town	1239
Rost	43 38 43N	095 17 40W	city/town	1441
Rosy	47 39 29N	094 18 21W	city/town	1355
Rothman	47 45 58N	091 57 51W	city/town	
Rothsay	46 28 30N	096 16 49W	city/town	1209
Round Lake	43 32 26N	095 28 05W	city/town	
Round Prairie	45 54 16N	094 53 07W	city/town	
Rowena	44 23 23N	095 09 07W	city/town	
Rowland	44 51 37N	093 25 31W	city/town	
Roy Lake	47 19 31N	095 33 05W	city/town	1506
Royalton	45 49 48N	094 17 36W	city/town	
Ruby Junction	47 26 06N	092 55 09W	city/town	
Rum River Golf	45 33 45N	093 34 35W	golf	
Rush City	45 41 08N	092 57 55W	city/town	917
Rush City Municip	45 41 52N	092 57 10W	airport	923
Rush Point	45 39 31N	093 06 14W	city/town	954
Rush River	44 28 02N	094 03 02W	city/town	948
Rushford	43 48 30N	091 45 10W	city/town	726

Minnesota GPS Companion

Place Name	Latitude	Longitude	Type	Elev
Rushford Municipal	43 48 56N	091 49 48W	airport	1211
Rushford Village	43 48 24N	091 47 29W	city/town	
Rushmore	43 37 10N	095 48 01W	city/town	
Ruskin	44 16 03N	093 09 42W	city/town	
Russell	44 19 09N	095 57 05W	city/town	1527
Rustad	46 44 00N	096 44 40W	city/town	
Ruthton	44 10 36N	096 06 13W	city/town	
Rutledge	46 15 52N	092 52 02W	city/town	1032
Ryan	44 25 26N	092 42 55W	city/town	
Ryan Village	47 21 32N	094 17 20W	city/town	

§

Place Name	Latitude	Longitude	Type	Elev
Sabin	46 46 47N	096 39 10W	city/town	
Saco	44 00 16N	093 15 58W	city/town	
Sacred Heart	44 47 13N	095 21 05W	city/town	
Saga Hill	44 57 17N	093 38 23W	city/town	
Saganaga Falls	48 13 44N	090 50 24W	falls	
Saginaw	46 51 33N	092 26 39W	city/town	1354
Saint Anna	45 39 42N	094 28 30W	city/town	
Saint Anthony (1)	45 01 14N	093 13 04W	city/town	920
Saint Anthony (2)	45 41 12N	094 36 43W	city/town	
Saint Anthony Fls	44 58 56N	093 15 19W	falls	

Minnesota GPS Companion

Place Name	Latitude	Longitude	Type	Elev
Saint Augusta	45 28 43N	094 09 14W	city/town	
Saint Benedict	44 35 17N	093 36 49W	city/town	
Saint Bonifacius	44 54 20N	093 44 50W	city/town	970
Saint Charles	43 58 10N	092 03 51W	city/town	1142
Saint Clair	44 04 55N	093 51 27W	city/town	
Saint Clair Jct	47 28 14N	092 50 40W	city/town	
Saint Cloud	45 33 39N	094 09 44W	city/town	
St Cloud Munic.	45 32 43N	094 03 30W	airport	1024
Saint Cloud State	45 33 10N	094 09 06W	univ/coll	
Saint Croix State	45 58 27N	092 35 00W	park	
Saint Francis (1)	45 23 13N	093 21 33W	city/town	918
Saint Francis (2)	45 45 36N	094 35 05W	city/town	
Saint George	44 23 22N	094 31 56W	city/town	
St Gerard Mission	45 49 24N	093 03 07W	locale	
Saint Henry	44 23 03N	093 47 18W	city/town	1010
Saint Hilaire	48 00 50N	096 12 52W	city/town	1089
Saint James	43 58 57N	094 37 36W	city/town	
St James Munic.	43 59 03N	094 33 11W	airport	1067
Saint Johns Landng	45 59 15N	092 31 36W	city/town	
Saint Johns Univ.	45 34 46N	094 23 18W	univ/coll	
Saint Joseph	45 33 54N	094 19 05W	city/town	
Saint Kilian	43 47 25N	095 52 15W	city/town	

Minnesota GPS Companion

Place Name	Latitude	Longitude	Type	Elev
Saint Leo	44 43 02N	096 03 07W	city/town	1119
Saint Louis Park	44 56 54N	093 20 52W	city/town	
Saint Martin	45 30 07N	094 40 07W	city/town	
Saint Mary	44 01 42N	093 36 06W	city/town	
Saint Marys Coll.	44 02 46N	091 41 43W	univ/coll	
Saint Marys Point	44 54 52N	092 45 56W	city/town	693
Saint Mathias	46 13 22N	094 15 03W	city/town	
Saint Michael	45 12 36N	093 39 53W	city/town	
Saint Nicholas	45 22 51N	094 26 11W	city/town	
Saint Olaf College	44 27 48N	093 11 05W	univ/coll	
Saint Patrick	44 35 41N	093 30 07W	city/town	1005
Saint Paul	44 56 40N	093 05 35W	city/town	
St Paul -Lake Elmo	44 59 47N	092 51 25W	airport	919
St Paul Downtown	44 56 15N	093 03 43W	airport	700
Saint Paul Bible C	44 57 54N	093 09 25W	univ/coll	
Saint Paul Cathed.	44 56 49N	093 06 32W	church	
Saint Paul Church	46 47 06N	092 12 41W	city/town	
Saint Paul Park	44 50 32N	092 59 28W	city/town	
Saint Peter	44 19 25N	093 57 28W	city/town	
Saint Rosa	45 43 50N	094 42 56W	city/town	
Saint Scholastica	46 48 58N	092 06 22W	univ/coll	
Saint Stephen	45 42 10N	094 16 27W	city/town	

Minnesota GPS Companion

Place Name	Latitude	Longitude	Type	Elev
Saint Thomas	44 29 52N	093 45 26W	city/town	
Saint Thomas Coll	44 56 32N	093 11 23W	univ/coll	
Saint Vincent	48 58 04N	097 13 29W	city/town	
Saint Vincent Jct	48 58 25N	097 11 55W	city/town	
Saint Wendel	45 39 58N	094 22 39W	city/town	1210
Sakatah State Park	44 13 16N	093 32 08W	park	
Salem Corners	43 59 09N	092 36 28W	city/town	
Salida	45 21 24N	093 49 09W	city/town	
Salo Corner	47 39 40N	092 16 40W	city/town	1447
Salol	48 51 58N	095 34 14W	city/town	
Sanborn	44 12 35N	095 07 42W	city/town	
Sand Dunes Lookout	45 25 39N	093 41 38W	tower	
Sandstone	46 07 52N	092 52 02W	city/town	
Sandstone Municip	46 06 59N	092 53 00W	airport	1089
Santiago	45 32 21N	093 49 11W	city/town	
Saratoga	43 53 31N	092 04 11W	city/town	
Sargeant	43 48 19N	092 48 07W	city/town	
Sartell	45 37 18N	094 12 24W	city/town	
Sauk Centre	45 44 15N	094 57 08W	city/town	1246
Sauk Centre Muni	45 42 31N	094 56 00W	airport	1244
Sauk Rapids	45 35 31N	094 09 57W	city/town	
Saum	47 58 29N	094 40 36W	city/town	

Minnesota GPS Companion

Place Name	Latitude	Longitude	Type	Elev
Savage	44 46 45N	093 20 10W	city/town	
Savanna Fairways	46 42 26N	093 20 35W	golf	
Savanna Portage S	46 50 15N	093 09 23W	park	
Sawbill Landing	47 42 55N	091 16 04W	city/town	
Sawyer	46 40 17N	092 37 59W	city/town	1330
Sax	47 12 42N	092 36 10W	city/town	1315
Scandia	45 15 13N	092 48 20W	city/town	
Scanlon	46 42 24N	092 25 41W	city/town	
Scenic Lookout	47 44 00N	093 34 04W	tower	
Scenic State Park	47 42 57N	093 33 46W	park	
Schechs Mill	43 40 03N	091 34 51W	city/town	
Schley	47 22 08N	094 24 57W	city/town	1309
School Craft St.	47 13 26N	093 48 11W	park	
Schroeder	47 32 40N	090 53 30W	city/town	
Scott	47 26 59N	092 46 10W	city/town	1406
Scott Junction	47 24 30N	091 36 37W	city/town	
Scotts Corner	46 35 53N	092 25 43W	city/town	1106
Scranton	47 25 33N	092 56 56W	city/town	
Scribner	47 32 04N	095 00 44W	city/town	
Seaforth	44 28 38N	095 19 34W	city/town	
Searles	44 13 43N	094 26 04W	city/town	
Sebeka	46 37 48N	095 05 19W	city/town	1385

Minnesota GPS Companion

Place Name	Latitude	Longitude	Type	Elev
Section Thirty	47 54 37N	091 46 49W	city/town	
Sedan	45 34 32N	095 14 52W	city/town	
Sedil	44 45 12N	092 58 23W	city/town	766
Sha-Sha Resort	48 35 47N	093 09 37W	city/town	1142
Shadow Falls	44 56 32N	093 11 49W	falls	
Shafer	45 23 13N	092 44 51W	city/town	
Shakopee	44 47 53N	093 31 36W	city/town	
Shanty Town	43 58 27N	092 38 23W	city/town	
Shaw	47 06 48N	092 21 10W	city/town	
Sheldon	43 40 42N	091 35 35W	city/town	
Shelly	47 27 29N	096 49 05W	city/town	
Shephard	46 12 50N	094 06 14W	city/town	
Sherack	48 01 15N	096 46 53W	city/town	
Sherburn	43 39 08N	094 43 36W	city/town	
Sherman	44 56 52N	094 08 00W	city/town	1045
Shermans Corner	47 46 45N	092 39 22W	city/town	1333
Sherwood	47 27 06N	092 44 27W	city/town	
Sheshebee	46 42 17N	093 14 32W	city/town	
Shevlin	47 31 49N	095 15 30W	city/town	
Shieldsville	44 21 58N	093 24 31W	city/town	
Shilling Dam	48 22 12N	095 07 24W	dam	
Shingobee Ski Area	47 02 07N	094 38 33W	ski area	

Place Name	Latitude	Longitude	Type	Elev
Shipwreck Island	48 29 37N	093 01 28W	island	1125
Shirley	47 52 08N	096 36 51W	city/town	902
Shoepack Lookout	48 29 12N	092 53 47W	tower	1346
Shogrean Dam Picn.	47 41 43N	094 03 20W	locale	1322
Shooks	47 52 27N	094 26 17W	city/town	1358
Shoreham	46 45 27N	095 53 55W	city/town	
Shoreland C C	44 18 53N	093 55 12W	golf	
Shoreview	45 04 45N	093 08 49W	city/town	950
Shorewood	44 54 03N	093 35 20W	city/town	
Shotley	48 02 56N	094 38 19W	city/town	1210
Shovel Lake	46 57 27N	093 45 12W	city/town	1340
Sibley State Park	45 19 11N	095 01 22W	park	
Side Lake	47 39 55N	093 00 56W	city/town	
Siegel	45 00 56N	092 48 24W	city/town	885
Sigsbee	43 41 36N	093 12 31W	city/town	
Silica	47 15 53N	093 01 14W	city/town	
Silver Bay	47 17 40N	091 15 26W	city/town	
Silver Bay C C	47 16 35N	091 18 43W	golf	912
Silver Bay Municip	47 14 56N	091 24 56W	airport	1089
Silver Creek (1)	45 18 54N	093 58 46W	city/town	
Silver Creek (2)	47 06 45N	091 36 04W	city/town	
Silver Lake	44 54 12N	094 11 43W	city/town	

Place Name	Latitude	Longitude	Type	Elev
Silver Rapids	47 54 14N	091 45 19W	city/town	
Silverdale	47 59 10N	093 06 34W	city/town	1311
Silverwood	47 19 04N	093 18 34W	city/town	
Simar	46 48 47N	092 20 37W	city/town	1393
Simpson	43 55 26N	092 24 35W	city/town	
Sioux Falls	48 06 15N	092 12 58W	falls	
Sioux River Lkt.	48 12 29N	092 14 34W	tower	
Sioux Valley	43 32 38N	095 18 16W	city/town	1474
Skibo	47 29 08N	091 59 39W	city/town	
Skibo Lookout	47 25 54N	092 00 55W	tower	1802
Skime	48 32 49N	095 36 09W	city/town	1186
Skyberg	44 12 41N	092 55 55W	city/town	
Skyline	44 08 32N	094 01 50W	city/town	
Slayton	43 59 16N	095 45 20W	city/town	1608
Slayton Municipal	43 59 10N	095 46 57W	airport	1623
Sleepy Eye	44 17 50N	094 43 26W	city/town	1030
Sleepy Eye Municip	44 14 59N	094 43 00W	airport	1004
Sleepy Eye State	44 18 31N	094 43 38W	park	
Smith Dam	47 08 37N	091 55 29W	dam	
Smith Lake	45 04 59N	094 06 53W	city/town	1053
Smiths Mill	44 08 16N	093 46 04W	city/town	1062
Smithville	46 42 13N	092 12 58W	city/town	710

Minnesota GPS Companion

Place Name	Latitude	Longitude	Type	Elev
Smoky Hills Lkt.	46 56 40N	095 20 32W	tower	
Snellman	46 53 22N	095 24 46W	city/town	
Snowden	47 27 19N	092 33 01W	city/town	
Sobieski	45 55 28N	094 27 32W	city/town	1133
Soderville	45 17 17N	093 14 05W	city/town	
Sogn	44 24 23N	092 55 40W	city/town	
Solana	46 19 04N	093 09 11W	city/town	
Solway	47 31 12N	095 07 44W	city/town	
Somerset C C	44 54 09N	093 06 43W	golf	
Sophie, Mount	47 57 10N	089 50 05W	summit	1814
Soudan	47 48 57N	092 14 15W	city/town	
Soudan Mine	47 49 11N	092 14 29W	mine	
South Branch	43 53 02N	094 32 57W	city/town	1115
South Haven	45 17 33N	094 12 42W	city/town	
South Hollandale	43 43 15N	093 11 22W	city/town	
South Int'l	48 35 12N	093 23 56W	city/town	
South Lake Portage	48 05 57N	090 30 18W	portage	1545
South Ridge	43 49 31N	091 25 37W	city/town	
South Rushford	43 47 46N	091 45 18W	city/town	
South Saint Paul A	44 51 25N	093 01 56W	airport	819
South Saint Paul	44 53 34N	093 02 05W	city/town	
South Silver Lake	44 53 06N	094 11 56W	city/town	

Place Name	Latitude	Longitude	Type	Elev
South Troy	44 12 20N	092 25 57W	city/town	
Southdale Center	44 52 05N	093 19 29W	locale	
Southview C C	44 53 05N	093 04 26W	golf	
Spafford	43 36 58N	095 22 18W	city/town	
Sparta	47 28 03N	092 28 38W	city/town	
Spaulding	45 46 34N	094 51 09W	city/town	
Spencer Brook	45 31 19N	093 26 25W	city/town	
Spicer	45 13 59N	094 56 23W	city/town	1171
Spider Lake Lkt.	46 41 33N	094 38 38W	tower	
Split Rock Cabins	47 10 33N	091 24 45W	locale	642
Split Rock Creek	43 53 53N	096 21 50W	park	
Split Rock Light	47 11 32N	091 23 34W	park	942
Split Rock Lighth.	47 12 01N	091 22 01W	lighthous	
Split Rock Point	47 11 17N	091 23 00W	cape	
Spring Creek	44 43 05N	095 50 54W	city/town	1078
Spring Grove	43 33 40N	091 38 09W	city/town	
Spring Hill	45 31 29N	094 49 45W	city/town	
Spring Lake (1)	44 42 23N	093 27 47W	city/town	
Spring Lake (2)	45 32 32N	093 03 56W	city/town	
Spring Lake (3)	47 38 33N	093 52 04W	city/town	
Spring Lake Park	45 06 28N	093 14 16W	city/town	
Spring Lodge Res.	48 35 52N	093 12 40W	city/town	1113

Minnesota GPS Companion

Place Name	Latitude	Longitude	Type	Elev
Spring Park	44 56 07N	093 37 55W	city/town	
Spring Valley	43 41 13N	092 23 20W	city/town	
Springfield	44 14 20N	094 58 32W	city/town	1026
Springfield C C	44 13 48N	094 58 31W	golf	
Springfield Muni	44 13 51N	094 59 56W	airport	1072
Springvale	45 37 50N	093 18 24W	city/town	935
Spruce	47 25 39N	092 33 46W	city/town	
Spruce Center	46 04 14N	095 13 24W	city/town	
Squaw Lake	47 37 57N	094 08 10W	city/town	1360
Squier	46 08 15N	096 04 53W	city/town	1150
Stacy	45 23 53N	092 59 14W	city/town	
Stairway Portage	48 05 33N	090 26 42W	portage	
Stanchfield	45 40 24N	093 10 59W	city/town	
Stanchfield Corner	45 40 25N	093 11 34W	city/town	941
Stanley	45 33 02N	093 09 09W	city/town	
Stanton	44 28 19N	093 01 22W	city/town	
Stanton Airfield	44 28 31N	093 00 58W	airport	920
Staples	46 21 20N	094 47 31W	city/town	
Staples Municipal	46 22 51N	094 48 23W	airport	1287
Starbuck	45 36 52N	095 31 51W	city/town	1162
Starbuck Municipal	45 35 59N	095 32 01W	airport	1141
Stark (1)	45 34 50N	093 03 37W	city/town	

Minnesota GPS Companion

Place Name	Latitude	Longitude	Type	Elev
Stark (2)	44 14 22N	094 38 58W	city/town	
Steele Center	43 59 22N	093 13 34W	city/town	
Steelton	46 40 13N	092 13 13W	city/town	664
Steen	43 30 53N	096 15 46W	city/town	
Stephen	48 27 00N	096 52 20W	city/town	
Stephen Municipal	48 27 29N	096 51 46W	airport	830
Sterling Center	43 54 22N	094 04 37W	city/town	1009
Stevenson	47 26 12N	093 03 28W	city/town	1630
Stewart (1)	44 43 29N	094 29 08W	city/town	1062
Stewart (2)	47 06 12N	091 42 33W	city/town	
Stewartville	43 51 20N	092 29 18W	city/town	1240
Stillwater	45 03 23N	092 48 21W	city/town	
Stockholm	45 02 11N	094 13 15W	city/town	
Stockton	44 01 39N	091 46 11W	city/town	
Stokes Lookout	47 39 06N	093 40 30W	tower	
Stony Lookout	47 36 15N	091 26 05W	tower	2080
Stony Ridge Lkt.	47 39 09N	093 11 20W	tower	1545
Stony Tower Hill	47 36 15N	091 26 07W	summit	2080
Storden	44 02 20N	095 19 09W	city/town	1390
Strandquist	48 29 25N	096 26 49W	city/town	
Strathcona	48 33 14N	096 10 07W	city/town	1124
Strawberry Mtn.	47 14 26N	095 32 56W	summit	1854

Place Name	Latitude	Longitude	Type	Elev
Stroden	44 02 16N	095 19 05W	city/town	
Stroms	44 37 46N	092 39 41W	city/town	688
Strout	45 01 48N	094 35 39W	city/town	1179
Stuart Portage	48 06 09N	091 59 23W	portage	
Stubbs Bay -subd.	44 58 30N	093 36 52W	city/town	935
Sturgeon	47 46 36N	092 52 07W	city/town	1296
Sturgeon Lake	46 22 52N	092 49 25W	city/town	1074
Sturgeon River Ldg	48 12 45N	093 53 10W	city/town	
Sugarbush Lookout	47 21 13N	095 25 05W	tower	1639
Sugarloaf	44 01 36N	091 37 23W	city/town	
Sugarloaf Bluff	44 27 21N	092 18 21W	cliff	1067
Sullivan Lake Lkt.	46 07 29N	093 56 07W	tower	
Sultan	48 59 27N	097 10 39W	city/town	
Summit	43 55 15N	093 11 07W	city/town	
Summit Lookout	47 30 05N	095 20 58W	tower	1614
Sumter	44 44 22N	094 15 47W	city/town	1030
Sunburg	45 20 52N	095 14 17W	city/town	
Sundal	47 27 23N	096 11 53W	city/town	
Sunfish Lake	44 52 15N	093 05 54W	city/town	
Sunrise	45 32 49N	092 51 17W	city/town	
Suomi	47 29 00N	093 44 28W	city/town	1363
Surfside Seaplane	45 08 59N	093 07 00W	airport	880

Minnesota GPS Companion

Place Name	Latitude	Longitude	Type	Elev
Svea	45 00 12N	095 01 16W	city/town	
Sveadahl	44 04 27N	094 44 21W	city/town	
Swan River	47 05 12N	093 11 41W	city/town	1293
Swanburg	46 44 25N	094 10 31W	city/town	1310
Swanville	45 54 37N	094 38 36W	city/town	1183
Swatara	46 53 44N	093 40 26W	city/town	1296
Swift	48 51 12N	095 13 16W	city/town	
Swift Falls	45 23 56N	095 25 25W	city/town	
Sylvan	46 20 06N	094 24 23W	city/town	1206
Sylvan Dam	46 18 17N	094 22 40W	dam	1177
Syre	47 10 49N	096 15 30W	city/town	1116

𝕋

Place Name	Latitude	Longitude	Type	Elev
Tabor	48 04 45N	096 51 45W	city/town	
Taconite	47 18 46N	093 22 55W	city/town	
Taconite Harbor	47 31 21N	090 55 43W	city/town	
Taconite Harbor R.	47 31 43N	090 55 15W	park	765
Taft	46 59 40N	092 19 57W	city/town	1345
Talmoon	47 36 00N	093 46 25W	city/town	1359
Tamarack	46 38 40N	093 07 37W	city/town	1269
Tansem	46 40 31N	096 14 09W	city/town	
Taopi	43 33 29N	092 38 33W	city/town	

Minnesota GPS Companion

Place Name	Latitude	Longitude	Type	Elev
Taplin Gorge Dam	46 22 59N	096 01 03W	dam	
Taunton	44 35 37N	096 03 56W	city/town	1175
Tawney	43 36 59N	091 47 23W	city/town	1169
Taylors Falls	45 24 07N	092 39 08W	city/town	744
Temperance River S	47 33 16N	090 52 20W	park	652
Tenmile Corner	43 58 43N	094 25 44W	city/town	1033
Tenney	46 02 40N	096 27 11W	city/town	
Tenstrike	47 39 24N	094 40 28W	city/town	1403
Terrace	45 30 36N	095 19 11W	city/town	
Terrace C C	46 24 37N	094 46 59W	golf	
Terrebonne	47 49 57N	096 07 59W	city/town	
Tetagouche Lake C.	47 20 55N	091 16 14W	campgrnd	1385
The Arches	44 00 02N	091 49 03W	locale	
Theilman	44 17 21N	092 11 31W	city/town	
Thief River Falls	48 03 55N	096 11 00W	airport	1116
Thief River Falls	48 07 09N	096 10 51W	city/town	1133
Thistledew Lookout	47 48 11N	093 13 49W	tower	
Thistledew Ranger	47 49 17N	093 14 43W	station	1393
Thompson Heights	45 10 59N	093 20 15W	city/town	870
Thompson Riverview	45 09 27N	093 19 54W	city/town	
Thomson	46 39 49N	092 23 52W	city/town	
Thor	46 28 34N	093 25 14W	city/town	1270

Minnesota GPS Companion

Place Name	Latitude	Longitude	Type	Elev
Thorhult	48 13 49N	095 14 52W	city/town	
Thorpe Lookout	47 05 47N	094 51 12W	tower	
ThreeWay Watershed	47 28 20N	092 57 49W	marker	
Thunderbird Resort	48 35 58N	093 11 14W	city/town	1112
Tianna C C	47 04 46N	094 35 20W	golf	
Tilden Junction	47 42 08N	096 17 19W	city/town	
Tintah	46 00 35N	096 19 20W	city/town	
Toad Mountain	46 52 10N	095 30 42W	summit	1755
Tobique	47 06 56N	094 02 22W	city/town	1316
Tofte	47 34 26N	090 50 10W	city/town	629
Togo	47 49 17N	093 09 21W	city/town	1357
Toimi	47 24 02N	091 46 03W	city/town	
Toivola	47 10 01N	092 48 39W	city/town	
Tom, Mount	45 19 34N	095 01 57W	summit	1375
Tonka Bay	44 54 31N	093 35 34W	city/town	
Torfin	48 35 52N	095 44 00W	city/town	1137
Tower	47 48 20N	092 16 28W	city/town	
Tower Hill	45 51 10N	095 37 06W	summit	1582
Tower Junction	47 48 18N	092 15 22W	city/town	1383
Tower Municipal	47 49 02N	092 17 51W	airport	1369
Tower-Soudan State	47 49 29N	092 15 22W	park	
Town and Country G	44 56 58N	093 11 53W	golf	

Minnesota GPS Companion

Place Name	Latitude	Longitude	Type	Elev
Tracy	44 14 00N	095 37 08W	city/town	1398
Tracy Country Club	44 14 17N	095 34 35W	golf	
Tracy Municipal	44 14 59N	095 36 16W	airport	1340
Trail	47 46 48N	095 41 31W	city/town	
Traverse	44 20 55N	094 01 02W	city/town	
Trimont	43 45 44N	094 42 25W	city/town	
Trommald	46 30 19N	094 01 05W	city/town	
Trondjem	44 28 45N	093 23 34W	city/town	1057
Trosky	43 53 21N	096 15 24W	city/town	
Troy	43 52 15N	092 04 04W	city/town	
Truman	43 49 40N	094 26 13W	city/town	
Tulaby Lookout	47 10 06N	095 38 09W	tower	1734
Turtle River	47 35 15N	094 45 05W	city/town	
Twig	46 53 40N	092 21 52W	city/town	
Twig Station	46 52 40N	092 20 46W	city/town	1385
Twin City Speedway	45 07 16N	093 11 37W	locale	
Twin Grove	43 42 10N	093 11 17W	city/town	1208
Twin Lakes	43 33 35N	093 25 22W	city/town	
Twin Valley	47 15 37N	096 15 31W	city/town	
Two Harbors	47 01 22N	091 40 14W	city/town	
Two Harbors Air.	47 03 00N	091 44 42W	airport	1080
Two Harbors Light	47 00 50N	091 39 49W	locale	605

Place Name	Latitude	Longitude	Type	Elev
Two Inlets	47 03 10N	095 13 02W	city/town	
Tyler	44 16 42N	096 08 04W	city/town	1733
Tyler Municipal	44 17 29N	096 09 01W	airport	1742
U. of MN Duluth	46 48 45N	092 04 33W	univ/coll	
U. of MN Golf C.	44 59 32N	093 11 42W	golf	
U. of MN Main Camp	44 58 28N	093 13 58W	univ/coll	
U. of MN Morris	45 35 29N	095 54 02W	univ/coll	
Ulen	47 04 44N	096 15 31W	city/town	
Underwood	46 17 07N	095 52 14W	city/town	
Union	43 53 31N	093 07 31W	city/town	1247
Union Depot	46 46 54N	092 06 13W	building	
Union Hill	44 32 37N	093 40 01W	city/town	1006
Union Mission Camp	45 04 34N	093 07 20W	locale	
Upper Sioux Agency	44 44 17N	095 27 13W	park	
Upsala	45 48 39N	094 34 16W	city/town	
Urbank	46 07 22N	095 30 42W	city/town	1477
Utica	43 58 32N	091 57 17W	city/town	

V

Vadnais Heights	45 03 27N	093 04 25W	city/town	
Valley High C C	43 45 26N	091 25 52W	golf	
Varco	43 36 21N	092 57 23W	city/town	1202

Minnesota GPS Companion

Place Name	Latitude	Longitude	Type	Elev
Vasa	44 30 12N	092 43 20W	city/town	
Vaseux Portage	48 06 43N	090 08 05W	portage	
Vawter	45 54 44N	094 14 41W	city/town	1108
Verdi	44 12 31N	096 21 07W	city/town	
Vergas	46 39 24N	095 48 18W	city/town	
Vermilion Dam	47 57 40N	092 28 33W	dam	
Vermilion Dam Lkt.	47 58 12N	092 28 38W	tower	1504
Vermilion Gorge	48 16 27N	092 30 52W	valley	
Vermillion	44 40 25N	092 58 01W	city/town	
Vermillion Fls Pic	48 15 51N	092 34 04W	locale	1222
Vern	47 18 14N	095 12 51W	city/town	1486
Verndale	46 23 54N	095 00 52W	city/town	1349
Vernon	43 54 12N	092 44 17W	city/town	
Vernon Center	43 57 43N	094 10 08W	city/town	
Veseli	44 30 54N	093 27 35W	city/town	
Vesta	44 30 28N	095 24 58W	city/town	
Victoria	44 51 31N	093 39 41W	city/town	
Viking	48 13 07N	096 24 20W	city/town	
Villard	45 42 56N	095 16 08W	city/town	
Vineland	46 09 49N	093 45 26W	city/town	1261
Vining	46 15 47N	095 32 12W	city/town	1387
Viola	44 03 48N	092 16 05W	city/town	

Place Name	Latitude	Longitude	Type	Elev
Virginia	47 31 24N	092 32 11W	city/town	1437
Vista	43 57 26N	093 27 59W	city/town	1178
Vlasaty	43 57 53N	092 50 56W	city/town	1335
Voyageurs National	48 30 01N	092 50 00W	park	

𝕎

Place Name	Latitude	Longitude	Type	Elev
Wabasha	44 23 02N	092 01 58W	city/town	
Wabasso	44 24 07N	095 15 20W	city/town	
Wabedo	46 55 14N	094 11 16W	city/town	1316
Waconia	44 51 03N	093 47 12W	city/town	991
Wacouta	44 32 42N	092 26 05W	city/town	
Wacouta Beach	44 32 45N	092 24 37W	city/town	
Wadena	46 26 33N	095 08 09W	city/town	
Wadena C C	46 29 15N	095 05 24W	golf	
Wadena Municipal	46 26 29N	095 07 01W	airport	1350
Wagner Lake Lkt.	47 45 20N	094 09 48W	tower	
Wahkon	46 07 06N	093 31 15W	city/town	
Wahlsten	47 44 09N	092 17 00W	city/town	1464
Waite Park	45 33 26N	094 13 26W	city/town	
Wakemup	47 55 27N	092 38 42W	city/town	
Walbo	45 35 14N	093 19 36W	city/town	
Walcott	44 14 00N	093 11 00W	city/town	1190

Minnesota GPS Companion

Place Name	Latitude	Longitude	Type	Elev
Waldeck	46 40 28N	093 36 27W	city/town	1211
Waldo	47 03 58N	091 41 56W	city/town	
Waldorf	43 56 06N	093 41 50W	city/town	
Wales	47 14 06N	091 44 48W	city/town	1640
Walker	47 06 05N	094 35 13W	city/town	
Walker Municipal	47 09 31N	094 38 35W	airport	1362
Wall Lake	46 17 27N	095 57 52W	city/town	
Walnut Grove	44 13 23N	095 28 09W	city/town	1212
Walters	43 36 21N	093 40 23W	city/town	
Waltham	43 49 18N	092 52 37W	city/town	
Wanamingo	44 18 16N	092 47 25W	city/town	
Wanda	44 18 59N	095 12 41W	city/town	
Wangs	44 24 24N	092 58 46W	city/town	
Wanless Lookout	47 39 10N	091 10 25W	tower	2045
Wannaska	48 39 30N	095 44 04W	city/town	1105
Warba	47 07 44N	093 15 59W	city/town	1280
Ward Springs	45 47 31N	094 48 17W	city/town	
Warman	46 03 30N	093 17 03W	city/town	
Warren	48 11 48N	096 46 21W	city/town	854
Warren Municipal	48 11 14N	096 43 01W	airport	880
Warroad	48 54 19N	095 18 51W	city/town	1070
Warroad Intl	48 56 11N	095 20 33W	airport	1075

Minnesota GPS Companion

Place Name	Latitude	Longitude	Type	Elev
Warsaw	44 14 58N	093 23 37W	city/town	
Waseca	44 04 40N	093 30 26W	city/town	1151
Waseca Municipal	44 04 24N	093 33 10W	airport	1126
Washington	43 46 33N	092 20 19W	city/town	1148
Wasioja	44 04 49N	092 49 09W	city/town	
Waskish	48 09 41N	094 30 44W	city/town	
Waskish Municipal	48 09 14N	094 31 00W	airport	1181
Wastedo	44 24 17N	092 51 04W	city/town	
Watab	45 40 35N	094 10 51W	city/town	1046
Waterford	44 29 02N	093 08 34W	city/town	
Watertown	44 57 49N	093 50 49W	city/town	
Waterville	44 13 08N	093 34 04W	city/town	
Watkins	45 18 55N	094 24 30W	city/town	
Watonwan County CC	43 58 47N	094 30 46W	golf	
Watson	45 00 35N	095 48 04W	city/town	1031
Waubun	47 10 50N	095 56 20W	city/town	
Waukenabo	46 44 24N	093 36 00W	city/town	1249
Waukon	47 22 08N	096 07 51W	city/town	1178
Waverly	45 04 00N	093 57 58W	city/town	998
Wawina	47 03 11N	093 07 08W	city/town	1267
Wayland	48 28 06N	094 19 13W	city/town	1144
Wayzata	44 58 27N	093 30 23W	city/town	

Minnesota GPS Companion

Place Name	Latitude	Longitude	Type	Elev
Wayzata C C	44 58 42N	093 31 42W	golf	
Wealthwood	46 21 47N	093 39 14W	city/town	1274
Weaver	44 12 54N	091 55 43W	city/town	686
Weber	45 28 30N	093 07 26W	city/town	
Weber, Mount	47 29 04N	091 39 22W	summit	1944
Webster	44 31 47N	093 21 09W	city/town	
Wegdahl	44 53 24N	095 38 42W	city/town	
Welch	44 34 06N	092 44 18W	city/town	
Welcome	43 40 01N	094 37 09W	city/town	1235
Wells	43 44 46N	093 43 43W	city/town	
Wells Municipal	43 43 59N	093 47 00W	airport	1119
Weme	47 38 39N	095 32 16W	city/town	
Wendell	46 02 08N	096 06 03W	city/town	
Werner	47 36 59N	094 55 21W	city/town	
Wescott	44 49 11N	093 06 20W	city/town	881
West Albany	44 18 05N	092 17 07W	city/town	
West Albion	45 11 45N	094 08 05W	city/town	
West Concord	44 09 13N	092 53 58W	city/town	
West Coon Rapids	45 09 35N	093 20 58W	city/town	853
West Duluth	46 44 08N	092 11 10W	city/town	
West Fargo	46 52 36N	096 52 20W	city/town	900
West Lake Francis	45 30 28N	093 20 14W	city/town	927

Minnesota GPS Companion

Place Name	Latitude	Longitude	Type	Elev
West Newton	44 15 54N	091 54 02W	city/town	
West Point	45 33 28N	093 23 20W	city/town	
West Saint Paul	44 54 58N	093 06 05W	city/town	
West Union	45 48 03N	095 04 59W	city/town	
West Virginia	47 30 56N	092 34 12W	city/town	
Westbrook	44 02 32N	095 26 09W	city/town	1422
Westbury	46 55 02N	095 54 34W	city/town	
Western	46 09 07N	096 10 58W	city/town	1109
Westfield Center	43 57 01N	092 57 54W	city/town	1305
Westfield Golf	44 03 22N	091 40 38W	golf	
Weston	45 11 20N	092 59 04W	city/town	934
Westport	45 42 54N	095 10 01W	city/town	
Whalan	43 43 56N	091 55 35W	city/town	793
Wheatland	44 27 53N	093 29 00W	city/town	
Wheaton	45 48 16N	096 29 56W	city/town	1019
Wheaton Municipal	45 46 49N	096 32 36W	airport	1025
Wheelbarrow Falls	48 07 03N	091 41 29W	falls	1263
Wheeler Landing	47 43 33N	091 17 24W	city/town	
Wheelers Point	48 50 16N	094 41 51W	city/town	1071
Whipholt	47 02 56N	094 21 54W	city/town	
Whipholt Lookout	47 00 39N	094 22 04W	tower	
White Bear Beach	45 05 59N	092 59 20W	city/town	

Minnesota GPS Companion

Place Name	Latitude	Longitude	Type	Elev
White Bear Lake	45 05 05N	093 00 35W	city/town	950
White Earth	47 05 48N	095 50 35W	city/town	
White Elk Lookout	46 47 57N	093 40 46W	tower	
White Hawk	46 23 53N	093 49 31W	city/town	1264
White Iron	47 54 12N	091 46 36W	city/town	
White Pine Lookout	46 19 59N	093 13 19W	tower	1324
White Rock	44 27 23N	092 46 01W	city/town	
White Rock Dam	45 51 41N	096 34 20W	dam	
White Willow	44 21 51N	092 39 04W	city/town	
Whiteface	47 11 12N	092 21 58W	city/town	
Whiteface R. Picn.	47 16 17N	092 12 16W	area	1439
Whitewater State	44 03 30N	092 03 31W	park	
Whitman	44 09 12N	091 48 21W	city/town	
Whyte	47 27 06N	091 33 43W	city/town	
Wilbert	43 32 38N	094 32 21W	city/town	
Wilder	43 49 36N	095 11 50W	city/town	
Wilder Center	44 56 54N	093 07 40W	building	
Wilds	47 44 44N	096 38 09W	city/town	
Wildwood	47 53 26N	093 58 00W	city/town	
Wilkinson	47 15 03N	094 37 39W	city/town	
Willernie	45 03 15N	092 57 23W	city/town	
William O'Brien St	45 13 10N	092 45 57W	park	

Minnesota GPS Companion

Place Name	Latitude	Longitude	Type	Elev
Williams	48 46 06N	094 57 18W	city/town	
Williams Narrows C	47 30 12N	094 04 37W	campgrnd	1320
Willington Grove	43 34 42N	091 34 44W	city/town	
Willmar	45 07 19N	095 02 35W	city/town	
Willmar Municipal	45 06 56N	095 05 19W	airport	1127
Willow Creek	43 53 41N	094 16 06W	city/town	
Willow Creek C C	43 57 04N	092 29 11W	golf	
Willow Green C C	43 51 22N	092 28 34W	golf	
Willow River	46 19 06N	092 50 28W	city/town	1038
Willow River Lkt.	46 21 02N	092 49 23W	tower	
Wilmington	43 32 49N	091 32 32W	city/town	
Wilmont	43 45 53N	095 49 37W	city/town	
Wilno	44 29 59N	096 13 52W	city/town	
Wilpen	47 26 26N	092 49 40W	city/town	1427
Wilson	43 57 36N	091 41 04W	city/town	
Wilton (1)	44 00 50N	093 32 03W	city/town	1109
Wilton (2)	47 30 13N	095 00 03W	city/town	
Win-E-Mac Golf	47 39 45N	095 58 52W	golf	
Windcrest Golf	44 09 15N	092 10 21W	golf	
Windom	43 51 59N	095 07 00W	city/town	1364
Windom Municipal	43 54 48N	095 06 33W	airport	1410
Winger	47 32 10N	095 59 17W	city/town	

Minnesota GPS Companion

Place Name	Latitude	Longitude	Type	Elev
Winnebago	43 46 04N	094 09 56W	city/town	
Winner	48 35 52N	095 26 23W	city/town	1234
Winnewissa Falls	44 00 55N	096 19 12W	falls	
Winnie Lookout	47 26 20N	094 01 58W	tower	
Winnipeg Junction	46 53 45N	096 14 47W	city/town	
Winona	44 03 00N	091 38 21W	city/town	
Winona C C	44 00 28N	091 36 19W	golf	
Winona Municipal	44 04 40N	091 42 30W	airport	657
Winona State Coll	44 02 51N	091 38 30W	univ/coll	
Winsted	44 57 50N	094 02 50W	city/town	
Winsted Municipal	44 56 59N	094 04 00W	airport	1030
Winter	47 31 38N	091 29 25W	city/town	
Winthrop	44 32 35N	094 21 58W	city/town	1018
Winton	47 55 35N	091 48 02W	city/town	1335
Wirock	43 53 13N	095 42 12W	city/town	
Wirt	47 43 50N	093 57 35W	city/town	
Wisner	48 18 25N	093 40 34W	city/town	1188
Withrow	45 07 27N	092 53 50W	city/town	
Witoka	43 56 00N	091 37 12W	city/town	
Wolf	47 27 02N	092 36 31W	city/town	
Wolf Lake	46 48 11N	095 21 08W	city/town	
Wolf Lake Lookout	46 51 24N	095 21 30W	tower	

Minnesota GPS Companion

Place Name	Latitude	Longitude	Type	Elev
Wolford	46 32 44N	093 58 44W	city/town	
Wolverton	46 33 48N	096 44 00W	city/town	
Wood Lake	44 39 10N	095 32 17W	city/town	
Woodbury (1)	46 40 45N	092 57 35W	city/town	1320
Woodbury (2)	44 55 26N	092 57 33W	city/town	1065
Woodhill C C	44 58 31N	093 32 40W	golf	
Woodland (1)	46 50 46N	092 04 56W	city/town	
Woodland (2)	46 06 57N	093 17 02W	city/town	1241
Woodland (3)	44 56 49N	093 30 14W	city/town	
Woodrow	46 23 18N	094 04 27W	city/town	1263
Woodstock	44 00 33N	096 06 01W	city/town	
Woodward Brook	45 40 34N	093 35 06W	city/town	998
Worthington	43 37 12N	095 35 46W	city/town	
Worthington C C	43 37 45N	095 37 20W	golf	
Worthington Muni	43 39 18N	095 34 45W	airport	1574
Wrenshall	46 37 01N	092 22 56W	city/town	1041
Wright	46 40 09N	093 00 24W	city/town	1303
Wrightstown	46 16 26N	095 11 09W	city/town	1425
Wyanett	45 35 13N	093 27 02W	city/town	969
Wyattville	43 56 27N	091 47 24W	city/town	1246
Wykoff	43 42 26N	092 16 05W	city/town	1322
Wylie	47 57 43N	096 21 10W	city/town	

Place Name	Latitude	Longitude	Type	Elev
Wyman	47 31 57N	092 06 27W	city/town	
Wynne Lake Lookout	47 34 22N	092 18 37W	tower	1844
Wyoming	45 20 11N	092 59 49W	city/town	

X

Y

Place Name	Latitude	Longitude	Type	Elev
Yankeetown	45 29 28N	096 44 23W	city/town	
Yola	47 13 56N	095 00 43W	city/town	
York (1)	47 07 37N	091 42 12W	city/town	
York (2)	43 31 59N	092 16 08W	city/town	
Young America	44 46 58N	093 54 48W	city/town	
Yucatan	43 40 50N	091 41 19W	city/town	

Z

Place Name	Latitude	Longitude	Type	Elev
Zemple	47 19 23N	093 47 07W	city/town	
Zerkel	47 18 39N	095 22 53W	city/town	1565
Zim	47 18 25N	092 36 11W	city/town	1339
Zippel Bay State	48 51 50N	094 51 33W	park	1075
Zumbro Falls	44 17 00N	092 25 19W	city/town	
Zumbrota	44 17 39N	092 40 08W	city/town	1005

Minnesota GPS Companion

Place Name	Latitude	Longitude	Type	Elev

Add your own coordinates here

Place Name	Latitude	Longitude	Type	Elev

Add your own coordinates here

NORTH
CENTRAL
GPS
COMPANION

WISCONSIN

DATA FORMAT: DD-MM-SS

DATUM: NAD27

CAUTION: Airport data is not approved for aerial navigation.

Place Name	Latitude	Longitude	Type	Elev
A				
Abbotsford	44 56 47N	090 18 57W	city/town	
Abells Corners	42 43 34N	088 32 33W	city/town	881
Abraham Reef	43 54 19N	088 25 34W	bar	
Abrams	44 46 45N	088 03 35W	city/town	
Ackerville	43 18 36N	088 15 29W	city/town	
Acme Mine	42 44 33N	090 26 57W	mine	
Ada	43 52 37N	087 53 44W	city/town	
Adams (1)	43 57 22N	089 49 05W	city/town	960
Adams (2)	42 48 02N	088 31 58W	city/town	919
Adams Beach	44 41 10N	088 40 05W	city/town	
Addison	43 25 22N	088 22 28W	city/town	
Adell	43 37 09N	087 57 07W	city/town	
Adella Beach	44 08 32N	088 27 42W	city/town	
Advance	44 47 16N	088 19 56W	city/town	859
Afton	42 36 14N	089 04 16W	city/town	
Alaska	44 32 26N	087 30 04W	city/town	
Alban	44 37 40N	089 17 05W	city/town	1141
Albany	42 42 28N	089 26 13W	city/town	
Albertville	44 57 36N	091 36 01W	city/town	
Albion	42 52 46N	089 04 11W	city/town	

Wisconsin GPS Companion

Place Name	Latitude	Longitude	Type	Elev
Alderley	43 13 03N	088 26 59W	city/town	
Algoma	44 36 32N	087 25 57W	city/town	600
Algoma Marina	44 36 34N	087 26 55W	marina	585
Allen	44 39 41N	091 22 00W	city/town	974
Allens Grove	42 34 49N	088 45 45W	city/town	
Allenton	43 25 14N	088 20 27W	city/town	
Allenville	44 07 59N	088 37 08W	city/town	
Allouez (1)	44 28 39N	088 00 58W	city/town	
Allouez (2)	46 41 19N	092 01 28W	city/town	636
Alma	44 19 12N	091 54 53W	city/town	687
Alma Center	44 26 14N	090 54 40W	city/town	
Almena	45 25 01N	092 01 58W	city/town	1187
Almond	44 15 32N	089 24 25W	city/town	
Alpha	45 46 21N	092 34 46W	city/town	
Alpine C C	45 02 47N	087 17 47W	golf	589
Alto	43 40 36N	088 47 42W	city/town	
Altoona	44 48 17N	091 26 35W	city/town	
Alverno	44 05 06N	087 44 23W	city/town	
Alverno College	42 58 59N	087 57 51W	univ/coll	
Alvin	45 59 06N	088 49 45W	city/town	
Amberg	45 30 11N	087 59 37W	city/town	893
Ambridge	46 38 12N	092 04 13W	city/town	

Wisconsin GPS Companion

Place Name	Latitude	Longitude	Type	Elev
Amery	45 18 25N	092 21 43W	city/town	
Amery Municipal	45 16 52N	092 22 30W	airport	1088
Amherst	44 27 03N	089 17 05W	city/town	
Amherst Junction	44 28 08N	089 18 45W	city/town	1126
Amnicon Falls	46 36 14N	091 53 23W	city/town	
Amnicon Falls	46 36 36N	091 53 32W	falls	
Anacker	43 37 32N	089 26 37W	city/town	782
Anderson	42 43 01N	089 01 00W	city/town	
Angelica	44 40 26N	088 18 49W	city/town	
Angelo	43 58 15N	090 46 40W	city/town	
Angus	45 38 52N	091 36 06W	city/town	
Aniwa	45 00 31N	089 12 51W	city/town	1414
Aniwa Lookout	45 01 52N	089 15 51W	tower	
Annaton	42 54 41N	090 32 15W	city/town	
Anson	44 58 51N	091 17 12W	city/town	946
Anston	44 37 02N	088 09 37W	city/town	747
Antigo	45 08 25N	089 09 08W	city/town	
Antigo -Langlade	45 09 20N	089 06 32W	airport	1521
Anton	46 37 09N	092 14 07W	city/town	813
Anvil Lake Lookout	45 58 08N	089 03 05W	tower	
Apollonia	45 27 00N	091 18 05W	city/town	1102
Apostle Islands N.	46 57 00N	090 53 00W	park	

271

Wisconsin GPS Companion

Place Name	Latitude	Longitude	Type	Elev
Apple Creek	44 19 32N	088 22 28W	city/town	
Apple River Falls	45 09 27N	092 42 43W	falls	744
Appleton	44 15 43N	088 24 55W	city/town	
Appleton-Outagamie	44 15 26N	088 31 09W	airport	917
Arbor Vitae	45 55 14N	089 39 48W	city/town	
Arcade Acres	43 51 31N	088 52 15W	city/town	
Arcadia	44 15 10N	091 30 05W	city/town	728
Arcadia C C	44 15 07N	091 28 47W	golf	
Archibald Lookout	45 15 46N	088 35 12W	tower	
Arena	43 09 56N	089 54 46W	city/town	735
Argonne	45 39 35N	088 52 45W	city/town	1641
Argyle	42 42 04N	089 52 01W	city/town	810
Arkansaw	44 38 02N	092 01 52W	city/town	
Arkdale	44 01 38N	089 53 16W	city/town	
Arland	45 20 18N	092 01 22W	city/town	1217
Arlington	43 20 17N	089 22 49W	city/town	1052
Armstrong	43 42 37N	088 11 41W	city/town	
Armstrong Creek	45 39 30N	088 26 46W	city/town	1516
Arnold	45 14 56N	091 00 15W	city/town	
Arnott	44 27 26N	089 26 48W	city/town	1135
Arpin	44 32 26N	090 02 06W	city/town	
Artesia Beach	43 56 05N	088 18 54W	city/town	

Wisconsin GPS Companion

Place Name	Latitude	Longitude	Type	Elev
Arthur	42 50 48N	090 26 47W	city/town	
Ashford	43 35 13N	088 22 14W	city/town	
Ashippun	43 12 43N	088 30 58W	city/town	858
Ashland	46 35 33N	090 53 01W	city/town	671
Ashland -JFK Mem	46 32 54N	090 55 07W	airport	826
Ashland Junction	46 34 26N	090 58 16W	city/town	649
Ashley	44 41 34N	089 36 29W	city/town	
Ashton	43 08 26N	089 32 29W	city/town	
Ashton Corners	43 08 25N	089 31 14W	city/town	974
Ashwaubenon	44 28 56N	088 04 12W	city/town	590
Askeaton	44 16 12N	088 06 39W	city/town	740
Astico	43 19 59N	088 56 23W	city/town	
Asylum Point	44 03 56N	088 30 36W	cape	
Athelstane	45 25 26N	088 05 43W	city/town	933
Athens	45 01 59N	090 04 26W	city/town	
Atkins	45 39 55N	089 01 23W	city/town	
Atlas	45 38 08N	092 35 26W	city/town	
Attica	42 46 12N	089 28 50W	city/town	
Atwater	43 33 39N	088 44 04W	city/town	932
Atwood	44 53 10N	090 28 54W	city/town	1291
Aubrey	43 18 53N	090 17 36W	city/town	753
Auburndale	44 37 37N	090 00 27W	city/town	1220

273

Wisconsin GPS Companion

Place Name	Latitude	Longitude	Type	Elev
Augusta	44 40 49N	091 07 11W	city/town	
Aurora (1)	43 25 39N	088 18 06W	city/town	
Aurora (2)	45 47 08N	088 06 03W	city/town	1072
Auroraville	44 03 07N	088 59 33W	city/town	775
Avalanche	43 36 08N	090 46 49W	city/town	859
Avalon	42 37 58N	088 52 03W	city/town	
Avoca	43 10 55N	090 19 28W	city/town	698
Avon (1)	42 32 36N	089 19 53W	city/town	
Avon (2)	42 40 04N	090 07 34W	city/town	
Aztalan	43 04 22N	088 51 44W	city/town	
Aztalan State Park	43 03 56N	088 51 46W	park	

B

Place Name	Latitude	Longitude	Type	Elev
Babcock	44 18 06N	090 06 40W	city/town	975
Bagley	42 54 20N	091 06 04W	city/town	
Bagley Junction	45 08 18N	087 45 04W	city/town	
Bagley Lookout	45 06 21N	088 19 00W	tower	
Baileys Harbor	45 03 31N	087 06 37W	bay	
Baileys Harbor	45 03 54N	087 07 27W	city/town	595
Baileys Harbor Yt.	45 03 55N	087 05 22W	locale	585
Bakerville	44 37 38N	090 13 05W	city/town	1318
Balancing Rock	46 56 48N	090 31 05W	pillar	

Place Name	Latitude	Longitude	Type	Elev
Baldwin	44 58 00N	092 22 27W	city/town	
Baldy Hill	45 26 14N	089 24 47W	summit	1831
Ballou	46 19 03N	090 35 04W	city/town	
Balls Bluff	43 52 51N	090 46 03W	cliff	1329
Balsam Lake	45 27 08N	092 27 16W	city/town	1155
Bancroft	44 18 35N	089 30 49W	city/town	
Bangor	43 53 35N	090 59 25W	city/town	
Banner	43 46 23N	088 12 34W	city/town	997
Bannerman	43 59 48N	089 13 30W	city/town	
Baraboo	43 28 16N	089 44 39W	city/town	894
Baraboo Airp.	43 31 19N	089 46 14W	airport	979
Bardwell	42 35 13N	088 45 02W	city/town	
Bark Point	46 53 06N	091 11 13W	cape	
Bark Point	46 53 15N	091 11 00W	city/town	
Barksdale	46 37 17N	090 55 55W	city/town	
Barnes	46 18 20N	091 29 16W	city/town	
Barneveld	43 00 56N	089 53 43W	city/town	
Barnum	43 13 08N	090 50 22W	city/town	680
Barre Mills	43 50 29N	091 06 50W	city/town	723
Barron	45 24 05N	091 50 56W	city/town	1115
Barron Municipal	45 24 27N	091 50 03W	airport	1113
Barronett	45 38 13N	091 59 34W	city/town	

Wisconsin GPS Companion

Place Name	Latitude	Longitude	Type	Elev
Barry Corner	44 31 05N	092 10 46W	city/town	
Barton	43 26 37N	088 10 50W	city/town	
Basco	42 54 43N	089 30 53W	city/town	895
Bass Lake C C	45 21 18N	089 11 11W	golf	1689
Bassett	42 32 26N	088 13 40W	city/town	
Basswood	43 15 45N	090 29 57W	city/town	732
Basswood Island	46 51 01N	090 44 46W	island	
Batavia	43 35 40N	088 03 03W	city/town	
Bateman	44 55 52N	091 16 04W	city/town	937
Bavaria	45 18 51N	089 21 50W	city/town	1613
Baxter	45 06 26N	091 56 45W	city/town	953
Bay City	44 35 08N	092 27 01W	city/town	
Bay Ridge Golf	45 11 12N	087 08 41W	golf	641
Bay Settlement	44 33 11N	087 53 26W	city/town	730
Bay View	44 37 58N	087 44 39W	city/town	730
Bayfield	46 48 39N	090 49 05W	city/town	
Bayside	43 10 50N	087 54 02W	city/town	
Beachs Corners	44 12 05N	091 14 14W	city/town	
Bear Creek	44 31 53N	088 43 35W	city/town	817
Bear Skull Rock	46 02 12N	090 20 06W	pillar	
Bear Valley	43 18 29N	090 11 42W	city/town	
Beartrap Falls	44 56 21N	088 40 27W	falls	

Wisconsin GPS Companion

Place Name	Latitude	Longitude	Type	Elev
Beaumont	42 44 32N	088 06 37W	city/town	801
Beaver	45 08 15N	088 01 04W	city/town	667
Beaver Brook	45 45 12N	091 50 20W	city/town	1302
Beaver Dam	43 27 28N	088 50 14W	city/town	879
Beaver Lookout	45 10 42N	088 06 34W	tower	
Beebe	46 24 26N	091 50 21W	city/town	
Beecher	45 35 18N	087 59 41W	city/town	977
Beecher Lake	45 34 09N	087 59 51W	city/town	
Beechwood	43 35 34N	088 07 13W	city/town	
Beetown	42 47 42N	090 53 07W	city/town	
Belcrest	42 32 29N	089 05 46W	city/town	
Beldenville	44 46 26N	092 30 27W	city/town	980
Belgium	43 29 59N	087 51 01W	city/town	736
Bell Center	43 17 30N	090 49 36W	city/town	
Bell Heights	44 16 50N	088 24 57W	city/town	
Belle Fountain	43 36 52N	089 15 48W	city/town	
Belle Plaine	44 42 55N	088 39 58W	city/town	
Belleville	42 51 35N	089 32 17W	city/town	870
Bellevue	44 26 39N	087 55 12W	city/town	759
Bellile Falls	45 45 18N	091 12 28W	falls	
Bellinger	45 04 31N	090 48 00W	city/town	1292
Bellwood	46 34 19N	091 38 15W	city/town	

Place Name	Latitude	Longitude	Type	Elev
Belmont	42 44 10N	090 20 03W	city/town	
Beloit	42 30 30N	089 01 54W	city/town	
Beloit Airport	42 29 54N	088 57 57W	airport	817
Beloit College	42 30 11N	089 01 51W	univ/coll	
Benderville	44 36 41N	087 51 18W	city/town	615
Bennett	46 26 55N	091 51 12W	city/town	
Benoit	46 30 07N	091 04 36W	city/town	900
Benson	45 43 02N	092 51 20W	city/town	877
Benton	42 34 11N	090 22 50W	city/town	932
Bergen	42 29 38N	088 51 55W	city/town	
Bergen Beach	43 51 38N	088 22 15W	city/town	
Berkshire Mine R.	46 18 04N	090 37 25W	ruins	
Berlin	43 58 05N	088 56 36W	city/town	764
Berlin Field	43 59 30N	088 57 45W	airport	773
Bethel	44 32 26N	090 05 23W	city/town	1236
Bethesda	42 59 16N	088 19 06W	city/town	839
Bevent	44 46 14N	089 23 22W	city/town	
Big Bend	42 52 53N	088 12 24W	city/town	
Big Eddy Falls	44 57 55N	088 38 07W	falls	
Big Falls	44 36 56N	089 00 58W	city/town	
Big Falls	44 49 15N	091 17 39W	falls	
Big Flats	44 06 43N	089 48 28W	city/town	1000

Place Name	Latitude	Longitude	Type	Elev
Big Foot Beach St.	42 34 11N	088 25 24W	park	
Big Fork Prairie	42 29 43N	088 35 58W	city/town	955
Big Manitou Falls	46 32 10N	092 07 16W	falls	
Big Rock 1	42 40 12N	089 01 46W	pillar	
Big Rock 2	43 02 49N	090 25 56W	pillar	
Big Smoky Falls	45 01 01N	088 38 12W	falls	
Big Spring	43 40 10N	089 38 37W	city/town	
Big T Dock & Ramp	45 55 36N	089 14 28W	locale	1620
Bigpatch	42 40 00N	090 28 34W	city/town	
Billings Park	46 43 06N	092 07 27W	city/town	
Billy Boy Dam	45 50 31N	091 24 25W	dam	1291
Binghamton	44 25 37N	088 28 26W	city/town	
Birch	46 32 18N	090 34 31W	city/town	
Birch Park Ski Ar.	45 03 12N	092 44 55W	ski area	
Birch Ridge Lookt.	46 31 23N	090 33 00W	tower	1102
Birchwood (1)	44 27 29N	087 34 17W	city/town	742
Birchwood (2)	45 39 59N	091 33 21W	city/town	1264
Birchwood Lookout	45 35 39N	091 31 50W	tower	1557
Birnamwood	44 56 00N	089 12 34W	city/town	1289
Biron	44 25 26N	089 46 49W	city/town	1026
Black Creek	44 28 39N	088 27 02W	city/town	790
Black Earth	43 08 14N	089 44 48W	city/town	818

Wisconsin GPS Companion

Place Name	Latitude	Longitude	Type	Elev
Black Hawk	43 16 09N	089 55 38W	city/town	775
Black River	46 33 44N	092 08 50W	city/town	
Black River Falls	44 15 02N	090 51 18W	airport	836
Black River Falls	44 17 41N	090 51 05W	city/town	796
Black Wolf	43 56 16N	088 31 25W	city/town	799
Black Wolf Point	43 55 39N	088 28 17W	city/town	
Blackbird Island	44 06 45N	088 27 42W	island	
Blackhawk C C	43 04 45N	089 27 21W	golf	
Blackhawk Island	42 53 54N	088 53 32W	city/town	781
Blackstone Mine	42 31 35N	090 15 27W	mine	
Blackwell	45 30 51N	088 36 45W	city/town	
Blackwell Junction	45 31 54N	088 39 15W	city/town	1523
Blaine	44 18 33N	089 18 56W	city/town	
Blair	44 17 40N	091 14 06W	city/town	859
Blair Airport	44 17 10N	091 13 35W	airport	865
Blanchardville	42 48 37N	089 51 43W	city/town	833
Blenker	44 36 48N	089 54 54W	city/town	
Bloom City	43 29 40N	090 27 53W	city/town	
Bloomer	45 06 01N	091 29 19W	city/town	1011
Bloomingdale	43 38 35N	090 46 39W	city/town	
Bloomington	42 53 07N	090 55 24W	city/town	
Bloomville	45 17 36N	089 31 39W	city/town	1434

Wisconsin GPS Companion

Place Name	Latitude	Longitude	Type	Elev
Blue Mound C C	43 04 03N	088 02 27W	golf	
Blue Mounds	43 01 03N	089 49 56W	city/town	1261
Blue Mounds State	43 01 41N	089 51 10W	park	
Blue River	43 11 18N	090 34 00W	city/town	676
Blueberry	46 34 49N	091 40 07W	city/town	1137
Bluff Siding	44 04 17N	091 37 04W	city/town	
Bluffview	43 22 16N	089 46 23W	city/town	869
Boardman	45 03 56N	092 35 59W	city/town	947
Boaz	43 19 53N	090 31 33W	city/town	740
Bolt	44 20 31N	087 42 19W	city/town	
Boltonville	43 31 38N	088 06 02W	city/town	869
Bonduel	44 44 25N	088 26 41W	city/town	
Bonita	45 07 11N	088 27 31W	city/town	875
Bonneval	45 39 02N	088 32 19W	city/town	1514
Boom Island	44 11 54N	088 49 07W	island	
Borea	46 35 08N	092 10 56W	city/town	754
Borth	44 05 28N	088 53 45W	city/town	
Boscobel	43 08 04N	090 42 19W	city/town	672
Boscobel Airport	43 09 30N	090 40 45W	airport	671
Bosstown	43 23 25N	090 36 36W	city/town	
Boulder Junction	46 06 48N	089 38 40W	city/town	
Boulder Jct Air.	46 08 15N	089 38 45W	airport	1665

Wisconsin GPS Companion

Place Name	Latitude	Longitude	Type	Elev
Boulder Lookout	46 06 23N	089 42 51W	tower	1735
Bowers	42 41 29N	088 26 40W	city/town	
Bowler	44 51 47N	088 58 55W	city/town	1080
Boyceville	45 02 37N	092 02 27W	city/town	948
Boyceville Municip	45 02 32N	092 01 45W	airport	960
Boyd	44 57 07N	091 02 05W	city/town	1105
Boydtown	43 06 38N	090 48 13W	city/town	
Boyer Bluff Light	45 25 12N	086 56 11W	lighthous	698
Boylston	46 35 51N	092 07 43W	city/town	707
Boylston Junction	46 36 51N	092 07 10W	city/town	690
Brackett	44 42 05N	091 21 03W	city/town	
Bradley (1)	44 48 04N	090 00 53W	city/town	1210
Bradley (2)	45 32 22N	089 45 18W	city/town	1458
Bradys Bluff	44 01 13N	091 28 59W	summit	1170
Branch	44 08 45N	087 45 40W	city/town	750
Branch River C C	44 08 14N	087 46 20W	golf	
Brandon	43 44 07N	088 46 52W	city/town	999
Branstad	45 44 15N	092 40 58W	city/town	
Brant	44 04 24N	088 12 13W	city/town	933
Brantwood	45 33 46N	090 06 54W	city/town	690
Breed	45 04 23N	088 25 27W	city/town	
Briarton	44 36 12N	088 25 35W	city/town	819

Wisconsin GPS Companion

Place Name	Latitude	Longitude	Type	Elev
Bridgeport	43 00 33N	091 03 28W	city/town	768
Briggsville	43 39 18N	089 35 07W	city/town	
Brighton	42 37 45N	088 05 59W	city/town	
Brighton Beach	44 12 12N	088 25 14W	city/town	
Brill	45 36 10N	091 40 19W	city/town	
Brillion	44 10 38N	088 03 51W	city/town	
Bristol	42 33 32N	088 02 57W	city/town	
British Hollow	42 42 21N	090 41 12W	city/town	
Brodhead	42 37 06N	089 22 34W	city/town	798
Brodhead Airport	42 35 30N	089 22 30W	airport	793
Brodtville	42 57 09N	091 02 47W	city/town	
Brokaw	45 01 38N	089 39 11W	city/town	
Brookfield	43 03 38N	088 06 23W	city/town	828
Brookfield -Capit.	43 05 15N	088 10 40W	airport	850
Brooklyn	42 51 13N	089 22 13W	city/town	
Brooks	43 49 31N	089 38 40W	city/town	957
Brookside (1)	43 51 40N	089 49 00W	city/town	
Brookside (2)	44 48 17N	087 59 52W	city/town	
Brothertown	43 58 05N	088 18 32W	city/town	
Brothertown Harbor	43 57 58N	088 19 14W	bay	
Brown Deer	43 09 48N	087 57 52W	city/town	679
Brownstone Falls	46 22 35N	090 38 27W	falls	

Wisconsin GPS Companion

Place Name	Latitude	Longitude	Type	Elev
Brownsville	43 36 59N	088 29 26W	city/town	
Browntown	42 34 40N	089 47 39W	city/town	
Brownville	45 01 53N	090 56 01W	city/town	1151
Bruce	45 27 25N	091 16 23W	city/town	1106
Bruce Mound	44 26 38N	090 47 32W	summit	1355
Bruemmerville	44 36 24N	087 28 12W	city/town	
Brule	46 33 11N	091 34 35W	city/town	
Brule Island Dam	45 56 52N	088 13 10W	dam	1205
Brule Lookout	46 27 56N	091 34 03W	tower	
Brunet Island St.	45 10 55N	091 09 21W	park	
Brunet Lookout	45 56 47N	090 46 32W	tower	
Brushville	44 10 12N	088 59 45W	city/town	
Brussels	44 44 10N	087 37 15W	city/town	754
Brussels Hill	44 45 06N	087 35 27W	summit	851
Bryant	45 12 29N	089 01 26W	city/town	1586
Brynwood C C	43 09 00N	087 59 19W	golf	
Buck Creek	43 25 14N	090 21 41W	city/town	
Buckbee	44 38 56N	088 50 06W	city/town	864
Buckeye Lookout	45 53 49N	088 14 43W	tower	1533
Buckhorn Corner	43 30 30N	088 48 21W	city/town	
Buckman	44 24 52N	087 47 07W	city/town	831
Bud	43 33 30N	090 59 16W	city/town	1220

Wisconsin GPS Companion

Place Name	Latitude	Longitude	Type	Elev
Budsin	43 55 10N	089 18 43W	city/town	822
Buena Park	42 47 34N	088 13 15W	city/town	
Buena Vista	43 03 56N	088 21 06W	city/town	
Buffalo City	44 13 50N	091 51 51W	city/town	
Buffalo Shore Est.	43 44 27N	089 28 15W	city/town	
Bull Falls	45 35 45N	088 07 16W	falls	
Bundy	45 29 59N	089 26 01W	city/town	
Bunker Hill	43 29 45N	090 15 25W	city/town	1257
Bunyan	45 28 34N	092 22 01W	city/town	1172
Burke	43 08 09N	089 16 34W	city/town	895
Burkett Mine	42 33 09N	090 25 21W	mine	
Burkhardt	45 01 18N	092 40 01W	city/town	
Burkhardt Station	45 00 52N	092 39 55W	city/town	927
Burlington	42 40 41N	088 16 34W	city/town	
Burlington Municip	42 41 24N	088 18 13W	airport	780
Burnett	43 30 17N	088 42 25W	city/town	875
Burns	43 56 42N	090 58 33W	city/town	
Burr Oak	44 03 26N	091 03 16W	city/town	
Burton	42 43 04N	090 49 02W	city/town	
Busseyville	42 53 55N	088 59 16W	city/town	796
Butler	43 06 21N	088 04 10W	city/town	
Butman Corners	44 04 41N	091 17 30W	city/town	751

Place Name	Latitude	Longitude	Type	Elev
Butte des Morts	44 05 58N	088 39 14W	city/town	
Butternut	46 00 47N	090 29 25W	city/town	1503
Byrds Creek	43 13 12N	090 32 54W	city/town	
Byron	43 39 08N	088 27 03W	city/town	

ℂ

Cable	46 12 29N	091 17 31W	city/town	1370
Cable Union Arpt	46 11 30N	091 15 00W	airport	1360
Cadott	44 56 53N	091 09 02W	city/town	979
Cainville	42 42 35N	089 15 07W	city/town	
Calamine	42 44 33N	090 09 43W	city/town	
Caldwell	42 50 07N	088 16 35W	city/town	845
Caledonia	42 48 28N	087 55 27W	city/town	730
Calhoun	43 00 48N	088 07 37W	city/town	
Callon	44 53 52N	089 30 17W	city/town	1238
Calumet & Hecla M.	42 32 31N	090 14 33W	mine	
Calumet Harbor	43 54 47N	088 19 56W	city/town	
Calumetville	43 56 10N	088 18 12W	city/town	802
Calvary	43 50 48N	088 14 38W	city/town	944
Calvert	43 45 15N	091 12 18W	city/town	
Cambria	43 32 32N	089 06 26W	city/town	868
Cambridge	43 00 13N	089 00 59W	city/town	

Wisconsin GPS Companion

Place Name	Latitude	Longitude	Type	Elev
Camelot C C	43 35 15N	088 24 20W	golf	
Cameron	45 24 31N	091 44 38W	city/town	1097
Camp Douglas	43 55 21N	090 16 17W	city/town	933
Camp Lake	42 32 05N	088 08 37W	city/town	
Camp Lake Airport	42 32 00N	088 09 30W	airport	755
Camp McCoy	44 01 28N	090 41 15W	locale	
Camp Ten Lookout	45 32 53N	089 30 35W	tower	
Camp Whitcomb	43 10 17N	088 19 37W	city/town	1014
Campbellsport	43 35 52N	088 16 44W	city/town	
Campia	45 32 15N	091 39 56W	city/town	
Cana Island Light	45 05 17N	087 02 52W	lighthous	585
Canton	45 25 41N	091 39 35W	city/town	1105
Carcajou	42 53 23N	088 57 43W	city/town	805
Cardinal Stritch C	43 08 25N	087 54 27W	univ/coll	
Carlsville	44 57 06N	087 20 12W	city/town	735
Carnegie	46 38 00N	092 11 33W	city/town	741
Carnot	44 42 18N	087 25 07W	city/town	678
Carol Beach	42 30 44N	087 48 33W	city/town	
Caroline	44 43 15N	088 53 29W	city/town	902
Carroll College	43 00 15N	088 13 40W	univ/coll	
Carrollville	42 52 48N	087 51 17W	city/town	
Carter (1)	45 23 27N	088 37 40W	city/town	

Wisconsin GPS Companion

Place Name	Latitude	Longitude	Type	Elev
Carter (2)	46 13 44N	090 07 49W	city/town	1626
Carthage College	42 37 27N	087 49 05W	univ/coll	
Cary Mine	46 26 11N	090 12 13W	mine	
Caryville	44 45 05N	091 40 28W	city/town	
Cascade	43 39 30N	088 00 25W	city/town	
Casco	44 33 28N	087 37 05W	city/town	
Casco Junction	44 31 50N	087 39 02W	city/town	726
Cashton	43 44 31N	090 46 45W	city/town	
Casimir	44 34 12N	089 36 27W	city/town	1095
Cassell	43 12 24N	089 52 30W	city/town	734
Cassville	42 42 52N	090 59 26W	city/town	621
Cassville Municip	42 42 15N	090 57 52W	airport	627
Castle Mound C C	44 02 01N	091 17 22W	golf	
Castle Rock	43 02 51N	090 31 53W	locale	
Castle Rock	44 09 09N	090 31 17W	summit	1157
Castle Rock 1	43 59 17N	090 51 44W	pillar	1335
Castle Rock 2	43 02 40N	090 31 13W	pillar	
Castle Rock 3	43 48 18N	089 53 57W	pillar	
Cataract	44 05 16N	090 50 32W	city/town	847
Cataract Lookout	44 01 25N	090 49 17W	tower	1365
Catawba	45 32 11N	090 31 47W	city/town	
Cathedral of Pines	45 17 35N	088 34 04W	locale	1340

Wisconsin GPS Companion

Place Name	Latitude	Longitude	Type	Elev
Cato	44 08 34N	087 51 40W	city/town	863
Cato Falls	44 05 37N	087 53 21W	falls	
Cave Point Park	44 55 49N	087 10 27W	park	612
Cave Rock	43 54 15N	090 42 03W	pillar	
Cavour	45 39 08N	088 37 46W	city/town	1479
Cayuga	46 14 40N	090 40 56W	city/town	
Cazenovia	43 31 23N	090 11 46W	city/town	951
Cecil	44 48 36N	088 27 08W	city/town	811
Cedar	46 30 26N	090 29 53W	city/town	
Cedar Creek	43 20 23N	088 13 22W	city/town	
Cedar Falls	44 56 09N	091 53 02W	city/town	
Cedar Grove	43 34 11N	087 49 24W	city/town	711
Cedar Island Est.	46 27 40N	091 37 11W	locale	
Cedar Lake	43 21 14N	088 17 33W	city/town	1078
Cedar Park	42 41 20N	088 13 50W	city/town	
Cedarburg	43 17 48N	087 59 15W	city/town	
Cedarville	45 27 13N	087 58 58W	city/town	830
Cedarville Lookout	45 27 20N	088 00 32W	tower	
Center House	43 47 26N	088 57 20W	locale	
Center Valley	44 24 08N	088 27 35W	city/town	
Centerville (1)	43 01 01N	090 25 42W	city/town	1115
Centerville (2)	44 04 12N	091 27 04W	city/town	737

Wisconsin GPS Companion

Place Name	Latitude	Longitude	Type	Elev
Centerville (3)	44 52 01N	092 24 48W	city/town	
Centuria	45 27 05N	092 33 14W	city/town	
Chaffey	46 23 54N	092 09 48W	city/town	1280
Chambers Island	45 10 56N	087 21 19W	island	
Chambers Island Lt	45 12 09N	087 21 53W	lighthous	
Champion	44 35 21N	087 47 39W	city/town	772
Chapel Ridge	44 31 54N	087 54 16W	city/town	
Chapultepee	44 13 23N	091 16 52W	city/town	1064
Charlesburg	43 58 11N	088 10 12W	city/town	
Charlie Bluff	42 50 25N	088 58 41W	city/town	784
Charme	43 10 04N	091 08 16W	city/town	
Chase	44 43 05N	088 09 24W	city/town	768
Chaseburg	43 39 28N	091 05 47W	city/town	728
Cheeseville	43 28 08N	088 04 50W	city/town	889
Chelsea	45 17 25N	090 18 26W	city/town	
Chenequa	43 06 42N	088 23 32W	city/town	
Chequamegon Bay	46 39 01N	090 50 49W	bay	602
Chequamegon Point	46 42 09N	090 45 14W	cape	
Chequamegon Pt Lt.	46 43 42N	090 48 33W	lighthous	
Cherneyville	44 25 44N	087 44 05W	city/town	
Cherneyville Hill	44 25 33N	087 43 50W	summit	1020
Cherokee	44 54 08N	090 13 04W	city/town	1282

Place Name	Latitude	Longitude	Type	Elev
Chetek	45 18 51N	091 39 03W	city/town	
Chicago	42 35 10N	087 49 29W	city/town	
Chicago Corners	44 27 32N	088 15 03W	city/town	
Chicago Junction	45 48 12N	091 53 11W	city/town	
Chicken Rock	43 54 06N	090 41 29W	pillar	
Chili	44 37 37N	090 21 23W	city/town	1235
Chilton	44 01 44N	088 09 46W	city/town	902
Chimney Rock 1	43 52 45N	090 42 36W	pillar	
Chimney Rock	44 28 09N	091 24 58W	locale	
Chimney Rock 2	45 06 20N	092 04 36W	pillar	
Chippewa Falls	44 56 13N	091 23 34W	city/town	
Chittamo	46 07 41N	091 42 59W	city/town	1108
Choate	45 22 41N	088 49 20W	city/town	
Christie	44 38 50N	090 35 47W	city/town	1176
Christie Mound	44 40 08N	090 35 52W	summit	1335
Christilla Heights	42 31 44N	089 04 22W	city/town	
Cicero	44 34 25N	088 23 14W	city/town	855
City Point	44 21 08N	090 19 17W	city/town	
City Rock	43 53 32N	090 42 24W	pillar	1360
Clam Falls	45 41 19N	092 17 36W	city/town	
Clam Lake	46 09 50N	090 54 08W	city/town	1421
Clark	45 01 45N	090 39 32W	city/town	

Place Name	Latitude	Longitude	Type	Elev
Clarks Mills	44 05 24N	087 51 51W	city/town	
Clarks Point	44 09 03N	088 42 37W	city/town	
Clarno	42 31 07N	089 38 52W	city/town	909
Clayton	45 19 53N	092 10 16W	city/town	
Clear Lake	45 15 07N	092 16 16W	city/town	1201
Clearwater Lake	45 51 13N	089 11 17W	city/town	
Cleghorn	44 41 01N	091 25 36W	city/town	
Cleveland	43 54 54N	087 44 50W	city/town	640
Clifford	45 33 19N	090 02 35W	city/town	
Clifton	43 52 45N	090 21 24W	city/town	
Clifton Highlands	44 47 21N	092 44 47W	golf	
Clifton Hollow G.	44 50 19N	092 44 40W	golf	
Clinton	42 33 28N	088 51 54W	city/town	949
Clintonville	44 37 14N	088 45 44W	city/town	825
Clintonville Munic	44 36 49N	088 43 52W	airport	822
Clover	44 02 17N	087 42 06W	city/town	671
Cloverdale	44 01 30N	090 10 44W	city/town	922
Cloverland	46 40 37N	091 40 44W	city/town	804
Clyde (1)	44 30 58N	087 34 58W	city/town	
Clyde (2)	43 07 10N	090 12 41W	city/town	734
Clyman	43 18 41N	088 43 12W	city/town	
Clyman Junction	43 19 31N	088 43 04W	city/town	893

Wisconsin GPS Companion

Place Name	Latitude	Longitude	Type	Elev
Cobb	42 58 03N	090 19 46W	city/town	1165
Cobb Town	44 22 32N	089 12 55W	city/town	
Cobban	45 06 11N	091 12 22W	city/town	
Cochrane	44 13 39N	091 50 06W	city/town	
Coddington	44 22 13N	089 32 53W	city/town	
Colburn	45 02 25N	091 02 41W	city/town	1128
Colby	44 54 36N	090 18 56W	city/town	1350
Cold Spring	42 53 27N	088 46 27W	city/town	
Cold Spring	45 57 11N	088 45 55W	spring	1595
Cold Springs	43 50 52N	091 12 45W	city/town	
Coleman	45 03 54N	088 02 03W	city/town	
Coles Peak	43 55 38N	090 37 51W	summit	1334
Colfax	44 59 51N	091 43 37W	city/town	
Colgate	43 11 35N	088 12 24W	city/town	
Collins	44 05 08N	087 58 58W	city/town	
Coloma	44 02 08N	089 31 17W	city/town	1044
Columbia	44 30 59N	090 43 11W	city/town	952
Columbus	43 20 17N	089 00 55W	city/town	871
Combined Locks	44 15 57N	088 18 51W	city/town	
Comfort	44 46 30N	092 02 07W	city/town	
Comfort, Point	43 56 01N	088 28 26W	city/town	
Commonwealth	45 54 49N	088 14 24W	city/town	

Wisconsin GPS Companion

Place Name	Latitude	Longitude	Type	Elev
Como	42 36 44N	088 28 56W	city/town	911
Comstock	45 28 40N	092 04 30W	city/town	
Concord	43 04 10N	088 35 55W	city/town	852
Concordia College	43 02 34N	087 57 14W	univ/coll	
Connorsville	45 08 10N	092 05 41W	city/town	996
Conover	46 03 17N	089 15 28W	city/town	1659
Conrath	45 23 10N	091 02 17W	city/town	1136
Consolidated Lkt.	45 39 34N	088 44 05W	tower	
Cooksville	42 50 07N	089 14 26W	city/town	877
Coomer	45 44 51N	092 15 25W	city/town	993
Coon Rock	43 09 03N	089 59 22W	city/town	724
Coon Rock	43 47 14N	090 06 57W	pillar	
Coon Valley	43 42 08N	091 00 47W	city/town	735
Cooper Hill	43 14 10N	090 33 10W	summit	980
Cooperstown	44 18 46N	087 46 28W	city/town	782
Coppens Corner	44 27 30N	087 47 08W	city/town	896
Copper Culture Mnd	44 53 17N	087 53 56W	park	
Copper Falls	46 22 23N	090 38 23W	falls	
Copper Falls State	46 22 28N	090 38 28W	park	
Coral City	44 22 46N	091 16 38W	city/town	834
Corinth	45 00 10N	090 08 21W	city/town	
Cormier	44 33 46N	088 04 41W	city/town	

Place Name	Latitude	Longitude	Type	Elev
Cornelia	42 41 22N	090 34 39W	city/town	
Cornell	45 10 02N	091 08 57W	city/town	
Cornell Municipal	45 09 56N	091 06 20W	airport	1154
Cornucopia	46 51 14N	091 06 06W	city/town	
Cottage Grove	43 04 34N	089 11 58W	city/town	888
Couderay	45 47 44N	091 18 24W	city/town	1265
Council Bay	44 03 27N	091 17 01W	city/town	
Council Grounds St	45 11 10N	089 44 58W	park	
Countryside Golf	44 15 27N	088 13 25W	golf	
County Line	44 59 25N	087 51 09W	city/town	626
Cowling Bay	44 06 45N	088 28 45W	bay	
Cozy Corner	46 09 53N	092 14 16W	city/town	1059
Cranberry Lake	45 38 25N	090 20 50W	city/town	
Cranberry Marsh	43 34 18N	088 05 08W	city/town	
Cranberry Rock Lkt	44 14 24N	089 59 42W	tower	
Crandon	45 34 19N	088 54 10W	city/town	
Cranmoor	44 18 53N	090 01 58W	city/town	982
Crawford Crossing	43 27 16N	089 43 45W	city/town	
Cream	44 18 58N	091 46 18W	city/town	775
Crescent	45 04 04N	091 08 48W	city/town	1138
Crescent Corner	45 34 12N	089 29 21W	city/town	1590
Crestview (1)	42 32 30N	089 01 52W	city/town	

Wisconsin GPS Companion

Place Name	Latitude	Longitude	Type	Elev
Crestview (2)	42 49 01N	087 48 36W	city/town	
Crivitz	45 13 57N	088 00 27W	city/town	681
Crivitz Municipal	45 12 52N	088 04 21W	airport	731
Cross Country Ski	46 05 32N	090 40 49W	ski area	1495
Cross Plains	43 06 12N	089 39 20W	city/town	859
Cuba City	42 36 20N	090 25 47W	city/town	1012
Cudahy	42 57 35N	087 51 41W	city/town	
Cullen	44 57 42N	087 51 11W	city/town	601
Cumberland	45 31 56N	092 01 09W	city/town	1251
Cumberland Municip	45 30 25N	091 58 50W	airport	1240
Curran	44 21 22N	087 44 44W	city/town	752
Curtiss	44 57 19N	090 26 04W	city/town	
Cushing	45 34 14N	092 39 03W	city/town	982
Cushing Memorial S	43 03 42N	088 24 55W	park	
Custer	44 30 38N	089 25 34W	city/town	1175
Cutler	44 01 33N	090 14 12W	city/town	925
Cutter	46 37 59N	091 57 31W	city/town	735
Cylon	45 07 20N	092 21 10W	city/town	1061
Czechville	44 11 14N	091 46 24W	city/town	682

𝔻

Dacada	43 32 36N	087 54 31W	city/town	839

Wisconsin GPS Companion

Place Name	Latitude	Longitude	Type	Elev
Dahl	44 59 25N	092 19 06W	city/town	1247
Dairyland	46 12 58N	092 09 19W	city/town	1122
Dairyland Lookout	46 14 39N	092 14 38W	tower	1216
Dakota	43 59 25N	089 21 23W	city/town	843
Dale	44 16 23N	088 40 42W	city/town	806
Daleyville	42 54 54N	089 48 53W	city/town	
Dallas	45 15 33N	091 48 53W	city/town	1054
Dalton	43 39 25N	089 12 23W	city/town	861
Danbury	46 00 24N	092 22 16W	city/town	
Danbury Lookout	45 57 50N	092 19 16W	tower	
Dancy	44 41 16N	089 42 47W	city/town	
Dane	43 15 02N	089 30 05W	city/town	
Danville	43 19 10N	088 57 20W	city/town	
Darboy	44 14 36N	088 19 26W	city/town	750
Darien	42 36 06N	088 42 27W	city/town	948
Darlington	42 40 59N	090 07 03W	city/town	817
Day Rock	43 07 58N	090 24 26W	pillar	1129
Daylight Hill	43 43 31N	090 12 07W	summit	1314
Dayton	42 49 37N	089 30 47W	city/town	
De Forest	43 14 52N	089 20 37W	city/town	949
De Pere	44 26 56N	088 03 37W	city/town	
De Soto	43 25 23N	091 11 56W	city/town	

Place Name	Latitude	Longitude	Type	Elev
Dead Creek Spring	46 03 54N	091 12 47W	spring	1390
Deadwood Point	43 50 27N	088 23 15W	cape	749
Deansville	43 10 54N	089 06 12W	city/town	884
Decker	43 28 14N	087 51 45W	city/town·	
Decker Corner	43 21 05N	088 02 42W	city/town	
Decorah Beach	43 55 22N	088 28 30W	city/town	
Dedham	46 32 32N	092 11 52W	city/town	797
Deepwood Golf	45 03 48N	091 48 10W	golf	
Deer Park	45 11 17N	092 23 07W	city/town	
Deer Shelter Rock	43 06 05N	090 08 05W	pillar	
Deerbrook	45 14 01N	089 09 20W	city/town	1530
Deerfield	43 03 07N	089 04 32W	city/town	
Dekorra	43 27 27N	089 28 03W	city/town	
Delafield	43 03 39N	088 24 13W	city/town	
Delavan	42 37 59N	088 38 37W	city/town	940
Delavan -Lk Lawn	42 37 55N	088 36 05W	airport	981
Delavan Lake	42 35 03N	088 37 57W	city/town	
Dells, The	43 38 30N	089 47 00W	area	
Dellwood (1)	43 33 48N	089 50 26W	city/town	855
Dellwood (2)	43 59 03N	089 56 19W	city/town	918
Delta	46 28 22N	091 16 12W	city/town	
Delta Lookout	46 25 56N	091 19 25W	tower	

Wisconsin GPS Companion

Place Name	Latitude	Longitude	Type	Elev
Denmark	44 20 52N	087 49 38W	city/town	
Denzer	43 20 39N	089 53 12W	city/town	816
Deronda	45 18 13N	092 25 41W	city/town	1069
Detroit Harbor	45 20 48N	086 55 26W	bay	
Detroit Harbor	45 21 24N	086 55 50W	city/town	
Detroit Island	45 19 00N	086 54 38W	island	
Devils Chimney	42 55 10N	089 37 52W	pillar	
Devils Corner	44 30 39N	092 08 06W	city/town	1134
Devils Head Golf	43 25 02N	089 37 07W	golf	
Devils Head Lodge	43 25 04N	089 37 38W	building	
Devils Island	47 04 14N	090 43 37W	island	
Devils Lake State	43 25 01N	089 42 13W	park	
Devils Monument	43 57 12N	090 18 50W	pillar	
Dewey	46 34 10N	092 14 41W	city/town	815
Dexter	43 50 33N	088 29 16W	city/town	
Dexterville	44 22 35N	090 06 38W	city/town	
Dheinsville	43 15 00N	088 08 34W	city/town	
Diamond Bluff	44 39 02N	092 37 44W	city/town	
Diamond Grove	42 47 33N	090 55 10W	city/town	
Dickeyville	42 37 38N	090 35 31W	city/town	957
Diefenbach Corners	43 21 13N	088 15 38W	city/town	1133
Dilly	43 38 32N	090 26 24W	city/town	

Wisconsin GPS Companion

Place Name	Latitude	Longitude	Type	Elev
Disco	44 15 44N	091 00 32W	city/town	969
Dobie (1)	45 33 07N	091 41 00W	city/town	1173
Dobie (2)	46 31 36N	091 48 16W	city/town	1139
Dodge	44 07 56N	091 33 07W	city/town	673
Dodgeville	42 57 37N	090 07 48W	city/town	1222
Doering	45 14 07N	089 27 29W	city/town	
Dominican College	42 47 52N	087 46 59W	univ/coll	
Donald	45 15 09N	090 53 49W	city/town	
Donald Rock	42 57 50N	089 40 30W	pillar	
Door Creek	43 01 51N	089 11 59W	city/town	946
Dorchester	45 00 11N	090 20 08W	city/town	
Dorns Faro Sprgs B	44 07 21N	088 19 09W	city/town	766
Dorns Twilight Bch	44 02 22N	088 19 14W	city/town	
Dorro Couche Lkt.	44 10 23N	089 47 02W	tower	1227
Doty Island	44 11 37N	088 26 51W	island	
Dotyville	43 45 08N	088 15 39W	city/town	1056
Dousman	43 00 51N	088 28 21W	city/town	
Dover	45 40 18N	090 11 15W	city/town	1660
Downing	45 02 47N	092 07 55W	city/town	983
Downsville	44 46 29N	091 55 55W	city/town	
Doylestown	43 25 40N	089 09 00W	city/town	
Draper	45 53 11N	090 49 51W	city/town	

Wisconsin GPS Companion

Place Name	Latitude	Longitude	Type	Elev
Dresser	45 21 22N	092 38 00W	city/town	
Druecker	43 26 24N	087 52 16W	city/town	772
Drummond	46 20 13N	091 15 28W	city/town	
Drummond -E.C. Lks	46 20 56N	091 29 53W	airport	1214
Drywood	45 02 54N	091 10 05W	city/town	
Duck Creek	44 33 43N	088 04 09W	city/town	
Ducknest Falls	45 02 50N	088 39 33W	falls	
Dudley	45 20 08N	089 27 55W	city/town	
Dunbar	45 39 03N	088 10 17W	city/town	
Dunbar Lookout	45 39 54N	088 06 34W	tower	1322
Dunbarton	42 33 42N	090 07 59W	city/town	992
Dundas	44 14 03N	088 11 54W	city/town	
Dundee	43 39 19N	088 09 52W	city/town	
Dunkirk	42 52 53N	089 12 35W	city/town	843
Dunnville	44 43 07N	091 54 19W	city/town	
Duplainville	43 04 26N	088 11 53W	city/town	856
Durand	44 37 35N	091 57 56W	city/town	721
Durham	42 51 59N	088 04 14W	city/town	796
Durwards Glen	43 26 19N	089 35 29W	city/town	
Dutchman Lookout	45 00 09N	088 52 17W	tower	1344
Duvall	44 39 40N	087 42 48W	city/town	
Duveneck	44 01 01N	087 42 42W	city/town	

Wisconsin GPS Companion

Place Name	Latitude	Longitude	Type	Elev
Dyckesville	44 38 36N	087 45 40W	city/town	

𝔼

Place Name	Latitude	Longitude	Type	Elev
Eadsville	45 00 35N	090 51 40W	city/town	1204
Eagle	42 52 46N	088 28 27W	city/town	949
Eagle Bluff Light	45 10 14N	087 13 30W	lighthous	585
Eagle Lake Manor	42 41 54N	088 08 06W	city/town	
Eagle Point	45 01 54N	091 23 45W	city/town	971
Eagle River	45 55 02N	089 14 39W	city/town	1647
Eagle River Union	45 55 55N	089 16 04W	airport	1642
Eagle Rock	43 25 43N	090 46 43W	pillar	
Eagles Peak	46 17 53N	090 37 56W	summit	1682
Eagleton	45 03 37N	091 23 21W	city/town	989
Eagleville	42 51 17N	088 25 58W	city/town	
Earl	45 54 38N	091 45 37W	city/town	
East Bristol	43 16 06N	089 09 09W	city/town	
East Delavan	42 36 32N	088 33 38W	city/town	
East Ellsworth	44 44 03N	092 28 04W	city/town	
East End	46 42 32N	092 03 33W	city/town	
East Farmington	45 15 11N	092 41 50W	city/town	1045
East Gate Basin	46 44 54N	092 05 39W	harbor	
East Krok	44 25 44N	087 36 08W	city/town	728

302

Wisconsin GPS Companion

Place Name	Latitude	Longitude	Type	Elev
East Pier Light	46 51 36N	091 05 40W	lighthous	599
East Troy	42 47 07N	088 24 18W	city/town	
East Troy Municip	42 47 50N	088 22 20W	airport	861
East Waupun	43 37 27N	088 41 26W	city/town	880
East Winona	44 02 52N	091 35 42W	city/town	
East.Cont'l Divide	45 56 23N	089 02 10W	locale	1699
Easter Rock	43 09 04N	090 43 15W	city/town	673
Eastman	43 09 59N	091 01 03W	city/town	1224
Easton	43 50 17N	089 48 24W	city/town	
Eau Claire	44 48 41N	091 29 54W	city/town	
Eau Claire County	44 51 55N	091 29 05W	airport	907
Eau Galle	44 41 32N	092 00 41W	city/town	
Ebenezer	43 08 18N	088 44 16W	city/town	854
Eckers Lakeland	44 00 12N	088 19 22W	city/town	
Eden	43 41 37N	088 21 39W	city/town	
Edgar	44 55 38N	089 57 48W	city/town	
Edgerton	42 50 07N	089 04 03W	city/town	
Edgerton -Jana	42 52 22N	089 04 32W	airport	842
Edgewater	45 44 32N	091 28 30W	city/town	
Edgewater Beach	44 37 25N	087 49 47W	city/town	
Edgewood	43 03 45N	088 18 06W	city/town	
Edgewood College	43 03 35N	089 25 20W	univ/coll	

Wisconsin GPS Companion

Place Name	Latitude	Longitude	Type	Elev
Edmund	42 58 03N	090 15 52W	city/town	1210
Edson	44 55 48N	091 02 05W	city/town	1082
Egg Harbor	45 02 47N	087 17 49W	city/town	
Egg Harbor	45 03 17N	087 17 27W	bay	
Eidsvold	44 57 51N	090 51 59W	city/town	
Eight Corners	44 28 04N	089 55 31W	city/town	
Eighteenfoot Falls	45 35 15N	088 07 47W	falls	
Eightfoot Falls	45 34 46N	088 08 03W	falls	
El Paso	44 46 11N	092 20 38W	city/town	
Eland	44 52 14N	089 12 54W	city/town	
Elcho	45 26 09N	089 11 00W	city/town	
Elderon	44 47 02N	089 14 41W	city/town	1199
Elderon Lookout	44 48 36N	089 19 13W	tower	
Eldorado	43 49 29N	088 37 18W	city/town	880
Eleva	44 34 33N	091 28 12W	city/town	
Elk Creek	44 25 37N	091 23 58W	city/town	
Elk Grove	42 40 18N	090 23 27W	city/town	
Elk Mound	44 52 23N	091 41 27W	city/town	
Elk Mound	44 52 44N	091 41 13W	summit	1200
Elkhart Lake	43 50 00N	088 01 04W	city/town	938
Elkhorn	42 40 22N	088 32 40W	city/town	1033
Elks Country Club	44 59 07N	091 20 58W	golf	

Place Name	Latitude	Longitude	Type	Elev
Ella	44 32 12N	092 03 00W	city/town	700
Ellenboro	42 47 00N	090 36 49W	city/town	
Ellis	44 34 31N	089 26 47W	city/town	1171
Ellison Bay	45 15 17N	087 04 17W	city/town	
Ellisville	44 27 28N	087 41 03W	city/town	
Ellsworth	44 43 56N	092 29 14W	city/town	1226
Elm Grove	43 02 35N	088 04 44W	city/town	746
Elm Tree Corners	44 33 17N	088 05 53W	city/town	636
Elmhurst	45 03 30N	089 11 03W	city/town	1476
Elmo	42 38 34N	090 26 09W	city/town	1014
Elmore	43 34 30N	088 18 10W	city/town	
Elmwood	44 46 52N	092 08 45W	city/town	
Elmwood Park	42 41 32N	087 49 20W	city/town	650
Elo	43 56 18N	088 42 22W	city/town	863
Elroy	43 44 27N	090 16 20W	city/town	959
Elroy Municipal	43 42 23N	090 15 27W	airport	944
Elton	45 10 06N	088 53 11W	city/town	
Elvers	43 04 11N	089 47 52W	city/town	809
Embarrass	44 39 56N	088 42 26W	city/town	
Emerald	45 04 59N	092 15 29W	city/town	1155
Emerald Grove	42 39 22N	088 52 50W	city/town	903
Endeavor	43 42 57N	089 27 58W	city/town	785

Wisconsin GPS Companion

Place Name	Latitude	Longitude	Type	Elev
Engine Rock	43 56 21N	090 36 45W	pillar	
Enterprise	45 29 50N	089 15 30W	city/town	1626
Ephraim	45 09 23N	087 10 05W	city/town	
Ephraim Yacht Harb	45 09 37N	087 10 16W	locale	598
Ephraim-Fish Creek	45 08 09N	087 11 28W	airport	773
Epsey Mound	44 31 40N	090 19 29W	summit	1209
Erdman	43 47 24N	087 45 34W	city/town	676
Erin Corner	45 04 46N	092 26 13W	city/town	1071
Esdaile	44 37 15N	092 26 19W	city/town	
Esofea	43 37 52N	090 57 47W	city/town	
Etna	42 33 57N	090 19 39W	city/town	768
Ettrick	44 10 06N	091 16 08W	city/town	771
Eureka	44 00 16N	088 50 30W	city/town	
Eureka Center	45 30 46N	092 39 05W	city/town	1062
Euren	44 37 06N	087 36 08W	city/town	751
Evansville	42 46 49N	089 17 57W	city/town	897
Evergreen Falls	45 03 46N	088 41 08W	falls	
Excelsior	43 15 06N	090 37 41W	city/town	
Exeland	45 40 05N	091 14 38W	city/town	
Exeter	42 47 26N	089 34 59W	city/town	
Exile	44 41 57N	092 09 56W	city/town	1172
Eysnogel Hill	43 31 02N	090 27 08W	summit	1148

Place Name	Latitude	Longitude	Type	Elev
F				
Face Rock	43 54 11N	090 40 18W	pillar	1318
Fahrney Point	43 56 45N	088 29 10W	cape	
Fair Play	42 32 08N	090 33 38W	city/town	885
Fairburn	43 58 16N	089 02 14W	city/town	774
Fairchild	44 36 01N	090 57 46W	city/town	1080
Fairfield	42 37 59N	088 46 35W	city/town	
Fairview	43 22 05N	090 56 34W	city/town	
Fairview Beach	44 05 06N	088 30 41W	city/town	
Fairwater	43 44 38N	088 52 01W	city/town	
Fall Creek	44 45 49N	091 16 37W	city/town	
Fall Hall Glen	44 11 47N	090 50 23W	city/town	
Fall River	43 23 04N	089 02 42W	city/town	858
Falls City	44 47 50N	091 46 07W	city/town	
Falun	45 46 19N	092 31 39W	city/town	
Fancher	44 27 47N	089 23 08W	city/town	1140
Fargo	43 27 21N	090 57 26W	city/town	
Farmersville	43 33 30N	088 31 53W	city/town	
Farmington	43 04 34N	088 40 19W	city/town	
Fayette	42 45 15N	090 02 07W	city/town	
Fence	45 44 40N	088 25 27W	city/town	1548

Place Name	Latitude	Longitude	Type	Elev
Fennimore	42 59 01N	090 39 19W	city/town	
Fenwood	44 51 58N	090 00 55W	city/town	
Fern	45 50 10N	088 23 09W	city/town	
Ferryville	43 21 02N	091 06 07W	city/town	634
Fifield	45 52 47N	090 25 19W	city/town	1451
Fifth Street Yacht	42 43 50N	087 47 29W	marina	590
Fillmore	43 29 54N	088 03 38W	city/town	848
Finley	44 12 48N	090 08 10W	city/town	952
First Capitol St.	42 46 06N	090 21 45W	park	
Fish Creek	45 07 40N	087 14 49W	city/town	583
Fishermans Landing	46 05 31N	090 10 12W	city/town	
Fisherville	44 14 26N	087 40 48W	city/town	651
Fisk	43 57 21N	088 40 41W	city/town	838
Fitchburg	42 57 39N	089 28 11W	city/town	
Fitzgerald	43 58 56N	088 37 16W	city/town	836
Five Corners (1)	44 48 40N	089 02 33W	city/town	
Five Corners (2)	44 24 53N	088 22 27W	city/town	818
Five Points (1)	42 48 52N	090 48 27W	city/town	
Five Points (2)	43 00 58N	089 31 59W	city/town	1008
Five Points (3)	43 19 11N	090 35 43W	city/town	
Fivemile Bluff	44 29 14N	092 03 40W	cliff	1180
Fivemile Lookout	46 06 26N	092 01 41W	tower	1092

Wisconsin GPS Companion

Place Name	Latitude	Longitude	Type	Elev
Flag Rock	43 42 47N	090 34 37W	pillar	
Flambeau Lkt 1	45 16 50N	091 12 58W	tower	
Flambeau Lkt 2	45 59 45N	089 50 42W	tower	
Flannagan Lookout	46 35 08N	091 56 09W	tower	
Flintville	44 38 48N	088 07 04W	city/town	
Flora Fountain	42 49 55N	090 50 23W	city/town	
Florence	45 55 20N	088 15 06W	city/town	1296
Florence Lookout	45 57 44N	088 29 57W	tower	
Folsom	43 26 18N	090 50 18W	city/town	1170
Fond du Lac	43 46 23N	088 26 49W	city/town	760
Fond Du Lac County	43 46 15N	088 29 18W	airport	807
Fontana	42 33 05N	088 34 30W	city/town	
Fontenoy	44 22 16N	087 47 10W	city/town	
Footville	42 40 15N	089 12 32W	city/town	
Forest	45 08 12N	092 15 34W	city/town	
Forest Glen Beach	43 49 01N	088 55 56W	city/town	
Forest Junction	44 12 45N	088 08 39W	city/town	828
Forest Rapids	45 55 05N	090 21 35W	rapids	1570
Forestville	44 41 24N	087 28 45W	city/town	633
Forks Dam	45 58 56N	088 56 31W	dam	1690
Fort Atkinson	42 55 44N	088 50 13W	city/town	790
Fort Atkinson Muni	42 57 47N	088 49 03W	airport	800

Wisconsin GPS Companion

Place Name	Latitude	Longitude	Type	Elev
Fort Wales Rock	43 33 53N	090 39 42W	pillar	
Forward	42 53 49N	089 45 22W	city/town	
Foster	44 38 35N	091 18 42W	city/town	
Foster Junction	46 18 49N	090 42 14W	city/town	
Fountain City	44 07 55N	091 43 07W	city/town	663
Fountain Valley	44 05 27N	088 59 10W	city/town	
Four Corners (1)	45 10 06N	088 50 41W	city/town	1375
Four Corners (2)	45 40 17N	092 35 26W	city/town	
Four Corners (3)	44 04 30N	090 54 49W	city/town	875
Fox Creek	45 29 01N	092 20 43W	city/town	
Fox Hills Country	44 13 56N	087 39 03W	golf	
Fox Lake	43 33 56N	088 54 23W	city/town	920
Fox Lake Junction	43 31 52N	088 54 09W	city/town	880
Fox Point	43 09 27N	087 54 06W	city/town	672
Fox River	42 33 25N	088 11 04W	city/town	
Fox Valley Golf	44 21 16N	088 16 41W	golf	
Foxboro	46 29 55N	092 17 16W	city/town	
Foxhollow	42 30 50N	088 54 28W	city/town	
Francis Creek	44 11 58N	087 43 17W	city/town	
Franklin (1)	43 50 08N	087 54 05W	city/town	
Franklin (2)	44 12 46N	091 07 25W	city/town	
Franklin (3)	42 53 19N	088 02 18W	city/town	

Place Name	Latitude			Longitude			Type	Elev
Franksville	42	45	36N	087	54	48W	city/town	735
Franksville -Gunt.	42	49	25N	088	05	40W	airport	790
Frazer Corners	44	40	28N	088	21	44W	city/town	957
Frederic	45	39	33N	092	28	01W	city/town	
Fredonia	43	28	14N	087	57	02W	city/town	
Freedom	44	23	11N	088	17	19W	city/town	
Freeman	45	20	59N	088	49	44W	city/town	
Freeman Falls	44	50	39N	088	44	14W	falls	
Freistadt	43	14	10N	088	02	33W	city/town	
Fremont	44	15	35N	088	51	53W	city/town	
Frenchville	44	08	59N	091	19	22W	city/town	
Friendship	43	58	14N	089	49	00W	city/town	
Friendship -Adams	43	57	45N	089	47	26W	airport	977
Friesland	43	35	19N	089	04	02W	city/town	
Fromm Lookout	45	07	51N	089	55	14W	tower	
Frostville	45	00	19N	088	19	30W	city/town	870
Fulton	42	48	29N	089	07	39W	city/town	796
Fussville	43	09	06N	088	04	40W	city/town	

G

Place Name	Latitude			Longitude			Type	Elev
Gagen	45	39	45N	089	08	17W	city/town	
Galesville	44	04	54N	091	20	56W	city/town	712

Place Name	Latitude	Longitude	Type	Elev
Galloway	44 42 46N	089 15 51W	city/town	1174
Garden Village	42 33 17N	089 01 45W	city/town	
Garfield	44 33 43N	089 17 39W	city/town	1147
Garnet	43 56 08N	088 15 46W	city/town	943
Gays Mills	43 19 03N	090 50 41W	city/town	
Genesee	42 57 10N	088 21 32W	city/town	896
Genesee Depot	42 58 00N	088 22 16W	city/town	909
Genoa	43 34 36N	091 13 27W	city/town	
Genoa City	42 29 54N	088 19 41W	city/town	
Genoa City -Vinc.	42 31 06N	088 18 01W	airport	880
Georgetown	42 37 27N	090 29 04W	city/town	996
Germania (1)	46 26 18N	090 13 28W	city/town	
Germania (2)	43 53 26N	089 15 25W	city/town	
Germantown (1)	43 13 43N	088 06 37W	city/town	863
Germantown (2)	43 31 33N	090 13 17W	city/town	
Giant Pine Grove	45 45 41N	088 59 08W	locale	1689
Gibbsville	43 39 08N	087 49 36W	city/town	722
Gibraltar Rock	43 20 35N	089 36 01W	pillar	1247
Gile	46 25 42N	090 13 30W	city/town	
Gillett	44 53 24N	088 18 26W	city/town	812
Gillingham	43 25 35N	090 26 42W	city/town	802
Gills Landing	44 18 10N	088 53 00W	city/town	

Wisconsin GPS Companion

Place Name	Latitude	Longitude	Type	Elev
Gills Rock	45 17 24N	087 01 18W	city/town	
Gilman	45 10 00N	090 48 27W	city/town	
Gilman Lookout	45 02 45N	090 53 20W	tower	
Gilmanton	44 28 15N	091 40 33W	city/town	786
Gilmer Falls	44 50 33N	088 43 21W	falls	
Girard Junction Lk	45 29 49N	088 12 12W	city/town	
Gladstone Beach	43 51 56N	088 22 08W	city/town	
Glandon	45 05 20N	089 25 37W	city/town	1461
Gleason	45 18 32N	089 29 47W	city/town	
Gleason Bay	43 54 47N	088 47 51W	bay	
Glen Flora	45 29 45N	090 53 38W	city/town	1276
Glen Haven	42 49 35N	091 04 15W	city/town	
Glen Oak	43 44 39N	089 21 41W	city/town	
Glenbeulah	43 47 50N	088 02 50W	city/town	
Glendale (1)	43 46 56N	090 20 44W	city/town	1073
Glendale (2)	43 08 07N	087 56 08W	city/town	
Glenmore	44 23 09N	087 55 38W	city/town	924
Glenn Oaks Beach	42 52 53N	088 59 55W	city/town	
Glenway Golf	43 03 31N	089 26 12W	golf	
Glenwood City	45 03 31N	092 10 20W	city/town	
Glidden	46 08 06N	090 34 42W	city/town	
Globe	44 39 16N	090 39 33W	city/town	1127

Wisconsin GPS Companion

Place Name	Latitude	Longitude	Type	Elev
Glover	44 54 47N	092 40 49W	city/town	981
Goerkes Corner	43 02 11N	088 09 58W	city/town	
Goldenthal	43 14 10N	088 09 43W	city/town	
Goll	45 16 49N	087 45 03W	city/town	692
Goodman	45 37 53N	088 21 12W	city/town	
Goodman Lookout	45 36 58N	088 19 48W	tower	
Goodnow	45 41 50N	089 40 18W	city/town	
Goodrich	45 08 58N	090 05 08W	city/town	1424
Gooseville	43 35 14N	088 01 16W	city/town	
Gordon	46 14 49N	091 47 54W	city/town	1035
Gotham	43 13 24N	090 17 29W	city/town	
Government Island	44 20 30N	089 08 44W	island	
Governor Dodge St	43 00 52N	090 06 36W	park	
Grafton	43 19 11N	087 57 12W	city/town	
Graham Corners	43 43 57N	088 10 30W	city/town	
Grand Crossing	43 50 43N	091 13 46W	city/town	
Grand Marsh	43 53 13N	089 42 22W	city/town	1010
Grand View	46 22 03N	091 06 29W	city/town	
Granddad Bluff	43 48 51N	091 12 32W	cliff	
Grandfather Falls	45 18 14N	089 47 25W	falls	
Grandmother Dam	45 22 00N	089 43 42W	dam	1427
Granite Heights	45 03 36N	089 38 22W	city/town	1215

Wisconsin GPS Companion

Place Name	Latitude	Longitude	Type	Elev
Granton	44 35 20N	090 27 40W	city/town	
Grantsburg	45 46 35N	092 40 57W	city/town	
Grantsburg Municip	45 47 55N	092 39 51W	airport	926
Granville	43 10 39N	088 02 38W	city/town	737
Gratiot	42 34 44N	090 01 21W	city/town	
Gravesville	44 02 11N	088 08 46W	city/town	
Graytown	45 11 58N	092 07 37W	city/town	
Great Div. Snowmob	46 12 03N	090 49 04W	trail	1510
Great Lks Dragway	42 39 45N	088 01 57W	locale	
Green Bay	44 31 09N	088 01 11W	city/town	594
Green Bay -Anton.	44 34 48N	088 03 23W	airport	587
Green Bay -Straub.	44 29 06N	088 07 43W	airport	695
Green Lake	43 50 39N	088 57 36W	city/town	828
Green Lake Terrace	43 46 57N	089 03 52W	city/town	
Green Valley	44 47 44N	088 16 13W	city/town	813
Greenbush	43 46 36N	088 05 02W	city/town	972
Greendale	42 56 26N	087 59 45W	city/town	
Greenfield	42 57 41N	088 00 45W	city/town	
Greenfield Fire	44 02 43N	090 37 40W	tower	1450
Greenleaf	44 18 48N	088 05 46W	city/town	
Greenville	44 18 01N	088 32 11W	city/town	
Greenwood (1)	44 46 13N	090 35 57W	city/town	1168

Wisconsin GPS Companion

Place Name	Latitude	Longitude	Type	Elev
Greenwood (2)	43 33 50N	090 25 06W	city/town	933
Gregorville	44 37 06N	087 32 47W	city/town	716
Grellton	43 08 06N	088 47 18W	city/town	
Gresham	44 51 11N	088 47 17W	city/town	930
Grimms	44 08 46N	087 54 06W	city/town	843
Gull Island Light	46 54 25N	090 26 31W	lighthous	604
Gurney	46 28 22N	090 30 29W	city/town	1094
Guthrie	42 55 30N	088 12 00W	city/town	970

ℍ

Place Name	Latitude	Longitude	Type	Elev
Haevers Corners	44 30 46N	087 58 40W	city/town	
Hager City	44 36 06N	092 32 17W	city/town	
Halder	44 47 57N	089 52 14W	city/town	
Hale	44 27 57N	091 15 44W	city/town	
Hale Corner	44 39 42N	091 16 35W	city/town	
Hales Corners	42 56 15N	088 02 55W	city/town	
Hall Rapids	46 31 28N	091 36 27W	rapids	982
Hallie	44 52 58N	091 25 57W	city/town	
Hamburg	45 05 26N	089 53 06W	city/town	1468
Hamilton (1)	43 17 03N	087 58 18W	city/town	
Hamilton (2)	43 41 51N	088 27 31W	city/town	
Hamilton Falls	44 47 47N	090 57 44W	falls	

316

Place Name	Latitude	Longitude	Type	Elev
Hamilton Fls Snowm	44 46 04N	090 58 30W	trail	
Hammond	44 58 44N	092 26 08W	city/town	
Hammond Hill	44 45 26N	092 10 18W	summit	1124
Hamples Corner	44 21 06N	088 28 31W	city/town	794
Hancock	44 08 01N	089 31 23W	city/town	1089
Hanerville	42 52 32N	089 09 41W	city/town	877
Hannibal	45 15 09N	090 47 20W	city/town	1267
Hanover	42 38 19N	089 09 43W	city/town	
Harbor Lite Yacht	42 43 57N	087 47 13W	marina	585
Harbor Springs	44 03 51N	088 41 08W	city/town	
Harmony	45 05 57N	087 49 11W	city/town	
Harmony Grove	43 22 18N	089 33 03W	city/town	782
Harmony Lookout	45 34 38N	090 33 41W	tower	1645
Harrison (1)	45 28 39N	089 30 24W	city/town	596
Harrison (2)	44 08 03N	088 17 30W	city/town	989
Harrisville	43 52 40N	089 24 19W	city/town	820
Harshaw	45 39 56N	089 39 19W	city/town	
Hartford	43 19 04N	088 22 44W	city/town	
Hartford Municipal	43 20 58N	088 23 28W	airport	1070
Hartland	43 06 18N	088 20 31W	city/town	
Hartman Creek St.	44 19 24N	089 13 02W	park	
Hatch Landing	45 20 19N	091 19 29W	city/town	

Wisconsin GPS Companion

Place Name	Latitude	Longitude	Type	Elev
Hatchville	44 51 29N	092 08 10W	city/town	1202
Hatfield	44 24 53N	090 43 50W	city/town	886
Hatley	44 53 15N	089 20 19W	city/town	
Hauer	45 48 10N	091 27 36W	city/town	
Haugen	45 36 32N	091 46 29W	city/town	1229
Haven	43 50 54N	087 45 12W	city/town	650
Hawkins	45 30 54N	090 43 11W	city/town	1369
Hawkins Corner	44 31 05N	092 09 55W	city/town	
Hawthorne	46 30 11N	091 51 38W	city/town	
Hay Creek	44 37 20N	091 04 29W	city/town	
Hay Stack Corner	45 38 55N	090 52 32W	city/town	
Hayen	43 50 57N	087 44 45W	city/town	635
Hayes	44 59 59N	088 25 22W	city/town	
Hayton	44 01 21N	088 06 58W	city/town	833
Hayward	46 00 47N	091 29 04W	city/town	1198
Hayward Municipal	46 01 31N	091 26 38W	airport	1215
Hazel Green	42 31 58N	090 26 04W	city/town	
Hazelhurst	45 48 28N	089 43 30W	city/town	1612
Heafford Junction	45 32 50N	089 42 55W	city/town	1491
Heart Prairie	42 45 56N	088 38 31W	city/town	
Heath Mills	42 59 02N	088 34 27W	city/town	
Hebron	42 55 31N	088 41 33W	city/town	840

Place Name	Latitude	Longitude	Type	Elev
Heffron	44 14 37N	089 18 22W	city/town	
Hegg	44 12 33N	091 11 32W	city/town	
Helena	43 10 17N	090 01 20W	city/town	
Helenville	43 00 43N	088 41 58W	city/town	845
Hematite	45 54 33N	088 12 34W	city/town	1326
Hemlock	44 49 25N	090 36 42W	city/town	
Henry Ford Dam	45 48 28N	088 07 31W	dam	1072
Henrysville	44 26 38N	087 47 09W	city/town	897
Herbster	46 49 57N	091 15 39W	city/town	614
Herman Center	43 24 50N	088 27 36W	city/town	1118
Hermans Landing	45 56 03N	091 11 15W	city/town	
Hermit Island	46 53 12N	090 41 06W	island	
Herold	44 18 20N	091 50 31W	city/town	1274
Herrington	43 46 42N	091 13 09W	city/town	
Hersey	44 57 46N	092 12 41W	city/town	
Hertel	45 48 31N	092 10 30W	city/town	
Hewitt	44 38 42N	090 06 00W	city/town	
Hickory Corners	45 00 17N	088 15 14W	city/town	837
Hickory Grove (1)	43 06 22N	090 35 57W	city/town	1106
Hickory Grove (2)	44 17 54N	087 52 03W	city/town	870
Hickory Hills C C	44 03 20N	088 11 33W	golf	
High Bridge	46 23 20N	090 44 10W	city/town	

Wisconsin GPS Companion

Place Name	Latitude	Longitude	Type	Elev
High Cliff	44 09 08N	088 18 00W	cliff	
High Cliff C C	44 10 20N	088 17 22W	golf	
High Cliff State	44 09 33N	088 17 22W	park	
Highland	43 02 48N	090 22 47W	city/town	
Highland Beach	44 11 12N	088 18 57W	city/town	
Highland Lookout	46 20 29N	091 34 59W	tower	
Highland Park	43 53 39N	088 20 51W	city/town	
Highland Shore	44 03 03N	088 37 50W	city/town	
Hilbert	44 08 25N	088 09 50W	city/town	839
Hilbert Junction	44 08 46N	088 09 34W	city/town	829
Hilburn	42 47 18N	088 21 18W	city/town	819
Hiles	45 42 14N	088 58 38W	city/town	
Hiles Lookout	45 42 23N	088 56 38W	tower	1804
Hill Point	43 25 28N	090 06 45W	city/town	1000
Hillcrest	46 30 11N	091 53 53W	city/town	1171
Hillcrest C C	44 47 38N	091 26 49W	golf	
Hillmoor C C	42 35 47N	088 25 21W	golf	880
Hillsboro	43 39 08N	090 20 38W	city/town	1001
Hillsdale	45 18 57N	091 51 34W	city/town	
Hillside	42 56 05N	089 02 34W	city/town	
Hilly Haven Golf	44 20 55N	088 02 49W	golf	
Hines	46 32 35N	091 54 29W	city/town	

Wisconsin GPS Companion

Place Name	Latitude	Longitude	Type	Elev
Hingham	43 38 20N	087 54 51W	city/town	
Hintz	44 54 57N	088 24 36W	city/town	
Hixton	44 23 09N	091 00 51W	city/town	
Hochheim	43 27 25N	088 28 09W	city/town	1164
Hofa Park	44 37 49N	088 19 58W	city/town	904
Hogarty	45 01 47N	089 18 20W	city/town	1408
Holcombe	45 13 28N	091 07 02W	city/town	
Holiday Heights	43 51 55N	091 12 03W	city/town	
Holiday Hills	42 32 53N	089 01 49W	city/town	
Holland	44 14 55N	088 10 18W	city/town	769
Hollandale	42 52 33N	089 56 10W	city/town	862
Hollister	45 14 53N	088 47 29W	city/town	1378
Holmen	43 57 48N	091 15 22W	city/town	718
Holt	44 43 03N	089 19 31W	city/town	1200
Holts Landing	46 00 36N	090 22 17W	city/town	
Holy Cross	43 28 13N	087 53 44W	city/town	782
Homestead Mine	42 44 28N	090 27 28W	mine	
Honey Creek	42 44 54N	088 18 28W	city/town	783
Honey Lake	42 42 57N	088 18 21W	city/town	
Hoopers Mill	43 05 48N	088 52 53W	city/town	
Hope	43 03 06N	089 14 46W	city/town	870
Hopokoekau Beach	43 49 20N	088 23 16W	city/town	

Wisconsin GPS Companion

Place Name	Latitude	Longitude	Type	Elev
Horicon	43 27 05N	088 37 52W	city/town	884
Horns Corner	43 20 29N	088 01 26W	city/town	
Horse Creek	45 15 27N	092 34 59W	city/town	
Horseman	45 29 40N	091 33 34W	city/town	1549
Horseshoe Falls	45 32 53N	088 08 12W	falls	
Horseshoe Reef	44 01 38N	088 30 24W	bar	
Hortonville	44 20 05N	088 38 17W	city/town	794
Houghton Rock	43 55 47N	089 48 15W	pillar	
Houlton	45 03 38N	092 47 28W	city/town	
Howard (1)	44 57 02N	091 32 15W	city/town	
Howard (2)	44 32 37N	088 05 17W	city/town	
Howards Bay	46 44 33N	092 05 56W	harbor	
Howards Grove	43 50 02N	087 49 12W	city/town	
Hoyt	46 24 38N	090 17 58W	city/town	
Hub City	43 28 16N	090 21 22W	city/town	
Hubbleton	43 11 37N	088 52 55W	city/town	794
Hubertus	43 14 12N	088 13 16W	city/town	1014
Hudson	44 58 29N	092 45 24W	city/town	
Hudson C C	44 57 51N	092 43 41W	golf	
Hughey	45 14 55N	090 42 00W	city/town	1278
Huilsburg	43 23 03N	088 27 38W	city/town	1119
Hulls Crossing	43 48 57N	088 06 41W	city/town	939

Wisconsin GPS Companion

Place Name	Latitude	Longitude	Type	Elev
Humbird	44 31 45N	090 53 21W	city/town	
Humboldt	44 30 07N	087 49 33W	city/town	
Hunting	44 41 00N	088 58 17W	city/town	
Huntington	45 11 31N	092 33 31W	city/town	
Hurley	46 26 59N	090 11 11W	city/town	
Huron	45 07 10N	090 58 57W	city/town	
Hurricane	42 47 05N	090 46 16W	city/town	986
Husher	42 48 51N	087 53 40W	city/town	
Hustisford	43 20 46N	088 36 02W	city/town	867
Hustler	43 52 48N	090 16 18W	city/town	929
Hyde	43 04 24N	089 58 54W	city/town	784

I

Place Name	Latitude	Longitude	Type	Elev
Idlewild	44 53 18N	087 25 38W	city/town	
Iduna	44 11 55N	091 18 45W	city/town	
Imalone	45 33 08N	091 13 38W	city/town	
Independence	44 21 25N	091 25 13W	city/town	782
Indian Creek	45 42 19N	092 12 26W	city/town	
Indian Lookout	45 48 32N	089 17 57W	tower	1716
Indian Shores	44 08 21N	088 42 06W	city/town	
Indianford	42 48 15N	089 05 28W	city/town	
Ingle	43 37 28N	089 07 40W	city/town	930

Place Name	Latitude	Longitude	Type	Elev
Ingram	45 30 18N	090 48 44W	city/town	
Inlet	42 37 38N	088 35 06W	city/town	
Ino	46 31 51N	091 10 43W	city/town	977
Institute	44 53 36N	087 17 13W	city/town	
Interstate State	45 23 21N	092 39 26W	park	
Interwald	45 13 26N	090 06 59W	city/town	
Iola	44 30 29N	089 07 50W	city/town	955
Iola -Central Cty	44 30 20N	089 01 30W	airport	876
Ipswich	42 42 27N	090 24 37W	city/town	1048
Irma	45 21 05N	089 39 59W	city/town	
Iron Belt	46 24 02N	090 19 27W	city/town	
Iron Ridge	43 23 59N	088 31 57W	city/town	
Iron River	46 33 52N	091 24 29W	city/town	
Iron River -Bayfld	46 34 35N	091 27 30W	airport	1143
Iron River Lookout	46 34 35N	091 19 25W	tower	
Ironton	43 32 46N	090 08 28W	city/town	954
Irvine	44 55 32N	091 25 11W	city/town	
Irvington	44 50 10N	091 57 16W	city/town	771
Isaar	44 34 18N	088 17 04W	city/town	
Island Beach	44 05 28N	088 30 10W	city/town	
Island Lake	45 19 08N	091 22 08W	city/town	
Island Park	44 01 22N	088 48 08W	city/town	

Wisconsin GPS Companion

Place Name	Latitude	Longitude	Type	Elev
Island Park	44 05 19N	088 28 54W	island	759
Itasca	46 40 29N	092 00 23W	city/town	647
Ithaca	43 20 27N	090 16 54W	city/town	734
Ives	42 46 12N	087 48 19W	city/town	649
Ives Grove	42 43 45N	087 57 58W	city/town	
Ixonia	43 08 38N	088 35 50W	city/town	870

J

Place Name	Latitude	Longitude	Type	Elev
Jack Pine Lookout	45 40 48N	089 47 53W	summit	1585
Jackson	43 19 26N	088 10 00W	city/town	896
Jackson Cty Iron M	44 17 35N	090 43 30W	mine	
Jacksonport	44 58 43N	087 11 08W	city/town	593
James Island	44 12 00N	088 27 50W	island	
Jamestown	42 35 16N	090 32 54W	city/town	923
Janesville	42 40 58N	089 01 07W	city/town	858
Janesville -Rock	42 37 10N	089 02 24W	airport	808
Jefferson	43 00 20N	088 48 26W	city/town	
Jefferson Junction	43 02 13N	088 47 24W	city/town	811
Jeffris	45 30 07N	089 25 49W	city/town	
Jenkinsville	42 38 05N	090 22 11W	city/town	
Jennings	45 30 27N	089 04 19W	city/town	
Jericho (1)	42 52 42N	088 25 22W	city/town	902

Wisconsin GPS Companion

Place Name	Latitude	Longitude	Type	Elev
Jericho (2)	43 58 12N	088 15 59W	city/town	
Jersey City	45 29 07N	089 44 40W	city/town	
Jewett	45 07 03N	092 26 10W	city/town	
Jim Falls	45 02 43N	091 16 22W	city/town	956
Jimtown	43 21 12N	090 38 18W	city/town	
Joel	45 21 38N	092 14 04W	city/town	
Johannesburg	45 09 55N	092 35 38W	city/town	
Johnsburg	43 52 38N	088 17 23W	city/town	
Johnson Creek	43 04 34N	088 46 27W	city/town	812
Johnsonville	43 47 54N	087 54 34W	city/town	
Johnstown	42 42 00N	088 48 22W	city/town	
Johnstown Center	42 41 45N	088 50 22W	city/town	
Jonesdale	42 53 56N	090 00 48W	city/town	
Jordan	44 34 29N	089 30 18W	city/town	
Juda	42 35 23N	089 30 21W	city/town	823
Jump River	45 21 11N	090 48 04W	city/town	
Jump River Fire	45 20 39N	090 36 17W	tower	1394
Junction	45 00 35N	090 54 08W	city/town	1162
Junction City	44 35 27N	089 46 02W	city/town	
Juneau	43 24 20N	088 42 18W	city/town	
Juneau -Dodge Cty	43 25 36N	088 42 03W	airport	936
Jute Lake Lookout	46 09 35N	089 29 35W	tower	1785

Place Name	Latitude	Longitude	Type	Elev
𝕂				
Kalinke	45 01 50N	089 23 49W	city/town	1468
Kansasville	42 40 57N	088 06 37W	city/town	823
Kaukauna	44 16 41N	088 16 19W	city/town	
Keene	44 22 01N	089 28 27W	city/town	
Keenville	44 03 41N	088 31 31W	city/town	
Kegonsa	42 58 38N	089 12 01W	city/town	
Kekoskee	43 31 48N	088 33 39W	city/town	909
Kellner	44 21 32N	089 43 29W	city/town	
Kellners Corners	44 07 34N	087 42 34W	city/town	
Kellnersville	44 13 33N	087 48 08W	city/town	827
Kelly (1)	43 58 00N	090 05 59W	city/town	903
Kelly (2)	44 54 48N	089 33 45W	city/town	1219
Kelly Brook	44 57 37N	088 12 57W	city/town	804
Kempster	45 17 23N	089 10 00W	city/town	1628
Kendall	43 47 32N	090 22 06W	city/town	1021
Kennan	45 31 53N	090 35 13W	city/town	
Kennedy	45 54 37N	090 39 26W	city/town	1476
Kennedy Lookout	45 55 07N	090 37 10W	tower	1617
Kenosha	42 35 05N	087 49 16W	city/town	
Kenosha C C	42 39 27N	087 49 46W	golf	

Wisconsin GPS Companion

Place Name	Latitude	Longitude	Type	Elev
Kenosha Light	42 35 19N	087 48 30W	lighthous	582
Kenosha Regional	42 35 43N	087 55 38W	airport	743
Kenosha Yacht Club	42 35 24N	087 48 58W	locale	600
Kent Lookout Tower	45 14 38N	088 53 04W	tower	1903
Keowns	43 22 07N	088 08 10W	city/town	908
Keshena	44 53 02N	088 38 01W	city/town	829
Keshena Falls	44 53 36N	088 39 14W	city/town	
Kewaskum	43 31 15N	088 13 44W	city/town	
Kewaunee	44 27 30N	087 30 11W	city/town	
Kewaunee Nucl Powr	44 20 32N	087 32 10W	plant	
Keyeser	43 17 48N	089 15 21W	city/town	
Keysville	43 20 23N	090 13 07W	city/town	
Kiel	43 54 45N	088 02 08W	city/town	933
Kieler	42 34 53N	090 36 09W	city/town	853
Kilbournville	42 48 28N	087 57 08W	city/town	
Kimball	46 28 55N	090 18 21W	city/town	
Kimball Crk Snowmo	45 48 56N	089 02 03W	locale	1682
Kimberly	44 16 20N	088 20 20W	city/town	734
Kimberly Park	44 11 07N	088 26 33W	park	
Kinepoway Lookout	44 59 55N	088 40 27W	tower	
King	44 20 15N	089 08 30W	city/town	898
Kingsbridge	44 12 41N	087 40 52W	city/town	622

Place Name	Latitude	Longitude	Type	Elev
Kingston	43 41 44N	089 07 39W	city/town	
Kinnickinnic State	44 49 55N	092 44 35W	park	
Kirby	44 05 26N	090 32 21W	city/town	
Kirchhayn	43 17 39N	088 05 42W	city/town	885
Klevenville	43 01 28N	089 40 04W	city/town	
Klondike (1)	45 04 05N	088 09 35W	city/town	792
Klondike (2)	42 35 24N	088 07 10W	city/town	838
Kloten	44 02 07N	088 15 57W	city/town	1024
Knapp	44 57 19N	092 04 31W	city/town	
Knapp Mound	44 13 25N	090 30 14W	summit	1347
Kneeland	42 49 36N	088 00 30W	city/town	
Knellsville	43 24 51N	087 52 15W	city/town	
Knowles	43 34 22N	088 30 15W	city/town	
Knowlton	44 42 59N	089 40 57W	city/town	
Kodan	44 39 40N	087 29 52W	city/town	656
Koehler Ford	44 44 18N	090 53 41W	city/town	
Koepenick	45 20 12N	089 10 00W	city/town	1692
Kohler (1)	43 29 47N	088 01 24W	city/town	
Kohler (2)	43 44 21N	087 46 54W	city/town	676
Kohlsville	43 28 16N	088 19 19W	city/town	
Kolb	44 25 22N	087 57 47W	city/town	829
Kolberg	44 43 09N	087 32 56W	city/town	705

Wisconsin GPS Companion

Place Name	Latitude	Longitude	Type	Elev
Kolpack Lookout	44 55 18N	089 00 24W	tower	
Konsin Beach	44 00 52N	088 19 15W	locale	
Koro	43 58 05N	088 50 40W	city/town	833
Koshkonong	42 50 46N	088 55 09W	city/town	820
Koshkonong Manor	42 54 05N	088 57 36W	city/town	
Koshkonong Mounds	42 52 27N	088 54 43W	city/town	
Krakow	44 45 42N	088 15 05W	city/town	
Kremlin	45 39 03N	087 50 41W	city/town	
Kroghville	43 03 42N	089 00 29W	city/town	
Krok	44 25 44N	087 37 59W	city/town	728
Krueger Hill	43 58 39N	091 02 12W	summit	1343
Kunesh	44 36 56N	088 11 25W	city/town	754

𝕃

Place Name	Latitude	Longitude	Type	Elev
La Belle Lookout	45 02 40N	088 35 01W	tower	
La Crosse	43 48 05N	091 14 22W	city/town	669
La Crosse Municip	43 52 45N	091 15 22W	airport	654
La Farge	43 34 29N	090 38 25W	city/town	797
La Grange	42 47 59N	088 36 08W	city/town	945
La Pointe	46 46 45N	090 47 11W	city/town	
La Pointe Light	46 46 43N	090 47 22W	lighthous	604
La Valle	43 34 56N	090 07 41W	city/town	896

Wisconsin GPS Companion

Place Name	Latitude	Longitude	Type	Elev
Lac du Flambeau	45 58 11N	089 53 31W	city/town	
Lac La Belle	43 08 39N	088 31 50W	city/town	
Ladd Creek Lookout	45 35 59N	090 47 49W	tower	1497
Ladoga	43 43 12N	088 40 27W	city/town	907
Ladysmith	45 27 47N	091 06 14W	city/town	1144
Ladysmith -Rusk C	45 29 57N	091 00 06W	airport	1238
Ladysmith Lookout	45 27 54N	091 08 02W	tower	
Lake Beulah	42 49 17N	088 19 15W	city/town	832
Lake Church	43 29 59N	087 49 14W	city/town	
Lake Como	42 35 25N	088 30 07W	city/town	882
Lake Delton	43 36 04N	089 47 37W	city/town	894
Lake Five	43 11 33N	088 16 15W	city/town	
Lake Geneva	42 35 30N	088 26 00W	city/town	889
Lake Hallie	44 52 33N	091 26 26W	city/town	
Lake Lawn	42 37 33N	088 35 39W	city/town	
Lake Mills	43 04 53N	088 54 42W	city/town	
Lake Nebagamon	46 30 54N	091 41 59W	city/town	
Lake Owen	46 16 05N	091 15 30W	city/town	1400
Lake Tomahawk	45 48 51N	089 35 37W	city/town	1632
Lake Tomahawk Lkt.	45 50 07N	089 36 40W	tower	
Lake Windsor	43 12 15N	089 20 52W	city/town	
Lake Wisconsin C C	43 18 47N	089 43 08W	golf	

Wisconsin GPS Companion

Place Name	Latitude	Longitude	Type	Elev
Lake Wissota	44 55 35N	091 18 03W	city/town	926
Lake Wissota State	44 58 19N	091 17 54W	park	
Lakefield	43 17 42N	087 55 32W	city/town	702
Lakeland Hills C C	43 18 55N	089 32 21W	golf	
Lakeport	44 26 55N	092 10 47W	city/town	
Lakeside Park	43 47 49N	088 26 41W	park	
Lakeview	42 58 31N	089 22 19W	city/town	
Lakewood	45 18 03N	088 31 24W	city/town	1271
Lakewood C C	45 17 40N	088 29 40W	airport	1229
Lamar	45 25 33N	092 34 12W	city/town	1218
Lamartine	43 44 00N	088 34 07W	city/town	
Lambeau Field	44 30 05N	088 03 44W	other	
Lamont	42 42 17N	089 59 07W	city/town	1071
Lampson	45 58 59N	091 48 58W	city/town	1137
Lampson Lookout	45 59 07N	091 48 03W	tower	
Lancaster	42 50 51N	090 42 38W	city/town	
Lancaster Junction	42 58 37N	090 36 50W	city/town	1178
Lancaster Municip	42 46 50N	090 40 51W	airport	1008
Land O Lakes Arpt	46 09 15N	089 12 42W	airport	1706
Landstad	44 39 38N	088 26 37W	city/town	838
Laneville	44 37 23N	091 57 24W	city/town	830
Laney	44 38 40N	088 17 21W	city/town	

Place Name	Latitude	Longitude	Type	Elev
Langes Corners	44 23 08N	087 51 39W	city/town	
Langlade	45 11 24N	088 43 56W	city/town	1257
Lannon	43 08 46N	088 09 58W	city/town	
Laona	45 33 53N	088 40 26W	city/town	1580
Laona Junction	45 39 22N	088 41 38W	city/town	1544
Laona Lookout	45 35 25N	088 38 16W	tower	
Lapham Junction	44 17 51N	090 28 41W	city/town	994
Lark	44 18 51N	087 56 59W	city/town	925
Larrabee	44 16 05N	087 42 54W	city/town	741
Larsen	44 11 30N	088 37 26W	city/town	
LaRue	43 26 10N	089 53 22W	city/town	
Lasleys Point	44 07 37N	088 42 23W	city/town	765
Lauderdale	42 45 55N	088 33 20W	city/town	
Laudolff Beach	43 52 40N	088 21 26W	city/town	
Lawrence	43 53 01N	089 32 40W	city/town	
Lawrence College	44 15 39N	088 23 51W	univ/coll	
Lawrence Lookout	45 27 53N	090 51 43W	tower	
Lawton	44 46 33N	092 24 56W	city/town	1096
Lead Mine	42 34 15N	090 20 43W	city/town	
Lebanon	43 15 19N	088 37 36W	city/town	
Ledge Rapids, The	45 59 58N	090 21 51W	rapids	1480
Leeds	43 18 38N	089 19 28W	city/town	1059

Wisconsin GPS Companion

Place Name	Latitude	Longitude	Type	Elev
Leeman	44 34 27N	088 33 23W	city/town	796
Lehigh	45 26 28N	091 33 03W	city/town	
Leipsig	43 24 03N	088 51 51W	city/town	
Leland	43 20 08N	089 56 51W	city/town	
Leland Natural Br.	43 20 54N	089 55 52W	arch	
Lemington	45 45 33N	091 21 10W	city/town	
Lemonweir	43 47 04N	090 01 01W	city/town	
Lena	44 57 04N	088 02 48W	city/town	714
Lenawee Lookout	46 40 38N	091 15 19W	tower	
Lennox	45 30 43N	089 04 18W	city/town	
Lenroot Landing	46 06 23N	091 27 18W	city/town	
Lenroot Ledges	46 37 51N	091 35 50W	rapids	837
Leo V Mine	42 39 02N	090 21 58W	mine	
Leon	43 52 39N	090 49 48W	city/town	783
Leonards	46 10 11N	091 19 16W	city/town	
Leonards Point	44 02 48N	088 37 21W	city/town	763
Leopolis	44 46 05N	088 50 41W	city/town	943
LeRoy	43 34 25N	088 33 38W	city/town	1052
Leslie	42 46 14N	090 21 59W	city/town	
Levis	44 32 19N	091 06 16W	city/town	1047
Lewis	45 42 39N	092 24 08W	city/town	1058
Lewiston	43 34 50N	089 38 08W	city/town	809

Place Name	Latitude	Longitude	Type	Elev
Leyden	42 43 51N	089 07 44W	city/town	
Liberty	43 30 59N	090 44 02W	city/town	771
Liberty Corners	42 31 15N	088 05 57W	city/town	841
Liberty Mine	42 38 58N	090 22 17W	mine	
Liberty Mound	43 00 56N	089 09 45W	summit	1075
Liberty Pole	43 29 24N	090 54 31W	city/town	
Lighthouse Reef	44 11 43N	088 25 11W	bar	
Lighthouse Rock 1	43 33 35N	090 02 02W	pillar	
Lighthouse Rock 2	43 54 33N	089 46 42W	pillar	
Lily	45 18 25N	088 51 14W	city/town	
Lima	44 38 02N	091 52 22W	city/town	877
Lima Center	42 47 22N	088 49 38W	city/town	
Lime Ridge	43 28 04N	090 09 17W	city/town	
Lincoln	44 37 05N	087 38 31W	city/town	842
Lind	45 44 24N	092 47 43W	city/town	
Linden	42 55 04N	090 16 24W	city/town	1101
Linden Beach	43 51 15N	088 22 24W	city/town	
Lindina	43 45 36N	090 08 49W	city/town	
Lindsey	44 33 21N	090 18 00W	city/town	1155
Linton	42 32 04N	088 30 06W	city/town	
Little Black	45 06 22N	090 19 46W	city/town	
Little Bull Fls 1	44 28 10N	090 07 45W	falls	

Wisconsin GPS Companion

Place Name	Latitude	Longitude	Type	Elev
Little Bull Fls 2	44 50 28N	088 43 07W	falls	
Little Chicago	45 02 50N	089 50 39W	city/town	1275
Little Chute	44 16 48N	088 19 06W	city/town	728
Little Chute Isl.	44 16 29N	088 17 49W	island	
Little Eau Claire	44 47 11N	089 26 51W	city/town	1233
Little Falls	45 16 26N	092 25 07W	city/town	
Little Falls 1	44 36 27N	089 00 05W	falls	
Little Falls 2	45 38 36N	090 44 18W	falls	
Little Grant Mine	42 41 24N	090 32 53W	mine	
Little Hope	44 19 06N	089 06 32W	city/town	
Little Manitou Fls	46 31 20N	092 07 33W	falls	
Little Norway	43 01 37N	089 47 22W	city/town	
Little Point	43 55 08N	088 28 07W	city/town	
Little Prairie	42 50 20N	088 32 20W	city/town	956
Little Quinnesec F	45 46 25N	087 59 21W	falls	
Little Rapids	44 22 49N	088 07 38W	city/town	
Little River C C	45 02 24N	087 37 37W	golf	
Little Rose	44 48 03N	090 10 13W	city/town	
Little Sturgeon	44 50 20N	087 33 45W	city/town	
Little Sturgeon B.	44 50 31N	087 32 47W	bay	
Little Suamico	44 43 03N	088 00 33W	city/town	
Little Waupon	44 35 38N	089 23 40W	city/town	

Place Name	Latitude	Longitude	Type	Elev
Livingston	42 54 00N	090 25 51W	city/town	1164
Lizard Mound State	43 27 48N	088 08 21W	park	
Loddes Mill	43 15 50N	089 48 02W	city/town	743
Lodi	43 18 50N	089 31 35W	city/town	833
Loganville	43 26 25N	090 02 09W	city/town	
Lohrville	44 02 14N	089 07 01W	city/town	802
Lombard	44 57 33N	090 44 21W	city/town	1232
Lomira	43 35 29N	088 26 37W	city/town	1039
London	43 02 52N	089 00 46W	city/town	
Lone Rock	43 52 56N	089 51 57W	pillar	
Lone Rock (1)	43 11 00N	090 11 52W	city/town	706
Lone Rock (2)	43 56 38N	090 12 50W	city/town	903
Lone Willow Island	44 08 03N	088 46 12W	island	
Long Lake	45 50 34N	088 40 04W	city/town	
Long Mile Lookout	46 17 59N	091 03 38W	tower	1605
Long Nebagamon Rap	46 31 52N	091 36 17W	rapids	971
Long Slide Falls	45 41 00N	087 56 00W	falls	
Long Tail Point	44 35 12N	087 58 49W	cape	589
Longwood	44 53 13N	090 35 53W	city/town	1245
Lookout	44 27 30N	091 34 45W	city/town	874
Loomis	45 11 33N	087 53 57W	city/town	
Loreta	43 20 44N	090 06 26W	city/town	1171

Wisconsin GPS Companion

Place Name	Latitude	Longitude	Type	Elev
Loretta	45 53 08N	090 51 10W	city/town	1443
Lost Creek Golf	44 52 03N	087 26 44W	golf	615
Lost Dauphin State	44 23 21N	088 07 26W	park	
Lost Lake	43 27 32N	088 59 20W	city/town	929
Louis Corners	43 56 07N	087 57 07W	city/town	912
Louisburg	42 34 45N	090 33 20W	city/town	896
Lowell	43 20 25N	088 49 01W	city/town	
Lowville	43 22 57N	089 19 37W	city/town	967
Loyal	44 44 13N	090 29 45W	city/town	
Loyd	43 25 23N	090 14 34W	city/town	813
Lublin	45 04 38N	090 43 28W	city/town	1289
Lucius Woods State	46 20 58N	091 49 05W	park	
Luck	45 34 34N	092 28 57W	city/town	
Luco	43 48 05N	088 25 09W	city/town	
Ludington	44 49 45N	091 07 38W	city/town	
Lufkin	44 45 04N	091 36 38W	city/town	778
Lugerville	45 46 32N	090 30 22W	city/town	
Lugerville Lookout	45 46 50N	090 31 16W	tower	1484
Lund	44 32 23N	092 12 21W	city/town	1139
Lunds	44 41 58N	088 32 43W	city/town	
Luxemburg	44 32 19N	087 42 14W	city/town	
Lykens	45 25 28N	092 28 08W	city/town	1092

Place Name	Latitude	Longitude	Type	Elev
Lymantown	45 56 03N	090 27 09W	city/town	
Lyndhurst	44 50 31N	088 48 45W	city/town	950
Lyndon Dale	43 34 38N	088 55 50W	city/town	
Lyndon Station	43 42 44N	089 53 58W	city/town	
Lynn	44 34 57N	090 24 35W	city/town	
Lynxville	43 14 47N	091 03 22W	city/town	638
Lyons	42 39 04N	088 21 30W	city/town	802

M

Place Name	Latitude	Longitude	Type	Elev
Mackville	44 20 37N	088 24 54W	city/town	815
Madeline Island	46 47 20N	090 45 30W	airport	679
Madeline Island	46 48 59N	090 41 20W	island	
Madge	45 44 45N	091 43 25W	city/town	1296
Madison	43 04 23N	089 24 04W	city/town	863
Madison -Blackhawk	43 06 15N	089 11 05W	airport	905
Madison -Dane Co.	43 08 22N	089 20 14W	airport	862
Madsen	44 04 52N	087 49 19W	city/town	813
Magnolia	42 42 57N	089 17 19W	city/town	943
Maiden Rock	43 05 31N	090 16 40W	pillar	
Maiden Rock	44 30 04N	092 17 21W	summit	725
Maiden Rock	44 33 39N	092 18 34W	city/town	689
Malone	43 51 37N	088 16 53W	city/town	

Wisconsin GPS Companion

Place Name	Latitude	Longitude	Type	Elev
Malvern	45 36 28N	089 17 06W	city/town	
Manawa	44 27 52N	088 55 11W	city/town	
Manchester	43 41 26N	089 02 54W	city/town	
Manitawoc Yacht Cl	44 06 17N	087 38 53W	locale	588
Manitou Island	46 58 00N	090 39 20W	island	
Manitowish	46 07 59N	090 00 48W	city/town	1592
Manitowish Waters	46 08 06N	089 53 15W	city/town	
Manitowoc	44 05 19N	087 39 27W	city/town	606
Manitowoc County	44 07 43N	087 40 49W	airport	651
Manitowoc Harbor	44 05 31N	087 38 50W	harbor	580
Manitowoc Rapids	44 05 57N	087 42 03W	city/town	
Mann	44 42 01N	090 13 01W	city/town	
Mansur Bay	44 08 47N	088 27 21W	bay	
Maple	46 35 23N	091 43 14W	city/town	1099
Maple Birch Golf	45 29 29N	089 40 51W	golf	
Maple Bluff	43 07 06N	089 22 46W	city/town	
Maple Grove (1)	44 11 22N	087 55 25W	city/town	904
Maple Grove (2)	43 44 58N	091 11 55W	city/town	652
Maple Grove C C	43 52 27N	091 06 42W	golf	
Maple Grove Golf	45 22 06N	086 55 43W	golf	632
Maple Heights	43 57 23N	088 19 03W	city/town	
Maple Hill	45 01 01N	090 59 01W	city/town	1160

Place Name	Latitude	Longitude	Type	Elev
Mapleton	43 10 44N	088 27 36W	city/town	
Maplewood	44 44 51N	087 28 45W	city/town	703
Marathon	44 55 45N	089 50 25W	city/town	1245
Marathon Lookout	44 53 16N	089 45 39W	tower	
Marblehead	43 42 15N	088 23 01W	city/town	1000
Marcellon	43 34 07N	089 15 56W	city/town	820
March Rapids	44 50 40N	090 09 00W	city/town	1283
Marcy	43 06 27N	088 07 58W	city/town	894
Marengo	46 25 21N	090 49 00W	city/town	
Marengo Lookout	46 22 04N	090 48 27W	tower	
Marian College	43 46 40N	088 25 54W	univ/coll	
Maribel	44 16 35N	087 48 26W	city/town	861
Maribel Caves Cty	44 16 53N	087 45 49W	park	
Marinette	45 06 00N	087 37 50W	city/town	598
Marion	44 40 15N	088 53 21W	city/town	850
Markesan	43 42 26N	088 59 24W	city/town	847
Markton	45 07 19N	088 39 53W	city/town	
Marlands	45 57 22N	089 48 58W	city/town	
Marquette	43 44 51N	089 08 19W	city/town	
Marquette Univers.	43 02 15N	087 55 47W	univ/coll	
Marshall	43 10 06N	089 04 00W	city/town	
Marshfield	44 40 08N	090 10 18W	city/town	

Wisconsin GPS Companion

Place Name	Latitude	Longitude	Type	Elev
Marshfield Municip	44 38 12N	090 11 21W	airport	1277
Marshland	44 04 25N	091 33 17W	city/town	
Martell	44 49 47N	092 23 51W	city/town	
Martinsville	43 10 49N	089 35 24W	city/town	
Martintown	42 30 30N	089 48 02W	city/town	
Marxville	43 11 28N	089 39 35W	city/town	
Mary Hill	43 47 12N	088 21 58W	summit	1092
Marytown	43 54 49N	088 12 08W	city/town	965
Mason	46 26 07N	091 03 35W	city/town	
Mather	44 08 34N	090 18 31W	city/town	
Mattoon	45 00 15N	089 02 31W	city/town	
Mauston	43 47 50N	090 04 38W	city/town	883
Maxville	44 31 54N	092 00 31W	city/town	776
Maxwelton C C	45 02 36N	087 08 09W	golf	653
May Corner	45 02 57N	087 51 02W	city/town	
May Ledges	46 38 16N	091 35 47W	rapids	800
Mayfield	43 19 45N	088 11 48W	city/town	
Mayville	43 29 39N	088 32 41W	city/town	
Mazomanie	43 10 36N	089 47 41W	city/town	
McAllister	45 19 38N	087 43 16W	city/town	
McCartney	42 41 00N	090 51 03W	city/town	
McCaslin Lookout	45 22 51N	088 27 10W	tower	1609

Wisconsin GPS Companion

Place Name	Latitude	Longitude	Type	Elev
McCaslin Mountain	45 23 43N	088 23 36W	summit	1632
McCord	45 33 19N	089 53 58W	city/town	1475
McFarland	43 00 45N	089 17 23W	city/town	
McKenzie Lake Lkt.	45 55 35N	092 00 48W	tower	
McKinley	45 34 17N	092 10 35W	city/town	
McKinley Marina	43 03 07N	087 53 10W	locale	
McNaughton	45 43 57N	089 32 39W	city/town	
Meadow Valley	44 12 55N	090 13 16W	city/town	
Meadowbrook C C	42 44 45N	087 49 49W	golf	
Mecan	43 47 46N	089 12 54W	city/town	817
Medary	43 51 19N	091 12 34W	city/town	
Medford	45 08 19N	090 20 24W	city/town	
Medford -Taylor C.	45 05 58N	090 18 20W	airport	1463
Medina	44 16 22N	088 38 16W	city/town	
Medina Junction	44 13 59N	088 37 18W	city/town	760
Meehan	44 26 10N	089 38 50W	city/town	1065
Meeker	43 13 18N	088 10 23W	city/town	
Meekers Grove	42 38 44N	090 22 10W	city/town	976
Meeme	43 55 14N	087 49 53W	city/town	777
Meggers	43 58 20N	088 02 29W	city/town	893
Mellen	46 19 32N	090 39 39W	city/town	
Mellen C C	46 21 33N	090 40 44W	golf	

Place Name	Latitude	Longitude	Type	Elev
Mellen Lookout	46 18 03N	090 37 02W	tower	1872
Melnik	44 14 51N	087 44 45W	city/town	801
Melrose	44 07 50N	090 59 53W	city/town	
Melrose Park	44 01 58N	088 35 41W	city/town	
Melvina	43 48 20N	090 46 19W	city/town	
Menasha	44 12 08N	088 26 47W	city/town	
Menasha Lock	44 12 10N	088 27 38W	dam	
Menchalville	44 13 33N	087 52 56W	city/town	862
Menomonee Falls	43 10 44N	088 07 02W	city/town	
Menomonee Fls Aero	43 06 30N	088 09 35W	airport	850
Menomonie	44 52 32N	091 55 09W	city/town	877
Menomonie -Score	44 53 42N	091 52 12W	airport	865
Menomonie C C	44 53 41N	091 56 36W	golf	
Menomonie Junction	44 54 51N	091 55 29W	city/town	
Mequon	43 14 11N	087 59 04W	city/town	
Mercer	46 09 56N	090 03 45W	city/town	
Meridean	44 44 17N	091 47 27W	city/town	
Merrick State Park	44 09 06N	091 44 53W	park	
Merrill	45 10 50N	089 41 00W	city/town	
Merrill Municipal	45 11 57N	089 42 40W	airport	1317
Merrillan	44 27 04N	090 50 28W	city/town	937
Merrimac	43 22 24N	089 37 24W	city/town	

Place Name	Latitude	Longitude	Type	Elev
Merton	43 08 48N	088 18 24W	city/town	
Meteor	45 41 22N	091 21 53W	city/town	
Meteor Hill	45 41 17N	091 23 48W	summit	1801
Metz	44 12 49N	088 53 11W	city/town	
Michigan Island	46 52 57N	090 28 51W	island	
Michigan Island Lt	46 52 17N	090 29 49W	lighthous	
Mid Vallee Golf	44 21 54N	088 11 09W	golf	
Middle Inlet	45 17 30N	087 59 32W	city/town	710
Middle Inlet Lkt.	45 18 01N	087 50 22W	tower	780
Middle Ridge	43 48 03N	090 56 48W	city/town	
Middleton	43 05 50N	089 30 15W	city/town	
Middleton Junction	43 03 37N	089 31 40W	city/town	1055
Midway (1)	42 47 32N	088 18 30W	city/town	
Midway (2)	43 55 45N	091 15 28W	city/town	657
Mifflin	42 52 16N	090 21 14W	city/town	955
Mifflin Mine	42 53 02N	090 23 15W	mine	
Mikana	45 35 31N	091 36 04W	city/town	
Milan	44 58 52N	090 10 46W	city/town	
Milford	43 06 03N	088 50 48W	city/town	811
Mill Bluff State	43 56 28N	090 19 08W	park	
Mill Center	44 35 17N	088 09 38W	city/town	760
Mill Creek	44 32 25N	089 40 39W	city/town	

Place Name	Latitude	Longitude	Type	Elev
Milladore	44 36 15N	089 51 17W	city/town	
Millard	42 44 04N	088 37 17W	city/town	938
Millhome	43 53 42N	087 57 44W	city/town	
Millston	44 11 35N	090 38 51W	city/town	
Milltown	45 31 34N	092 30 30W	city/town	1246
Millville	43 02 00N	090 55 48W	city/town	
Milton	42 46 32N	088 56 38W	city/town	
Milton Junction	42 46 57N	088 57 46W	city/town	889
Milwaukee	43 02 20N	087 54 23W	city/town	634
Milwaukee -Timmer	43 06 40N	088 02 04W	airport	745
Milwaukee C C	43 09 48N	087 56 16W	golf	
Milwaukee Downer C	43 04 44N	087 52 43W	univ/coll	
Milwaukee Mitchell	42 56 48N	087 53 48W	airport	723
Milwaukee Passeng.	43 03 09N	087 53 09W	pier	590
Minahan Stadium	44 27 35N	088 03 06W	locale	
Minawa Beach	43 50 47N	088 22 53W	city/town	751
Mindoro	44 01 16N	091 06 06W	city/town	786
Mineral Lake Lkt.	46 17 04N	090 48 03W	tower	1766
Mineral Point (1)	42 42 43N	089 28 00W	city/town	847
Mineral Point (2)	42 51 36N	090 10 47W	city/town	1135
Mineral Pt -Iowa C	42 53 12N	090 13 52W	airport	1174
Minersville	46 24 25N	090 47 50W	city/town	811

Wisconsin GPS Companion

Place Name	Latitude	Longitude	Type	Elev
Minnesota Junction	43 27 09N	088 41 49W	city/town	923
Minocqua	45 52 17N	089 42 39W	city/town	1603
Minong	46 05 58N	091 49 29W	city/town	1064
Mirror Lake State	43 33 54N	089 49 07W	park	
Misha Mokwa	44 29 50N	092 00 37W	city/town	
Mishicot	44 14 21N	087 38 28W	city/town	
Mission House Col.	43 50 29N	087 52 55W	univ/coll	785
Modena	44 27 27N	091 47 47W	city/town	
Moeville	44 41 19N	092 31 38W	city/town	995
Moldenhauer Hill	44 43 38N	091 13 32W	summit	1104
Mole Lake	45 28 47N	088 58 59W	city/town	
Monahan Lookout	46 04 59N	089 23 05W	tower	
Monches	43 11 28N	088 20 37W	city/town	
Mondeaux Dam	45 20 01N	090 26 58W	dam	
Mondovi	44 34 04N	091 40 15W	city/town	
Monico	45 34 35N	089 09 18W	city/town	
Monona	43 03 44N	089 20 02W	city/town	
Monroe	42 36 04N	089 38 18W	city/town	1099
Monroe Center	44 06 43N	089 56 22W	city/town	945
Monroe Municipal	42 36 54N	089 35 23W	airport	1079
Montana	44 20 29N	091 39 53W	city/town	812
Montello	43 47 29N	089 19 11W	city/town	782

Place Name	Latitude	Longitude	Type	Elev
Monterey	43 10 16N	088 29 58W	city/town	
Montfort	42 58 18N	090 25 59W	city/town	
Montgomeryville	43 21 23N	090 44 23W	city/town	1114
Monticello	42 44 44N	089 35 41W	city/town	847
Montreal	46 25 41N	090 14 45W	city/town	
Montrose	42 52 58N	089 34 38W	city/town	985
Moon	44 46 18N	089 47 16W	city/town	1256
Moon Valley	43 22 13N	089 40 21W	city/town	
Moonlight Bay	45 05 03N	087 04 54W	bay	
Moose Junction	46 17 15N	092 09 17W	city/town	1229
Moquah	46 34 14N	091 04 59W	city/town	849
Moquah Lookout	46 35 13N	091 09 48W	tower	1333
Moraine Lookout	44 33 46N	090 39 36W	tower	
Morey Airport	43 06 51N	089 31 50W	airport	928
Morgan (1)	44 47 38N	088 11 24W	city/town	797
Morgan (2)	44 53 06N	088 49 28W	city/town	1005
Morgan Falls	46 20 50N	090 54 58W	falls	
Morgan Fls & St P.	46 20 50N	090 54 50W	locale	1400
Morris Lookout	44 49 14N	089 04 16W	tower	1278
Morris, Mount	44 07 05N	089 11 04W	summit	1137
Morrison	44 17 57N	087 59 20W	city/town	919
Morrisonville	43 16 38N	089 21 34W	city/town	964

Place Name	Latitude	Longitude	Type	Elev
Morse	46 13 20N	090 37 39W	city/town	
Morton Corner	44 47 26N	092 28 19W	city/town	1053
Moscow	42 50 00N	089 51 18W	city/town	
Mosel	43 48 20N	087 44 25W	city/town	642
Mosinee	44 47 35N	089 42 11W	city/town	1153
Mosinee Central	44 46 42N	089 39 58W	airport	1277
Mosinee Hill	44 53 16N	089 39 01W	summit	1587
Mosinee Lookout	44 47 22N	089 40 59W	tower	
Mosling	44 52 08N	088 22 10W	city/town	849
Mount Calvary	43 49 35N	088 14 46W	city/town	
Mount Hope	42 58 02N	090 51 32W	city/town	
Mount Hope Corners	44 44 04N	091 34 07W	city/town	883
Mount Horeb	43 00 31N	089 44 18W	city/town	
Mount Ida	42 58 19N	090 45 39W	city/town	
Mount Mary College	43 04 22N	088 01 50W	univ/coll	
Mount Morris	44 06 52N	089 11 26W	city/town	
Mount Senario Col.	45 27 19N	091 07 09W	univ/coll	
Mount Sterling	43 18 55N	090 55 43W	city/town	
Mount Tabor	43 42 02N	090 27 15W	city/town	
Mount Telemark W.	46 11 05N	091 15 01W	ski area	1650
Mount Valhalla Ski	46 43 08N	091 02 51W	ski area	1338
Mount Vernon	42 56 49N	089 39 21W	city/town	

Place Name	Latitude	Longitude	Type	Elev
Mount View	44 57 06N	089 43 36W	city/town	
Mount Zion	43 15 24N	090 44 01W	city/town	1178
Mountain	45 11 05N	088 28 25W	city/town	
Mountain Lookout	45 12 56N	088 27 54W	tower	
Mukwonago	42 52 00N	088 20 00W	city/town	837
Mulcahy Mine	42 32 16N	090 16 38W	mine	
Murat	45 11 22N	090 26 44W	city/town	
Murphy Corner	44 23 11N	088 20 05W	city/town	
Murrays Landing	46 04 55N	090 04 47W	city/town	
Murry	45 36 02N	091 12 02W	city/town	1164
Muscoda	43 11 06N	090 26 35W	city/town	
Muskeg	46 34 14N	091 29 26W	city/town	
Muskego	42 54 21N	088 08 20W	city/town	
Muskellunge Lkt.	45 59 27N	089 36 11W	tower	
Myers Field	43 52 36N	088 54 02W	airport	935
Myra	43 24 57N	088 05 44W	city/town	

ℕ

Nabob	43 25 13N	088 16 15W	city/town	
Nakoma C C	43 02 30N	089 26 25W	golf	
Namekagon	46 12 46N	091 02 43W	city/town	
Namur	44 44 05N	087 40 12W	city/town	

Place Name	Latitude	Longitude	Type	Elev
Nasbro	43 35 41N	088 30 17W	city/town	
Nashotah	43 05 52N	088 24 08W	city/town	
Nashville	45 31 22N	089 01 29W	city/town	1700
Nasonville	44 35 56N	090 15 30W	city/town	
Natural Bridge St.	43 20 39N	089 55 43W	park	
Naugart	45 04 34N	089 47 18W	city/town	1311
Navarino	44 36 40N	088 29 31W	city/town	
Necedah	44 01 34N	090 04 26W	city/town	
Necedah Airport	44 02 00N	090 05 05W	airport	720
Neda	43 25 17N	088 32 15W	city/town	
Neenah	44 11 09N	088 27 45W	city/town	
Neenah -Brennand	44 09 36N	088 33 34W	airport	850
Neenah Channel	44 11 04N	088 26 46W	channel	
Neenah Point	44 11 06N	088 26 35W	cape	
Neillsville	44 33 36N	090 35 46W	city/town	
Neillsville Muni	44 33 29N	090 30 40W	airport	1236
Nekoosa	44 18 45N	089 54 15W	city/town	
Nekoosa Junction	44 20 16N	089 53 21W	city/town	
Nekoosa Lookout	44 14 56N	089 48 20W	tower	
Nelma	46 01 11N	088 49 04W	city/town	
Nelson	44 25 13N	092 00 29W	city/town	
Nelson Dewey State	42 44 06N	091 01 08W	park	

Wisconsin GPS Companion

Place Name	Latitude	Longitude	Type	Elev
Nelsonville	44 29 42N	089 18 35W	city/town	
Nelsonville -hist.	44 39 15N	091 34 11W	city/town	994
Nemadji Golf Club	46 40 23N	092 04 30W	golf	
Nenno	43 26 46N	088 23 29W	city/town	
Neopit	44 58 51N	088 49 51W	city/town	
Neosho	43 18 37N	088 31 05W	city/town	883
Neptune	43 22 23N	090 16 02W	city/town	
Nerike	44 33 02N	092 04 56W	city/town	
Neshkoro	43 57 57N	089 13 03W	city/town	800
Neureru	44 30 07N	087 43 29W	city/town	848
Neva	45 14 22N	089 06 47W	city/town	
Neva Corners	45 13 12N	089 08 40W	city/town	
Nevins	44 29 47N	090 21 54W	city/town	
New Amsterdam	43 58 58N	091 18 59W	city/town	
New Auburn	45 12 15N	091 33 29W	city/town	
New Berlin	42 58 35N	088 06 30W	city/town	
New Dall Mine	42 38 07N	090 21 29W	mine	
New Diggings	42 32 07N	090 20 07W	city/town	
New Fane	43 33 18N	088 11 09W	city/town	978
New Franken	44 31 51N	087 49 33W	city/town	813
New Glarus	42 48 52N	089 38 06W	city/town	
New Glarus Woods S	42 47 14N	089 37 47W	park	1068

Wisconsin GPS Companion

Place Name	Latitude	Longitude	Type	Elev
New Holstein	43 57 00N	088 05 03W	city/town	935
New Holstein Muni	43 56 41N	088 06 57W	airport	992
New Hope	44 30 13N	089 15 49W	city/town	1154
New Lisbon	43 52 45N	090 09 55W	city/town	891
New London	44 23 34N	088 44 23W	city/town	789
New Miner	44 10 11N	090 02 10W	city/town	
New Munster	42 34 46N	088 13 40W	city/town	771
New Paris	43 43 59N	087 58 19W	city/town	
New Post	45 53 45N	091 11 09W	city/town	1328
New Prospect	43 36 57N	088 10 43W	city/town	978
New Richmond	45 07 23N	092 32 11W	city/town	982
New Richmond Muni	45 08 39N	092 32 10W	airport	996
New Rome	44 13 10N	089 52 51W	city/town	
Newald	45 44 19N	088 42 19W	city/town	1569
Newald Lookout	45 43 57N	088 33 42W	tower	1518
Newark	42 32 32N	089 13 39W	city/town	817
Newbold	45 41 53N	089 30 36W	city/town	
Newburg	43 25 54N	088 02 47W	city/town	850
Newman Springs Ski	45 56 49N	090 11 45W	ski area	1617
Newport Marina	44 53 21N	087 50 40W	locale	583
Newry	43 42 42N	090 49 02W	city/town	
Newton (1)	43 59 38N	087 43 35W	city/town	659

Wisconsin GPS Companion

Place Name	Latitude	Longitude	Type	Elev
Newton (2)	43 35 23N	091 03 46W	city/town	733
Newtonburg	44 03 06N	087 45 42W	city/town	810
Newville	42 49 44N	089 01 17W	city/town	
Niagara	45 46 17N	087 59 41W	city/town	
Nichols	44 33 47N	088 27 48W	city/town	
Nichols Shore Acr.	44 05 50N	088 38 23W	city/town	
Niebauer Springs	45 45 04N	090 32 52W	spring	1403
Nobleton	45 40 45N	091 42 09W	city/town	
Nora	43 01 51N	089 09 00W	city/town	953
Norma	44 57 06N	091 22 10W	city/town	
Norman	44 22 15N	087 36 12W	city/town	
Norrie	44 53 08N	089 15 15W	city/town	
Norske	44 39 09N	089 12 30W	city/town	
North Andover	42 48 56N	090 57 57W	city/town	
North Bay (1)	42 45 53N	087 46 47W	city/town	
North Bay (2)	45 08 46N	087 04 58W	city/town	
North Bend	44 05 29N	091 07 00W	city/town	
North Bluff	44 19 19N	090 10 55W	summit	1182
North Branch	44 26 51N	090 59 56W	city/town	975
North Bristol	43 16 00N	089 12 44W	city/town	941
North Brook C C	44 33 32N	087 42 15W	golf	
North Cape	42 46 43N	088 04 15W	city/town	801

Place Name	Latitude	Longitude	Type	Elev
North Cape -Valh.	42 45 45N	088 02 33W	airport	805
North Clayton	43 22 51N	090 42 34W	city/town	
North Creek	44 16 15N	091 25 55W	city/town	824
North Fond du Lac	43 48 41N	088 29 00W	city/town	
North Freedom	43 27 35N	089 52 06W	city/town	867
North Grimms	44 09 12N	087 54 08W	city/town	858
North Hudson	44 59 35N	092 45 24W	city/town	
North La Crosse	43 50 47N	091 14 53W	city/town	654
North Lake	43 09 22N	088 22 14W	city/town	
North Leeds	43 19 55N	089 19 31W	city/town	
North Lowell	43 22 13N	088 47 46W	city/town	
North Menomonie	44 53 52N	091 55 54W	city/town	
North Pierce Light	44 27 30N	087 29 25W	lighthous	580
North Point Light	43 02 59N	087 52 12W	lighthous	655
North Prairie	42 56 04N	088 24 19W	city/town	
North Readfield	44 17 12N	088 46 10W	city/town	817
North Red Wing	44 34 38N	092 32 51W	city/town	
North Shore	42 54 40N	088 55 13W	city/town	
North Shore C C	44 11 47N	088 20 15W	golf	
North Star	44 37 03N	089 25 21W	city/town	1217
North York	46 23 34N	090 46 39W	city/town	
Northeim	43 59 39N	087 41 55W	city/town	

Place Name	Latitude	Longitude	Type	Elev
Northfield	44 27 33N	091 05 58W	city/town	950
Northland	44 35 42N	089 12 28W	city/town	1046
Northland College	46 34 50N	090 52 27W	univ/coll	
Northline	44 59 21N	092 42 54W	city/town	
Northport (1)	44 24 35N	088 47 38W	city/town	
Northport (2)	45 17 31N	086 58 48W	city/town	
Northwestern Col.	43 11 18N	088 42 43W	univ/coll	
Northwoods Beach	45 54 51N	091 24 12W	city/town	
Norton	45 00 59N	091 50 03W	city/town	931
Norwalk	43 49 50N	090 37 17W	city/town	1030
Norway Grove	43 14 55N	089 24 09W	city/town	
Norway Ridge	44 07 29N	090 19 45W	city/town	
Norway Ridge Lkt.	44 07 05N	090 20 42W	tower	
Nutterville	45 00 14N	089 31 38W	city/town	
Nye	45 18 52N	092 34 49W	city/town	967

◯

Place Name	Latitude	Longitude	Type	Elev
Oak Center	43 39 39N	088 36 00W	city/town	899
Oak Creek	42 53 09N	087 51 47W	city/town	
Oak Creek Harbor	42 50 46N	087 49 36W	locale	580
Oak Grove	43 23 10N	088 44 44W	city/town	
Oak Grove -hist.	44 40 21N	091 36 18W	city/town	955

Wisconsin GPS Companion

Place Name	Latitude	Longitude	Type	Elev
Oak Hall	42 57 02N	089 26 13W	city/town	969
Oak Hill	42 56 09N	088 35 12W	city/town	827
Oak Knoll	42 52 07N	088 20 16W	city/town	
Oak Orchard	44 46 53N	087 55 33W	city/town	
Oak Ridge Fire T.	44 12 49N	090 43 21W	tower	
Oakdale	43 57 35N	090 22 54W	city/town	956
Oakfield	43 41 10N	088 32 47W	city/town	894
Oakland (1)	45 56 15N	092 22 07W	city/town	1004
Oakland (2)	42 58 36N	088 57 20W	city/town	
Oakley	42 31 37N	089 28 04W	city/town	854
Oakridge	44 35 18N	092 23 43W	city/town	1129
Oakwood (1)	44 02 47N	088 36 10W	city/town	751
Oakwood (2)	42 51 29N	087 55 28W	city/town	699
Oakwood Hills Golf	44 15 58N	088 17 55W	golf	
Observatory Hill	43 42 19N	089 20 37W	summit	
Oconomowoc	43 06 42N	088 29 57W	city/town	873
Oconomowoc Lake	43 06 16N	088 27 33W	city/town	
Oconto	44 53 14N	087 51 52W	city/town	591
Oconto Falls	44 52 26N	088 08 34W	city/town	735
Oconto Municipal	44 52 32N	087 54 31W	airport	603
Oconto Yacht Club	44 53 09N	087 51 02W	locale	583
Odana Hills Golf	43 02 52N	089 27 30W	golf	

Wisconsin GPS Companion

Place Name	Latitude	Longitude	Type	Elev
Odanah	46 36 30N	090 41 48W	city/town	610
Ogdensburg	44 27 07N	089 01 54W	city/town	861
Ogema	45 26 37N	090 17 53W	city/town	1583
Oil City	43 45 02N	090 35 12W	city/town	
Ojibwa	45 47 53N	091 07 00W	city/town	1254
Ojibwa Golf Club	44 57 43N	091 23 44W	golf	
Ojibwa State Park	45 48 28N	091 04 40W	park	
Okauchee	43 06 49N	088 26 09W	city/town	
Okee	43 21 28N	089 34 48W	city/town	
Old Albertville	44 56 12N	091 36 00W	city/town	
Old Ashippun	43 13 29N	088 31 11W	city/town	892
Old Hickory Golf	43 26 52N	088 46 45W	golf	
Old Lebanon	43 13 34N	088 37 49W	city/town	
Old Tyrone -hist.	44 42 50N	091 50 33W	city/town	760
Old Wade House St.	43 46 45N	088 05 33W	park	
Oliver	46 39 27N	092 11 42W	city/town	649
Olivet	44 47 11N	092 15 25W	city/town	
Omro	44 02 22N	088 44 39W	city/town	
Onalaska	43 53 04N	091 14 06W	city/town	716
Oneida	44 29 55N	088 10 58W	city/town	
Oneida Golf Course	44 32 18N	088 06 39W	golf	
Ono	44 39 20N	092 15 22W	city/town	1146

Wisconsin GPS Companion

Place Name	Latitude	Longitude	Type	Elev
Ontario	43 43 33N	090 35 29W	city/town	
Oostburg	43 37 22N	087 47 40W	city/town	
Orange Mill	43 54 06N	090 13 56W	city/town	
Orchard Grove	43 29 54N	088 08 27W	city/town	947
Oregon	42 55 34N	089 23 04W	city/town	949
Orfordville	42 37 39N	089 15 11W	city/town	
Orihula	44 12 33N	088 49 58W	city/town	
Orion	43 12 11N	090 25 40W	city/town	
Ormsby	45 15 22N	089 15 09W	city/town	
Orva	46 27 07N	090 13 53W	city/town	
Osceola	45 19 14N	092 42 17W	city/town	
Osceola Municipal	45 18 28N	092 41 11W	airport	903
Osh-O-Nee Mdwy Bt.	44 06 19N	088 29 02W	ramp	
Oshkosh	44 01 29N	088 32 33W	city/town	
Oshkosh -Wittman	43 59 03N	088 33 24W	airport	808
Oshkosh Reefs	44 00 08N	088 30 43W	bar	
Osman	43 58 07N	087 49 15W	city/town	
Osseo	44 34 20N	091 13 38W	city/town	959
Ostrander	44 23 34N	088 50 16W	city/town	
Otis	45 16 08N	089 41 36W	city/town	
Otsego	43 24 08N	089 09 58W	city/town	
Ottawa	42 58 34N	088 26 59W	city/town	927

Place Name	Latitude	Longitude	Type	Elev
Otteson Bluff	44 58 03N	091 54 32W	summit	1258
Ottman Corners	44 42 12N	092 31 01W	city/town	1029
Oulu	46 37 59N	091 31 54W	city/town	998
Ourtown	43 41 50N	087 49 16W	city/town	
Outer Island	47 02 07N	090 25 51W	island	
Outer Island Light	47 04 36N	090 24 58W	lighthous	655
Owen	44 56 55N	090 33 51W	city/town	1245
Owens Rock	44 12 16N	089 39 29W	pillar	
Oxbo	45 51 46N	090 42 15W	city/town	
Oxford	43 46 53N	089 34 21W	city/town	857

ℙ

Place Name	Latitude	Longitude	Type	Elev
Packard	45 21 17N	087 41 39W	city/town	693
Packwaukee	43 45 48N	089 27 30W	city/town	
Paddock Lake	42 34 39N	088 06 18W	city/town	
Padus	45 29 35N	088 39 51W	city/town	1593
Padus Lookout	45 29 42N	088 39 07W	tower	
Palmer	44 54 20N	092 23 41W	city/town	1060
Palmyra	42 52 40N	088 35 10W	city/town	848
Palmyra Municipal	42 53 00N	088 35 45W	airport	854
Paoli	42 55 46N	089 31 25W	city/town	
Pardeeville	43 32 16N	089 18 00W	city/town	815

Wisconsin GPS Companion

Place Name	Latitude	Longitude	Type	Elev
Parfreyville	44 18 46N	089 07 52W	city/town	
Paris	42 38 01N	088 03 05W	city/town	755
Park Falls	45 56 04N	090 26 29W	city/town	1490
Park Falls Municip	45 57 22N	090 25 28W	airport	1502
Park Ridge	44 31 10N	089 32 45W	city/town	
Parkland	46 38 52N	091 59 51W	city/town	693
Parnell Observatn.	43 41 59N	088 05 22W	tower	1312
Parrish	45 25 11N	089 24 09W	city/town	
Patch Grove	42 56 25N	090 58 19W	city/town	
Pattison State	46 31 36N	092 07 20W	park	
Patzau	46 29 29N	092 13 14W	city/town	
Paukotuk	43 58 05N	088 31 15W	city/town	
Paul Bunyon Ski	45 19 26N	088 31 27W	ski area	1300
Pearson	45 21 51N	089 00 59W	city/town	
Pearson Hill	45 26 52N	090 10 42W	summit	1950
Peavey Falls	44 57 58N	088 46 13W	falls	
Peebles	43 48 59N	088 22 35W	city/town	816
Peeksville	46 05 53N	090 31 48W	city/town	1538
Pelican Lake	45 29 58N	089 10 00W	city/town	1604
Pell Lake	42 32 17N	088 21 03W	city/town	871
Pella	44 44 33N	088 48 12W	city/town	
Pembine	45 38 07N	087 59 27W	city/town	968

Wisconsin GPS Companion

Place Name	Latitude	Longitude	Type	Elev
Pemene Falls	45 35 39N	087 46 38W	falls	
Pence	46 24 55N	090 16 17W	city/town	
Pence Lake Lookout	45 19 50N	089 03 50W	tower	
Peninsula State	45 08 49N	087 12 51W	park	
Pennington	45 31 55N	090 23 32W	city/town	
Penninsula Golf	45 08 58N	087 11 27W	golf	697
Pensaukee	44 49 23N	087 54 47W	city/town	591
Pensaukee Harb Lt.	44 49 17N	087 53 46W	lighthous	583
Pepin	44 26 28N	092 08 52W	city/town	720
Peplin	44 47 10N	089 37 08W	city/town	1211
Percussion Rock	43 06 11N	090 08 04W	pillar	
Perkinstown	45 12 15N	090 36 53W	city/town	
Perkinstown Lkt.	45 11 12N	090 37 25W	tower	1599
Perkinstown Winter	45 10 56N	090 37 57W	ski area	1551
Perrot State Park	44 01 04N	091 27 56W	park	
Peru	44 34 12N	089 14 36W	city/town	1117
Peshitigo Reef Lt.	44 56 59N	087 34 40W	lighthous	
Peshtigo	45 03 16N	087 44 57W	city/town	
Peshtigo Harbor	44 58 23N	087 39 11W	bay	
Peshtigo Lookout	45 05 19N	087 45 22W	tower	
Peshtigo Point	44 59 04N	087 37 45W	cape	584
Petenwell Rock	44 02 45N	090 01 13W	summit	

Wisconsin GPS Companion

Place Name	Latitude	Longitude	Type	Elev
Petersburg	43 16 20N	090 50 15W	city/town	
Petes Landing	46 02 59N	090 19 38W	city/town	
Pewaukee	43 04 50N	088 15 40W	city/town	
Pewaukee West	43 04 29N	088 19 51W	city/town	
Peyton	46 39 01N	092 01 16W	city/town	
Pheasant Branch	43 06 15N	089 29 02W	city/town	
Phelps	46 03 52N	089 05 15W	city/town	1770
Phillips	45 41 48N	090 24 01W	city/town	
Phillips -Price C.	45 42 19N	090 24 10W	airport	1472
Phipps	46 03 46N	091 24 48W	city/town	1233
Phlox	45 03 04N	089 00 51W	city/town	
Piacenza	44 08 47N	088 42 26W	city/town	
Pickerel	45 21 34N	088 54 39W	city/town	
Pickerel Lookout	45 58 08N	089 25 11W	tower	1724
Pickett	43 54 41N	088 43 47W	city/town	
Piehl Lookout	45 43 07N	089 07 54W	tower	1722
Pierceville	43 08 09N	089 09 11W	city/town	952
Pierhead Light	43 01 32N	087 53 43W	lighthous	590
Pigeon Falls	44 25 35N	091 12 37W	city/town	882
Pike Lake	43 18 50N	088 20 31W	city/town	
Pike Lake State	43 19 12N	088 18 53W	park	
Pike River	46 27 36N	091 14 23W	city/town	961

Place Name	Latitude	Longitude	Type	Elev
Pikes Peak	43 59 10N	090 36 35W	summit	1345
Pikeville	42 29 46N	088 01 28W	city/town	
Pillar Rock	43 19 14N	089 57 46W	pillar	
Pilot Island	45 17 06N	086 55 11W	island	
Pilot Island Light	45 17 04N	086 55 09W	lighthous	594
Pilsen	44 26 37N	087 43 30W	city/town	888
Pine Aire C C	43 39 37N	089 46 53W	golf	
Pine Bluff	43 03 39N	089 39 20W	city/town	993
Pine Bluff Observ.	43 04 39N	089 40 18W	observtry	
Pine Creek	44 08 04N	091 31 36W	city/town	768
Pine Grove (1)	44 53 59N	091 37 49W	city/town	
Pine Grove (2)	44 24 59N	087 53 19W	city/town	
Pine Lake	46 15 22N	090 08 26W	city/town	
Pine Lake Lookout	46 15 43N	090 07 26W	tower	1744
Pine River (1)	44 09 08N	089 04 37W	city/town	
Pine River (2)	45 08 03N	089 37 19W	city/town	1250
Pine River Lookout	45 56 58N	088 49 34W	tower	1737
Pinehurst	44 51 30N	091 27 45W	city/town	
Pinewood C C	45 41 26N	089 40 07W	golf	
Pioneer Airport	43 59 22N	088 34 42W	airport	826
Pioneer State Col.	42 44 06N	090 29 10W	univ/coll	
Pipe	43 54 51N	088 18 45W	city/town	

Place Name	Latitude	Longitude	Type	Elev
Pipersville	43 08 32N	088 39 00W	city/town	
Pipestone Falls	45 51 19N	091 14 12W	falls	
Pipestone Lookout	45 51 09N	091 12 16W	tower	
Pittsfield	44 35 58N	088 14 42W	city/town	806
Pittsville	44 26 21N	090 07 28W	city/town	1032
Pixley Dam	45 52 49N	090 30 42W	dam	1458
Plain	43 16 44N	090 02 37W	city/town	
Plainfield	44 12 50N	089 29 32W	city/town	
Plainville	43 42 32N	089 48 45W	city/town	
Plat	43 12 28N	088 16 51W	city/town	
Platteville	42 44 03N	090 28 42W	city/town	994
Platteville -Grant	42 41 16N	090 26 41W	airport	1022
Pleasant Lake Lkt.	46 14 39N	090 21 08W	tower	1875
Pleasant Prairie	42 33 11N	087 56 00W	city/town	
Pleasant Ridge	43 03 17N	090 04 24W	city/town	
Pleasant Valley	43 43 16N	091 10 24W	city/town	
Pleasant View Golf	43 05 16N	089 32 35W	golf	
Pleasantville	44 27 13N	091 18 17W	city/town	
Plover	44 27 23N	089 32 38W	city/town	1075
Plugtown	43 13 21N	090 44 54W	city/town	
Plum City	44 37 45N	092 11 32W	city/town	
Plum Island	45 18 26N	086 57 06W	island	

Wisconsin GPS Companion

Place Name	Latitude	Longitude	Type	Elev
Plum Light Range L	45 18 28N	086 57 28W	locale	588
Plummer Point	44 05 15N	088 37 45W	city/town	
Plymouth	43 44 55N	087 58 37W	city/town	
Point Comfort	44 37 11N	087 51 23W	cape	
Pokegama	46 38 49N	092 08 46W	city/town	688
Poland	44 26 37N	087 49 34W	city/town	
Polar	45 10 07N	088 59 24W	city/town	
Pollard Rock	43 44 09N	090 01 15W	pillar	
Polley	45 08 28N	090 48 25W	city/town	
Polonia	44 34 12N	089 24 47W	city/town	
Pompeys Pillar	43 04 38N	090 18 39W	pillar	
Poniatowski	44 59 42N	089 59 36W	city/town	
Poplar	46 35 02N	091 47 56W	city/town	
Popple Ridge Snowm	45 15 17N	088 41 21W	trail	1460
Popple River	45 47 29N	088 41 06W	city/town	1523
Porcupine	44 35 02N	092 05 44W	city/town	
Porcupine Lookout	45 34 14N	089 31 45W	tower	
Porcupine Mountain	45 24 22N	089 35 18W	summit	
Port Andrew	43 12 26N	090 34 02W	city/town	699
Port Arthur	45 25 45N	091 09 43W	city/town	1095
Port Edwards	44 21 03N	089 51 55W	city/town	975
Port Washington	43 23 14N	087 52 32W	city/town	612

Wisconsin GPS Companion

Place Name	Latitude	Longitude	Type	Elev
Port Washington Yt	43 23 29N	087 51 57W	locale	590
Port Wing	46 46 29N	091 23 11W	city/town	
Portage	43 32 21N	089 27 45W	city/town	
Portage Municipal	43 33 36N	089 28 58W	airport	820
Porterfield	45 09 16N	087 47 40W	city/town	
Porters	42 31 43N	088 57 33W	city/town	
Portland (1)	43 11 56N	088 58 29W	city/town	809
Portland (2)	43 46 08N	090 51 29W	city/town	1312
Poskin	45 24 33N	091 57 41W	city/town	1191
Post Lake	45 26 27N	089 04 49W	city/town	
Postville	42 47 57N	089 45 10W	city/town	
Potato Rapids Dam	45 06 52N	087 45 37W	dam	621
Potato River Falls	46 27 40N	090 31 44W	falls	
Potawatomi State	44 51 52N	087 24 54W	park	
Potosi	42 41 22N	090 42 43W	city/town	
Pottawatomie Light	45 25 40N	086 49 43W	lighthous	
Potter	44 07 14N	088 05 57W	city/town	
Pound	45 05 39N	088 02 02W	city/town	
Powell	46 05 19N	089 57 30W	city/town	1596
Powers Lake	42 33 13N	088 17 40W	city/town	
Poy Sippi	44 08 14N	088 59 43W	city/town	778
Poynette	43 23 25N	089 24 10W	city/town	847

Place Name	Latitude	Longitude	Type	Elev
Praag	44 22 41N	091 45 02W	city/town	855
Prairie Corners	42 32 09N	090 32 00W	city/town	906
Prairie Du Chien	43 01 18N	091 07 28W	airport	660
Prairie Du Chien	43 03 06N	091 08 28W	city/town	632
Prairie du Sac	43 17 13N	089 43 26W	city/town	
Prairie Farm	45 14 14N	091 58 53W	city/town	
Pratt Junction	45 28 57N	089 09 52W	city/town	
Pray	44 22 24N	090 29 50W	city/town	978
Preble	44 29 51N	087 58 11W	city/town	
Prentice	45 32 46N	090 17 11W	city/town	
Prentice Airport	45 32 35N	090 16 45W	airport	1578
Prescott	44 44 56N	092 48 07W	city/town	
Presque Isle	46 14 50N	089 43 45W	city/town	
Preston	42 58 30N	090 32 49W	city/town	
Price	44 34 54N	091 03 16W	city/town	1082
Primrose	42 54 05N	089 39 44W	city/town	1002
Princeton	43 51 03N	089 07 18W	city/town	
Prospect	42 56 40N	088 09 32W	city/town	
Pt Beach Nucl Pow.	44 16 52N	087 32 11W	plant	
Pucketville	44 34 10N	092 32 21W	city/town	
Pugh's Peerless M.	42 44 04N	087 47 48W	marina	585
Pukwana Beach	43 55 40N	088 19 01W	city/town	751

Wisconsin GPS Companion

Place Name	Latitude	Longitude	Type	Elev
Pulaski	44 40 20N	088 14 33W	city/town	
Pulaski -Carter	44 38 28N	088 12 53W	airport	783
Pulcifer	44 50 39N	088 21 36W	city/town	
Purdy	43 31 01N	091 02 53W	city/town	704
Pureair	46 47 25N	090 50 50W	city/town	

Q

Place Name	Latitude	Longitude	Type	Elev
Quarry Lookout	44 42 37N	089 30 36W	tower	
Quarterdeck Marina	44 49 26N	087 22 23W	marina	580
Queenstown	45 21 07N	090 17 17W	city/town	
Quinney	44 00 52N	088 18 26W	city/town	
Quiver Falls	45 39 28N	087 49 20W	falls	

R

Place Name	Latitude	Longitude	Type	Elev
Racine	42 43 34N	087 46 58W	city/town	
Racine -JH Batten	42 45 39N	087 48 49W	airport	673
Racine Reef Light	42 44 23N	087 43 10W	lighthous	
Racine Yacht Club	42 44 15N	087 46 40W	locale	582
Radisson	45 46 08N	091 13 16W	city/town	1245
Radspur	46 10 43N	091 19 00W	city/town	
Ragged Rock	43 57 47N	090 18 09W	pillar	
Rainbow Beach	44 09 24N	088 26 42W	city/town	750

Place Name		Latitude		Longitude		Type	Elev
Rainbow Falls		44 58 29N	088 47 40W			falls	
Rainbow Rapids		45 48 38N	089 32 30W			falls	
Randall		45 41 45N	092 50 06W			city/town	
Randolph		43 32 21N	089 00 24W			city/town	964
Random Lake		43 33 08N	087 57 42W			city/town	901
Range		45 23 44N	092 17 04W			city/town	1168
Rangeline		44 44 37N	089 57 50W			city/town	1204
Rankin		44 35 46N	087 30 12W			city/town	
Rantz		45 49 54N	089 43 46W			city/town	
Rasque Mine		42 41 39N	090 26 13W			mine	
Rat Lake Perm. Lkt		45 33 27N	088 48 49W			tower	1939
Rawley Point		44 12 45N	087 30 28W			cape	
Raymond		42 48 03N	088 00 45W			city/town	742
Raymore		43 59 51N	090 37 09W			city/town	982
Readfield		44 16 21N	088 46 11W			city/town	
Readstown		43 26 58N	090 45 33W			city/town	760
Red Banks (1)		44 16 37N	088 51 31W			city/town	
Red Banks (2)		44 36 40N	087 51 47W			city/town	
Red Cedar		44 41 21N	091 53 03W			city/town	758
Red Cliff		46 51 20N	090 47 16W			city/town	640
Red Mound		43 28 21N	091 08 41W			city/town	
Red River		44 49 30N	088 42 16W			city/town	

Wisconsin GPS Companion

Place Name	Latitude			Longitude			Type	Elev
Red Rock	42	38	33N	090	02	51W	city/town	
Red Wing Municipal	44	35	24N	092	29	10W	airport	784
Redgranite	44	02	31N	089	05	54W	city/town	789
Reedsburg	43	31	57N	090	00	09W	city/town	926
Reedsburg C C	43	32	00N	089	57	46W	golf	
Reedsburg Municip	43	31	33N	089	58	58W	airport	905
Reedsville	44	09	13N	087	57	24W	city/town	
Reeseville	43	18	18N	088	50	41W	city/town	856
Reeve	45	14	19N	092	07	33W	city/town	
Regina	44	53	41N	089	01	18W	city/town	
Reifs Mills	44	10	56N	087	47	57W	city/town	
Reighmoor	44	03	27N	088	40	25W	city/town	
Renet Lake	42	29	53N	088	04	54W	city/town	
Requa	44	35	12N	091	08	41W	city/town	1016
Reseburg	44	54	55N	090	45	36W	city/town	1217
Reserve	45	52	53N	091	23	11W	city/town	
Retreat	43	26	44N	091	04	50W	city/town	
Rewey	42	50	34N	090	23	43W	city/town	1140
Rhine	43	51	46N	087	57	24W	city/town	
Rhinelander	45	38	12N	089	24	43W	city/town	1554
Rhinelander-Oneida	45	37	51N	089	27	56W	airport	1623
Rib Falls	44	58	16N	089	54	13W	city/town	

Wisconsin GPS Companion

Place Name	Latitude	Longitude	Type	Elev
Rib Lake	45 19 03N	090 12 30W	city/town	
Rib Mountain	44 55 15N	089 41 40W	summit	1924
Rib Mountain State	44 55 14N	089 41 14W	park	
Rib River Lookout	45 12 27N	090 10 16W	tower	
Rice Lake	45 30 22N	091 44 17W	city/town	
Rice Lake C C	45 29 31N	091 46 21W	golf	
Rice Lake Municip	45 28 45N	091 43 20W	airport	1138
Richardson	45 19 09N	092 11 59W	city/town	1194
Richfield	43 15 22N	088 11 38W	city/town	974
Richford	44 01 25N	089 26 07W	city/town	
Richland Center	43 16 59N	090 17 54W	airport	726
Richland Center	43 20 05N	090 23 12W	city/town	731
Richmond	42 42 53N	088 44 57W	city/town	
Richwood	43 14 29N	088 46 59W	city/town	
Ricker Bay	44 07 52N	088 28 14W	city/town	
Ridgeland	45 12 13N	091 53 43W	city/town	
Ridgetop	45 55 47N	088 16 12W	city/town	
Ridgeway	43 00 08N	089 59 25W	city/town	
Ridgeway C C	44 11 56N	088 32 42W	golf	902
Riley	43 01 24N	089 37 21W	city/town	999
Ring	43 54 33N	088 38 25W	city/town	
Ringle	44 53 28N	089 25 32W	city/town	1334

Place Name	Latitude	Longitude	Type	Elev
Rio	43 26 52N	089 14 23W	city/town	974
Rio -Cowgill Fld	43 27 00N	089 15 00W	airport	925
Rio Creek	44 35 21N	087 32 28W	city/town	703
Riplinger	44 49 30N	090 24 11W	city/town	1294
Ripon	43 50 32N	088 50 09W	city/town	943
Ripon College	43 50 40N	088 50 24W	univ/coll	
Rising Sun	43 25 05N	090 57 29W	city/town	
River Falls	44 51 41N	092 37 25W	city/town	
River Falls Arpt	44 50 32N	092 36 59W	airport	922
River Falls Golf	44 51 35N	092 35 30W	golf	
River Hills	43 10 27N	087 55 27W	city/town	
Riverhills C C	45 04 24N	089 34 17W	golf	
Rivermoor	44 04 22N	088 41 10W	city/town	
Riverside (1)	46 04 35N	092 14 51W	city/town	893
Riverside (2)	42 35 38N	090 01 21W	city/town	
Riverside Golf	44 38 06N	088 46 12W	golf	
Riverview	46 40 35N	092 11 06W	city/town	
Riverview Golf	45 08 19N	089 14 55W	golf	
Road America Racew	43 47 51N	087 59 38W	track	
Roberts	44 59 02N	092 33 21W	city/town	
Roche a Cri	44 00 10N	089 49 07W	summit	
Roche a Cri State	44 00 06N	089 49 04W	park	

Wisconsin GPS Companion

Place Name	Latitude	Longitude	Type	Elev
Rochester	42 44 29N	088 13 27W	city/town	777
Rochester -Fox Riv	42 45 00N	088 15 03W	airport	822
Rock Dam County Pk	44 44 00N	090 51 02W	falls	
Rock Elm	44 44 12N	092 12 59W	city/town	
Rock Falls	44 43 07N	091 41 23W	city/town	861
Rock Falls Lookout	45 20 11N	089 42 50W	tower	1672
Rock Island Ferry	45 24 01N	086 51 23W	locale	582
Rock River C C	43 38 37N	088 45 37W	golf	
Rock Springs	43 29 33N	089 55 08W	city/town	
Rockaway Beach (1)	44 02 47N	088 30 35W	city/town	
Rockaway Beach (2)	44 05 52N	088 19 37W	city/town	
Rockbridge	43 26 50N	090 21 53W	arch	
Rockbridge	43 26 54N	090 21 50W	city/town	777
Rockdale	42 58 19N	089 01 51W	city/town	
Rockfield	43 15 27N	088 07 34W	city/town	890
Rockland	43 54 23N	090 55 09W	city/town	752
Rockmont	46 35 09N	091 54 31W	city/town	
Rockton	43 38 28N	090 36 06W	city/town	884
Rockville (1)	43 55 12N	087 59 52W	city/town	
Rockville (2)	42 43 38N	090 40 55W	city/town	
Rockwood	44 10 05N	087 42 20W	city/town	
Rocky Arbor State	43 38 32N	089 48 29W	park	

Place Name	Latitude	Longitude	Type	Elev
Rocky Corners	44 42 51N	089 36 28W	city/town	1201
Rocky Run	44 32 40N	089 38 25W	city/town	
Rodell	44 43 12N	091 11 17W	city/town	
Rogersville	43 44 57N	088 37 56W	city/town	915
Rolling Ground	43 19 46N	090 44 25W	city/town	1230
Rolling Prairie	43 27 33N	088 44 03W	city/town	941
Romance	43 33 08N	091 08 41W	city/town	
Rome	42 58 49N	088 37 52W	city/town	832
Roosevelt	45 40 19N	089 18 53W	city/town	
Rose Lawn	44 36 05N	088 19 30W	city/town	890
Rosecrans	44 16 36N	087 49 37W	city/town	872
Rosendale	43 48 28N	088 40 29W	city/town	
Rosendale Center	43 51 06N	088 43 13W	city/town	892
Rosewood	42 40 33N	088 10 07W	city/town	
Rosholt	44 37 40N	089 18 31W	city/town	
Rosiere	44 40 32N	087 36 43W	city/town	818
Ross	43 32 28N	090 45 11W	city/town	
Ross Crossing	42 49 45N	089 33 08W	city/town	
Rostok	44 30 06N	087 30 05W	city/town	
Rothschild	44 53 14N	089 37 12W	city/town	
Round Top Hill	43 17 27N	089 42 35W	summit	959
Rouse	46 21 23N	090 27 56W	city/town	1488

Wisconsin GPS Companion

Place Name	Latitude	Longitude	Type	Elev
Rowley Bay	45 13 05N	087 01 11W	bay	
Rowleys Bay	45 13 11N	087 02 07W	city/town	595
Roxbury	43 14 58N	089 40 31W	city/town	868
Royalton	44 24 46N	088 51 46W	city/town	822
Rozellville	44 44 36N	090 01 28W	city/town	1259
Rube	44 03 06N	087 48 05W	city/town	768
Rubicon	43 20 25N	088 27 27W	city/town	1013
Ruby	45 10 38N	090 59 17W	city/town	1140
Rubys Corner	45 10 44N	087 44 23W	city/town	634
Rudd Hills	44 09 38N	090 34 50W	summit	1160
Rudolph	44 29 46N	089 48 27W	city/town	1138
Rugby Junction	43 17 31N	088 13 07W	city/town	
Rural	44 18 47N	089 09 11W	city/town	876
Rush Lake	43 55 26N	088 50 21W	city/town	861
Rusk	44 54 28N	091 50 02W	city/town	905
Rutland	42 52 44N	089 21 00W	city/town	
Rutledge	42 33 17N	090 38 01W	city/town	
Ryans Corner	44 30 48N	087 36 28W	city/town	

𝕊

Sabin	43 25 49N	090 34 07W	city/town	
Saint Anna	43 53 36N	088 07 17W	city/town	

Wisconsin GPS Companion

Place Name	Latitude	Longitude	Type	Elev
Saint Anthony	43 26 33N	088 20 30W	city/town	
Saint Cloud	43 49 22N	088 10 01W	city/town	930
Saint Croix Falls	45 24 36N	092 38 22W	city/town	
Saint Francis	42 58 03N	087 52 39W	city/town	
Saint Germain	45 54 06N	089 29 14W	city/town	
Saint John	44 10 08N	088 12 14W	city/town	
Saint Joseph	43 47 08N	091 02 30W	city/town	1301
Saint Joseph Col.	42 52 26N	089 01 03W	univ/coll	
Saint Kilian	43 32 35N	088 21 41W	city/town	1121
Saint Lawrence	43 22 11N	088 19 58W	city/town	1071
Saint Martins	42 54 08N	088 03 23W	city/town	
Saint Marys	43 47 53N	090 41 14W	city/town	1379
Saint Michaels	43 30 48N	088 09 38W	city/town	1054
Saint Nazianz	44 00 29N	087 55 20W	city/town	
Saint Norbert Col.	44 26 40N	088 03 58W	univ/coll	
Saint Peter	43 50 11N	088 20 29W	city/town	1076
Saint Rose	42 37 26N	090 26 04W	city/town	
Salem (1)	42 33 17N	088 06 39W	city/town	
Salem (2)	44 37 23N	092 21 26W	city/town	1027
Salem Oaks	42 33 31N	088 05 32W	city/town	
Sally, Mount	43 45 35N	090 33 34W	summit	963
Salmo	46 46 53N	090 51 54W	city/town	

Wisconsin GPS Companion

Place Name	Latitude	Longitude	Type	Elev
Salona	44 44 44N	087 21 23W	city/town	675
Sampson	44 45 54N	088 11 10W	city/town	
Sanborn	46 25 59N	090 54 31W	city/town	
Sand Bay	46 56 45N	090 53 27W	city/town	
Sand Creek	45 10 01N	091 41 10W	city/town	
Sand Island	46 58 45N	090 56 54W	island	
Sand Lake	45 22 06N	092 33 30W	city/town	1145
Sand Lake Lkt 1	45 48 16N	091 26 23W	tower	1548
Sand Lake Lkt 2	44 52 50N	088 33 20W	tower	
Sand Portage Falls	45 45 36N	087 57 52W	falls	
Sand Prairie	43 12 19N	090 36 41W	city/town	691
Sandalwood C C	44 46 53N	088 05 23W	golf	
Sandrock	46 18 49N	090 08 42W	city/town	1628
Sandstone Bluff	43 49 02N	088 58 01W	city/town	
Sandusky	43 23 43N	090 09 07W	city/town	
Sandy Hook	42 32 36N	090 36 36W	city/town	885
Sarona	45 42 40N	091 48 23W	city/town	1300
Sauk City	43 16 15N	089 43 19W	city/town	757
Sauk Hill	43 24 07N	089 45 33W	summit	1461
Saukville	43 22 54N	087 56 26W	city/town	
Saunders	46 38 19N	092 06 32W	city/town	679
Sauntry	46 22 28N	091 49 21W	city/town	1147

Wisconsin GPS Companion

Place Name	Latitude	Longitude	Type	Elev
Savoy -hist.	44 31 25N	092 02 27W	city/town	691
Saxeville	44 10 34N	089 06 52W	city/town	
Saxon	46 29 36N	090 24 51W	city/town	1115
Saxon Falls	46 32 10N	090 22 46W	falls	
Saylesville (1)	42 56 58N	088 19 13W	city/town	812
Saylesville (2)	43 18 01N	088 26 21W	city/town	924
Sayner	45 59 10N	089 31 57W	city/town	
Scandinavia	44 27 42N	089 08 57W	city/town	931
Schmidt Corner	44 36 11N	089 07 21W	city/town	
Schnappsville	44 58 24N	090 01 30W	city/town	1438
Schneyville	42 31 01N	089 38 22W	city/town	895
Schofield	44 54 35N	089 36 16W	city/town	1198
School Hill	43 57 00N	087 53 38W	city/town	
Schultz	42 41 24N	089 36 09W	city/town	974
Scotts Junction	43 57 53N	090 40 09W	city/town	984
Seagull Marina	44 08 42N	087 33 57W	locale	584
Sechlerville	44 22 22N	091 01 51W	city/town	927
Sedgwick	46 28 01N	090 36 19W	city/town	
Seeley	46 07 16N	091 21 40W	city/town	1271
Seeley Lookout	46 08 52N	091 17 01W	tower	
Seminary Springs	43 06 31N	089 14 55W	city/town	
Seneca	43 15 54N	090 57 30W	city/town	

Wisconsin GPS Companion

Place Name	Latitude	Longitude	Type	Elev
Sentinal Point Lkt	45 58 15N	090 04 52W	tower	1676
Sextonville	43 16 42N	090 17 27W	city/town	
Seymour	44 30 54N	088 19 49W	city/town	
Shady Dell	42 57 32N	090 47 28W	city/town	979
Shalagoco C C	44 49 53N	088 31 55W	golf	
Shale Falls	46 41 28N	091 36 00W	falls	692
Shamrock	44 10 27N	090 48 16W	city/town	842
Shanagolden	46 07 03N	090 38 09W	city/town	1529
Shangri La Point	44 03 59N	088 36 27W	city/town	
Shantytown	44 41 16N	089 25 26W	city/town	1175
Sharon	42 30 09N	088 43 44W	city/town	1027
Shaw Landing	44 21 59N	088 48 33W	city/town	
Shawano	44 46 56N	088 36 32W	city/town	821
Shawano Municipal	44 47 14N	088 33 34W	airport	810
Shawtown	44 47 42N	091 32 13W	city/town	
Shea Dam	46 14 12N	089 59 39W	dam	1610
Sheboygan	43 45 03N	087 42 52W	city/town	
Sheboygan County	43 46 10N	087 51 05W	airport	749
Sheboygan Falls	43 43 45N	087 48 38W	city/town	659
Sheboygan Point	43 45 49N	087 41 52W	cape	631
Sheboygan Yacht	43 45 01N	087 42 12W	locale	585
Shelby	43 46 09N	091 09 39W	city/town	694

Wisconsin GPS Companion

Place Name	Latitude	Longitude	Type	Elev
Sheldon	45 18 38N	090 57 21W	city/town	1129
Shell Lake	45 44 22N	091 55 31W	city/town	
Shell Lake Municip	45 43 48N	091 55 14W	airport	1232
Shelton Lookout	45 43 52N	091 49 40W	tower	
Shennington	44 01 33N	090 19 03W	city/town	911
Shepley	44 51 44N	089 06 10W	city/town	1175
Sheppard	44 15 39N	090 46 50W	city/town	
Sheridan	44 23 45N	089 11 53W	city/town	
Sherry	44 35 03N	089 54 56W	city/town	
Sherry Junction	45 13 09N	088 59 16W	city/town	1627
Sherwood (1)	44 28 03N	090 21 20W	city/town	1065
Sherwood (2)	44 10 25N	088 15 35W	city/town	
Sherwood Point Lt.	44 53 33N	087 25 59W	lighthous	583
Shiocton	44 26 41N	088 34 44W	city/town	
Shiocton Airport	44 27 17N	088 33 42W	airport	770
Ship Rock	44 01 31N	089 40 30W	summit	
Shirley	44 21 25N	087 56 51W	city/town	941
Shoemaker Point	44 43 14N	087 43 14W	city/town	590
Shopiere	42 34 21N	088 56 18W	city/town	
Shorewood	43 05 21N	087 53 15W	city/town	679
Shorewood Golf	44 32 04N	087 55 22W	golf	
Shorewood Hills	43 04 39N	089 26 44W	city/town	

Place Name	Latitude	Longitude	Type	Elev
Shortville	44 29 42N	090 30 59W	city/town	1007
Shoto	44 10 31N	087 38 57W	city/town	
Shullsburg	42 34 24N	090 13 51W	city/town	1021
Sidney	44 33 10N	090 38 19W	city/town	1089
Silica	43 51 01N	088 20 30W	city/town	
Silver Creek	43 33 25N	088 01 30W	city/town	912
Silver Lake (1)	42 32 46N	088 09 56W	city/town	
Silver Lake (2)	44 03 19N	089 13 34W	city/town	
Sinsinawa	42 31 25N	090 32 21W	city/town	
Sioux	46 44 14N	090 52 48W	city/town	608
Siren	45 47 09N	092 22 51W	city/town	996
Siren -Burnett Cty	45 49 22N	092 22 20W	airport	989
Siren Lookout	45 47 02N	092 25 53W	tower	1131
Siskiwit Massacre	46 51 41N	091 05 33W	site	668
Sister Bay	45 11 14N	087 07 15W	city/town	587
Ski Hill Winter Sp	46 08 08N	089 11 57W	ski area	1770
Skillet Falls	43 26 48N	089 46 22W	falls	
Slab City	44 43 13N	088 26 44W	city/town	904
Slabtown	42 58 01N	088 38 06W	city/town	
Slades Corners	42 34 55N	088 17 38W	city/town	862
Slateford	42 47 08N	090 11 36W	city/town	851
Slinger	43 20 01N	088 17 10W	city/town	1069

Wisconsin GPS Companion

Place Name	Latitude	Longitude	Type	Elev
Slovan	44 31 51N	087 34 59W	city/town	
Smalley Falls	45 41 42N	087 56 49W	falls	
Smith Landing	44 41 21N	092 41 30W	city/town	
Smoky Hill	46 13 55N	091 29 39W	summit	1506
Snell	45 03 31N	089 17 06W	city/town	1450
Snells	44 08 30N	088 29 26W	city/town	760
Sniderville	44 21 06N	088 11 28W	city/town	678
Snow Crest Ski	45 05 42N	092 44 03W	ski area	919
Snows Corner	44 40 26N	092 29 48W	city/town	
Snug Harbor Yacht	44 49 21N	087 21 04W	marina	586
So Milwaukee Yacht	42 54 25N	087 50 40W	marina	595
Sobieski	44 43 15N	088 04 19W	city/town	657
Sobieski Corners	44 43 16N	088 03 08W	city/town	642
Soldiers Grove	43 23 43N	090 46 27W	city/town	
Solon Springs	46 21 12N	091 49 20W	city/town	
Solon Springs Muni	46 18 53N	091 38 58W	airport	1101
Somers	42 38 25N	087 54 37W	city/town	
Somerset	45 07 28N	092 40 24W	city/town	
Sono Junction	44 59 22N	092 40 43W	city/town	
Soperton	45 26 18N	088 38 10W	city/town	
South Beaver Dam	43 26 27N	088 53 10W	city/town	892
South Breakwater L	46 42 36N	092 00 22W	light	604

Wisconsin GPS Companion

Place Name	Latitude	Longitude	Type	Elev
South Byron	43 38 20N	088 29 11W	city/town	
South Chase	44 41 24N	088 09 04W	city/town	779
South Itasca	46 39 42N	092 00 18W	city/town	
South Jetty Light	43 23 00N	087 51 51W	locale	582
South Kenosha	42 32 25N	087 50 03W	city/town	
South Milwaukee	42 54 38N	087 51 38W	city/town	
South Pierhead Lt.	43 44 55N	087 41 41W	light	581
South Randolph	43 30 40N	088 59 56W	city/town	
South Range	46 36 29N	091 59 00W	city/town	763
South Shore Marina	46 51 29N	091 05 36W	marina	599
South Shore Yacht	42 59 51N	087 52 57W	marina	585
South Superior	46 40 10N	092 05 42W	city/town	
South Wayne	42 34 08N	089 52 47W	city/town	803
Sparta	43 56 39N	090 48 46W	city/town	793
Sparta Ft. McCoy	43 57 30N	090 44 18W	airport	837
Spaulding	44 21 21N	090 24 56W	city/town	
Speck Oaks	44 18 01N	090 34 14W	city/town	953
Spencer	44 45 28N	090 17 48W	city/town	
Spencerian College	43 03 53N	087 56 56W	univ/coll	
Spirit	45 27 15N	090 06 51W	city/town	1685
Spirit Falls	45 27 11N	089 58 50W	city/town	1487
Split Rock	44 42 18N	089 01 33W	city/town	

Place Name	Latitude	Longitude	Type	Elev
Spokeville	44 42 45N	090 26 03W	city/town	1273
Spooner	45 49 21N	091 53 21W	city/town	1065
Sprague	44 08 52N	090 07 53W	city/town	
Spread Eagle	45 52 55N	088 08 23W	city/town	1196
Spring Bank Park	44 00 24N	090 37 15W	city/town	
Spring Camp Falls	46 20 52N	090 14 21W	falls	
Spring Green	43 10 31N	090 04 04W	city/town	729
Spring Grove	43 48 54N	088 56 29W	city/town	
Spring Lake	44 01 24N	089 09 31W	city/town	
Spring Prairie	42 41 29N	088 24 15W	city/town	1018
Spring Valley (1)	43 56 20N	087 50 22W	city/town	
Spring Valley (2)	44 50 43N	092 14 19W	city/town	
Springbrook	45 56 55N	091 41 17W	city/town	
Springdale -hist	44 31 38N	091 46 32W	city/town	960
Springfield	42 38 30N	088 24 43W	city/town	851
Springfield Corn.	43 11 31N	089 33 59W	city/town	
Springstead	46 01 31N	090 08 12W	city/town	1619
Springstead Lkt.	46 02 59N	090 09 28W	tower	
Springstead Lndng.	46 04 25N	090 10 26W	city/town	
Springville	43 35 01N	090 56 23W	city/town	
Spruce	44 57 09N	088 09 53W	city/town	
Spruce Lake Bog N.	43 40 11N	088 11 58W	landmark	

Wisconsin GPS Companion

Place Name	Latitude	Longitude	Type	Elev
St Catherines Bay	44 05 00N	088 19 28W	city/town	781
Stanberry	46 00 26N	091 37 34W	city/town	
Stand Rock	43 40 31N	089 48 53W	pillar	
Stang Lookout	45 17 06N	091 28 17W	tower	
Stangelville	44 24 01N	087 41 04W	city/town	804
Stanley	44 57 36N	090 56 13W	city/town	
Stanton	45 10 23N	092 28 01W	city/town	1058
Star Lake	46 02 18N	089 28 20W	city/town	
Star Praire	45 11 48N	092 31 42W	city/town	940
Star Prairie	45 11 49N	092 31 50W	city/town	
Starks	45 39 47N	089 13 18W	city/town	1630
Starks Mound	44 48 36N	092 45 06W	summit	1022
State Line	42 29 40N	087 49 15W	city/town	
Stateline Lookout	46 14 36N	089 38 06W	tower	1802
Steamboat Rock 1	43 45 26N	090 06 32W	pillar	
Steamboat Rock 2	43 39 57N	089 47 13W	pillar	
Stearns	42 39 23N	089 36 26W	city/town	
Stebbinsville	42 50 40N	089 10 23W	city/town	
Steinthal	43 58 57N	088 00 08W	city/town	
Stephensville	44 22 24N	088 35 03W	city/town	
Sterling Lookout	45 37 47N	092 48 46W	tower	
Stetsonville	45 04 37N	090 18 54W	city/town	

Wisconsin GPS Companion

Place Name	Latitude	Longitude	Type	Elev
Stettin -hist	44 58 23N	089 48 27W	city/town	1382
Steuben	43 10 52N	090 51 31W	city/town	675
Stevens Hill	44 50 25N	087 22 10W	city/town	
Stevens Point	44 31 25N	089 34 28W	city/town	1093
Stevens Point C C	44 31 12N	089 31 53W	golf	
Stevens Point Muni	44 32 42N	089 31 48W	airport	1110
Stevenstown	44 02 11N	091 10 17W	city/town	
Stiles	44 51 40N	088 02 54W	city/town	
Stiles Junction	44 53 00N	088 02 48W	city/town	656
Stiles Lookout	44 49 50N	088 04 25W	tower	
Stillwell Dam	43 59 25N	090 38 42W	dam	939
Stitzer	42 55 36N	090 37 23W	city/town	1191
Stockbridge	44 04 18N	088 17 56W	city/town	
Stockbridge Harbor	44 04 11N	088 19 45W	bay	
Stockholm	44 29 00N	092 15 43W	city/town	690
Stockton	44 30 41N	089 28 01W	city/town	1133
Stockton Island	46 56 17N	090 34 42W	island	
Stoddard	43 39 43N	091 13 06W	city/town	646
Stone	42 52 29N	089 18 36W	city/town	
Stone Lake	45 50 44N	091 32 25W	city/town	
Stonebank	43 08 33N	088 24 38W	city/town	
Stony Beach	43 59 17N	088 31 40W	city/town	

Wisconsin GPS Companion

Place Name	Latitude	Longitude	Type	Elev
Stop n Dock Marina	44 09 25N	087 34 43W	marina	585
Stoughton	42 55 01N	089 13 04W	city/town	
Stout State Univ.	44 52 24N	091 55 38W	univ/coll	
Stratford	44 48 04N	090 04 45W	city/town	
Strawbridge	42 31 58N	090 22 43W	city/town	
Strickland	45 26 12N	091 31 16W	city/town	1275
Stringer Hill	44 42 07N	092 03 47W	summit	1160
Stroebe Island	44 14 06N	088 27 17W	island	
Strong Falls	45 31 05N	088 20 23W	falls	
Strongs Prairie	44 03 41N	089 58 33W	city/town	913
Strum	44 32 59N	091 23 33W	city/town	
Sturgeon Bay	44 50 03N	087 22 37W	city/town	588
Sturgeon Bay	44 51 15N	087 23 40W	bay	
Sturgeon Bay -Door	44 50 56N	087 25 11W	airport	724
Sturgeon Bay Can L	44 47 40N	087 18 45W	light	582
Sturgeon Bay Canal	44 48 02N	087 19 19W	canal	
Sturgeon Yacht Hrb	44 49 32N	087 22 32W	marina	582
Sturtevant	42 41 53N	087 53 40W	city/town	727
Sturtevant -Sylv.	42 42 11N	087 57 30W	airport	790
Suamico	44 37 55N	088 02 21W	city/town	593
Sugar Bush (1)	44 28 54N	088 44 09W	city/town	829
Sugar Bush (2)	44 30 06N	087 47 08W	city/town	

Place Name	Latitude	Longitude	Type	Elev
Sugar Camp	45 47 40N	089 18 50W	city/town	
Sugar Camp Hill	46 37 15N	091 36 41W	summit	1256
Sugar Grove	43 25 33N	090 41 01W	city/town	
Sugar Island	43 13 33N	088 34 47W	city/town	
Sugarbush Hill	45 33 29N	088 48 47W	summit	1939
Sugarloaf Hill	43 17 33N	089 41 31W	summit	1141
Sullivan	43 00 46N	088 35 17W	city/town	860
Sullivan Falls	45 03 10N	088 39 33W	falls	
Summit Corners	43 04 36N	088 28 12W	city/town	884
Summit Lake	45 22 40N	089 11 41W	city/town	1727
Summit Lookout	46 21 55N	092 07 23W	tower	1369
Sumner	45 23 11N	091 39 08W	city/town	1089
Sun Prairie	43 11 01N	089 12 49W	city/town	951
Sundown Golf	45 16 02N	088 02 07W	golf	
Sunnyside	46 36 15N	092 03 23W	city/town	
Sunrise Bay	44 09 49N	088 26 19W	city/town	748
Sunset	45 00 12N	089 29 31W	city/town	1399
Sunset Beach (1)	43 30 06N	088 51 56W	city/town	
Sunset Beach (2)	44 03 51N	088 19 35W	city/town	
Sunset Point	44 03 20N	088 35 15W	city/town	749
Sunset Rock	43 03 22N	090 27 22W	pillar	
Superior	46 43 15N	092 06 14W	city/town	642

Place Name	Latitude	Longitude	Type	Elev
Superior -R. Bong	46 40 53N	092 05 33W	airport	674
Superior Falls	46 33 40N	090 24 58W	falls	
Superior Harbor	46 42 22N	092 01 41W	harbor	
Superior Village	46 39 25N	092 06 15W	city/town	
Suring	44 59 57N	088 22 19W	city/town	804
Sussex	43 08 02N	088 13 19W	city/town	
Sutherland	46 26 15N	091 10 35W	city/town	935
Swayne Lookout	45 41 17N	091 03 27W	tower	1326
Sweetheart City	45 18 33N	087 58 34W	city/town	
Sylvan	43 25 21N	090 37 41W	city/town	1257
Sylvan Mounds	42 59 57N	088 58 42W	city/town	
Sylvania	42 41 55N	087 57 30W	city/town	767
Symco	44 30 48N	088 54 14W	city/town	

T

Place Name	Latitude	Longitude	Type	Elev
Tabor	42 48 56N	087 50 06W	city/town	
Taegesville	45 02 48N	089 43 35W	city/town	1390
Tamarack	44 10 30N	091 26 52W	city/town	815
Tarrant	44 35 48N	091 50 35W	city/town	818
Taus	44 11 21N	087 51 43W	city/town	860
Tavera	43 17 03N	090 38 44W	city/town	708
Taycheedah	43 48 32N	088 23 42W	city/town	

Place Name	Latitude	Longitude	Type	Elev
Taylor	44 19 16N	091 07 11W	city/town	
Telemark, Mount	46 11 06N	091 15 01W	summit	1650
Tell	44 22 50N	091 51 58W	city/town	
Tennyson	42 41 24N	090 41 06W	city/town	
Terrace Beach	43 50 00N	088 55 51W	beach	
Terrell Island	44 04 18N	088 39 47W	island	
Terry Andrae State	43 39 36N	087 43 22W	park	
Tess Corners	42 55 20N	088 05 58W	city/town	
Theresa	43 31 02N	088 27 04W	city/town	
Theresa Station	43 31 36N	088 25 40W	city/town	
Thiensville	43 14 15N	087 58 43W	city/town	
Thiry Daems	44 36 11N	087 41 35W	city/town	727
Thompson	43 15 31N	088 22 14W	city/town	
Thompsonville	42 46 43N	087 57 10W	city/town	
Thornapple	45 24 35N	091 13 10W	city/town	
Thornton	44 47 48N	088 41 28W	city/town	860
Thorp	44 57 40N	090 47 59W	city/town	
Thorp Hill	43 58 09N	090 40 21W	summit	1063
Thousand Island St	44 16 25N	088 15 17W	park	
Three Chimneys	43 36 39N	090 54 19W	pillar	
Three Lakes	45 47 54N	089 09 46W	city/town	1666
Three Lakes Muni	45 47 25N	089 07 15W	airport	1636

Wisconsin GPS Companion

Place Name	Latitude	Longitude	Type	Elev
Tibbets	42 44 05N	088 34 53W	city/town	938
Tichigan	42 49 44N	088 11 51W	city/town	796
Tiffany	42 34 57N	088 55 37W	city/town	
Tigerton	44 44 27N	089 03 47W	city/town	
Tilden	45 00 24N	091 26 15W	city/town	
Tilleda	44 48 56N	088 54 40W	city/town	
Timberland	45 40 34N	092 06 21W	city/town	
Timms Hill	45 27 04N	090 11 42W	highest	1951
Tioga	44 41 03N	090 47 35W	city/town	1082
Tipler	45 55 30N	088 38 05W	city/town	1537
Tisch Mills	44 19 38N	087 37 25W	city/town	638
Tobin	42 30 27N	087 50 26W	city/town	
Token Creek	43 11 40N	089 17 37W	city/town	882
Tomah	43 58 43N	090 30 14W	city/town	
Tomah Bloyer	43 58 30N	090 29 00W	airport	963
Tomahawk	45 28 16N	089 43 47W	city/town	
Tomahawk Regional	45 28 10N	089 48 15W	airport	1486
Tonet	44 35 21N	087 44 01W	city/town	717
Tony	45 28 59N	090 59 33W	city/town	
Topside	46 33 33N	091 19 21W	city/town	
Torun	44 36 49N	089 30 34W	city/town	1135
Tower Bay Slip	46 44 29N	092 06 07W	harbor	

Wisconsin GPS Companion

Place Name	Latitude	Longitude	Type	Elev
Tower Hill State	43 09 10N	090 02 41W	park	
Tower Rock	43 19 08N	089 53 50W	pillar	
Towerville	43 24 27N	090 53 21W	city/town	
Townsend	45 19 41N	088 35 22W	city/town	1361
Trade Lake	45 41 23N	092 35 34W	city/town	
Trade River	45 38 54N	092 40 21W	city/town	
Trego	45 53 59N	091 49 15W	city/town	1086
Tremble	44 38 17N	088 04 10W	city/town	
Trempealeau	44 00 20N	091 26 31W	city/town	691
Trempealeau Mt.	44 01 17N	091 29 47W	summit	1034
Trenton	44 36 14N	092 33 53W	city/town	
Trevino	44 25 43N	092 04 04W	city/town	684
Trevor	42 30 45N	088 07 15W	city/town	776
Trimbelle	44 43 54N	092 34 47W	city/town	
Tripoli	45 33 19N	089 59 38W	city/town	
Tripoli Golf Club	43 09 10N	087 57 58W	golf	
Trippville	43 42 33N	090 24 15W	city/town	
Troste Lookout	46 15 06N	089 54 30W	tower	1806
Troy	42 46 44N	088 26 41W	city/town	
Troy Center	42 48 35N	088 27 54W	city/town	
Truax	44 50 57N	091 34 09W	city/town	898
Truesdell	42 34 00N	087 54 04W	city/town	

Wisconsin GPS Companion

Place Name	Latitude	Longitude	Type	Elev
Truman	42 43 10N	090 13 47W	city/town	1048
Tuckaway C C	42 56 56N	087 57 31W	golf	
Tuleta Hills	43 48 31N	088 58 52W	city/town	
Tunnel City	44 00 26N	090 33 56W	city/town	1053
Tunnelville	43 33 11N	090 39 30W	city/town	
Turtle Dam	46 04 13N	090 13 24W	dam	1577
Turtle Lake	45 23 40N	092 08 32W	city/town	1264
Tuscobia	45 34 01N	091 45 29W	city/town	
Tustin	44 09 46N	088 53 32W	city/town	
Twelve Corners	44 24 06N	088 26 05W	city/town	
Twelvefoot Falls	45 34 52N	088 08 02W	falls	
Twin Bluffs	43 16 26N	090 18 46W	city/town	707
Twin Grove	42 31 53N	089 32 35W	city/town	948
Twin Lakes	42 31 52N	088 14 53W	city/town	
Twin Peaks	44 01 58N	090 58 54W	summit	1148
Twin Town	45 21 36N	092 01 56W	city/town	1225
Two Creeks	44 18 08N	087 33 47W	city/town	
Two Rivers	44 09 14N	087 34 09W	city/town	
Tyler Forks	46 20 09N	090 31 39W	city/town	
Tyran	45 56 56N	088 18 19W	city/town	1297

Wisconsin GPS Companion

Place Name	Latitude	Longitude	Type	Elev
U				
U of W -Baraboo	43 28 54N	089 45 56W	univ/coll	
U of W -Eau Claire	44 47 54N	091 30 02W	univ/coll	
U of W -Exp. Stat.	46 34 21N	090 58 13W	univ/coll	
U of W -Great Lks.	43 01 03N	087 54 22W	univ/coll	
U of W -Green Bay	44 31 48N	087 55 15W	univ/coll	
U of W -La Crosse	43 48 49N	091 13 47W	univ/coll	
U of W -Madison	43 04 26N	089 24 39W	univ/coll	
U of W -Marshfield	44 38 28N	090 08 00W	univ/coll	
U of W -Medford	45 07 46N	090 20 08W	univ/coll	
U of W -Milwaukee	43 04 32N	087 52 44W	univ/coll	692
U of W -Oshkosh	44 01 35N	088 33 01W	univ/coll	
U of W -Rice Lake	45 29 01N	091 44 47W	univ/coll	
U of W -River Fls.	44 51 12N	092 37 20W	univ/coll	
U of W -Rock Co	42 38 55N	089 03 24W	univ/coll	
U of W -Stevens Pt	44 31 41N	089 34 13W	univ/coll	
U of W -Superior	46 43 05N	092 05 26W	univ/coll	637
U of W -Wausau	44 57 31N	089 38 39W	univ/coll	
U of W -Whitewater	42 50 18N	088 44 31W	univ/coll	
U of W Arboretum	43 02 48N	089 24 58W	univ/coll	
U of W Exper. Farm	43 18 02N	089 19 37W	univ/coll	

Wisconsin GPS Companion

Place Name	Latitude	Longitude	Type	Elev
Ubet	45 21 14N	092 31 45W	city/town	1116
Ulao	43 19 14N	087 54 59W	city/town	
Underhill	44 52 31N	088 23 04W	city/town	
Union (1)	42 49 49N	090 31 34W	city/town	1097
Union (2)	44 50 36N	091 32 55W	city/town	915
Union (3)	42 49 28N	089 18 06W	city/town	945
Union Center	43 41 07N	090 16 00W	city/town	922
Union Church	42 50 37N	088 04 09W	city/town	822
Union Grove	42 41 17N	088 03 05W	city/town	
Unity	44 51 06N	090 18 59W	city/town	1338
Upper French Creek	44 13 03N	091 19 29W	city/town	824
Upson	46 22 09N	090 24 24W	city/town	1497
Upson Lookout	46 25 12N	090 23 04W	tower	1819
Urne	44 29 55N	091 53 32W	city/town	825
Utica (1)	42 57 56N	089 07 19W	city/town	956
Utica (2)	43 01 20N	088 29 05W	city/town	
Utley	43 43 39N	088 54 22W	city/town	
Utowana Beach	44 12 18N	088 21 49W	city/town	

𝕍

Place Name	Latitude	Longitude	Type	Elev
Valders	44 03 58N	087 53 03W	city/town	840
Valley	43 38 30N	090 32 30W	city/town	

Wisconsin GPS Companion

Place Name	Latitude	Longitude	Type	Elev
Valley Golf Course	44 35 03N	091 38 35W	golf	
Valley Junction	44 03 12N	090 24 44W	city/town	
Valmy	44 54 29N	087 15 47W	city/town	
Valton	43 34 23N	090 16 27W	city/town	1031
Van Buskirk	46 23 14N	090 08 36W	city/town	1513
Van Dyne	43 53 15N	088 30 15W	city/town	
Van Hise Rock	43 30 16N	089 54 56W	pillar	
Vaudreuil	44 18 23N	090 48 35W	city/town	
Veedum	44 24 35N	090 10 24W	city/town	
Veefkind	44 41 30N	090 22 24W	city/town	
Vermont	43 04 20N	089 47 08W	city/town	
Vernon	42 54 13N	088 15 08W	city/town	
Verona	42 59 27N	089 31 59W	city/town	
Verona Airport	42 59 00N	089 31 00W	airport	960
Vesper	44 28 56N	089 57 50W	city/town	1110
Vette Seaplane B.	43 56 28N	088 29 37W	airport	750
Victory	43 29 08N	091 12 45W	city/town	629
Victory Center	43 12 25N	088 04 57W	city/town	
Victory Heights	42 32 34N	089 05 26W	city/town	
Vignes	44 43 34N	087 22 39W	city/town	
Viking	44 51 42N	092 21 32W	city/town	1096
Vilas	43 05 23N	089 14 05W	city/town	

397

Place Name	Latitude	Longitude	Type	Elev
Vilas Lookout	45 14 14N	089 18 22W	tower	1673
Villa Marina Docks	42 35 27N	087 49 10W	locale	585
Vinnie Ha Ha	42 52 50N	088 54 17W	city/town	
Viola	43 30 22N	090 40 05W	city/town	
Viroqua	43 33 25N	090 53 19W	city/town	
Viroqua C C	43 32 26N	090 52 49W	golf	
Viroqua Municipal	43 34 45N	090 54 03W	airport	1291
Viterbo College	43 48 12N	091 14 39W	univ/coll	
Voyager Village	45 58 00N	092 08 45W	airport	1020

W

Wabeno	45 26 19N	088 39 37W	city/town	1540
Wagner	45 18 08N	087 44 08W	city/town	1700
Waino	46 38 23N	091 34 24W	city/town	
Waldo	43 40 29N	087 56 55W	city/town	838
Waldwick	42 49 32N	090 02 23W	city/town	
Wales	43 00 16N	088 22 36W	city/town	1002
Walhain	44 32 43N	087 45 15W	city/town	784
Walsh	45 10 46N	087 45 45W	city/town	
Walworth	42 31 52N	088 35 58W	city/town	998
Walworth -Big Foot	42 31 40N	088 39 14W	airport	951
Wanderoos	45 18 31N	092 29 39W	city/town	

Wisconsin GPS Companion

Place Name	Latitude	Longitude	Type	Elev
Wangreen Hill	44 17 34N	090 31 40W	summit	1097
Wanless Hill	44 00 21N	090 58 12W	summit	1368
Warrens	44 07 52N	090 29 59W	city/town	
Warrentown	44 34 33N	092 21 30W	city/town	
Wascott	46 10 21N	091 47 53W	city/town	1090
Washburn	46 40 24N	090 53 41W	city/town	
Washburn Lookout	46 44 12N	091 01 28W	tower	1415
Washington	45 23 41N	086 55 53W	city/town	
Washington Harbor	45 24 24N	086 55 23W	bay	
Washington Island	45 22 38N	086 54 03W	island	
Washington Island	45 23 15N	086 55 30W	airport	656
Washington Pk Zoo	43 03 11N	087 58 04W	park	
Waterbury	44 23 07N	090 35 54W	city/town	
Waterford	42 45 47N	088 12 51W	city/town	
Waterloo	43 11 02N	088 59 18W	city/town	819
Watertown	43 11 41N	088 43 44W	city/town	823
Watertown Municip	43 10 11N	088 43 23W	airport	820
Waterville	43 01 12N	088 26 17W	city/town	
Waubeka	43 28 30N	087 59 25W	city/town	
Waucousta	43 39 09N	088 15 37W	city/town	
Waukau	43 59 21N	088 46 18W	city/town	
Waukesha	43 00 42N	088 13 53W	city/town	821

Wisconsin GPS Companion

Place Name	Latitude	Longitude	Type	Elev
Waukesha County	43 02 27N	088 14 13W	airport	911
Waumandee	44 18 11N	091 42 20W	city/town	
Waunakee	43 11 31N	089 27 20W	city/town	925
Waunakee Airport	43 11 00N	089 27 00W	airport	950
Waupaca	44 21 29N	089 05 09W	city/town	
Waupaca C C	44 21 26N	089 03 55W	golf	
Waupaca Municipal	44 19 59N	089 01 23W	airport	827
Waupun	43 38 00N	088 43 46W	city/town	904
Wausau	44 57 33N	089 37 48W	city/town	
Wausau Junction	44 56 28N	089 36 31W	city/town	
Wausau Municipal	44 55 33N	089 37 31W	airport	1201
Wausaukee	45 22 15N	087 57 08W	city/town	744
Wautoma	44 04 29N	089 17 16W	city/town	867
Wautoma Municipal	44 02 29N	089 18 15W	airport	859
Wauwatosa	43 02 58N	088 00 27W	city/town	672
Wauzeka	43 05 07N	090 52 59W	city/town	657
Waverly	44 43 43N	092 15 24W	city/town	1097
Waverly Beach	44 12 37N	088 24 16W	city/town	749
Waxdale	42 41 53N	087 52 40W	city/town	
Wayka Falls	44 55 50N	088 39 16W	falls	
Wayne	43 30 51N	088 19 17W	city/town	1054
Wayside	44 15 19N	087 57 09W	city/town	

Wisconsin GPS Companion

Place Name	Latitude	Longitude	Type	Elev
Webb Lake	46 00 34N	092 07 57W	city/town	
Webster	45 52 39N	092 22 02W	city/town	
Weedens	43 41 16N	087 46 19W	city/town	688
Weirgor	45 41 24N	091 16 04W	city/town	
Weisinger Hill	44 39 55N	092 06 34W	summit	1160
Welch Point -hist	44 42 10N	092 00 45W	city/town	770
Wellers Dock	44 38 44N	087 45 38W	locale	581
Welling Beach	43 52 14N	088 21 50W	city/town	
Wells	44 05 44N	088 02 36W	city/town	
Wendts Siding	43 57 40N	088 54 20W	locale	
Wentworth	46 36 00N	091 50 09W	city/town	939
Wequiock	44 34 03N	087 52 52W	city/town	724
Werley	43 01 10N	090 45 55W	city/town	766
West Allis	43 01 00N	088 00 25W	city/town	730
West Almond	44 17 10N	089 27 39W	city/town	
West Bancroft	44 18 17N	089 31 51W	city/town	
West Baraboo	43 28 28N	089 46 13W	city/town	886
West Bend	43 25 31N	088 11 00W	city/town	893
West Bend Municip	43 25 19N	088 07 40W	airport	888
West Bloomfield	44 13 15N	088 58 18W	city/town	828
West De Pere	44 26 44N	088 04 31W	city/town	607
West Denmark	45 34 12N	092 30 34W	city/town	1257

Wisconsin GPS Companion

Place Name	Latitude	Longitude	Type	Elev
West Fork Lookout	46 01 22N	091 06 22W	tower	1495
West Gate Basin	46 44 54N	092 06 11W	harbor	
West Granville	43 08 26N	088 02 42W	city/town	
West Kraft	45 26 47N	089 44 57W	city/town	
West La Crosse	43 50 44N	091 15 44W	city/town	643
West Lima	43 32 47N	090 31 49W	city/town	1291
West Milwaukee	43 00 45N	087 58 21W	city/town	
West Prairie (1)	43 28 00N	091 01 21W	city/town	
West Prairie (2)	44 03 51N	091 30 56W	city/town	
West Rosendale	43 49 21N	088 43 30W	city/town	924
West Salem	43 53 57N	091 04 52W	city/town	742
West Sweden	45 42 21N	092 29 48W	city/town	
Westboro	45 21 19N	090 17 45W	city/town	
Westby	43 39 25N	090 51 15W	city/town	1298
Westfield	43 53 01N	089 29 36W	city/town	865
Westmoor C C	43 01 50N	088 06 20W	golf	
Weston	44 48 45N	092 04 17W	city/town	
Westport	43 12 18N	090 38 28W	city/town	
Westview C C	44 36 41N	090 13 20W	golf	
Weyauwega	44 19 17N	088 56 01W	city/town	
Weyerhaeuser	45 25 25N	091 24 30W	city/town	1203
Wheatland	42 35 38N	088 12 30W	city/town	763

Wisconsin GPS Companion

Place Name	Latitude	Longitude	Type	Elev
Wheeler	45 02 40N	091 54 31W	city/town	938
Whispering Pines	44 16 49N	088 23 03W	city/town	763
Whitcomb	44 47 00N	089 07 07W	city/town	
White City	43 37 07N	090 27 11W	city/town	
White Creek	43 49 33N	089 51 17W	city/town	
White Lake	45 09 26N	088 45 52W	city/town	1286
White Oak	42 31 06N	090 16 37W	city/town	965
White River	46 32 09N	090 51 02W	city/town	
Whitefish Bay (1)	43 06 48N	087 54 00W	city/town	
Whitefish Bay (2)	44 54 21N	087 13 02W	city/town	605
Whitehall	44 22 03N	091 18 59W	city/town	820
Whitelaw	44 08 41N	087 49 17W	city/town	857
Whitewater	42 50 01N	088 43 56W	city/town	
Whiting	44 29 37N	089 33 31W	city/town	1069
Whittlesey	45 13 23N	090 19 43W	city/town	
Whittlesey, Mount	46 18 03N	090 37 02W	summit	1872
Wickware	45 21 05N	091 47 10W	city/town	1208
Wiemer Dam	45 42 13N	090 34 58W	dam	1416
Wien	44 54 07N	090 01 28W	city/town	1320
Wilcox	44 59 52N	087 50 07W	city/town	
Wild Rose (1)	44 10 43N	089 14 56W	city/town	
Wild Rose (2)	43 17 13N	090 34 54W	city/town	1170

Place Name	Latitude	Longitude	Type	Elev
Wild Rose Idlewild	44 11 52N	089 13 04W	airport	908
Wildcat Lookout	46 11 14N	089 38 39W	locale	1820
Wildcat Mountain S	43 42 02N	090 33 41W	park	
Wildwood	44 53 31N	092 17 57W	city/town	
Willard	44 44 06N	090 43 09W	city/town	1179
Williams Bay	42 34 41N	088 32 27W	city/town	
Willow Creek	43 12 26N	088 09 30W	city/town	
Willow Harbor	43 56 49N	088 29 41W	bay	
Willow River State	45 01 23N	092 41 29W	park	
Willow Springs	43 08 20N	088 11 03W	city/town	
Wills	46 32 21N	091 32 21W	city/town	
Wilmoore Heights	43 53 19N	088 48 30W	city/town	
Wilmot	42 30 46N	088 10 55W	city/town	
Wilmot Hills Racew	42 29 56N	088 11 16W	track	
Wilson (1)	44 49 41N	091 01 21W	city/town	
Wilson (2)	44 57 13N	092 10 24W	city/town	
Wilson Lookout	44 47 31N	090 59 33W	tower	
Wilton	43 48 49N	090 31 40W	city/town	995
Winchester (1)	44 11 55N	088 39 53W	city/town	
Winchester (2)	46 13 19N	089 53 52W	city/town	
Wind Lake	42 49 46N	088 09 31W	city/town	797
Wind Point	42 46 51N	087 45 27W	cape	

Wisconsin GPS Companion

Place Name	Latitude	Longitude	Type	Elev
Wind Point	42 47 04N	087 45 58W	city/town	
Windsor	43 13 06N	089 20 29W	city/town	902
Winnebago	44 04 33N	088 31 30W	city/town	
Winnebago Heights	43 54 01N	088 20 33W	city/town	763
Winnebago Mission	44 20 46N	090 45 17W	city/town	
Winnebago Park	43 53 07N	088 21 09W	city/town	
Winnebago Point	43 58 58N	088 19 38W	cape	
Winneboujou	46 31 03N	091 36 03W	city/town	1036
Winneconne	44 06 39N	088 42 45W	city/town	753
Winter	45 49 11N	091 00 42W	city/town	
Winter Lookout	45 48 36N	090 55 28W	tower	
Wiota	42 38 12N	089 57 09W	city/town	
Wisconsin Dells	43 37 39N	089 46 15W	city/town	912
Wisconsin Dells Sp	43 40 34N	089 50 43W	track	
Wisconsin Int Racw	44 14 43N	088 15 37W	track	
Wisconsin Junction	45 39 22N	088 54 40W	city/town	
Wisconsin Rapids	44 21 37N	089 50 17W	airport	1021
Wisconsin Rapids	44 23 01N	089 49 02W	city/town	
Wisconsin River CC	44 28 19N	089 35 39W	golf	
Wisconsin St. Cap.	43 04 28N	089 23 03W	building	917
Wisconsin St. Off.	43 02 23N	087 55 17W	building	
Withee	44 57 23N	090 35 51W	city/town	1272

Wisconsin GPS Companion

Place Name	Latitude	Longitude	Type	Elev
Wittenberg	44 49 38N	089 10 10W	city/town	
Witwen	43 17 07N	089 53 14W	city/town	
Wolf Creek	45 33 22N	092 43 21W	city/town	
Wolf River Headwtr	45 39 36N	088 59 41W	locale	1639
Wolf River Lookout	45 33 18N	089 00 24W	tower	1884
Wonewoc	43 39 10N	090 13 24W	city/town	938
Woodboro	45 36 27N	089 33 15W	city/town	1619
Wooddale	45 41 06N	091 27 39W	city/town	
Woodford	42 38 55N	089 51 45W	city/town	793
Woodhull	43 46 39N	088 34 23W	city/town	
Woodland	43 22 13N	088 31 07W	city/town	952
Woodland Corner	46 08 36N	092 14 18W	city/town	1037
Woodlawn	45 25 56N	088 49 17W	city/town	
Woodman	43 05 24N	090 48 04W	city/town	
Woodruff	45 53 47N	089 41 56W	city/town	
Woodstock	43 28 21N	090 25 38W	city/town	
Woodville	44 57 11N	092 17 28W	city/town	
Woodworth	42 33 29N	088 00 04W	city/town	752
Worcester	45 36 13N	090 17 31W	city/town	
Wrightstown	44 19 33N	088 09 46W	city/town	
Wuertsburg	44 57 37N	090 05 56W	city/town	1442
Wyalusing	42 56 38N	091 08 29W	city/town	

Place Name	Latitude	Longitude	Type	Elev
Wyalusing State	42 59 30N	091 07 20W	park	
Wyeville	44 01 42N	090 23 04W	city/town	
Wyocena	43 29 45N	089 18 30W	city/town	826
Wyoming	43 07 34N	090 06 42W	city/town	738

𝕏

𝕐

Yarnell	45 43 37N	091 25 09W	city/town	
Yellow Lake	45 56 12N	092 23 24W	city/town	930
Yellowstone	42 47 54N	089 58 13W	city/town	913
Yerkes Observatory	42 34 13N	088 33 22W	locale	
York	44 27 00N	091 08 42W	city/town	
York Center	43 14 21N	089 04 13W	city/town	
York Island	46 58 59N	090 51 48W	island	
Yorkville	42 44 31N	088 01 36W	city/town	753
Young America	43 27 06N	088 11 09W	city/town	
Yuba	43 32 20N	090 25 47W	city/town	1868

ℤ

Zachow	44 43 56N	088 21 49W	city/town	862
Zander	44 18 47N	087 42 19W	city/town	733

407

Wisconsin GPS Companion

Place Name	Latitude	Longitude	Type	Elev
Zenda	42 30 43N	088 28 54W	city/town	979
Zenith Lookout	45 27 45N	089 51 19W	tower	
Zion	43 59 49N	088 39 43W	city/town	847
Zittau	44 13 00N	088 47 10W	city/town	774
Zoar	45 00 54N	088 53 56W	city/town	1214

Add your own coordinates here

Place Name	Latitude	Longitude	Type	Elev

Add your own coordinates here

Wisconsin GPS Companion

Place Name	Latitude	Longitude	Type	Elev

Add your own coordinates here

ABOUT LATITUDE AND LONGITUDE

Latitude and Longitude coordinates are commonly expressed two ways: Degrees, Minutes, and Seconds such as DD-MM-SS or Degrees and Minutes where minutes may be stated to one-tenth minute resolution, such as DD-MM.M. Just as 30 seconds equals one half minute on the clock, 30 seconds of Latitude or Longitude equals one half (0.5) minutes on the coordinate system.

Locations North of the equator often include the letter (N) to indicate North Latitude. These are sometimes given a (+) value. Locations South of the equator would be (S) or (-). Locations West of Greenwich, England often include the letter (W) to indicate West Longitude. These are sometimes given a (+) value. Locations East of Greenwich would be (E) or (-).

Most GPS units accept data in either the "tenth minute" format or the "minutes and seconds" format. Quick conversion charts follow for your convenience.

FROM DD-MM.M	to	DD-MM-SS
DD-MM.1	=	DD-MM-06
DD-MM.2	=	DD-MM-12
DD-MM.3	=	DD-MM-18
DD-MM.4	=	DD-MM-24
DD-MM.5	=	DD-MM-30
DD-MM.6	=	DD-MM-36
DD-MM.7	=	DD-MM-42
DD-MM.8	=	DD-MM-48
DD-MM.9	=	DD-MM-54

```
FROM
DD-MM-SS          to    DD-MM.M
DD-MM-00 to 03  =    DD-MM.0
DD-MM-04 to 09  =    DD-MM.1
DD-MM-10 to 15  =    DD-MM.2
DD-MM-16 to 21  =    DD-MM.3
DD-MM-22 to 27  =    DD-MM.4
DD-MM-28 to 33  =    DD-MM.5
DD-MM-34 to 39  =    DD-MM.6
DD-MM-40 to 45  =    DD-MM.7
DD-MM-46 to 51  =    DD-MM.8
DD-MM-52 to 57  =    DD-MM.9
DD-MM-58 to 60  =    DD-M+1.0 (next minute)
```

HOW FAR IS A MINUTE?

When using your GPS you will notice the coordinates
indicated for a certain location will vary slightly with time.
To get a better understanding of the actual distances
represented by these values, you may use the following
approximations. The number of statute miles represented
by a unit of Latitude is constant wherever you go.

So when traveling North-South:
1 Degree=69 miles, 1 Minute=1.15 miles, 1 Second=101 ft.

The number of statute miles represented by a unit of Longitude varies with location, since the lines of Longitude converge at the North and South poles.

For this reason, in Northern Minnesota (Warroad) when traveling East-West:
1 Degree=45.6 miles, 1 Minute=0.76 miles, 1 Second=67 ft.

In Southern Wisconsin (Beloit) when traveling East-West:
1 Degree=50.8 miles, 1 Minute=0.85 miles, 1 Second=75 ft.

NOTES

Points Around the USA

Place Name	Latitude	Longitude	Type	Elev
Aberdeen SD	45 27 53N	098 29 10W	city/town	1304
Akron OH	41 04 53N	081 31 09W	city/town	1050
Albany NY	42 39 09N	073 45 24W	city/town	
Albuquerque NM	35 05 04N	106 39 02W	city/town	4955
Amarillo TX	35 13 19N	101 49 51W	city/town	
Anchorage AK	61 13 05N	149 54 01W	city/town	101
Ann Arbor MI	42 16 15N	083 43 35W	city/town	
Appomattox Mem VA	37 22 38N	078 47 44W	site	
Ashland WI	46 35 33N	090 53 01W	city/town	671
Atlanta GA	33 44 56N	084 23 17W	city/town	1050
Austin TX	30 16 01N	097 44 34W	city/town	501
Baltimore MD	39 17 25N	076 36 45W	city/town	100
Bangor ME	44 48 04N	068 46 42W	city/town	158
Barrow AK	71 17 26N	156 47 19W	city/town	
Baton Rouge LA	30 27 02N	091 09 16W	city/town	53
Bellingham WA	48 45 35N	122 29 13W	city/town	100
Billings MT	45 47 00N	108 30 00W	city/town	3124
Biloxi MS	30 23 45N	088 53 07W	city/town	25
Birmingham AL	33 31 14N	086 48 09W	city/town	600
Bismarck ND	46 48 30N	100 47 00W	city/town	1700
Boise ID	43 36 49N	116 12 09W	city/town	2730
Boston MA	42 21 30N	071 03 37W	city/town	20

Place Name	Latitude	Longitude	Type	Elev
Boundary Peak NV	37 50 46N	118 21 00W	summit	13140
Branson MO	36 38 37N	093 13 06W	city/town	722
Brownsville TX	25 54 05N	097 29 50W	city/town	
Buffalo NY	42 53 11N	078 52 43W	city/town	
Burlington VT	44 28 33N	073 12 45W	city/town	113
Cape Hatteras NC	35 13 28N	075 31 50W	cape	
Carbondale IL	37 43 38N	089 13 00W	city/town	415
Casper WY	42 52 00N	106 18 45W	city/town	
Cedar Rapids IA	42 00 30N	091 38 38W	city/town	
Charleston SC	32 46 35N	079 55 52W	city/town	118
Charleston WV	38 20 59N	081 37 58W	city/town	606
Charlotte NC	35 13 37N	080 50 36W	city/town	850
Cheyenne WY	41 08 24N	104 49 11W	city/town	6067
Chicago IL	41 51 00N	087 39 00W	city/town	596
Cincinnati OH	39 09 43N	084 27 25W	city/town	683
Cleveland OH	41 29 58N	081 41 44W	city/town	690
Columbia SC	34 00 02N	081 02 06W	city/town	314
Concord NH	43 12 29N	071 32 17W	city/town	288
Corpus Christi TX	27 48 01N	097 23 46W	city/town	
Corvallis OR	44 33 53N	123 15 39W	city/town	225
Dallas TX	32 47 00N	096 48 00W	city/town	463
Dayton OH	39 45 32N	084 11 30W	city/town	750

Points Around the USA

Place Name	Latitude	Longitude	Type	Elev
Denver CO	39 44 21N	104 59 03W	city/town	5260
Des Moines IA	41 36 02N	093 36 32W	city/town	
Detroit MI	42 19 53N	083 02 45W	city/town	
Disney World FL	28 24 41N	081 34 58W	park	
Disneyland CA	33 48 37N	117 55 05W	locale	
Duluth MN	46 47 00N	092 06 23W	city/town	
El Paso TX	31 45 31N	106 29 11W	city/town	
Empire State B. NY	40 44 55N	073 59 11W	building	
Evansville IN	37 58 29N	087 33 21W	city/town	388
Fairbanks AK	64 50 16N	147 42 59W	city/town	440
Fargo ND	46 52 38N	096 47 22W	city/town	900
Flagstaff AZ	35 11 53N	111 39 02W	city/town	
Ford Museum MI	42 18 12N	083 14 02W	museum	
Fort Sumter SC	32 45 08N	079 52 29W	park	
Fort Wayne IN	41 07 50N	085 07 44W	city/town	781
Gallup NM	35 31 41N	108 44 31W	city/town	6508
Gannett Peak WY	43 11 04N	109 39 12W	summit	13804
Gateway Arch MO	38 37 28N	090 11 14W	other	
Gettysburg PA	39 49 00N	077 14 00W	memorial	
Graceland TN	35 02 46N	090 01 25W	mansion	
Grand Canyon WY	44 20 09N	104 11 47W	valley	
Grand Junction CO	39 03 50N	108 33 00W	city/town	4597

Points Around the USA

Place Name	Latitude	Longitude	Type	Elev
Grand Teton WY	43 44 28N	110 48 06W	summit	13770
Granite Peak MT	45 09 48N	109 48 26W	summit	12799
Greenville SC	34 51 09N	082 23 39W	city/town	966
Hartford CT	41 45 49N	072 41 08W	city/town	
Helena MT	46 35 34N	112 02 07W	city/town	4090
Hilo HI	19 43 47N	155 05 24W	city/town	38
Hilton Head SC	32 11 37N	080 44 18W	island	
Honolulu HI	21 18 25N	157 51 30W	city/town	18
Hoover Dam NV	36 01 00N	114 44 12W	dam	
Houston TX	29 45 47N	095 21 47W	city/town	
Huntsville AL	34 43 49N	086 35 10W	city/town	641
Indianapolis IN	39 46 06N	086 09 29W	city/town	717
Indianapolis S. IN	39 47 41N	086 14 06W	speedway	
Jackson MS	32 17 55N	090 11 05W	city/town	294
Jacksonville FL	30 19 55N	081 39 21W	city/town	12
Jefferson Mem. DC	38 52 53N	077 02 13W	memorial	
Juneau AK	58 18 07N	134 25 11W	city/town	
Kansas City MO	39 05 59N	094 34 42W	city/town	
Kill Devil Hls NC	36 01 00N	075 40 00W	summit	78
Kings Peak UT	40 46 43N	110 22 28W	summit	13528
Knoxville TN	35 57 38N	083 55 15W	city/town	889
Kodiak AK	57 47 24N	152 24 26W	city/town	

Points Around the USA

Place Name	Latitude	Longitude	Type	Elev
Lansing MI	42 43 57N	084 33 20W	city/town	
Las Vegas NV	36 10 30N	115 08 11W	city/town	2000
Lexington KY	37 59 19N	084 28 40W	city/town	
Little Rock AR	34 44 47N	092 17 22W	city/town	350
Los Angeles CA	34 03 08N	118 14 34W	city/town	330
Louisville KY	38 15 15N	085 45 34W	city/town	462
Lubbock TX	33 34 40N	101 51 17W	city/town	
Lynchburg VA	37 24 49N	079 08 33W	city/town	818
Macon GA	32 50 26N	083 37 57W	city/town	400
Madison WI	43 04 23N	089 24 04W	city/town	863
Manassas Battle VA	38 49 19N	077 31 24W	battlefld	
Marquette MI	46 32 37N	087 23 43W	city/town	628
Mayo Clinic MN	44 01 20N	092 27 56W	hospital	
Medford OR	42 19 36N	122 52 28W	city/town	383
Memphis TN	35 08 58N	090 02 56W	city/town	254
Miami FL	25 46 26N	080 11 38W	city/town	11
Milwaukee WI	43 02 20N	087 54 23W	city/town	634
Minneapolis MN	44 58 48N	093 15 49W	city/town	
Missoula MT	46 52 20N	113 59 35W	city/town	3200
Mobile AL	30 41 39N	088 02 35W	city/town	16
Montgomery AL	32 22 00N	086 18 00W	city/town	250
Montpelier VT	44 15 36N	072 34 33W	city/town	525

Points Around the USA

Place Name	Latitude	Longitude	Type	Elev
Mt Elbert CO	39 07 04N	106 26 41W	summit	14433
Mt Hood OR	45 22 25N	121 41 33W	summit	11239
Mt McKinley AK	63 04 10N	151 00 13W	summit	20320
Mt Rainier WA	46 51 10N	121 45 31W	summit	14410
Mt Rushmore SD	43 52 49N	103 27 30W	summit	5725
Mt St Helens WA	46 11 52N	122 11 28W	summit	9677
Mt Whitney CA	36 34 45N	118 17 30W	summit	14491
Mukilteo Light WA	47 56 56N	122 18 12W	lighthous	28
Mystic Seaport CT	41 21 40N	071 58 01W	city/town	
Air & Space Mus OH	40 33 58N	084 10 33W	museum	
Nags Head NC	35 57 26N	075 37 28W	city/town	10
Nantucket Is. MA	41 17 00N	070 05 00W	island	
Nashville TN	36 09 57N	086 47 04W	city/town	440
New Haven CT	41 18 29N	072 55 43W	city/town	
New Orleans LA	29 57 16N	090 04 30W	city/town	11
New York NY	40 42 51N	074 00 23W	city/town	
Newark NJ	40 44 08N	074 10 22W	city/town	95
Newport News VA	36 58 43N	076 25 42W	city/town	15
Newport RI	41 29 24N	071 18 48W	city/town	96
Niagara Falls NY	43 05 00N	079 04 15W	falls	
Nome AK	64 30 04N	165 24 23W	city/town	
North Platte NE	41 07 26N	100 45 54W	city/town	

422

Points Around the USA

Place Name	Latitude	Longitude	Type	Elev
Oklahoma City OK	35 28 03N	097 30 58W	city/town	
Old Faithful WY	44 27 38N	110 49 41W	geyser	
Omaha NE	41 15 31N	095 56 15W	city/town	
Orlando FL	28 32 17N	081 22 46W	city/town	106
Oshkosh WI	44 01 29N	088 32 33W	city/town	
Peoria IL	40 41 37N	089 35 20W	city/town	
Philadelphia PA	39 57 08N	075 09 51W	city/town	40
Phoenix AZ	33 26 54N	112 04 24W	city/town	
Pierre SD	44 22 06N	100 21 02W	city/town	1484
Pikes Peak CO	38 50 26N	105 02 38W	summit	14110
Pima Air Mus. AZ	32 07 00N	110 51 29W	museum	
Pittsburgh PA	40 26 26N	079 59 46W	city/town	770
Plymouth Rock MA	41 57 30N	070 39 45W	rock	10
Pocatello ID	42 52 17N	112 26 41W	city/town	4464
Portland ME	43 39 41N	070 15 21W	city/town	
Portland OR	45 31 25N	122 40 30W	city/town	50
Providence RI	41 49 26N	071 24 48W	city/town	
Pueblo CO	38 15 16N	104 36 31W	city/town	4662
Raleigh NC	35 46 19N	078 38 20W	city/town	350
Rapid City SD	44 04 50N	103 13 50W	city/town	3247
Redding CA	40 35 12N	122 23 26W	city/town	557
Reno NV	39 31 47N	119 48 46W	city/town	4498

Points Around the USA

Place Name	Latitude	Longitude	Type	Ele
Richmond Battle VA	37 25 45N	077 22 26W	battlefld	
Richmond VA	37 33 13N	077 27 38W	city/town	190
Sacramento CA	38 34 54N	121 29 36W	city/town	20
Saint George UT	37 06 15N	113 35 00W	city/town	2761
Saint Louis MO	38 37 38N	090 11 52W	city/town	
Salina KS	38 50 25N	097 36 40W	city/town	1225
Salt Lake City UT	40 45 39N	111 53 25W	city/town	4266
San Antonio TX	29 25 26N	098 29 36W	city/town	
San Diego CA	32 42 55N	117 09 23W	city/town	40
San Francisco CA	37 46 30N	122 25 06W	city/town	63
Santa Fe NM	35 41 13N	105 56 14W	city/town	6989
Scranton PA	41 24 32N	075 39 46W	city/town	754
Seattle WA	47 36 23N	122 19 51W	city/town	350
Sheridan WY	44 47 50N	106 57 20W	city/town	3742
Sioux City IA	42 30 00N	096 24 00W	city/town	1117
Sioux Falls SD	43 33 00N	096 42 00W	city/town	1442
Smithsonian I. DC	38 53 19N	077 01 34W	museum	
South Bend IN	41 41 00N	086 15 00W	city/town	725
Spokane WA	47 39 32N	117 25 30W	city/town	2000
Springfield IL	39 48 06N	089 38 37W	city/town	
Springfield MA	42 06 05N	072 35 25W	city/town	70
Syracuse NY	43 02 53N	076 08 52W	city/town	